IRISH HISTORICAL DOCUMENTS
1172—1922

IRISH HISTORICAL DOCUMENTS

1172—1922

Edited by

EDMUND CURTIS, M.A., LITT.D.

LECKY PROFESSOR OF HISTORY AT TRINITY COLLEGE, DUBLIN

and

R. B. McDOWELL, PH.D.

SOMETIME SCHOLAR, TRINITY COLLEGE, DUBLIN

BARNES & NOBLE, Inc.
New York
METHUEN & CO. Ltd
London

First published in 1943

Reprinted, 1968
by
Barnes & Noble, Inc., New York
and
Methuen & Co. Ltd, London

Printed in the United States of America

FOREWORD

THE want of a general and representative source-book of the chief documents of Irish history has long been felt. Even for limited periods and subjects such works are few. The texts of such famous enactments as the Bull *Laudabiliter*, the Statutes of Kilkenny, ' Poynings' law ' and the Union of 1800, which are known by name or general purport to most of us, are only to be found scattered through various publications, often of an antiquarian nature.

In this present work the editors have aimed at collecting in one volume for reference purposes the principal Irish constitutional and political documents, together with a number of other documents and extracts illustrating the main trends of Irish history from the introduction of English rule and the discipline of the medieval catholic church in the twelfth century to our own time.

Our work has, we are aware, many limitations besides those imposed by considerations of space. Purely Gaelic sources, which reflect an archaic order of law, custom and institutions far removed from the normal medieval, and still more from modern, European civilization, are a world to themselves and must be left to the experts in this rare field of learning. The contacts, however, between the English Crown, the Anglo-Irish and the native race are reflected throughout our documents. Social, economic, ecclesiastical and municipal history, though finding place in some of our pages, are each a subject demanding more treatment than we have been able to give them. Our work must be taken as confining itself to the main course of Anglo-Irish history, and to those written sources in French, Latin and English in which the constitutional and official life of Ireland has been expressed since the twelfth century. The medieval period, important as it is, is somewhat briefly represented in view of the fact that the material available for later periods is not only more abundant but probably more interesting to most modern readers. We venture therefore to claim for our work, in spite of limitations and omissions, the merit of being the first collection of Irish historical documents of a varied and representative nature yet published, covering the last eight centuries of Irish history.

Spelling and punctuation have been modernized throughout, and documents in Latin or French have been translated into English. For the convenience of readers it may be pointed out that, since the book is divided into sections with the documents numbered within each section, editorial references in the introduction and in the sections are indicated by roman and the documents by arabic numerals (e.g. II, 7).

For section I (the medieval portion) Edmund Curtis is responsible; for the subsequent sections R. B. McDowell.

To the Board of Trinity College we offer grateful thanks for a generous grant in aid of the publication of this volume. For criticism and advice our thanks are due to Dr. T. W. Moody, Fellow of Trinity College, Dublin, and Dr. D. B. Quinn of Queen's University, Belfast. To Dr. Moody we owe the document printed on page 281, to Dr. Quinn that printed on page 94. For permission to include in this volume extracts from government publications we wish to express our gratitude to the Controller of H.M. Stationery Office, and to the Controller of the Irish Stationery Office. Our thanks are also due to Messrs. Benn for leave to include the address by Dr. Douglas Hyde printed in the *Revival of Irish literature and other addresses* (published by Messrs. Fisher Unwin), to the Clarendon Press for permission to reprint the writ establishing the court of Castle Chamber published in *Select statutes and other constitutional documents* by G. W. Prothero, and to the Wood Printing Works, Dublin for permission to print extracts from the *Minutes and proceedings of the first parliament of the republic of Ireland*.

EDMUND CURTIS
R. B. McDOWELL

Trinity College, Dublin
March 1943

Professor Curtis died on 25th March 1943. Before his death he had corrected the first proofs of this work.

R. B. McD.

CONTENTS

3

SECTION II. THE TUDOR PERIOD

SECTION III. THE SEVENTEENTH CENTURY

SECTION IV. THE EIGHTEENTH CENTURY

SECTION V.   THE NINETEENTH CENTURY, AND AFTER

INTRODUCTION

IF we divide Irish history from 1172 into two great periods, the first extending from the Anglo-Norman invasion in the twelfth century to the beginnings of the Tudor regime in 1485, and the second from the latter date to the present day, the differences are many and striking. The lack of any real unity is very pronounced in medieval Ireland, even more than in other contemporary states. As against this, in the later or modern period there are visible a growing unity enforced by the Crown as expressed in the Kingdom of Ireland (1541), and an Irish nation formed by the blending of the native Gaelic race with the Anglo-Normans and some later settlers, the chief bond being in the Catholic Church. Our documents reflect the difference of the two periods. Those in Section I are selected from a large mass of sources illustrative of the many aspects of a country which, owing to an imperfect conquest, finally became a patchwork of units almost totally lacking in a recognized obedience and willing co-operation. They could hardly be other than selective, and the whole medieval period needs a volume or several volumes to itself.

The documents that illustrate the later Tudor reconquest and Stuart centralization naturally have more cohesion than those of the earlier age, and represent the growing unity of a positive state (' the Kingdom of Ireland ') which for some four centuries embodied the established and lawful sovereignty.

For both of these periods, therefore, a certain obvious difference of treatment was essential. The failure of the ' Pax Normannica ' and of all effective royal control from England is reflected in the earlier documents : in the later the growing unity of the island, both central and local, under one Monarchy and law and an established Church. The unity seemed assured under James I : that actually it was more obvious than real took some long generations to perceive.

MEDIEVAL IRELAND TO 1494

The English conquest of Ireland began with a fair show of completeness, and under the Angevin ' Lord of Ireland ' who was also King of England, an active Norman aristocracy, full of the vigour of their race, seemed like to conquer and organize the whole island. The institutions of the greater kingdom, monarchy, English law, counties, towns, baronies, and a Church organized like that of England, were in the thirteenth century so far extended as to promise that Ireland would become a complete replica of the greater island, in language, law and organization.

This prospect, however, soon receded and after a century or so Ireland was committed to the evils of an incomplete conquest and a war of races which lasted till the end of the Tudor age. Instead of cohesion under the royal suzerain, the baronial class dissolved into feudal anarchy and local independence, while through gaelicization large numbers of them came to be described as the ' degenerate English.' The ' Lordship of Ireland,' originally due to papal grant and so reckoned as a papal fief by the Irish, though itself the only possible centre of unity under the circumstances, steadily lost all true control force and efficiency from 1327 and kept only a nominal and absentee authority which it was left to the Tudors to re-integrate.

The main features of this period are reflected in the documents given. They are as follows (excluding that purely Gaelic world which either was never conquered or which subsequent to the thirteenth century reverted to Irish law, kingship, language and land tenure).

(1) English sovereignty. Henry II, partly by conquest, partly by native submission, partly by papal grant, acquired the Lordship of all Ireland and handed it over to his son John. The latter succeeding to the English throne, the Lordship of Ireland became vested in the Kings of England, his heirs. At first the Irish state was simply ruled by royal edicts and writs. Later it acquired a parliament of its own, which could legislate for the whole island subject to royal permission.

Finally, under Henry VIII (1541), the Lordship of Ireland was turned into the Kingdom of Ireland, which lasted as a separate realm till 1800.

(2) English institutions were extended as a body to Ireland, but naturally took real effect only in the counties which were nearer to Dublin, the seat of Anglo-Irish rule. There was a replica, but on a small and embryonic scale, of all that England possessed but which in the larger island grew into an efficient parliamentary monarchy. To the ' English of Ireland ' were secured, first by Henry and more particularly by John, Henry III and Edward I, all the laws of English ' liege subjects,' which status the colonial stock never lost, however rebellious and ' degenerate ' (hibernicized) they became in time. Magna Carta in its final issue became also their heritage (I, 8, 9).

(3) Among these institutions were the feudal ones of manorial and baronial jurisdiction, reaching their height in the palatine earldoms of Desmond and Ormond, and the system of chartered boroughs with the characteristic Anglo-Norman civic liberties. Dublin, the capital, was a supreme instance of a ' royal borough,' while, more restricted in their liberties, there were many ' lords' towns ' such as Wexford, and others, which enjoyed ' Breteuil rights ' from barons or bishops (I, 6, 7, 16). The Church, as in medieval England, had also its rights constantly recognized or insisted upon.

(4) The internal government of Ireland. The King being almost permanently an absentee, his government at Dublin was exercised by his viceroys, often English-born, styled Justiciar, Lieutenant, ' Custos,' etc. Their commissions varied in the extent of powers conveyed, the Lieutenant coming nearest to full regal

authority. In the latter half of the fifteenth century Lord Deputies begin, representing royal princes who had the title of Lieutenant but seldom came over. The system reached its height in the Earls of Kildare who, from about 1470 till 1534, practically ruled the country more in their own interests and those of the Anglo-Irish nobility than those of the English Crown (I, 19, 22, 23).

(5) The legal and political status of the native Gaelic race towards the English Crown, the Anglo-Norman lords and the colonial element in general. This makes a complicated story. Attempts were made from the time of Henry II to Edward III to extend English law in some fashion to the Irish. Henry at least accepted Rory O'Conor as King of Connacht, and John and Henry III admitted Irish kingships, while the chief Irish dynasts of the five provinces had in theory at least a legal standing in the Anglo-Irish courts. With Edward I the question became acute and this monarch seems to have genuinely wished to bring the Irish, or at least those who wished it, within the benefits and the duties of English law, custom and allegiance. Edward II, and Edward III in the earlier part of his reign, attempted this policy but it would appear that the selfish interest of the Anglo-Irish obstructed the royal will. At all events no Irish parliament of the medieval period passed a general statute of emancipation. It must be admitted that the practical difficulties were great, and it can be questioned if the mass of the native race under their proud chiefs really wished for the position of English subjects after the first impact of the Conquest. Finally the Statutes of Kilkenny (1366) settled the question in a sense adverse to the Irish by excluding from the rights of English law and land tenure, as enjoyed by the English in Ireland, those who lived under Irish law and the rule of their own chiefs. By these statutes, designed to check the ' degeneracy ' of ' the great of lineage ' and preserve an English enclave in Ireland, the English subjects and the Irish ' inter anglicos ' in some eight counties are ordered under severe penalties to speak English, have English surnames, and forsake Irish law, language and intermarriage with ' the Irish enemies.' The latter, the ' mere ' or pure Irish, who continue to live under their own chiefs by Brehon law, are regarded as outside the protection of ' English law and liberty.' This made them incapable of offices in Church, state and towns, or to trade freely and hold freehold land within ' the obedient shires,' i.e. wherever the King's writ ran. The Irish chiefs and their septs might be treated occasionally as vassals, but legally they were not regarded as liege subjects.[1]

[1] For this difficult and complicated subject see Curtis, *Hist. of Medieval Ireland* (2nd ed. 1938), pp. 231–4 and Appendix IV, ' Legal treatment of the Irish in Medieval Ireland.' This quotes several instances of grants of English liberty and release from Irish servitude. What Irish servitude and exclusion from English rights meant for the Irish see *Cal. of Ormond Deeds*, III, pp. 263 and 302, where such grants are made by Henry VII to Cormac MacCarthy lord of Muskerry, and to William Casshene (' Irishman '). One of our documents here (I, 15) gives a picture of the ' betaghs ' or Irish villeins as they existed on a Norman manor in 1333.

In this rightless position the mass of the native Irish existed till Chichester's parliament (1613–15) declared the Statutes of Kilkenny and all such anti-Irish laws null and void ; consequent upon which all natives of Ireland became common subjects of the Crown. In the middle ages, however, the King, through his viceroy in Ireland, granted many charters of ' English law and liberty ' to individual Irishmen, or to petty septs with their ruling chiefs as a matter of grace or policy (I, 4, 10, 13, 14, 15, 21).

The great Anglo-Irish lords practised also this royal prerogative of denization, and the Earl of Ormond, for example, as Palatine lord of Tipperary by royal grant, made numerous treaties with subject or adjacent Gaelic chiefs and admitted many of his Irish tenants and townsmen to English law and liberty.

(6) The ' degeneracy ' of the Anglo-Irish. This was a phenomenon appearing within a century after the first landing of the Cambro-Normans under Strongbow, they themselves being in reality a French-speaking and feudal race in no way yet anglicized, or bridled by the strong hand of Angevin monarchy. The falling away of numbers of them in the remoter parts to Irish ways of dress, law, war, and warlike habits is noted and denounced as early as the parliament of 1297. In various ways and by various events too long to retail here, this hibernization continued to grow and the Statutes of Kilkenny recognized it as an almost universal evil. By the time of Poynings' parliament (1494) when the royal authority in Ireland was at its lowest ebb, little but the four counties round Dublin (with, of course, the chartered towns) obeyed the laws of the State and held true to English order, speech and tradition. The rest was divided into great lordships of the feudal type and petty kingships of the Gaelic order, speech and culture. Frequently these were intermingled, and Gaelic or ' Brehon ' law, and feudal custom mixed with Irish (' loi de March '), ran side by side (I, 11, 17, 22).

Nevertheless the Fitzgerald earls of Kildare and Desmond and the Butler earls of Ormond maintained a princely and more or less English state and form of local sovereignty. They were the Irish counterpart of the ' overmighty subject ' common in England in the fifteenth century. Part of their power rested upon the vassalage of Irish chiefs, and agreements of military service and ' retainer ' with prominent Anglo-Irishmen who were their neighbours or vassals (I, 16, 27).

(7) The Irish Parliament. The beginnings of an Irish representative system began under Edward I, and in 1297 practical convenience led to the deputies of counties, liberties, towns and Church receiving the summons to supplement the barons and prelates who with the council met to advise the justiciar. The system as far as it developed in Ireland was completed late in Edward III's reign. But the Irish parliament, though it claimed to bind all Ireland, remained in fact representative only of the prelates and magnates, the counties and the towns, of the English Pale, an area which steadily dwindled during the fifteenth century. The alliance

of the Anglo-Irish with the House of York, begun under the viceroyalty of Richard, Duke of York, who came as Lord Lieutenant for Henry VI in 1449, enabled the leaders of the ' English by blood ' to get practical control of the petty but self-important parliament of Dublin. In 1460 it took the opportunity of England's fatal divisions to declare its legislative independence as far as Ireland was concerned (I, 28). This internal autonomy, owing to the feebleness of English rule, henceforth till 1534 had all the aspect of ' Home Rule ' of an aristocratic and colonial type but suffered its first reverse at the Parliament of Drogheda in 1494 when the famous Lord Deputy, Sir Edward Poynings, got passed the restrictive act known by his name which lasted till 1782 and in some sense till the Union.

MODERN IRELAND FROM 1494

The Tudor period (to which the early years of James I's reign form an epilogue) marked the end of Gaelic and feudal Ireland. The Dublin administration was brought under English control (II, 2, 4, 16) ; the area under the effectual rule of the Crown was steadily enlarged (II, 19, 20) ; the Norman palatinates were abolished (save that of Ormond which lasted till 1715) ; the great Gaelic princes and lords, formerly petty kings, were banished or reduced to the position of ordinary landlords ; English settlers were encouraged ; and a series of colonization projects, of which the plantation in Ulster was the best planned, were set on foot (III, 2, 3). The way seemed clear for the enforcement of English law and the spread of English civilization and language.

But the ecclesiastical legislation of the sixteenth century had erected a new obstacle to the formation of a united Irish community owing allegiance to the English crown. Liege subjects in Ireland, as elsewhere, were supposed to be members of the State Church, in spite of the fact that most Irishmen would have nothing to do with it. Twice in the seventeenth century the Gaelic and Old English catholics rose in defence of their religion and lands, and the confiscations which followed these revolts transferred to the protestant interest the bulk of the land of Ireland and established a harsh form of landlordism which was only remedied in the nineteenth century. Meanwhile the catholics, whether of Gaelic or English stock, were fused into a united community by common tribulations. For they were driven out of political life and severely hampered in their religious, educational and economic activities by the penal laws enacted during the seventeenth and early eighteenth centuries (IV, 4).

The Tudor ideal of government for Ireland was a vigorous administrative monarchy unifying the country by energetic executive action. Parliament, while regarded as a useful instrument of government, occupied a relatively subordinate place. But in Chichester's parliament (1613–15) the politico-religious opposition of the Irish catholics to the government programme was a precursor of later demands for self-government through a free parliament. In the

2

parliament of 1640 catholics and protestants united in upholding the rights of parliament and criticising the executive (III, 9). The outbreak of the Irish rebellion of 1641, coinciding with the beginning of a critical stage in the conflict between the crown and parliament in England, led to parliamentary intervention in the affairs of Ireland. In addition, since during the seventeenth and most of the eighteenth centuries, mercantilism dominated economic thinking, the parliament at Westminster was induced by considerations of imperial economic policy besides those of prestige, to treat Ireland as under its jurisdiction (III, 19–23). Irishmen hotly resented this claim. The catholic assembly at Kilkenny asserted that the Irish parliament was a 'free parliament of itself'; James II's Irish parliament declared it was a sovereign legislature ; and finally towards the close of the eighteenth century the protestant ruling caste led by the 'patriot party' in the house of commons successfully asserted the legislative independence of Ireland.

The settlement of 1782 in so far as it regulated Anglo-Irish relations, was a delicately adjusted—and, it might be argued, incomplete—arrangement. The British parliament had renounced the right to legislate for Ireland, but the Irish executive was controlled by the British cabinet.

At home, the Irish parliament, after a decade of independence, had to deal not only with the catholics who began to demand the repeal of the penal laws, but also with middle-class radicals who believed in liberty and equality and resented the practical monopoly of political power possessed by the landed gentry (IV, 24). The extreme reformers might not in themselves have been dangerous, but they were supported by a discontented and organized peasantry. Parliament, rejecting the whig policy of concession (IV, 23), met the situation by enacting the emergency legislation which the government declared was required (IV, 12). After the rebellion of 1798 Pitt made a bold attempt to solve Ireland's problems, external and domestic, by a union with Great Britain (IV, 13, 22).

The union issued in a century of almost continuous strife. The catholics led by O'Connell, a brilliant innovator in the technique of mass organization, fought for complete emancipation which was not obtained until 1829 (V, 1, 2). Shortly afterwards the struggle for self-government began. O'Connell simply asked for the repeal of the Union (V, 11). Later this sweeping, and apparently impracticable, programme was superseded by a more modest demand for some form of federal Home Rule (V, 12–14). But Parnell, at least, always made it clear that any measure of self-government would probably be used for winning further concessions. To the national claim for Home Rule, Davitt and Parnell linked the urgent and popular cause of agrarian reform. By the beginning of the twentieth century the economic and political power of the landed gentry had been almost completely destroyed, and rural Ireland was well on the way to becoming a country of peasant proprietors (V, 1–10).

Unionists throughout the British Isles defended the union with essentially the same arguments as Pitt had used when advocating it. In the three southern provinces of Ireland they were relatively too few and scattered to influence seriously the course of events. But in Ulster they were numerous, comparatively concentrated, and quite prepared to defy parliament rather than be excluded from its jurisdiction.

O'Connell and the Home Rule leaders believed they could obtain their ends by peaceful and strictly legal methods. But there was another tradition in Irish nationalism, going back to the closing years of the eighteenth century, which despised constitutional action, relied on physical force, and regarded a republic as the ideal form of government. Successive exponents of this outlook were Young Irelanders such as Mitchel, the Fenians, the Irish Republican Brotherhood and many of those associated with Sinn Féin. At the end of the nineteenth century came an attempt to revive the then rapidly dying Irish language and give Irish nationalism a cultural basis (V, 24). With this conception of a Gaelic community the older nationalist leaders, Grattan, Tone, O'Connell and Parnell, whose nationalism was political and economic, had showed no sympathy whatever. The Gaelic movement claimed to be non-political. In fact, naturally enough, it inspired the more extreme nationalists.

After the constitutional Home Rulers had been thrice thwarted when apparently on the brink of success (in 1886, 1893 and 1914) the political situation was more and more controlled by those who believed in direct action. In 1916 there was an armed rising which was suppressed. In 1919, when democracy and national self-determination were being enunciated as the guiding principles which ought to govern political development, a national assembly, claiming to derive its power from the people and to be alone entitled to act for Ireland, met in Dublin and set up an administration which strove to supersede the existing governmental machinery (V, 31–33). After nearly three years of civil strife the imperial government yielded, and by the terms of the treaty of 1921 Ireland was given the status of a British dominion. This implied a far greater degree of self government than any of the Home Rule bills had offered, and, when the constitutional developments of the following decade are taken into account, may be said to have given Ireland virtual independence, together with opportunities for co-operation with an important group of nations speaking the same language and upholding similar democratic ideals.

In one respect the settlement disappointed and shocked nationalist opinion. The new Irish government had jurisdiction over only twenty-six counties. The last of the Home Rule bills, the government of Ireland act of 1920, while trying to preserve at least a tenuous Irish unity, had dealt with the Ulster question by giving six of the northern counties a legislature of their own, and in 1922 Northern Ireland, exercising its right of choice under the treaty, decided to remain part of the United Kingdom. The Ulster unionists were determined not to be a minority in a united Ireland, even though

their decision involved the creation or intensification of a proportionately greater minority problem in the six county area.
However, a discussion of these developments would remove us from
the sphere of history to that of politics.

ABBREVIATIONS

Acts privy council, 1554–6 [etc.] . *Acts of the privy council of England*,
                                   1554–6 [etc.] (London, 1890–).

Acts privy council, Ire., 1556–71 . ' Acts of the privy council in Ireland,
                                   1556–71,' ed. J. T. Gilbert in
                                   Hist. MSS. Comm., 15*th rep.*,
                                   app. 3 (London, 1897).

Analecta Hib. .   .   . Analecta Hibernica.

Berry, Early Statutes .   . *Statutes and ordinances and acts of*
                                   the parliament of Ireland, King
                                   John to Henry V., ed. H. F. Berry
                                   (Dublin, 1907).

Cal. Doc. Ire., 1171–1251 .   . Calendar of documents relating to
                                   Ireland, 1171–1251 (London, 1875).

Cal. Ormond Deeds .   .   . Calendar of Ormond deeds, ed. E.
                                   Curtis (Irish MSS. Commission,
                                   1932–43).

Commons journ. .   .   . Journals of the house of commons
                                   of England.

Commons journ., Ire. .   . Journals of the house of commons
                                   of the kingdom of Ireland, 1613–
                                   1800 (19 vols., Dublin, 1796–1800).

Ir. Stat. .   .   .   . Statutes at large passed in the
                                   parliaments held in Ireland, 1310–
                                   1800 (20 vols., Dublin, 1786–1801).

Lords journ., Ire. .   .   . Journals of the house of lords of
                                     Ireland, 1634–1800 (8 vols., Dublin,
                                   1779–1800).

Proc. RIA .   .   .   . Proceedings of the Royal Irish
                                   Academy.

S.P. Henry VIII .   . State papers, Henry VIII (11 vols.,
                                   London, 1830–52).

Stat. of realm .   .   . Statutes of the realm of England
                                   (10 vols., 1810–22).

SECTION I. FROM THE NORMAN CONQUEST TO THE TUDOR PERIOD

1. THE BULL *LAUDABILITER*, POPE ADRIAN IV'S GRANT OF IRELAND TO HENRY II

ADRIAN, bishop, servant of the servants of God, to our well-beloved son in Christ the illustrious king of the English, greeting and apostolic benediction.

Laudably and profitably does your majesty contemplate spreading the glory of your name on earth and laying up for yourself the reward of eternal happiness in heaven, in that, as becomes a catholic prince, you purpose to enlarge the boundaries of the Church, to proclaim the truths of the Christian religion to a rude and ignorant people, and to root out the growths of vice from the field of the Lord ; and the better to accomplish this purpose you seek the counsel and goodwill of the apostolic see. In pursuing your object, the loftier your aim and the greater your discretion, the more prosperous, we are assured, with God's assistance, will be the progress you will make : for undertakings commenced in the zeal of faith and the love of religion are ever wont to attain to a good end and issue. Verily, as your excellency doth acknowledge, there is no doubt that Ireland and all islands on which Christ the sun of righteousness has shone, and which have accepted the doctrines of the Christian faith, belong to the jurisdiction of the blessed Peter and the holy Roman Church ; wherefore the more pleased are we to plant in them the seed of faith acceptable to God, inasmuch as our conscience warns us that in their case a stricter account will hereafter be required of us.

Whereas then, well-beloved son in Christ, you have expressed to us your desire to enter the island of Ireland in order to subject its people to law and to root out from them the weeds of vice, and your willingness to pay an annual tribute to the blessed Peter of one penny from every house, and to maintain the rights of the churches of that land whole and inviolate : We therefore, meeting your pious and laudable desire with due favour and according a gracious assent to your petition, do hereby declare our will and pleasure that, with a view to enlarging the boundaries of the Church, restraining the downward course of vice, correcting evil customs and planting virtue, and for the increase of the Christian religion, you shall enter that island and execute whatsoever may tend to the honour of God and the welfare of the land ; and also that the people of that land shall receive you with honour and revere you as their lord : provided always that the rights of the churches remain whole and inviolate, and saving to the blessed Peter and the Holy Roman Church the annual tribute of one penny from every house. If then you should carry your project into effect, let it be your care to instruct that people in good ways of life, and so act, both in person and by agents whom you shall have found in faith, in word, and in deed fitted for the task, that the Church there may be adorned, that the Christian religion may take root and grow, and that all things appertaining to the honour of God and the salvation of souls may be so ordered that you may deserve at God's hands the fullness of an everlasting reward, and may obtain on earth a name renowned throughout the ages.

[The original Latin text of this famous document is found in Giraldus Cambrensis, *Expugnatio Hibernica*, Bk. II, chap. vi. It was granted during the pontificate of the English pope, Adrian IV (1154–59), probably in 1155, but was not acted upon until 1172.]

2. THE CONSTITUTIONS OF THE SYNOD OF CASHEL, 1172

In the year of our Lord 1172, being the first year in which Henry, king of England and conqueror of Ireland, obtained the dominion of that island, Christian, bishop of Lismore and legate of the Apostolic see, Donatus, archbishop of Cashel, Laurence, archbishop of Dublin, and Catholicus [Cadhla], archbishop of Tuam, together with their suffragans and fellow-bishops, and many abbots, archdeacons, priors, and other Irish prelates, assembled by the conqueror's command at the city of Cashel, and there held a synod concerning the well-being of the Church and the reformation thereof.

At this synod were present, on the King's behalf, Ralph, abbot of Buildewas, Ralph, archdeacon of Llandaff, Nicholas the chaplain, and other clerks, having the commision of our lord the King. The decrees of the synod were subscribed by the prelates, and confirmed by the royal authority ; as follows :

' First. That all the faithful throughout Ireland shall eschew concubinage with their cousins and kinsfolk, and shall contract and adhere to lawful marriages.

' Second. That children shall be catechized outside the church doors, and infants baptized at the consecrated fonts in the baptisteries of the churches.

' Third. That all good Christians shall pay the tithes of beasts, corn, and other produce, to the church of the parish in which they live.

' Fourth. That all the lands and possessions of the church be entirely free from all exactions of secular [lay] persons ; and especially, that neither the petty kings [*reguli*], earls, or other great men in Ireland, nor their sons, nor any of their household, shall exact provisions and lodgings from any ecclesiastical territories, as the custom is, nor under any pretence presume to extort the same by violent means ; and that the detestable practice of extorting a loaf four times a year from the vills belonging to the churches, by neighbouring lords, shall henceforth be utterly abolished.

' Fifth. That in the case of a homicide committed by laymen, when it is compounded for by the adverse parties, none of the clergy, though of kindred to the perpetrators of the crime, shall contribute anything ; that, as they were free from the guilt of the homicide, so they shall be also exonerated from any payment in satisfaction therefor.

' Sixth. That every good Christian, being sick and weak, shall solemnly make his last will and testament in the presence of his confessor and neighbours, and that, if he have wife and children, all his moveable goods (his debts and servants' wages being first paid) shall be divided into three parts, one of which he shall bequeath to his children, another to his lawful wife, and the third to such uses as he shall declare. And if it shall happen that there be no lawful child or children, then his goods shall be equally divided between his wife and legatees. And if his wife die before him, then his goods shall be divided into two parts, of which the children shall take one, and his residuary legatees the other.

' Seventh. That those who depart this life after a good confession shall be buried with masses and vigils and all due ceremonies.

' Finally. That divine offices shall be henceforth celebrated in every part of Ireland according to the forms and usages of the church of England.'

[For it is right and just that, as by divine Providence Ireland has received her lord and king from England, she should also submit to a reformation from the same source. Indeed both the realm and church of Ireland are indebted to this mighty King for whatever they enjoy of the blessings of peace and the growth of religion ; as, before his coming to Ireland, all sorts of wickedness had prevailed among this people for a long series of years, which now, by his authority and careful administration, are abolished.

The primate of Armagh was not present at this synod by reason of his infirmities and advanced age, but he afterwards came to Dublin and gave his assent to the royal will in all these matters.] [1]

[From Giraldus Cambrensis, *Expugnatio Hibernica*, Bk. I, chap. xxxiv.]

3. THE THREE LETTERS OF POPE ALEXANDER III, CONFIRMING HENRY II'S CONQUEST OF IRELAND, 1172

Letter 1

Alexander, bishop, servant of the servants of God, to the venerable brothers Christian, bishop of Lismore, legate of the apostolic See, and Gelasius of Armagh, Donatus of Cashel, Laurence of Dublin, and Catholicus [Cadhla] of Tuam, archbishops, and their suffragans, greeting and apostolic blessing. With what shocking abuses the Irish people are infected and how, lapsed from the fear of God and reverence for the Christian faith, they follow those things which lead to the peril of their souls, has been made known

[1] The portion in brackets is not part of the decrees, but the comment of Giraldus, the historian.

to Us in a series of letters from you, and also has often come to the knowledge of the Apostolic See by the trustworthy accounts of others.

Hence it is that—understanding from your letters that our dear son in Christ, Henry, illustrious King of England, stirred by divine inspiration and with his united forces, has subjected to his dominion that people, a barbarous one uncivilized and ignorant of the Divine law, and that those evils which were unlawfully practised in your land are now, with God's help, already beginning to diminish— We are overjoyed and have offered our grateful prayers to Him who has granted to the said King so great a victory and triumph, humbly beseeching that by the vigilance and care of the same King that most undisciplined and untamed nation may in and by all things persevere in devotion to the practice of the Christian faith, and that you and your ecclesiastical brethren may rejoice in all due honour and tranquillity.

Since therefore it is fitting that you should afford all your due care and support to carry on such things which have had so pious and happy a beginning, We command and enjoin upon you by these our Apostolic letters that you will diligently and manfully and as far as you are able, saving your order and office, assist the above-said King, so great a man and so devout a son of the Church, to maintain and preserve that land and to extirpate the filthiness of such great abominations.

And if any of the Kings, princes or other persons of that land shall rashly attempt to go against his due oath and fealty pledged to the said King and does not at your admonition promptly, as he ought, return to his allegiance, then you, trusting in the Apostolic authority and putting aside every pretext and excuse, shall lay ecclesiastical censure on such a one, diligently and effectively executing this our injunction so that—even as the said King, like a most Catholic and Christian prince is said to have obeyed our wishes in pious and generous fashion in restoring to you the tithes and other ecclesiastical rights and all things which belong to the liberties of the Church—you also will do, if you firmly respect those things which belong to the royal dignity and to the best of your ability make them to be respected by others.

Given at Tusculum on the 12th of the Kalends of October [September 20, 1172].

Letter 2

Alexander, bishop, servant of the servants of God, to his dear son in Christ, Henry, illustrious king of England, greeting and apostolic blessing.

By frequent report and trustworthy evidence and with much joy, we have been assured how that, like a pious king and magnificent prince, you have wonderfully and gloriously triumphed over that people of Ireland, who, ignoring the fear of God, in unbridled fashion at random wander through the steeps of vice, and have renounced all reverence for the Christian faith and virtue, and who destroy themselves in mutual slaughter, and over a kingdom which the Roman emperors, the conquerors of the world, left (so we read) untouched in their time, and, by the will of God (as we firmly believe), have extended the power of your majesty over that same people, a race uncivilized and undisciplined. For, while we for the present omit other monstrous abuses which the same race, neglecting the observances of the Christian faith, irreverently practice, even as the venerable our brothers, Christian, bishop of Lismore, legate of the Apostolic See, and the archbishops and bishops of that land, have made known to us in their letters, and our dear son Ralph, archdeacon of Landaff, an intelligent and discreet man and bound by the chain of peculiar devotion to your royal majesty, who with his own eyes has seen all these things and made them known to you in person, both carefully and clearly, it appears that the aforesaid people, as perhaps has more fully come to your know-ledge, marry their stepmothers and are not ashamed to have children by them ; a man will live with his brother's wife while the brother is still alive ; one man will live in concubinage with two sisters ; and many of them, putting away the mother, will marry the daughters.

And all from time to time eat meat in Lent ; nor do they pay tithes, or respect as they ought the churches of God and ecclesiastical persons.

And because (for so the said archbishops and bishops have signi-fied to Us and the aforesaid archdeacon has more fully and expressly informed us) We understand that you, collecting your splendid naval and land forces, have set your mind upon subjugating that people to your lordship and, by the Divine grace, extirpating the filthiness of such abomination, We hold your purpose good and acceptable in all ways, and therefore render to Him from who all good proceeds, and who disposes the pious deeds of his faithful ones at his good pleasure, all our grateful prayers, beseeching the Almighty Lord with fervent prayer that, even as by your influence those evils which so wickedly are practised in that land begin already to diminish and the seeds of virtue to flourish instead, so also by you with God's aid the said people, with the stains of vice cast away, may receive the whole discipline of the Christian faith, to the glory of an unfading crown for you and the health of their souls.

And so we exhort and beseech your majesty and enjoin upon you for the remission of your sins that in this work which you have so laudably begun you will even more intently and strenuously continue, so that, even as you have to the remission of your sins undertaken so great a task as regards that people, so also for the benefit to their souls you shall be worthy of an eternal crown.

And because, owing to your majesty's greatness, the Roman Church has a different right in islands than on the mainland, We (holding this hope and trust, through the fervour of your devotion that wills not only to preserve the rights of the Church but even to increase them and, where She has no rights, feels bound to confer them upon Her) beseech and earnestly enjoin upon your majesty that you will carefully seek to preserve the rights of the see of Saint Peter for us in the abovesaid land and that, even if it has none there, you will appoint and assign those rights to the Church, so that in return we may owe your highness the fullest gratitude and that you may be seen to offer to God the first fruits of your glory and your triumph.

Given at Tusculum, the twelfth of the Kalends of October.

Letter 3

Alexander, bishop, servant of the servants of God, to our dear and noble sons, the Kings and Princes of Ireland, greeting and apostolic blessing.

Whereas by common report and the assured relation of many it has been made known to us that you have received our dear son in Christ, Henry, the illustrious king of England, as your king and lord, and have sworn fealty to him, the greater is our joy in that, by God's aid and the power of the said King, there shall reign in your land greater peace and tranquillity and that the Irish people, in proportion as, through the enormity and filthiness of their vices, they have fallen away so far from the Divine law, so they shall be all the more surely moulded in it and receive all the more fully the discipline of the Christian faith.

Wherefore, in that you have of your free will submitted to so powerful and magnificent a king and so devoted a son of the Church, we commend your wise forethought as most worthy of praise, seeing that from it great advantage can be looked for alike to you, to the Church and to the whole people of that land.

' We moreover warn and admonish your noble order to strive to preserve the fealty which by solemn oath you have made to so great a king firm and unbroken with due submission towards him. And may you so show yourselves, in all humility and meekness, submissive and devoted towards him that you may be able ever to win his abundant favour and that we may be able to commend fully your prudence and foresight.

Given at Tusculum, 12th day of the Kalends of October.

[Translated from the Latin text of the three letters of Pope Alexander III, respectively addressed to the bishops of Ireland, to Henry II, and to the kings and princes of Ireland, confirming Henry's conquest of the country in 1171–2. The originals are printed in Hearne, *Black Book of the Exchequer* (1728) pp. 42–7 ; Rymer's *Foedera* (1816) I, p. 45 ; and *Opera Alex.* III, Migne, 200, col. 883–6.]

4. THE TREATY OF WINDSOR, 1175, BETWEEN HENRY II AND RORY O'CONOR, HIGH KING

This is the agreement which was made at Windsor in the octaves of Michaelmas [October 6] in the year of Our Lord 1175, between Henry, king of England, and Roderic [Rory], king of Connaught, by Catholicus, archbishop of Tuam, Cantordis, abbot of Clonfert, and Master Laurence, chancellor of the king of Connaught, namely :

The king of England has granted to Roderic [Rory], his liege-man, king of Connacht, as long as he shall faithfully serve him, that he shall be king under him, ready to his service, as his man. And he shall hold his land as fully and as peacefully as he held it before the lord king entered Ireland, rendering him tribute. And that he shall have all the rest of the land and its inhabitants under him and shall bring them to account [*justiciet eos*], so that they shall pay their full tribute to the king of England through him, and so that they shall maintain their rights. And those who are now in posses-sion of their lands and rights shall hold them in peace as long as they remain in the fealty of the king of England, and continue to pay him faithfully and fully his tribute and the other rights which they owe to him, by the hand of the king of Connaught, saving in all things the right and honour of the king of England and of Roderic. And if any of them shall be rebels to the king of England and to Roderic and shall refuse to pay the tribute and other rights of the king of England by his hand, and shall withdraw from the fealty of the king of England, he, Roderic, shall judge them and remove them. And if he cannot answer for them by himself, the constable of the king of England in that land [Ireland] shall, when called upon by him, aid him to do what is necessary.

And for this agreement the said king of Connaught shall render to the king of England tribute every year, namely, out of every ten animals slaughtered, one hide, acceptable to the merchants both in his land as in the rest ; save that he shall not meddle with those lands which the lord king has retained in his lordship and in the lordship of his barons ; that is to say, Dublin with all its appurten-ances ; Meath with all its appurtenances, even as Murchat Ua Mailethlachlin [Murchadh O' Melaghlin] held it fully and freely [*melius et plenius*] or as others held it of him ; Wexford with all its appurtenances, that is to say, the whole of Leinster ; and Waterford with its whole territory from Waterford to Dungarvan, including Dungarvan with all its appurtenances.

And if the Irish who have fled wish to return to the land of the barons of the king of England they may do so in peace, paying the said tribute as others pay it, or doing to the English the services which they were wont to do for their lands, which shall be decided by the judgment and will of their lords. And if any of them are unwilling to return and their lords have called upon the king of Connaught, he shall compel them to return to their land, so that they shall dwell there in peace.

And the king of Connaught shall accept hostages from all whom the lord king of England has committed to him, and he shall him-self give hostages at the will of the king.

The witnesses are Robert, bishop of Winchester ; Geoffrey, bishop of Ely ; Laurence, archbishop of Dublin ; Geoffrey Nicholas and Roger, the king's chaplains ; William, Earl of

Essex ; Richard de Luci ; Geoffrey de Purtico, and Reginald de Courtenea.

[For the Latin text of this document see Rymer's *Foedera* I, p. 31 ; *Gesta Henrici* I, pp. 101–3, and Rog. Howden's chronicle I, pp. 83, 84.]

5. GRANT OF PRINCE JOHN TO THEOBALD WALTER OF LANDS IN IRELAND (1185)

John, son of the King of England, Lord of Ireland, to all archbishops, bishops, abbots, earls, barons, justices, etc., and lieges, French, English and Irish, cleric and lay, present and to come, greeting. Know that we have enfeoffed Ranulf de Glanville and Theobald Walter, our lieges, in 5½ cantreds of land in Limerick, viz. the burgh of Kildelo [Killaloe] with half of the cantred called Truohekedmalech in which that burgh is situate ; the whole cantred of Elykaruel [Ely O'Carroll] ; the whole cantred of Elyhogarthi ; the whole cantred of Ewermun [Ormond] ; the whole cantred of Areth and Wetheni [Arra and Owney] ; and the whole cantred of Owethenihokathelan and Owethenihoiffernan [Owney O'Cathelan and Owney O'Hiffernan]. These five and a half cantreds I have given them for their homage and service with all their appurtenances in wood and plain, in castles and fortresses, meadows and pastures, etc. ; also the donations of parish churches which are in those lands or shall be there. To hold of me and my heirs for ever to them and their heirs in fee and heritage by service of a fee of twenty-two knights for all service. In the same lands also I have given and granted them and their heirs sac and soc, toll and theam, infangenthef and all other liberties and free customs which pertain to the same lands, except crosses and donations of bishoprics and abbeys and dignities which belong to the royal Crown, which I have retained to myself. Wherefore I wish and ordain that they shall hold all the above well and in peace, freely fully and entirely in all free customs, etc., as above-said. And this I have confirmed by my seal.

Witnesses : Hugh de Lacy, our constable, Bertram de Verdon, our seneschal, Gilbert Pipard, William de Wennevail, our steward, John de Curcy, Alard, ' camerarius,' William the chaplain, Richard clerk ' de camera nostra,' etc., given at Waterford.

[This fine specimen of a feudal grant from the Lord of Ireland, on which the greatness of the Butlers, later Earls of Ormond, was founded is taken from the *Calendar of Ormond Deeds* (ed. Curtis), II, No. 426. See also *ibid.* I, p. 12.]

6. GRANT OF CIVIC LIBERTIES TO DUBLIN, BY PRINCE JOHN, 1192

John, Lord of Ireland and Earl of Mortain, to all his men and friends, French, English, Irish and Welsh, present and to come, greeting.
Know that I have given, granted and by this my charter con-

firmed to my citizens of Dublin dwelling both without the walls as within, even to the boundaries of the town : That they may have their boundaries even as they were perambulated by the oath of lawful men of the same city by command of King Henry my father, viz. from the eastern part of Dublin, and on the southern part the meadow which goes to the gate of St Kevin's church and so by the road even to Kilmerecaregan and so by the boundary of land from Donnybrook to the Dodder and from the Dodder to the sea, viz. to Clarade near the sea and from Clarade even to Renniuelan [Ringsend], and in the western part of Dublin from St Patrick's by the valley even to Karnaclonegunethe [Dolphin's Barn] and thence to the boundary of Kilmainham and beyond the water (stream) of Kilmainham near Avon Liffey even to the fords of Kylmehavoc and beyond the water of Avon Liffey to the north by Ennecnegavhoc (or ' ganhoc ') and thence to the granges [orrea] of Holy Trinity and from those granges to the Forks [furcas] and so by the boundary between Clonliffe and Crinan even to the Tolka and thence to the church of Houstmanebi.

And that they have all liberties and customs and the undermentioned liberties.

The liberties which I have granted them to have, are as follows : that no citizen of Dublin shall plead outside the walls on any plea save for the pleas of external tenements which do not belong to the Hundred court of the town.

And that they shall be free of *murdrum* within the boundaries of the town.

And that no citizen shall make *duellum* [ordeal of Battle] in the city for any appeal [charge] which anyone may make against him, but he shall clear himself by oath of 40 lawful men of the same said city.

And that no one shall take forced quarters within the walls by assise or by order of any marshal against the will of the citizens.

And that they shall be free of toll, lastage, passage and pontage and all other duties throughout my whole land and jurisdiction.

That no one shall be put into mercy for a fine except according to the law of the Hundred [court], viz. by forfeiture of 40^s for which he who falls into mercy shall be quit of half and shall give the other half as a fine, excepting the three fines for bread, ale, and the watch, which are fines of 2^s 6^d, of which one half shall be pardoned and the other paid.

That the Hundred court shall be held once in the week.

That no one shall in any plea be debarred by miskenning.

That they shall justly have their lands, tenures, pledges and debts throughout all my land and jurisdiction whosoever shall owe them, and that they may distrain their debtors by their pledges in Dublin.

That of the lands and tenures which are within the walls justice shall be done to them according to the custom of the city.

That of debts which are arranged and pledges given within the city the pleas shall be held according to the custom of the city.

And if any one anywhere in our land or jurisdiction shall take toll of the men of the city and does not return it after being summoned to do so, the reeve of the city shall take pledge therefor in Dublin and distrain for its return.

That no extern merchant shall buy within the city of any extern man corn, hides or wool save from the citizens.

That no extern merchant shall have a tavern for wine, save on a ship. But this liberty is reserved to me, that from each ship which happens to come thither with wine, my bailiff in my place shall choose two tuns of wine according as he wishes in the ship ; namely, one before the mast and one behind the mast to my use, for 40^8 ; one for 20^8 and the other for 20^8 ; and he shall take nothing further therefrom, save at the will of the merchant.

That no extern merchant shall sell cloth in the city by cutting [ad decisionem].

That no extern merchant shall stay in the town with his wares, for the purpose of selling his wares, more than 40 days.

Also no Dublin citizen anywhere in my land or jurisdiction shall be pledged or distrained for any debt, unless he himself be debtor or pledge.

And that they [my citizens] may marry, both themselves, their sons, daughters and widows, without leave of their lords.

Also that none of their lords, on the ground of extern estates, shall have wardship or giving [in wardship] of their sons, daughters or widows, but only the wardship of their lands which are in their [the lords'] fee, until they come of age.

That no assise [recognitio] be made in the city.

Also that they shall have all their rightful gilds, as fully as the burgesses of Bristol have or are accustomed to have.

That no citizen shall be compelled to repledge anyone, unless he wishes to do so, although he may be dwelling on his land.

I have granted also all tenures within and without the walls up to the abovesaid boundaries, to be disposed of according to their will by common assent of the city, in messuages, thickets and buildings on the water [river] and elsewhere wherever they shall be in the town, to be held in free burgage, viz. by the service of land-gable which they pay within the walls.

I have granted also that each of them may improve himself, as far as he is able, in making buildings wherever he shall wish upon the water [river], without damage however to the citizens and the town.

Also that they may have and possess all vacant lands and plots which are contained within the said boundaries ; to build on at their will.

Also that neither Templars nor Hospitallers shall have any man or any messuage free of the common duties of the city, within the said boundaries, save one only.

All these things I have granted, saving the tenures and lands of all those who have lands and tenures by charter from me outside the walls up to the said boundaries, so that the city may not dispose of these as it may of others, but let them all obey all the customs of the city like other citizens. Of those however I say this, who had my charter for any lands within the same boundaries outside the walls, before We granted to the city the aforesaid liberties and this charter.

Wherefore I well and firmly command, that my abovesaid citizens of Dublin and their heirs after them shall have and hold all the abovesaid liberties and free customs, as is written above, of me and my heirs as fully entirely and well as they ever had them, in peace and honourably, without any impediment or hindrance which anyone may make against them.'

Witnesses : Stephen Ridell, my chancellor ; William de Kahaignes, my seneschal, Theobald Walter, my butler, Hamo de Valognes, etc.

[For the Latin text see Gilbert, *Historic and Municipal Documents of Ireland*, 1172–1320, pp. 51–5. In 1229 Henry III granted to the citizens the right to elect a mayor annually (in place of the reeve who was their chief officer up to that date) from among themselves.]

7. GRANT OF URBAN LIBERTIES (THE LAW OF BRETEUIL) TO DROGHEDA
BY WALTER DE LACY, EARL OF MEATH, 1194

Walter de Lacy, Earl of Meath, to all his men and friends, French, English and Irish, greeting. Know that I have given, granted and by this present charter confirmed to all my burgesses of Drogheda dwelling on that side of the bridge which is next to our castle of Drogheda, that is, the southern side, the town and the burgages assigned to them formerly by lawful consideration and oath of lawful knights and burgesses, namely, so that each burgage assigned to them should have fifty feet of front and three acres in the [common] field. I have granted also to them the river of Boyne from the sea to the bridge of Trim, free of all obstacle and impediment of any weir, pool, or fishery, so that with other boats and merchandise they may [freely] go and return there. Further, I have granted to them the free Law of Breteuil [*legem Britolli*] even as such [liberties] are most fully and freely held in the land of the King of England. And all the above-said town, burgages and three acres, and the free law of Breteuil aforesaid I have given, granted and by this present charter confirmed to my said burgesses and to their heirs after them, to have and to hold in heritage in free burgage of me and my heirs, rendering yearly for each burgage 12ᵈ, namely 6ᵈ at Easter and 6ᵈ at Michaelmas, for all service. Wherefore I will and firmly enjoin that the aforesaid burgesses and their heirs shall have and hold in heritage the abovesaid town, burgages and three acres, well and in peace, freely and quietly, peaceably and honorably, fully and entirely, in wood and plain, in meadows and pastures, in ways and paths, with all the free liberties and customs appertaining to the free law of Breteuil.

[From the Inspeximus and confirmation of the original made by King Edward III, on 23 May, 1340. See *Cal. Pat. Rolls*, Ed. III, 1338–40, p. 525. Text in Latin.]

8. MAGNA CARTA HIBERNIAE (THE GREAT CHARTER OF IRELAND), 1216

Henry, by the grace of God, King of England, Lord of Ireland, etc., to all his archbishops, bishops, abbots, earls, barons, justices, sheriffs, reeves, ministers etc., and to all his faithful people, greeting.

Know that to the honour of God, the exaltation of Holy Church, and the amendment of our kingdom, by advice of Gualo, cardinal priest of St. Martin's, Legate of the Apostolic See, Peter, bishop of Winchester [and ten other bishops], William the Marshal, earl of Pembroke [and other earls and nobles], Hubert de Burgh, our justiciar, and others.

Firstly, we have granted to God, and by this present charter confirmed for us and our heirs for ever, that the Irish Church shall be free, and have all her rights entire and her liberties inviolable.

We have also granted to all free men of our kingdom, for us and our heirs for ever, all the liberties underwritten, to have and to hold to them and their heirs of us and our heirs.

[The principal liberties that follow are here summarized.]

If any earl, baron or other holding of us in chief by knight-service die, and at the time of his death his heir is of full age and owes relief, he shall have his heritage by the old relief, viz. a hundred pounds for the whole barony of an earl, a hundred pounds for the whole barony of a baron, and a hundred shillings at most for the whole knight's fee of a knight ; and he who owes less shall give less, according to the ancient custom of fees.

But if the heir of any such be under age, his lord shall not have wardship of him before he take homage of him, and when he comes to age, that is to say twenty-one years, he shall have his heritage without relief or fine ; provided that, if while under age he becomes a knight, nevertheless his land shall remain in the wardship of his lord up to that time.

The guardian of such an heir under age shall not take of his land aught save rightful issues, customs and services, and these without destruction of men [tenants] or goods. And if we commit the custody of such land to the sheriff or any other and he make destruction or waste of what is in his custody, we shall take amends of him, and commit the land to two lawful and discreet men of that fee, who shall answer for the issues to us or to him to whom we assign them. And if we give or sell to anyone the custody of such land and he make destruction or waste thereof, he shall lose the custody, and it shall be committed to two lawful men of that fee, who shall likewise answer to us thereof, as aforesaid.

The guardian as long as he has custody, shall keep up the houses, parks, ponds, mills etc. pertaining to that land out of the issues thereof, and restore to the heir when he shall have come of age, all his land stocked with ploughs etc. as fully as he received them.

And similarly with the custody of vacant archbishops, bishoprics, abbeys, priories, churches and ecclesiastical dignities, save that such custodies ought not to be sold.

Heirs shall be married without disparagement. A widow, immediately on her husband's death, shall have her marriage portion and inheritance ; nor shall she give anything for her dower, marriage portion, or inheritance which she and her husband held at his death. No widow shall be compelled to marry again as long as she wishes to live unmarried, provided that she give security not to marry without our assent, if she hold of us, or her lord's assent, if she hold of another.

The city of Dublin shall have all its ancient liberties and free customs. We further will and grant that all other cities, towns, boroughs and ports shall have their liberties and free customs. No one shall be distrained to do more service for a knight's fee or any other freehold than is due therefrom.

Common pleas shall not follow our court but shall be held in some certain place.

Assises of Novel Disseisin, Mort D'Ancestor and Darrein Presentment shall not be taken save in their own counties, and in this way. We, or if we are out of the realm, our Chief Justiciar, shall send two justices through each county four times in the year, who, with four knights of every county elected by the county, shall take, both in the county [court] and on the day and place of the county, the aforesaid assises ; and if on the day of the county [court] the aforesaid assises cannot be taken, so many knights and free tenants of those who were present at the county [court] on that day shall remain, by whom it may be competent to make judgements, according as the business shall be more or less.

No freeman shall be amerced for a small fault, but according to the measure of the fault, and for a great fault according to the magnitude of the fault, saving his tenement ; and a merchant in the same way, saving his merchandise ; and a villein in the same way, saving his warnage, if he fall into our mercy. And none of the said amercements shall be assessed but by the oath of good and lawful men of the venue. Earls and barons shall not be amerced except by their peers, and according to the measure of their fault. No clerk shall be amerced except as aforesaid, and not according to the quantity of his ecclesiastical benefice.

No town nor individual shall be distrained to make bridges over rivers, except those who of from old and of right ought to make them.

No sheriff, constable, coroners, or other our bailiffs shall hold pleas of our crown.

We will not hold the lands of those who shall be convicted of

3

felony, save for a year and a day, and then the lands shall be restored to the lords of the fees.

Also all weirs shall henceforth be put down through the whole of the Anna Liffey and all Ireland, except by the sea coast.

The writ which is called ' precipe ' from henceforth shall not be granted to anyone of any tenement whereby a freeman may lose his court.

There shall be one measure of wine throughout our entire kingdom, and one measure of ale, and one measure of corn, that is to say, the quarter of Dublin ; and one breadth of dyed cloth, russets and habergets, that is to say, two ells within the lists.

Nothing shall henceforth be given for the writ of inquisition of life or limbs, but it shall be freely granted and not denied.

No freeman shall be taken or imprisoned or disseised or outlawed or exiled, or in any otherwise destroyed ; nor will we pass upon him nor send upon him but by the lawful judgment of his peers or by the law of the land. We will sell to no man, we will deny to no man, or delay, right or justice.

All merchants, unless they were before publicly prohibited, shall have safe and secure [conduct] to depart from Ireland, and come into Ireland, and to tarry in and go through Ireland, as well by land as by water, to buy and sell, without all the evil extortions, by the old and rightful customs, except in time of war.

All men who have founded abbeys, for which they have charters of the Kings of England or ancient tenure, shall have the custody of them when they become vacant, as they ought to have, and as is above declared.

All forests which were afforested in the time of King John, our father, shall be immediately disafforested ; and so let it be done in the case of rivers which were placed in defence by the said John in his time.

And all those customs and liberties, aforesaid, which we have granted to be held in our kingdom, as far as to us appertains towards our men, everyone in our realm, as well clergy as laymen, shall observe, as far as appertains to them, towards their men.

Given by the hands of the aforesaid Legate and Marshal at Bristol, the twelfth day of November, in the first year of our reign [1216].

[The full text of this document and translation is given in Berry, *Early Statutes of Ireland* (pp. 5–19). It represents the Magna Carta as granted by Henry III on 12 November, 1216, with some changes applicable to Ireland. The Charter of 1216 was a re-issue in modified terms of John's original ' Great Charter of Liberties ' (granted on 19 June, 1215), now confirmed by his infant son as a royal concession and sealed with the seals of the Papal Legate and William the Marshal, the Regent. This (the first re-issue) was sent over to Ireland on 6 February, 1217 ; a summary of its more important provisions seems sufficient for our purposes. The original of the charter thus sent over has not survived and is known only from the copy in the ' Red Book of the Exchequer of Ireland,' a MS. volume compiled in the 14th century. From this book Berry took the foregoing ' Magna Carta Hiberniae,' as it is there called.

The Red Book has subsequently perished in the destruction of the Irish Record Office in 1922. At some time subsequent to 1216, the 'Magna Carta Hiberniae' was adapted to the King's Lordship of Ireland and to the case of his Anglo-Irish subjects, who were thus confirmed in the same liberties and rights as his English subjects. The differences are in those clauses in which 'Ireland' is substituted for 'England,' the Irish Church for the Church of England, the Liffey for the Thames and Medway, Dublin for London, and the standard measures of wine, corn, cloth, etc., by 'the quarter of Dublin' instead of the quarter of London.

The 'Magna Carta Hiberniae,' thus adapted to Ireland and entered into the Red Book of the Exchequer, seems to have become the accepted form for Ireland. For England the third re-issue (in 1225) of Magna Carta became the final form. Confirmed by Edward I in 1297 it was frequently published by subsequent Kings of England and still remains on the Statute Book. There is no evidence that the 1225 version was officially transmitted to Ireland, but we can hardly doubt that it was in force here too. Its 37 clauses practically repeat all the 33 clauses of the *Magna Carta Hiberniae*. For a different view of the matter see 'Magna Carta Hiberniae' by R. Dudley Edwards in *Féil-sgríbhinn Eóin Mhic Néill*, pp. 307–18, and H. G. Richardson in *Irish Historical Studies*, iii, 31–3.

9. THE LAWS OF ENGLAND TO BE OBSERVED IN IRELAND, 1246

The King, to the archbishops, bishops, abbots, priors, earls, barons, knights and all free tenants of Ireland. Forasmuch as for the common benefit of the land of Ireland and the unity of the King's dominions, the King wills, and by the Common council of the King it is provided, that all the laws and customs which are observed in the realm of England should be observed in Ireland and the said land should be subject to the said laws, and should be ruled by the same, as the lord King John, when he was last in Ireland, ordained and ordered to be done. Forasmuch also as the King wills that all writs of common right which run in England should likewise run in Ireland under the King's new seal, it is commanded to the said archbishops, bishops, earls, barons, etc. of Ireland, that for the peace and quiet of the said land they permit them to be ruled and governed by the same laws and follow them in all things. Witness the King, at Woodstock, the 9th day of September.

[From the text printed in Rymer's *Foedera*, I, p. 266, which is taken from Patent Roll (Eng.), 30 H. III, m. i.]

10. PROPOSED EXTENSION OF ENGLISH LAW TO THE NATIVE IRISH, 1277

Edward, King of England, Lord of Ireland etc., to his faithful Robert de Ufford, his justiciar in Ireland, greeting.

Touching the improvement in the state and peace of our land of Ireland, concerning which you have lately informed us by your letters, we greatly rejoice and highly commend your diligence in this matter, hoping by the help of God that what you have so laudably begun you may as far as in you lies continue even more happily and vigorously in the future.

And in particular, as the community of Ireland have offered us 8,000 marks if we will grant them the laws of England to be used in that country, we wish you to know that, after diligent discussion and fullest deliberation with our Council in the matter and inasmuch as the laws which the Irish use are detestable to God and contrary to all law so much so that they ought not to be deemed law, it seems to us and our Council expedient to grant them the laws of England, provided however that in this the common assent of the people or at least of the prelates and magnates of that land, who are well disposed, should uniformly concur.

We therefore enjoin on you that discussion be had with them on this matter and that the wishes of the people, prelates and magnates who are well disposed should be diligently examined, and agreement made upon a higher sum of money to be paid to us such as you may be able to arrange, by consent of all or at least the greater and more serious part of them, according as your perseverance in our honour and advantage may find befitting. Provided also that they shall furnish men, footmen good and strong, up to a certain number according as you are able to arrange with them, who shall be ready to come to us at any given time whenever we shall think fit to demand them.

[From the *Liber Munerum Publicorum Hiberniae* I, pt. iv, p. 3 (translated from the Latin). In this order Edward I raised the question of the extension of English law and liberty to the Irish race, as a result of a report made to him by his justiciar in Ireland, Robert D'Ufford, sent in 1277 (see *Cal. Docs. Ireland*, II, No. 1400). D'Ufford in his report says that ' the Irish have offered 7,000 (*recte* 8,000) marks for a grant from the King for the common laws of the English, and much desire to have an answer thereupon.']

11. PARLIAMENT OF IRELAND, 1297 (25 EDWARD I)

Of the Council of Ireland by the magnates of all that island.

The Justiciar, with the common council of the lord the king in this land, in order to establish peace more firmly, ordained and appointed a general parliament here at this day. And it was commanded to the archbishops, bishops, abbots, and priors, whose presence seems to be hereunto necessary, also to the earls, barons, and other chief persons of this land, to wit, to each of them severally, that they should be here at this day, etc. And likewise it was commanded to the sheriffs of Dublin, Louth, Kildare, Waterford, Tipperary, Cork, Limerick, Kerry, Connaught, and Roscommon, and also to the seneschals of the liberties of Meath, Wexford, Carlow, Kilkenny, and Ulster, that each of them by himself, to wit, the sheriff in his full county court, and the seneschal in his full court of the liberty, by the assent of his county or liberty, should cause to be elected two of the most honest and discreet knights of the several counties and liberties, that they should now be present here, having full power from the whole community of the county and liberty, etc., to do and to receive, etc., and that each sheriff and seneschal should be here in their proper persons, etc. And Thomas, bishop of Meath, Nicholas, bishop of Leighlin, etc., and Richard de

Burgo, earl of Ulster, now come, and in like manner Richard Taff, sheriff of Dublin, William de Hacche, sheriff of Louth, etc., Walter Trouman, seneschal of Trim, etc., likewise came, and their writs returned, and Walter de la Haye and Eustace le Poer, elected by the community of the liberty of Kilkenny, George de Rupe elected by the community of the county of Limerick, etc., came. And Nicholas, archbishop of Armagh and the others, excusing their absence, sent here their proctors or attorneys, to wit, the said archbishop I. and N., etc., but William, archbishop of Tuam, etc., came not.

And in like manner Hugh de Leis, one of those elected by the county of Limerick, etc., came not. Therefore they in mercy. And in presence of the aforesaid bishops of Meath and Leighlin and the earl and barons, and other chief persons here appearing of the common council of the lord the King in this land, certain provisions were made and by all unanimously agreed to and granted, saving the right of the lord the King, etc.

I. Firstly, whereas it is seen that the county of Dublin is too much scattered, and the parts thereof too far removed from each other and dispersed, as well Ulster and Meath, and then Leinster with the Vale of Dublin, etc., whereby it less competently obeys the lord the King in his precepts and those of his court, and also his people is less adequately ruled or governed, it is agreed that henceforward there be a sheriff in Ulster, as well of the Crosses of Ulster, as to carry out executions in the liberty of Ulster, when default is found in the seneschal of the aforesaid liberty, and that the sheriff of Dublin intermeddle not henceforth in Ulster. It is also agreed that Meath be a county by itself, to wit, as well the land of the liberty of Trim as the land of Theobald de Verdon, and all the lands of the Crosses being within the precinct of Meath, and that there be henceforth a sheriff there, and that he hold his county court at Kells on each Thursday after the county court of Dublin, and he shall make executions in the aforesaid liberty of Trim when default is found, etc. And the aforesaid Theobald de Verdon, for himself and Almaric de Saint Amand his tenant and their heirs, granted that they will henceforth do suit at the said county court of Meath aforesaid, so that they be absolved from the suits which they owe at the county court of Dublin, and it is granted unto them. Moreover that the county of Kildare, which was formerly a liberty intentive to the county of Dublin, be henceforth a county by itself, together with the Cross lands and other lands of the parceners of the lordship of Leinster, contained within the precinct of the same, totally discharged from the jurisdiction of the sheriff of Dublin. And that a sheriff be there as now is, etc.

II. Likewise, whereas some great persons and others who have divers lands in the marches near the Irish, and other lands in a land of peace, remain and dwell in their manors in a land of peace, their lands in the marches being left waste and uncultivated and without a guard ; and Irish felons by means of such waste lands in their marches, pass freely through to perpetrate robberies, homicides, and other mischiefs upon the English, and return through them without arrest, hue-and-cry, or hindrance ; whereby very many marches are either altogether destroyed or are for the greater part ruinous, and the English inhabitants either obey felons or are driven as it were into exile, it is agreed that tenants of this kind, of whatever authority or condition they be, place and have wards in their lands in the march, according to the quantity of those lands, lest malefactors pass through those lands unpunished or not pursued, and as often as it shall be necessary, tenants of this kind may be distrained thereunto, by taking their lands into the hand of the lord the King, and by other methods which the court of the lord the King shall see most expedient.

III. Frequently also it happens that felons escape with their booty, sometimes taken in a land of peace, because the country people have not armed horse to pursue them as would be expedient. Wherefore it is agreed and granted that every tenant holding xx. librates of land, whether in the march or in land of peace, of whatsoever condition he be, have a horse suitably caparisoned, together with the other arms which hereunto pertain, constantly ready in his dwelling. And that other tenants have hobbies and other horses unarmed according to their abilities. And as often as default shall be found in any one, that the defaulter be distrained and punished, according to the discretion of the Justice, sheriff, and seneschal. The magnates also and others who reside in England or elsewhere out of this land, who cause the profits of their land to be transmitted to them from this land, leaving nothing here to protect their tenements or the tenants thereof, shall from henceforth permit a competent portion to remain at least in the hands of their bailiffs, whereby their own lands may be sufficiently saved and defended, if it happen that war or disturbance of peace should be excited there by any persons. And that when it shall be necessary they shall be effectually distrained by the sheriff or the seneschal to do this.

IV. Frequently also felons escape with their spoils, by reason that the country people do not rise together with them [i.e. those plundered], but some of them, as if exulting in the damage and ruin of their neighbour, at which they ought justly to grieve, feign and conceal themselves, permitting such felons to pass unhurt with their spoils.

Wherefore it is agreed and granted that when thieves or robbers shall come into any country to take spoils or to do any other mischief, all the country people, as soon as their approach can come to their knowledge, rise together and effectually pursue them. And whosoever of those country people can be convicted of having been negligent or remiss in rising or in pursuing them shall be heavily punished towards the lord the King, and shall restore to the injured party a proportion of the property lost, according to the criminality of his negligence or remissness, and according to the discretion of the Justice assigned to hear such complaint.

V. Because also the commonalty of this land was hitherto much aggrieved by armies, which great men have led without warrant through the midst of a land of peace and of marches where there was no war, it is agreed and granted that from henceforth it shall not be lawful to anyone to lead an army out of his own land, unless he shall have had a licence for this from the Chief Justiciar, or a special mandate, and then all, as many as he shall have led, shall receive their wages from their leader, that they may be reasonably supported on their expedition. And he who shall contravene this ordinance shall be heavily punished towards the lord the King, and restore to the injured their damages to be assessed by a competent [jury of] the neighbourhood.

VI. The same commonalty has also on many occasions been aggrieved by magnates and others having kerns, continually living at other people's expense, as well in the marches as in land of peace, whereby the people is excessively impoverished. Whereupon it is agreed and granted that no person henceforward, of whatsoever authority or condition he be, shall keep kerns or idle men more or other than he himself can and will, out of his own resources, support ; nor shall any of such idle men henceforth take anything from any neighbour of his lord or other, against the unconstrained will of the giver ; which if it be done henceforward, he who shall have kept such idle men shall be heavily punished by the Justice, sheriff and seneschal, and indemnify the injured, and that such idle man be taken and imprisoned until he shall have deserved to obtain grace from the court of the lord the King ; nor shall he be discharged from prison without bail for his good behaviour in future.

VII. Frequently also Irish felons are better enabled to perpetrate crimes by this means, namely, that when they happen to be at war, or intend to destroy any person, they demand truces or armistices to be given to them by some of the English of their neighbours for a certain time, that they may be more completely and securely at leisure to destroy their other neighbours, whom, when they have destroyed, it often happens that the same Irishmen within the time of the truce or armistice attack those whose friends they had before pretended to be, and destroy and burn their forcelets and manors. Therefore lest such a danger occur hereafter, it is agreed and granted that it shall not be lawful to any person henceforth to have or to hold truces or armistices with the Irish, being at war or out of the peace, unless that truce or armistice be universal and equal towards all, none of the lieges being excepted or left out ; and that he who otherwise shall have taken or granted a truce or armistice to Irishmen being out of the peace, shall be punished towards the lord the King as a partaker of the guilt of such Irishmen, and shall restore to the injured party a proportion of the property lost, as is above said of a countryman not willing to rise with his neighbour against a felon.

VIII. Frequently also the Irish are stirred up to war by this, that when they are at peace or have had a general truce or armistice for a certain time, or protection of the peace has been granted to them by the Court of the lord the King, some, led by covetousness, others from motives of revenge, envy, or of taking pledges, lying in wait for them, rush suddenly or by night upon them, enter their lands, carry off spoils or take and lead away their cattle or the men found in their marches, who at least in the meantime are committing no mischief against any person ; whereby those Irish, as they are excitable, rush instantly to war, and wherever the country is believed to be weakest, there they plunder, as well those who were in nothing partakers of the wrong done them, nor did they know thereof or consent to it, as the friends and kin of such transgressors, whereby the countries are devastated in many places and so much the sooner, because it rarely happens that such transgressors interfere loyally to support the peace of the marches. Therefore, to avoid such mischief hereafter, it is agreed and granted that it shall not be lawful to any person in future for any cause or pretence to invade or attack any Irishmen being at peace, or having a fixed truce or armistice, during the time of the truce or armistice or during the time of the protection of the peace granted to them, provided those Irishmen shall have kept the peace during such time, nor to seize or take anything from them against their unconstrained will ; which if any person shall presume to contravene, he shall be heavily punished towards the lord the King as a disturber of his peace, and shall also restore to the Irish so injured, their damages to be assessed by a competent [jury of] the neighbourhood.

IX. Frequently also it happens that when the Irish have betaken themselves suddenly or unexpectedly to war, the Chief Justiciar acting then in remote parts, few or none are found who can resist and repress or interrupt their ravages ; whereby the lands of the marches are very often extensively devastated. To obviate which danger in future, it is agreed and granted that as soon as the Irish by homicides or burnings or plunderings shall have set themselves to war, all persons dwelling in the county or liberty where those Irish are remaining, and also their neighbours on the confine of their marches, shall with one accord and jointly rise upon the Irish and maintain war upon them at their own expense, until those Irishmen shall have rendered themselves to peace or obtained truces or armistices from the magnates of that land, hereunto deputed, or the Chief Justiciar shall have determined to order anything else therein. And that he who is not obedient to this ordinance shall also by the Justice, sheriff or seneschal be distrained and punished for his rebellion according to the deserts of his crime.

X. Likewise the Irish, confiding in the thickness of the woods and the depth of the adjacent bogs become more rapidly daring in doing mischief, especially when the King's highway in very many places is now so closed up and obstructed by the thickness of quickly growing wood, that scarcely any person, even on foot, can pass through them, whereby when the Irish returning after their misdeeds can reach a wood of this kind or a bog, although the country people in a body should wish to pursue them, and do pursue them, they often escape without hurt, whereas if access were open, they would be caught by those who pursue them. Whereupon it is ordained and granted that the lords of the woods through the midst whereof the King's highway anciently was, shall with their tenants cause passes, where the King's highway should be, to be cut and cleared low down, close to the ground, and sufficiently wide, at their own expense, and that of their tenants, so that a road of a sufficient width may be opened, and totally cleared from briars and trees as well standing as lying. But if the lord and his tenants of the place where the pass should be cut cannot without great loss support the costs necessary for such cutting, that then the lord the King or the Chief Justiciar do cause them to have aid from the whole adjacent country. And if that lord with his tenants shall have neglected to do, that he be distrained by the sheriff to do the same, or the Chief Justiciar may cause it to be done at their expense, and that they nevertheless be heavily punished towards the lord the King. That bridges also and causeways be repaired in their places as they ought and used to be, and where either bridges or causeways shall be broken and demolished, and he who is bound to repair them is not sufficient for such great expense, that the districts for whose benefit they shall be raised shall find means in common to rebuild them, and that when rebuilt he who is bound shall maintain them, and that nevertheless when ability shall serve him he shall restore to every person what he has paid. And that the Chief Justiciar heavily punish those whom he shall find adverse or rebellious to this ordinance. Also that the whole community of Leinster, which formerly was one liberty, shall together levy, together contribute to, together maintain, war against the Irish, be led by a common counsel, and that the refractory and discordant be heavily punished.

XI. Englishmen also, who have become degenerate in recent times, dress themselves in Irish garments and having their heads half shaven, grow the hair from the back of the head, which they call the ' culan,' conforming themselves to the Irish as well in garb as in countenance, whereby it frequently happens that Englishmen reputed as Irishmen are slain, although the killing of Englishmen and of Irishmen requires different modes of punishment. And by such killing matter of enmity and rancour is generated amongst many. The kindred also, as well of the slayer as of the slain, are often by turns struck down as enemies. And therefore it is agreed and granted that all Englishmen in this land wear, at least in that part of the head which presents itself most to view, the mode and tonsure of Englishmen, nor longer presume to turn their hair in the ' culan,' which if they shall do, that the Justice, sheriff, seneschal distrain and compel those Englishmen by their lands and chattels, and also, if it shall be necessary, by arrest of their body and imprisonment, to relinquish the Irish dress at least in the head or hair, and that there be no further answer made to an Englishman having his head transformed in the fashion of an Irishman, than would be made to an Irishman if he could complain in the like case.

XII. That there be henceforth assigned in every county and every liberty where the Irish are inhabitants, two magnates, who when the Chief Justiciar happen to be in remote parts, may lawfully treat for the good of peace with the Irish of those parts who are in a state of war, placing themselves in a state of war, and, for the common advantage, may grant them, for some short space of time, a general truce or armistice, under good security to be given hereupon, and shall immediately send to the Chief Justiciar what is done hereupon, distinctly and openly, that the Justiciar himself may cause a sufficient remedy to be ordained hereupon.

[For the Latin text of these acts see Berry, *Early Statutes*, pp. 194–213, and *Miscell. Irish Arch. Soc.* (1846). This parliament was held under Sir John Wogan, the King's Justiciar.]

12. THE REMONSTRANCE OF THE IRISH PRINCES TO POPE JOHN XXII, 1317

To the most holy Father in Christ, John, by the grace of God sovereign Pontiff, his devoted children, Donald O'Neill, king of Ulster and by hereditary right true heir to the whole of Ireland, and also the under-kings and nobles and the whole Irish people, with humble recommendation of themselves and devout kisses of his blessed feet.

Lest the sharp-toothed and viperous calumny of the English and their untrue representations should to any degree excite your mind against us and the defenders of our right, which God forbid, and so that there may be no ground for what is not well known and is falsely presented to kindle your displeasure, for our defence we pour into yours ears with mighty out-cry by means of this letter an entirely true account of our origin and our form of government, if government it can be called, and also of the cruel wrongs that have been wrought inhumanly on us and our forefathers by some kings of England, their evil ministers and English barons born in Ireland, wrongs that are continued still ; and this we do in order that you may be able to approach the subject and see in which party's loud assertion the truth bears company. And thus being carefully and sufficiently informed so far as the nature of the case demands, your judgment, like a naked blade, may smite or correct the fault of the party that is in the wrong.

Know then, most Holy Father, that since the time when our early ancestors, the three sons of Milesius or Micelius of Spain, by God's will came into Ireland (then destitute of all inhabitants) with a fleet of thirty ships from Cantabria, a city of Spain standing on the bank of the river Ebro or Hiberus (from which we take the name we bear), 3,500 years and more have passed, and of those descended from these men 136 kings without admixture of alien blood assumed the monarchical rule over all Ireland down to king

Legarius, from whom I, Donald, have derived my descent in a straight line. It was in days that our chief apostle and patron S. Patrick, sent us at the inspiration of the Holy Ghost by your predecessor Celestine in the year CCCCXXXV [*recte* CCCCXXXII] taught the truths of the Catholic faith with the fullest success to our fathers.

And after the faith had been preached and received, 61 kings of the same blood, without intervention of alien blood, kings admirably in the faith of Christ and filled with works of charity, kings that in temporal things acknowledged no superior, ruled here uninterruptedly in humble obedience to the Church of Rome until the year 1170.

And it was they, not the English nor others of any nation who eminently endowed the Irish Church with lands, ample liberties and many possessions, although at the present time she is, for the most part, sadly despoiled of those lands and liberties by the English.

And although for so long a time those kings with their own power had stoutly defended against tyrants and kings of divers countries the inheritance that God had given them and had always kept their birthright of freedom unimpaired, yet at last, in the year of the Lord MCLXX,[1] at the false and wicked representation of King Henry of England, under whom and perhaps by whom St. Thomas of Canterbury, as you know, in that very year suffered death for justice and defence of the church, Pope Adrian, your predecessor, an Englishman not so much by birth as by feeling and character, did in fact, but unfairly, confer upon that same Henry (whom for his said offence he should rather have deprived of his own kingdom) this lordship of ours by a certain form of words, the course of justice entirely disregarded and the moral vision of that great pontiff blinded, alas! by his English proclivities. And thus, without fault of ours and without reasonable cause, he stripped us of our royal honour and gave us over to be rent by teeth more cruel than any beast's ; and those of us that escaped half-alive and woefully from the deadly teeth of crafty foxes and greedy wolves were thrown by violence into a gulf of doleful slavery.

For, from the time when in consequence of that grant the English iniquitously but with some show of religion entered within the limits of our kingdom, they have striven with all their might and with every treacherous artifice in their power, to wipe our nation out entirely and utterly to extirpate it. By base and deceitful craftiness they have prevailed against us so far that, with no authority from a superior, they have driven us by force from the spacious places where we dwelt and from the inheritance of our fathers ; they have compelled us to seek mountains, woods, bogs, barren tracts and even caverns in the rocks to save our lives, and for a long time back to make our dwellings there like beasts. Yet even in such places as these they harass us continually and endeavour all they can to expel us from them and seek unduly to usurp to themselves

[1] *Recte* 1155, for the Bull of Adrian IV.

every place we occupy, mendaciously asserting in their blind madness that there is to be no free abode for us in Ireland but that all the land is entirely theirs by right.

Whence, by reason of all this and much more of the same kind, relentless hatred and incessant wars have arisen between us and them, from which have resulted mutual slaughter, continual plundering, endless rapine, detestable and too frequent deceits and perfidies. But alas! all correction and due reform fail us, for want of a head. And so for many years the native Irish clergy and people have stood in too serious and terrible danger not alone as regards what is perishable and bodily, but further still, through this want, the greatest danger, that of souls, is hanging over them, and that beyond an ordinary degree. For we hold it as an established truth that more than 50,000 human beings of each nation, in addition to those cut off by famine, distress and prison, have fallen by the sword in consequence of that false representation and the grant resulting from it, since the time when it was made. Let these few general particulars of the origin of our ancestors and the wretched position in which a Roman Pontiff placed us suffice on this occasion.

Know, most holy Father, that King Henry of England, who was authorized in the manner already stated to enter Ireland, and also the four kings his successors have clearly gone beyond the limits of the grant made them by the Pope's bull in certain definite articles, as appears plainly from the very text of the bull.

For the said Henry, as is embodied in the bull, undertook to extend the bounds of the Irish Church, to preserve its rights uninjured and entire, to bring the people under the rule of law and to train them in a good way of life, to implant virtue and to root out the weeds of vice and to make a yearly payment of one penny from every house to blessed Peter the apostle.

Henry himself, as well as his aforesaid successors and their wicked and crafty English ministers in no respect indeed keeping this promise, but departing altogether from the terms of the grant, have of set purpose and design accomplished in fact the opposite of all the foregoing engagements. For by them the bounds of the Church have been so far restricted, curtailed, and cut down that some cathedral churches have been forcibly despoiled of a half of their lands and possessions and even more, while nearly every liberty of the Church has been by these same persons cast adrift. For bishops and dignitaries are summoned, arrested, taken and imprisoned without respect by the king of England's ministers in Ireland; and though they suffer repeated and serious wrongs of this kind they are so overpowered with slavish fear that they in no wise dare to intimate them to your Holiness, and since they themselves are shamefully mute, we also will keep silent in this matter.

Likewise, the Irish people, whom in set terms they had promised to shape to good morals and to bring under laws, they so shape that its holy and dove-like simplicity has been surprisingly altered into a serpentine craftiness through daily life with them and through their bad example ; and they also deprive it of the written laws by which, for the most part, it was formerly governed, and of all other law, save what could not be uprooted, enacting for the extermination of our race most pernicious laws, beyond measure wicked and unjust, some of which are here inserted as instances.

In the King of England's court in Ireland these laws are rigidly observed, viz. that any person that is not an Irishman may bring any Irishman into court on any cause of action without restriction ; but every Irishman, cleric or lay, excepting only prelates, is refused all recourse to law by the very fact [of being Irish].

Also, as usually happens for the most part when by perfidy and guile some Englishman kills an Irishman, however noble and inoffensive, whether cleric or lay, regular or secular, even if an Irish prelate should be killed, no punishment or correction is inflicted by the said court on such a nefarious murderer ; nay more, the better the murdered man was and the greater the place be held among his people, the more his murderer is honoured and rewarded by the English, not merely by the populace but even by English religious and bishops, and most of all by those to whom it falls through their positions to inflict just punishment and due correction on such evil-doers.

Also, every Irishwoman, whether noble or otherwise, who marries any Englishman, is entirely deprived, after her husband's death, of the third part of his lands and possessions, her rightful dowry, precisely because she is Irish.

Likewise, wherever the English can oppress an Irishman by main force they in no way suffer the Irish to dispose of their property by their last wishes or to make a last will and testament ; nay, they appropriate to themselves all the goods of those persons, and deprive the Church of its right and of their own authority make serfs by violence of the blood that has been free from all antiquity.

Likewise, by the common council of this king of England and also by the action of certain English bishops, of whom the chief is a man of small wit and no learning, the archbishop of Armagh, an unjust statute has been lately made in the city of Kilkenny in this form of deformity :

' It is agreed that it be enjoined on all religious that abide in the land of peace among the English that they do not receive into their order or religion any except those that are English by nation ; and if they do otherwise the Lord King will take them as contemners of his command, and their founders and patrons will take them as disobedient and in opposition to this ordinance made by the common counsel of the whole land of Ireland among the English.' [1]

And even before this statute was made, and afterwards, the friars, preachers, minorites, monks, canons and other English religious have been observing it strictly enough, in the highest

---

[1] For this statute of the Parliament at Kilkenny in 1310 see Curtis, *Medieval Ireland* (1938), I, p. 180. It was immediately revoked by order of the king. The Archbishop of Armagh referred to is Walter Joce or Jorz.

degree being acceptors of persons ; yet the monasteries of monks and canons where at the present day the Irish are refused were, generally speaking, founded by them.

Likewise, where they were bound to implant virtues and root up the weeds of vice, they have cut out by the root the virtues already planted and of themselves have brought in vices.

Also of the same and the banquets of the English. For the English inhabiting our land, who call themselves of the middle nation, are so different in character from the English of England and from other nations that with the greatest propriety they may be called a nation not of middle [*medium*], but of utmost, perfidy. For, from of old they have had this wicked unnatural custom, which even yet has not ceased among them but every day becomes stronger and more established, viz. when they invite noblemen of our nation to a banquet, during the very feast or in the time of sleep they mercilessly shed the blood of their unsuspicious guests, and in this way bring their horrible banquet to an end. When this has been thus done they have cut off the heads of the slain and sold them for money to their enemies, as did the baron Peter Brunechehame (Bermingham), a recognized and regular betrayer, in the case of his gossip Maurice de S.[1] and his brother Caluache, men of high birth and great name among us. Inviting them to a banquet on Trinity Sunday, on that same day when the repast was finished, as soon as they had risen from the table he cruelly murdered them with twenty-four of their following and sold their heads dear to their enemies. And when he was afterwards accused to the king of England, the present king's father, of this crime, the king inflicted no punishment on so nefarious a traitor.

Likewise Sir Thomas de Clare, brother of the Earl of Gloucester, summoning to his house Brian Ruadh, prince of Thomond, his gossip, though as a token of closer confederacy and friendship he had communicated of the same host divided into two parts, at last by counsel of the aforesaid unspeakable nation he suddenly tore him from the table and the feast, had him dragged at horses' tails, and having cut off his head had the headless corpse hung by the feet from a beam.[2]

Likewise, Geoffrey de Pencoyt, of the same nation, after a feast which he had made for them in his house, on that same night, as they were sleeping in their beds, killed Maurice, king of Leinster, and Arthur, his father, men of very high nobility and authority.

Likewise, John fitz Thomas, Earl of Kildare, three days after

[1] Muircheartach O'Conchobhair, his kinsman Maelmordha, and Calbhach O'Conchobhair with 29 chiefs of his people were slain by Sir Piarus MacFeoruis by treachery and deceit in MacFeorais's castle (*F.M. ann.* 1305). For the treacherous murder of Murchertach O'Connor of Offaly and his leading men by Sir Piers Bermingham in 1305, see Curtis, *Medieval Ireland* (p. 181). Maurice de S. in the text is a scribe's error.

[2] ' Brian Ruadh Ua Briain was treacherously taken by the son of the earl of Clare (*sic*) and afterwards drawn between horses, and this after both had entered into gossipred with each other, and taken vows by bells and relics to retain mutual friendship ' (*F.M. ann.* 1277).

the killing, had the head of an Irish nobleman, his gossip (accident-ally slain not by him but by others), cut off in order to basely sell it. And likewise, the same Earl John, after the execrable death of the father as above narrated, thrust into a filthy prison John, son of the aforesaid most distinguished Caluache, a handsome youth who, from the time when he had been lifted from the baptismal font by the earl himself, had been reared continuously in his house ; and after a few days he had the guiltless youth not guiltlessly put to death in the prison.

Let these few cases, notorious to everyone, out of the countless misdeeds of that nation suffice as instances, on this occasion.

And though acts of this kind apppear horrible and detestable to all Christians, yet to those of that oft-mentioned nation, as by too hard a daily experience we feel, they seem honourable and praise-worthy, since those that do them reap not at all the punishment of which they are deserving, but by a too flagrant antithesis the reward of praise which they do not merit is heaped upon them. For not only their laymen and secular clergy but some also of their regular clergy dogmatically assert the heresy that it is no more sin to kill an Irish-man than a dog or any other brute. And in maintaining this heretical position some monks of theirs affirm boldly that if it should happen to them, as it does often happen, to kill an Irishman, they would not on that account refrain from saying mass, not even for a day.

And as, beyond all doubt, the monks of the Cistercian order of Granard, in Ardagh diocese, so too the monks of Inch, of the same order, in Down diocese, shamelessly fulfil in deed what they proclaim in word. For, bearing arms publicly, they attack the Irish and slay them, and nevertheless they celebrate their masses.

And in like manner friar Simon of the Order of Friars Minors, brother of the bishop of Connor, is the chief formulator of this heresy ; and in the year just passed, unable from the fulness of his malignant heart to keep silent he shamelessly burst out in words into a declaration of this kind in the court of Lord Edward de Broyse (Bruce), Earl of Carrick and in the presence of the said lord, as he himself testifies, viz. that it is no sin to kill a man of Irish birth and if he were to commit it himself he would none the less for that celebrate mass.

And falling out of this heresy into another error, all of them indifferently, secular and regular, assert with obstinacy that it is lawful for them to take away from us by force of arms whatever they can of our lands and possessions of every kind, making no conscientious scruple about it even when they are at the point of death. And all the land they hold in Ireland they hold by usurpation in this way.

And of whatever condition or station he may be that should withstand this error or preach in opposition to them, for that alone he is proclaimed an enemy to the king and kingdom of England, as guilty of death and outlawed by the King's council. For, lusting eagerly for our lands, they it is that, to the no small loss of the kings and kingdom of England, by sowing perpetual dissensions between them and us, have craftily and deceitfully kept us apart from them, lest of our own free will we should hold from the King directly the lands that are rightfully our due.

That this is a characteristic policy of theirs is well established, and from it spring frequent acts of bad faith and treachery. For they never cease from sowing similar dissentions not merely between persons of remote consanguinity but even between brothers and near relations. And as in way of life and speech they are more dissimilar from us and in their actions from many other nations than can be described by us in writing or in words, there is no hope whatever of our having peace with them. For such is their arrogance and excessive lust to lord it over us and so great is our due and natural desire to throw off the unbearable yoke of their slavery and to recover our inheritance wickedly seized upon by them, that as there has not been hitherto, there cannot now be or ever henceforward be established, sincere good will between them and us in this life. For we have a natural hostility to each other arising from the mutual, malignant and incessant slaying of fathers, brothers, nephews and other near relatives and friends so that we can have no inclination to reciprocal friendship in our time or in that of our sons.

Likewise it cannot escape you, since it is manifest to everyone, that the Roman curia does not receive a penny from every house in Ireland as was promised.

In this way then, and no other nor otherwise, have the kings of England and their often-mentioned subjects observed the articles of the above-said Bull to the Irish church and nation.

Since then such injustices and abominations of the said nation were clearly and openly intimated to that King's [Edward II] counsel and also to the King himself about two years past in letters of several noblemen of our nation by means of John de Hutome (now, as we have understood, bishop of Ely), in order to have redress, and as we also offered him [i.e. the King] generally that, to his greater advantage and to our peace we would hold our land, due by right to us alone, from him immediately without any opposition, according to the conditions and articles laid down and contained in Adrian's bull (of which we transmit you a copy) or that he should make a friendly arrangement between our said adversaries and us, himself dividing up reasonably with consent of the parties and to avoid unlimited bloodshed our own land that belonged to us ; but since then we have received no answer from him or his council in that matter.

Let no one wonder then that we are striving to save our lives and defending as we can the rights of our law and liberty against cruel tyrants and usurpers, especially since the said King, who calls himself lord of Ireland, and also the said kings his predecessors have wholly failed in this respect to do and exhibit orderly government to us and several of us.

Wherefore, if for this reason we are forced to attack that King and our said enemies that dwell in Ireland, we do nothing unlawful but rather our action is meritorious and we neither can nor should be held guilty of perjury or disloyalty on this account, since neither we nor our fathers have ever done homage or taken any other oath of fealty to him or his fathers. And therefore, without any conscientious misgivings, so long as life endures we will fight against them in defence of our right and will never cease to attack and assail them until through want of power they shall desist from unjustly injuring us and the justest of Judges shall take evident and condign vengeance upon them for their tyrannous oppression and other most wicked deeds ; and this with a firm faith we believe will soon come to pass.

Furthermore, we are ready and prepared to maintain by the testimony of twelve bishops at least and of many other prelates the articles here set forth and to prove the wrongs herein recited, lawfully in due time and place and by way of law which is due to us of right ; not like the English, who in the time of their prosperity and power will never stand to any due course of proceedings or process of law ; and if prosperity and power were with them now they would have been far from taking shelter under the wings of the Roman Curia, nay rather would they be fiercely afflicting all nations round about with their wonted tyranny, despising the power of God and that of the Roman Curia, which we declare to be one and the same ordinance. Whence, if the said Curia were fully instructed concerning their deeds, they would be ill satisfied by the comfort they would receive from it, for comfort is not merited by their wickedness.

Therefore, on account of the aforesaid wrongs and infinite other wrongs which cannot easily be comprehended by the wit of man and yet again on account of the [injustice] of the kings of England and their wicked ministers and the constant treachery of the English of mixed race, who, by the ordinance of the Roman curia, were bound to rule our nation with justice and moderation and have set themselves wickedly to destroy it ; and in order to shake off the hard and intolerable yoke of their slavery and to recover our native liberty, which for a time through them we lost, we are compelled to wage deadly war with them, aforesaid, preferring under stress of necessity to put ourselves like men to the trial of war in defence of our right, rather than to bear like women their atrocious outrages.

And that we may be able to attain our purpose more speedily and fitly in this respect, we call to our help and assistance Edward de Bruyis, illustrious earl of Carrick, brother of Robert by the grace of God most illustrious king of the Scots, who is sprung from our noblest ancestors.

And as it is free to anyone to renounce his right and transfer it to another, all the right which is publicly known to pertain to us in the said kingdom as its true heirs, we have given and granted to him by our letters patent, and in order that he may do therein judgment and justice and equity which through default of the prince

4

[i.e. the King of England] have utterly failed therein, we have unanimously established and set him up as our king and lord in our kingdom aforesaid, for in our judgment and the common judgment of men he is pious and prudent, humble and chaste, exceedingly temperate, in all things sedate and moderate, and possessing power (God on high be praised) to snatch us mightily from the house of bondage with the help of God and our own justice, and very willing to render to everyone what is due to him of right, and above all is ready to restore entirely to the Church of Ireland the possessions and liberties of which she was damnably despoiled, and he intends to grant greater liberties than ever otherwise she has been wont to have.

May it please you therefore, most Holy Father, for the sake of justice and general peace mercifully to approve what we have done as regards our said lord and king, forbidding the King of England and our aforesaid adversaries henceforward to molest us, or at least be pleased to render us with fitting favour our due complement of justice in respect of them.

For know, our revered Father, that besides the kings of lesser Scotia who all drew the source of their blood from our greater Scotia, retaining to some extent our language and habits, a hundred and ninety seven kings of our blood have reigned over the whole island of Ireland.

Here ends the process set on foot by the Irish against the king of England.

[This case, or Remonstrance, of the Irish chiefs, led by Donal O'Neill, king of Cenel Eoghain or Tyrone, against English oppression, was addressed to the Avignon Pope John XXII in the latter part of 1317, apparently through two papal nuncios, Luke and Gaucelin, who were then in England attempting to make peace between Edward II and Robert Bruce. For a summary of it and a comment upon the charges contained in it against the English and Anglo-Irish, see Curtis, *Medieval Ireland*, pp. 191–3.

The Latin original of the Remonstrance is found only in the *Scotichronicon* of John Fordun, a Scottish historian of the Bruce wars, who died about 1384. It has been printed, in imperfect form, by Thomas Hearne in 1722 in his edition of the *Scotichronicon*, vol. III, pp. 908–26. My friend Mr. Charles MacNeill has compared this with the Harleian text in the British Museum and kindly allowed me to use it as well as his translation.]

13. THE IRISH ADMITTED TO ENGLISH LAW, 1321

The King to his Justiciar of Ireland, who now is and who for the time shall be, or to his lieutenant, greeting. Know ye that whereas in the time of the lord Edward, formerly King of England, our father, and afterwards in our time, it has been frequently shewn to our said father and to us, with heavy complaint, that because the Irish admitted to English law in the said land did not previously enjoy the said law concerning life and limb, our peace in the said regions was disturbed in many ways, and evil-doers there not being punished, were emboldened to commit divers felonies, to the grievous injury of our people of the said regions ; and [whereas] at length in our Parliament summoned at Westminster in the octave of St Michael last past, prayer was made to us that we should cause a remedy to be applied hereupon, We therefore, wishing to provide for the peace and quietness of our said people, will that all the Irish previously admitted to English law and those who hereafter shall happen to be admitted thereto, do use henceforth the said law concerning life and limb, and by these presents we command that the Irish so admitted and to be admitted to the said law, as well within liberties as without, be treated according to the custom of the English, always saving in all things the right of us and of other lords, in the goods and chattels of the ' nativi ' who are commonly called in those regions ' betaghes,' who may happen to be admitted to the said law, and of their issue, as regards the possession of those goods and chattels.

Witness the King at Westminster the twentieth day of January. (To last for five years.)

By the King himself and by petition of the Council.

[From Berry, *Early Statutes*, p. 292. It is a royal order, directed by Edward II, entitled ' De Lege Anglicana de vita et membris in Hibernia utenda.']

14. BETAGHS ON THE MANOR OF LISRONAGH, 1333

The Works of the Betaghs

Each Betagh who has a plough shall plough one acre of wheat and the ploughing of the acre is worth 6^d. Also he shall plough one acre of oats and the ploughing is worth 8^d. Whoever of them has not a whole plough shall join his plough animals to those of his fellow-betaghs until they have a whole plough-team for doing the said work. So that each of the said ploughs shall plough one acre of wheat and one of oats as aforesaid. And they shall have for each crop of the lord 2s. Whosoever holds 30 acres shall find for each three acres 3 men in autumn for one day to reap the wheat and 2 men to reap the oats, and the work of each man is worth for the day 1½^d. And all other betaghs shall reap for one day at wheat and so much at oats as above and the value of the day's work is as above. And also all betaghs who have one farm-beast shall carry wheat from day to day with the wagons or carts of the lord to the haggard until all is carted in and they shall have food and drink once a day and the day's work with man and beast apart from food is 1½^d. And they shall " ted " [spread] the lord's meadow and make hay therefore and stack it in the meadow and carry it to the lord's haggard and shall have nothing therefor. Those who have horses shall do carriage for the lord at their own expense, provided they are able to return home that night and if they cannot they shall be at the lord's costs, and they shall carry the lord's letters or that of his ministers touching the state of the manor within the county at their own proper cost. And they shall find fuel for the lord or his chief ministers until they shall be residing in the said manor. Also whatsoever victuals which may be in their possession, viz. gross meat, geese and hens, and provision of this kind or of corn and straw also the lord or his chief minister shall have the right to purchase such for money at a reasonable estimate. And they shall do services at the will of the lord ; and of those who have 3 animals the lord shall have the best of them as heriot and of those who have less 12^{d}. for heriot. Also they shall come to the lord's court as often as [unstated].

[The total valuation of the betaghs' land is given as 32^{l}. 14^{s}. o$\frac{3}{4}$^{d}., and the rents of their hand mills 23^{s}. 4^{d}.]

[The original document (in Latin) is given in a paper by Edmund Curtis, ' Rental of a Manor of Lisronagh, 1333, and notes on Betagh tenure in medieval Ireland,' in *Proc.R.I.A.*, February, 1936. For the Betaghs (*betagii*) or villein class whom the Normans found universal in Ireland and who retained their identity for some two or three centuries, see also Appendix IV to Curtis, *Medieval Ireland* (1938) on ' The Betagh class and the legal treatment of the Irish in medieval Ireland.']

15. TWO TREATIES BETWEEN JAMES, EARL OF ORMOND, AND THE
O'KENNEDYS, 1336 AND 1356

(1) Indenture of agreement and concord between James, Earl of Ormond, on the one hand and O'Kennedy and Clangillekevynboy on the other, concerning all preys, homicides, and other transgressions made on either side up to the present. The Earl grants to O'Kennedy and those of his nation thirteen carucates [plowlands] of land in Meianarge and one carucate in Clomolyn, paying therefor *per annum* to the Earl 20.1 per annum for eleven carucates ; the other three to be free of rent. The Earl also grants that the said Irish shall make no suit at all assizes or county court but they shall make suit at the court of Nenagh during four years until they shall have come to complete peace with the men of the Marches. Also a seneschal acceptable to them and to the lord shall come to Rathirdill or Galnegarthe as often as is necessary, and if it is found by inquisition that O'Kennedy or any of his men have done damage to the lord or his betaghs they shall atone three-fold, and if they have done any damage to the English of the lord they shall atone two-fold, the lord to have half the fine and the injured person the other. Justice shall be done to the injured Irish on the part of the English. Further, O'Kennedy shall do suit at the court of Nenagh, and if it is found by inquisition that he has done any damage to the lord or his betaghs he shall atone three-fold and towards the English of the lord three-fold ; half to the lord, etc., as above.

He shall not be arrested in person for any such damage, but the lord's serjeant shall levy the damages upon him, unless before the lord's departure he has given pledge to make atonement of the same. Further O'Kennedy agrees to serve his lord [the Earl] in his army as he was wont to do to him and his ancestors and to make war upon such English or Irish as shall rise against the lord. Similarly it is agreed that if any of the Earl's men, English or Irish, slay O'Kennedy or any of his men by treachery, the body of the traitor shall be handed over for the body of the slain if he can be found, and if the lord or his sept cannot be found, compensation shall be levied and paid to the kindred of the same, and he shall have no peace from the lord for ever without the consent of O'Kennedy and his kin. For the full observance of all the above, the Earl and O'Kennedy each for himself and his men have found pledges, namely the Archbishop of Cashel, etc. who shall make war upon O'Kennedy or his men if they violate these terms. Further the Earl grants to O'Kennedy and his brothers as far as he is concerned all the lands from Belacharri to the Shannon, paying therefor to the lords of those lands as much rent as three on the side of the English and three on the side of O'Kennedy agree upon.

Given at Nenagh on the 5th day of March in the 10th year of Edward III.

[March 5, 1336.]

(2) This indenture lately made, viz. on the 16th of May in the 30th year of King Edward III at Cashel between Lord James le Botiller, Earl of Ormond, and his people and liegemen on one side and Rotheric, principal of his nation in Ormond on the other, attests that the Earl and O'Kennedy have come together wholly and unanimously and have agreed that the peace made between them before the said Earl set out to cross over into England (as contained in the indentures made between them under their seals more fully contains) should be firmly held.[1] Adding this, that all offences done to the Earl or his men against the said peace as far as they touch the lordship of the Earl shall be amended by O'Kennedy and his men according as eight men, four to be chosen on each side, shall decide and ordain. And if these eight cannot agree in all things, let them choose by their common assent another competent person and by the judgment of the five each of the two parties shall be bound, and for whatever trespasses take place between O'Kennedy and his men on one side and the common [English] people on the other, these shall deliver into the hands of the Earl satisfactory pledges.

Moreover O'Kennedy is bound according to the form of peace made between him and the Earl to be obedient and respondent to the Earl. And if it happen that any of the nation or subjects of O'Kennedy infringe in any way against the said peace, O'Kennedy ought to restrain and punish the transgressor of the peace according to the counsel of the Earl. Also the Earl and his men shall be bound to aid O'Kennedy in the punishment and restraint of said

---

[1] These provisions would seem to refer to the former treaty of 1336 (see page 48).

transgressor and ought not to charge such transgressions against O'Kennedy if it happens that he is unable to punish them. Otherwise O'Kennedy shall be bound to be faithful in the above said cases, according to the effect and force of the former indentures and the tenour of this indenture.[1]

The said Earl is also bound as his lord to aid the said O'Kennedy for the sake of justice, against all who are rebels and opponents of O'Kennedy in the matter of this peace. Also the same O'Kennedy now and for ever firmly promises and pledges himself on the holy gospels to do all that is contained in the above indentures, in the presence of the venerable the archbishop of Cashel, the bishop of Killaloe and many other great men of the land, that he will faithfully keep the said peace according to the terms of these indentures and will submit to the commands of the Earl and will be faithful and obedient to him and for this he submits himself to the distraint, coercion, excommunication and interdict of the said bishops if imposed. The Earl also promises that whenever O'Kennedy comes to him he will make no capture or attachment of O'Kennedy or any of his sons or others coming with him.

In witness whereof each party has alternatively set his seal. May 16, 1356.

[From the *Cal. Ormond Deeds*, I, No. 682, and II, No. 34. See also I, No. 700 and II, ix, x, and Nos. 35, 46, 48.

It would appear that the O'Kennedy in the treaty of 1336 was Rory, chief of the sept, whose name occurs in a grant by the Earl to Roderic, son of Alan O'Kennedy, in 1337, and also in the treaty of 1356, for mention is made in the latter of these earlier treaties.

' Clangillekevynboy ' (in the treaty of 1336) seems to have originated with one Giollacaoimhghin O'Kennedy who flourished in the latter half of the thirteenth century. See Gleeson, ' Castle and Manor of Nenagh,' in Journal of the *R.S.A.I.*, 1936, pp. 247–69.]

16. LIBERTIES GRANTED TO THE TOWN OF CARRICKMAGRIFFIN (CARRICK-ON-SUIR), BY JAMES, EARL OF ORMOND, 1366

James le Botiller, Earl of Ormond and of Carrick, gives and grants to the burgesses of Carrickmagriffin all the liberties which burgesses may have and which he can confer, to have and to hold to them and their heirs, from him and his heirs for ever.

First, that no burgess shall be drawn into any case or answer to any plea which comes within the boundaries of the borough in the castle or elsewhere but only in the Hundred of the town.[2]

The Hundred shall be held in the town.

No homicide done within the town shall be taken for ' murdrum.'

No burgess shall be put to the duel for any plea which may be made against him for the death of a man or theft or any other plea for which duel can be done.

[1] These provisions would seem to refer to the former treaty of 1336 (see formerly).
[2] The Hundred is the town or borough court.

The burgesses shall be free of toll, lastage, pontage and all other customs throughout all the Earl's land and power.

No burgess shall be put in the mercy of fine save by consideration of the Hundred, and the fine shall be fixed by the burgesses.

The Hundred shall be held once a fortnight.

No burgess shall be drawn into a plea for miskenning.

The burgesses may plead without [previous] motion.

They may distrain their debtors by their pledges which are found in the town. And if a plea arise of wagers or pledges for debts taken it shall be held in the Hundred. And if toll be taken of any burgess within our land and power, if he who took it has been requested to return it and has refused, then by pledges of the same place where he is, if they are so found in the town, they [i.e. he] shall be compelled to return it.

No merchant shall have the cutting of cloth or a tavern for wine in the town except for forty days and if he wish to do so longer it shall be by consent of the community of the burgesses and for the profit of the town that he remain.

No burgess shall be pledged or distrained in the Earl's land or power for any outside debt except he be a principal debtor or pledge.

No burgess shall be compelled to be a pledge of anyone if he holds of him except by his own consent.

The burgesses shall have their merchant gild with all liberty pertaining thereto as is the custom of other good towns.

The burgesses may freely dispose of their tenements which they hold in burgage in the said town without unlawful disturbance by their neighbours, and sell or pledge their houses, gardens and thickets saving the services which are due therefrom.

The burgesses may claim and prove their debts by suit of lawful men.

No burgess shall be compelled to lend his chattels unless security be previously made for a return at a certain term. And if any burgess shall have willingly lent his goods to the Earl's bailiffs and if they are not restored on the fixed date for return then they shall be so restored within forty days.

And if there is a change of bailiffs, then the Earl or the new bailiff shall compel the retiring one to make rightful return.

Also the burgesses shall have their milling in the Earl's mill at a reasonable toll.

Further the burgesses shall have and hold all the said liberties of the Earl and his heirs for ever.

The Earl grants also that if discords, pleas or lawsuits arise between the men of his hostel there dwelling, and any man of the community of the town, inquiry shall be made thereon before the sovereign of the town and the seneschal of the Earl's hostel by consideration of same in the said town. Also amendment of the same shall be done within three days.

No assize of victuals shall be made in the borough there save by the burgesses by consideration of the Earl's bailiff and seneschal.

Given in our castle of Carrick on Monday in the feast of St. Margaret in the 40th year of Edward III.

Witnesses : Peter le Botiller, seneschal of the Liberty of Kilkenny, David de Cauntewell, sheriff of the same Liberty, Edmund le Botiller, William Ilger, then Escheator of Ireland, Thomas le Botiller, Sir William, vicar of Carrick, Thomas Holhurst, seneschal of the Earl's hostel, and Thomas Brikyn, clerk.

July 20, 1366.

[From *Cal. Ormond Deeds*, II, No. 123. Carrickmagriffin is the present Carrick-on-Suir.]

17. THE STATUTES OF KILKENNY, 1366

Whereas at the conquest of the land of Ireland and for a long time after, the English of the said land used the English language, mode of riding and apparel and were governed and ruled, they and their subjects called *Betaghes*, by the English law ; in which time the rights of God and of Holy Church and their liberties according to their conditions were maintained in due obedience. But now many English of the said land, forsaking the English language, fashion, mode of riding, laws, and usages, live and govern themselves according to the manners, fashion and language of the Irish enemies, and also have made divers marriages and alliances between themselves and the Irish enemies aforesaid ; whereby the said land and the liege people thereof, the English language, the allegiance due to our lord the King, and the English laws there are put in subjection and decayed and the Irish enemies exalted and raised up contrary to right. Now therefore our lord the King, considering the mischiefs aforesaid, in consequence of the grievous complaints of the commons of his said land summoned to his Parliament held at Kilkenny the Thursday next after Ash Wednesday in the fortieth year of his reign [February 18, 1366], before his well-beloved son Lionel, Duke of Clarence, his Lieutenant in Ireland, to the honour of God and of his glorious Mother and of Holy Church and for the good government of the said land and quiet of the people and for the better observance of the laws and the punishment of evil doers, there are ordained and established by our said lord the King and his said Lieutenant and council there with the assent of the archbishops, bishops, abbots and priors (in that which appertains to them to assent to), the Earls, barons, and others the commons of the said land at the said parliament there assembled the ordinances and articles under-written to be held and kept perpetually, upon the penalties contained therein.

Firstly, it is ordained, agreed, and established that Holy Church be free and have all her franchises without infringement according to the franchises ordained and granted by our lord the King or his progenitors by statute or ordinance heretofore made in England or in Ireland, etc.

Also it is ordained and established that no alliance by marriage, gossipred, fostering of children, concubinage or amour or in any other manner be henceforth made between the English and Irish on the one side or on the other. And that no Englishman or other person being at peace shall give or sell to any Irish in time of peace or war horses or armour or any manner of victuals in time of war. And if any do to the contrary and thereof be attaint, that he shall have judgment of life and limb as a traitor to our lord the King.

Also it is ordained and established that every Englishman shall use the English language and be named by an English name, leaving off entirely the manner of naming used by the Irish ; and that every Englishman use the English custom, fashion, mode of riding and apparel according to his estate ; and if any English or Irish living amongst the English use the Irish language amongst themselves contrary to this ordinance and thereof be attaint, that his lands and tenements, if he have any, be seized into the hands of his immediate lord until he come to one of the places of our lord the King and find sufficient surety to adopt and use the English language and then that he have restitution of his said lands by writ to issue out of the same place. In case that such person have not lands or tenements, then his body shall be taken by some of the officers of our lord the King and committed to the next gaol, there to remain until he or another in his name find sufficient surety in the manner aforesaid. And that no Englishman who has to the value of one hundred shillings of lands or tenements or of rent by the year shall ride otherwise than on a saddle in the English fashion, and he that shall do the contrary and be thereof attaint his horse shall be forfeited to our lord the King and his body committed to prison until he make fine according to the King's pleasure for the contempt aforesaid. And also that beneficed persons of Holy Church living amongst the English shall use the English language ; and if they do not, then their ordinaries shall have the issues of their benefices until they use the English language as aforesaid ; and they shall have respite in order to learn the English language and to provide saddles between this and the feast of Saint Michael next coming.

Also, whereas diversity of government and divers laws in one land cause diversity of allegiance and disputes among the people, it is agreed and established that no English having disputes with other English henceforth make distraint or take pledge, distress, or vengeance against any other whereby the people may be troubled, but that they shall sue each other at the common law, and that no English be governed in the settlement of their disputes by March or Brehon law, which by right ought not to be called law but bad custom ; but that they be governed by the common law of the land as the lieges of our lord the King ; and if any do to the contrary and thereof be attaint then he shall be taken and imprisoned and adjudged as a traitor. And that no difference of allegiance henceforth be made between the English born in Ireland and the English born in England by calling them ' English hobbe ' or ' Irish dog,' but that all shall be called by one name [viz.] the English lieges of our lord the King, and that any one found doing to the contrary shall be punished by imprisonment for a year and afterwards fined at the King's will. And by this ordinance it is not the intention of our lord the King but that it may be lawful for any one who can to take distress for services and rents due to them and for damage feasant as the common law requires.

Also, whereas a land which is at war requires that every person do render himself able to defend himself, it is ordained and established that the commons of the said land of Ireland who are in divers marches of war use not henceforth the games which men call ' hurlings ' with great clubs at ball upon the ground, from which great evils and maims have arisen to the weakening of the defence of the said land, and other games which men call ' coitings,' but that they apply and accustom themselves to use and draw bows and throw lances and other gentle games which appertain to arms, whereby the Irish enemies may be the better checked by the liege commons of these parts ; and if any do or practice the contrary and of this be attaint that he shall be taken and imprisoned and fined at the will of our lord the King.

Also, whereas divers wars have often heretofore been commenced and not continued or brought to a good termination but by the party taking from the enemies at their departure a small tribute, whereby the said enemies were and are the more emboldened to renew the war, it is agreed and established that any war which shall be commenced hereafter shall be undertaken by the Council of our lord the King, by advice of the lords, commons, and marchers of the county where the war shall arise, and shall be continued and finished by their advice and counsel ; so that the Irish enemies shall not be admitted to peace until they are finally destroyed or shall make restitution fully of the costs and charges expended upon that war by their default and rebellion, and shall make reparation to those by whom the said charges and costs were incurred, and moreover shall make fine for the contempt at the King's will. And in case that hostages be taken and given to our lord the King or to his officers for keeping the peace by any of the Irish, that, if they renew the war contrary to the form of their peace, execution of their said hostages be made without delay or favour according to the ancient customs of the said land in such case used.

Also, for the better maintaining of the peace and doing right as well to the Irish enemies being at peace as to the English, it is ordained and established that if any Irish being at peace by bargain or purchase of merchandise or in any other manner become debtor to English or Irish being at peace, that for such cause no other Irish person with him, under him, or in subjection to him or his goods, shall be seized or attached for such debt if he be not pledge for the same debt ; but that his recovery shall be against the principal debtor as the law requires, etc.

Also it is ordained and established that in every peace henceforth to be made between our lord the King and his English lieges of the one part and the Irish of the other part in every march of the land, there shall be comprised the point which follows, that is to say that no Irishmen shall pasture or occupy upon the lands belonging to English or Irish being at peace, against the will of the lords of the said lands ; and, if they so do, that it be lawful for the said lords to lead with them to their pound the said beasts so feeding or occupying their said lands by way of distress for their rent and their damages ; so however that the beasts shall not be divided or separated as heretofore has been done but shall be kept altogether as they were taken, in order to deliver them to the party in case he come to make satisfaction to the lords of the said lands reasonably according to their demand ; and in case any one divide or separate the beasts so taken that he shall be punished as a robber and breaker of the peace of our lord the King. And if any Irish rise by force to the rescue of those reasonably taken, that it shall be lawful for the said English to assist themselves by strong hand without being impeached in the court of our lord the King on this account ; and that no English shall take any distress upon any Irish of any part between this and the feast of St. Michael next to come ; so that the Irish of every part may be warned in the mean time.

Also it is ordained that no Irish of the nations [septs] of the Irish shall be admitted into any cathedral or collegiate church by provision, collation, or presentation of any person whatsoever or to any benefice of Holy Church amongst the English of the land ; and that if any be admitted, instituted, or inducted into such benefice it shall be held void and the King have his presentation of the said benefice for that vacancy to what person soever the advowson of such benefice may belong, saving their right to present or make collation to the said benefice when it shall be vacant at another time.

Also it is agreed and established that no house of religion which is situate among the English, whether it be exempt or not, shall henceforth receive any Irishmen [to their] profession but shall receive Englishmen, without taking into consideration that they be born in England or in Ireland, and that [in the case of] any that shall do otherwise and thereof be attaint, the temporalities shall be seized into the hand of our lord the King to remain at his will. And that no prelate of Holy Church receive any villein to any orders without the assent and testimony of his lord made to him under his seal.

Also, whereas the Irish minstrels coming among the English spy out the secrets, customs and policies of the English whereby great evils have often happened, it is agreed and forbidden that any Irish minstrels, that is to say tympanours, poets, story-tellers, babblers, rymours, harpers or any other Irish minstrels [in the original, ' tympanours, fferdanes, skelaghes, bablers, rymours, clarsaghours '] shall come amongst the English ; and that no English receive them or make gift to them. And that he who does so and is thereof attaint, shall be taken and imprisoned, as well the Irish minstrels as the English that receive them or give them anything, and that afterwards they shall be fined at the King's will and the instruments of their minstrelsy forfeited to our lord the King.

Also it is agreed and assented that no man of whatever estate or condition shall, upon forfeiture of life and limb, keep kerns, hobelers or idlemen in the land of peace to aggrieve the loyal people of our lord the King ; but that he who wishes to keep them shall keep them in the March at his own expense without taking anything from any person against their will. And if it happen that any man, whether kern, or any other, take any manner of victuals or other goods of any man against his will, that Hue and Cry be raised against him and he shall be taken and committed to gaol if he surrender himself, and if he does not, but makes resistance and force and will not suffer the attachment, it shall be done to him as to an open robber ; and such manner of taking [of victuals] shall be considered a robbery. And, in case such malefactors fly from the attachment so that no man can take them, that then their lord or leader shall answer for him and make satisfaction to the party who has been so damaged. And if he make not satisfaction to the party that the King shall have the suit against him as well for himself as for the party. And that those who do not rise at such Hue and Cry shall be held and punished as maintainers of felons ; and if any man keep or lead kerns, hobelers or idlemen otherwise than is abovesaid that he shall have judgment of life and limb, and his lands and tenements shall be forfeited.

Also that it be proclaimed that all those who are now idlemen and are willing to take lands of the King may come to our lord Duke, lieutenant of our lord the King in Ireland, or to the chancellor or treasurer of the King and take waste lands of the King in fee or in farm ; and if they wish to take [such lands] of other lords that they may come to them or to their seneschal in like manner.

Also that no Marchers or others shall hold parley or intercourse with any Irish or English rebels who are against the peace without leave of the Court or in the presence of the sheriff of our lord the King or the wardens of the peace, so that they may see that such parley or intercourse is for common and not for individual benefit ; and that he who does it shall be imprisoned and fined at the King's will.

Also it is ordained and established that if any of the lineage, adherents or retainers of any chieftain of English lineage within the land of Ireland whom the said chieftain can chastise commit any trespass or felony the said chieftain, after he has had notice thereof, shall cause the said malefactor to be taken and committed to the nearest gaol there to remain until he be delivered by the law ; and if the said chieftain will not do so, then his body shall be taken for the said malefactor and detained in prison until the body of the malefactor be given up to the Court of our lord the King to be amenable to justice as is above said ; and nevertheless that the said chieftain for the contempt shall be fined at the King's will and make satisfaction to the party so aggrieved.

Also it is agreed and assented that one peace and one war shall be throughout the entire land, so that if any Irish or English be at war in one county the counties around them shall make war and harass them in their Marches as soon as they shall be warned by the wardens of the peace of the said county or by the sheriff where the war arises ; and if they do not they be held as maintainers of felons ; and if those of the country where the war arises suffer their marches to be laid waste by the enemy and will not rise to check the malice of the enemy after they be reasonably warned by the wardens of the peace or by the sheriff or cry raised in the countries of the said county, that then they be held as maintainers of felons.

Also in every county that there shall be ordained four of the most substantial of the county to be Wardens of the peace who shall have full power to assess horsemen-at-arms, hobelers and footmen each according to the value and quantity of his lands, goods and chattels so that they be ready whensoever there shall be need to arrest the malice of the enemy according to what they shall be assessed by the wardens aforesaid. And that the said wardens after array made in manner aforesaid shall make view of the said men-at-arms, hobelers and footmen from month to month in a certain place of the county where they shall see that it be best to be done in ease of the people. And if the said wardens find any rebel who will not obey their mandates, that they shall have power to attach and commit them to the nearest gaol there to remain until the law be made of them. And if the wardens of the peace be remiss or negligent in executing their office and thereof be attaint, that then they shall be taken and imprisoned and fined at the King's will. And if any one so chosen a warden refuse to receive the King's commission that he be taken and imprisoned and his lands seized into the hand of our lord the King and so remain until the King have otherwise ordained therein, and that the said wardens make oath to use their office lawfully in the manner abovesaid.

Also that if truce or peace be made by the Justiciar or wardens of the peace or sheriffs between English and Irish, and it be broken by any Englishman and he be thereof attainted, that he shall be taken and put in prison until satisfaction be made by him to those who are robbed and injured on that account and further that he be fined at the King's will ; and if he have not wherewith to make restitution to those who are so injured that he have perpetual imprisonment.

Also it is ordained that, if dispute arise between English and English whereby the English on one side and on the other gather to themselves English and Irish in the country there to remain to make war upon and aggrieve the other to the great damage and destruction of the King's liege people, it is agreed and assented that no English shall be so daring as to stir up war with each other to draw away henceforward any English or Irish for such purpose, and he that does it and thereof is attaint shall suffer judgment of life and limb and his lands be forfeited.

Also, whereas the commons of the land complain that they are in divers ways distressed by want of servants, for which the assigned Justices of Labourers are much the cause by reason that the common labourers are for a great part absent and fly out of the said land ; it is agreed and assented that, because living and victuals are much dearer than they were wont to be, each labourer, reasonably in his degree according to the discretion of two of the most substantial and discreet men of the city, town, borough, vill, village or hamlet in the country where he shall perform his labour, shall receive his maintenance in gross or by the day ; and if they will not do so nor be obedient, that they shall be taken by the mayor, seneschal, sovereign, provost, or bailiff of the cities and towns where they are, or by the sheriff of the county, and put in prison until the coming of the justices assigned who shall come twice in the year into each county, or by the Justice of the Chief Place, who shall award due punishment for the same and do right to the parties who shall feel themselves aggrieved thereby. And that no labourer shall pass beyond sea ; and in case he do so and return, that he be taken and put in prison for a year and afterwards be fined at the King's will. And moreover that writs shall be sent to the sheriffs, mayors, seneschals, sovereigns and bailiffs of counties, cities and towns throughout the land where is a seaport, commanding them that they do not suffer any such passage of labourers. And it is also agreed that the commissions made to Justices of labourers in every county be repealed and that henceforth none such shall be granted.

Also it is agreed and established that, in maintenance of the execution of the statutes aforesaid, two prudent men learned in the law, having associated with them by the King's council two of the most substantial men of the county shall be assigned by commission to inquire twice a year in every county respecting those who break the articles aforesaid, and to hear and determine such cases thereunder as shall come before them by indictment or at the suit of the party and of the different other articles which shall be contained in the said commission, according to the penalties thereof in the said statutes contained, without doing favour to anyone, and to certify into the Chancery from time to time that which shall have been done by them therein.

Also our lord the Duke of Clarence, lieutenant of our said lord the King in Ireland, and the Council of our said lord the King there, the earls, barons, and commons of the land aforesaid at this present Parliament assembled, have requested the archbishops, bishops, abbots, priors and other persons of religion that they shall cause to be excommunicated and do excommunicate the persons contravening the statutes and ordinances aforesaid, and to fulminate other censures of Holy Church against them, if any by rebellion of heart act contrary to the statutes and ordinances aforementioned. And we, Thomas, archbishop of Dublin, Thomas, archbishop of

Cashel, John, archbishop of Tuam, Thomas, bishop of Lismore and Waterford, Thomas, bishop of Killaloe, William, bishop of Ossory, John, bishop of Leighlin, and John, bishop of Cloyne, being present in the said parliament at the request of our said most gracious lord the Duke of Clarence, lieutenant of our lord the King in Ireland, and the lords and commons aforesaid, passing over the time preceding, do fulminate sentence of excommunication against those contravening the statutes or ordinances aforesaid, and do excommunicate them by this present writing, reserving and each of us reserving, the absolution of ourselves and of our subjects if they be in peril of death.

[The text (in French) of these memorable statutes is given in Berry, *Early Statutes*, pp. 431–69. In all they number thirty-six, of miscellaneous character. Those given above represent the general purpose of the statutes, as determining the relations of the English and Irish race in Ireland, from the legal point of view, until the reign of James I.]

18. ACT OF ABSENTEES, 1368

Lately, by the grievous and frequent complaint of our faithful subjects, prelates, earls, barons, and other magnates, and the commons of our land and lordship of Ireland, it was shown to us and to our great council how the Irish and others our enemies there rode in hostile array through every part of the said land committing homicides, robberies, arsons, pillaging, spoiling and destroying of monasteries, churches, castles, towns and fortresses without reverence or respect to God or Holy Church or to any person, to the great shame and disherison of the King and of his loyal subjects, so that the land was at point to be lost if remedy and help were not immediately supplied.

Whereupon our lord the King, desiring very earnestly to bring the matter to a good and speedy relief, and thinking that by his faithful subjects of Ireland who suffer and have suffered such injuries and mischiefs and who live continually therein he could be the better advised, and good counsel and ordinance be given in this case, by his special mandate made under his Great seal and passed by the advice of his great council by sufficient notice and summons beforehand caused to be set and established in his said Lordship a general Parliament of the prelates, earls, barons and other lords, wise men, and commons, his liege and faithful subjects there, to advise and counsel him upon the said matter which so highly touched his estate and that of his Crown.

The which subject having been well and long debated between them in the said parliament held at the city of Dublin on the Monday next before the feast of the Invention of the Holy Cross last past [May 1, 1368], at length it appeared and seemed to them in particular and in general that the said mischiefs could not in any wise be redressed and amended nor the said land succoured except by the coming and continuous residence of the earls, nobles and others of his realm of England who have inheritance in the said land of Ireland in their own persons, or by their strong men sufficient and well equipped for war upon their lordships, lands, possessions and inheritances within the said Lordship of Ireland for recovering their inheritances there lost, opposing the said mischiefs, and for the preservation of the estate of our lord the King and the rights of his Crown and the aid of the lands aforesaid. And that they and each of them might and ought to be driven and compelled to do this quickly and within short space, considering that upon the first Conquest of the land of Ireland made by his good ancestors, then Kings of England, many honours, lands, possessions and inheritances within the said Lordship of Ireland were given and granted in inheritance by his said ancestors to many noble persons and others of his realm of England in order that they should continually reside and dwell in their own persons with their families upon the said conquest to defend and maintain it for ever thereafter against all men who should attempt to rise or to rebel against the said conquest on his fealty and allegiance. And that his said subjects of England, having inheritances in such manner in his lordship of Ireland, have, since obtaining their inheritance, for the most part dwelt in England and elsewhere and drawn and levied the fruits and revenues of their said inheritances without defending them and without doing their duty in this case, whereby all the said evils and mischiefs without any opposition have occurred.

And upon these points they agreed finally. The which advice and agreement was fully reported and notified to the King and to his council by the prelates and other magnates of the said parliament under their seals. And afterwards postponing the matters under consideration, our said lord the King was again fully assured by his said magnates and subjects of Ireland that the said evils and mischiefs were renewed, multiplied and greatly increased so much so that his said lordship of Ireland was for the most part destroyed and lost as they caused him to know by their letters requiring aid and help in the way which was agreed upon, assented and required by their said parliament.

Our said lord the King having had long and mature consultation and advice upon all the said matters and the circumstances thereof for the said and other reasonable causes which moved him hereto and especially for the preservation, recovery, and defence of his lordship aforesaid, by the advice and express consent of the peers, prelates, dukes, earls, barons, nobles, magnates and wise men of his council for this purpose in his presence assembled, and of his certain knowledge and royal authority accepting and adopting the advice and assent of the parliament aforesaid, seeing clearly the need and want to be so very great that otherwise his said land and lordship would be utterly destroyed and lost has declared, willed and ordained that all those of the realm of England, be they prelates, dukes, earls, barons or others of whatsoever estate, degree or condition, who have or claim to have any lordships, lands, or possessions or other inheritances whatsoever within his said lordship of Ireland, shall go thither and each of them henceforth reside continuously upon their lordships, lands, possessions, and inheritances aforesaid, and that they shall go thither each of them in his own person with their families and men-at-arms and others, according to the proportion and quantity of the inheritances which they have and claim to have there, all excuses delays or essoins ceasing.

And if, for great and urgent necessity or other reasonable cause whatsoever they cannot in any way go and dwell there in their own persons, the which cause shall be shown to, discussed, and approved by the King and his council, then each of them shall send men-at-arms and others sufficient and well equipped to remain and dwell on their said inheritances in Ireland at their own costs and expense for the defence, government, and conquest of the lands, lordships, and inheritances aforesaid as if they and each of them were there in their own persons, ceasing all impediment.

And if such sufficient impediment thereto be approved as is aforesaid, that they send thither men-at-arms and others in a sufficient number and according to the proportion and quantity of their inheritances in Ireland as is aforesaid before the feast of Easter next ensuing. And if they are not there in their own persons with their families and men-at-arms and others, or send not thither at the time and in the manner which is aforesaid, then immediately all the lords and others of England, of whatever estate, degree or condition they be, shall be deprived of their lands, lordships, possessions and inheritances situated within the King's said lordship of Ireland ; and they shall be applied to his own use, to ordain and dispose of them at his free will and as it shall seem good to him for the preservation, defence and support of his lordship aforesaid. Any challenge or contradiction whatsoever in any case whatsoever for the time to come notwithstanding.

By the King himself and council.

[For this act or rather ' ordinance made concerning the Land of Ireland,' see Berry, *Early Statutes*, pp. 470–1. The King, Edward III, by advice of his Council in England had ordered a Parliament to meet in Ireland and advise him on the evils of absenteeism ; acting upon its advice, he and his Council in England issued the above ordinance. A further and final act was passed in the English Parliament in 1380 by which the penalty of absenteeism was to be the confiscation of two-thirds of the profits of lands, rents, offices and other possessions to the State, to be employed in the guard and defence of Ireland, saving such as were in the King's service or students in the universities. (See Berry, *Early Statutes*, pp. 476–7.)]

19. COMMISSION OF A JUSTICIAR, 1376

Edward, King of England, etc. Know that we, fully confiding in the fidelity and circumspection of James Botiller, Earl of Ormond, Justiciar of our land of Ireland, have given him by these presents power to admit to our peace both English and Irish who are rebels

5

to us, and to grant pardon to each or all of them both generally and particularly, for all murders, robberies, felonies, thefts, conspiracies, rebellions, etc., whatsoever, done in our said land, and have made our letters patent to that effect.

Also to receive fines and redemptions from those who wish to make them for our use ; to supervise the conduct of all our ministers there ; to remove those who shall be found unprofitable to us (the Chancellor, Treasurer and any other ministers and officers, there appointed by our letters and under our great seal of England, excepted), by due counsel and deliberation of the said Chancellor, Treasurer and other better and discreet men of our council there ; and to appoint others useful and profitable in their places, for the good of our said land and people there. Also to do full justice to all according to the laws and customs of that land, and to perform all and sundry for the good rule, safety and recovery of our land and people there as is necessary and opportune.

We have also ordered the Chancellor of our land of Ireland who now is, to have drawn up in the accustomed forms all such charters, etc., as the above Justiciar, in virtue of such power to pardon, etc., shall think fit to have made.

In witness whereof we have had these our letters patent made.

Teste ourself at Westminster on the 6th day of August in the 50th year of our reign.

August 6, 1376.

[From *Cal. Ormond Deeds*, II, No. 215.]

20. AN IRISH PARLIAMENT, 1380

Summons to a Parliament, September 1380 : to be held before Edmund Mortimer, Earl of March, Lord Lieutenant

The King to the venerable in Christ R[obert], Archbishop of Dublin, greeting. Whereas for certain urgent reasons specially concerning us and the state of our land of Ireland, we have thought fit to hold our parliament at Dublin on Saturday in the morrow of All Souls Day next coming by advice of our Lieutenant and Council in Ireland, enjoining you firmly in the faith and affection which you owe us, we order that you in person, along with sufficient proctors for the Dean and chapter of your cathedral church of Dublin and others of the clergy of your diocese, having sufficient power for themselves and the said Dean, chapter, and clergy and constituted by the assent of the same, shall be there on that day present to treat, agree, and consent, and to give your counsel on those things which in the same parliament shall be proposed on our part. And you shall have there the names of the said proctors and this writ. Witness the said Lieutenant at Trim the 12th day of September.

Similar writs are addressed to the archbishops, bishops and other persons following, under the same date, viz.

The archbishop of Cashel or his Vicar general.

The archbishop of Tuam.

The Guardian of the spiritualities of the archbishop of Armagh.

The Guardian ditto of the bishopric of Meath.

The bishops of Kildare, Leighlin, Ossory, Ferns, Lismore and Waterford, Cork, Limerick, Cloyne, Clogher, Ardfert, Killaloe, Emly, Elphin, Down, Killala, Clonfert, Ross, Connor, Clonmacnois, Raphoe, Breffny, Derry.

Similar writs are addressed to the abbots and priors following, viz.

The Prior of the Hospital of St. John of Jerusalem in Ireland.

The abbots of St. Thomas the Martyr near Dublin, St. Mary's near Dublin, Mellifont, Baltinglass, Dunbrody, Tracton (' de Albo Tractu ') Magio (Monasteraneany) and the Prior of Connal.

' The King to his dear cousin and liege, James le Botiller, Earl of Ormond, greeting. Whereas for certain urgent reasons etc. (as above), we enjoin on you in the faith and homage which you owe us that you be present etc. on that day (as above) and have this writ with you. Witness the aforesaid Lieutenant ' (as above).

Similar writs are addressed to the following persons, viz.

Gerald, Earl of Desmond, Maurice, Earl of Kildare, William de Loundres, knight, Thomas Fitzjohn, knight, Patrick de la Freigne, knight, Robert de la Freigne, knight, Simon Cusak, knight, Walter Cusak, knight, Hugh Byset, knight, Henry Savage, knight, Thomas Tuyt, knight, Thomas Vernayll, knight, David Barry, knight, Richard de Burgo, knight, and Edmund Husee.

Similar writs are addressed to the following persons, of the King's Council :

Robert Preson, knight, John Keppok, Stephen Braye, Richard Plunket, John Tyrell.

Also to the following :

Maurice FitzRichard, John Roche of Fermoy, Walter Bermyngham of Athenry, Philip son of William de Barry, Nicholas le Poer.

' The King to the sheriff of Dublin, greeting. Whereas for certain urgent reasons etc. (as above) : we order you that by common assent of the county court of your county you make to be chosen two of the most worthy and lawful knights of the same county and most fitted to act, having obtained full power to act for themselves and the said county, whom you shall make to come on the day and place aforesaid to treat etc. [as above]. And you shall have there the names of the said two knights and this writ.' Witness (as above).

Similar writs addressed to the sheriffs and seneschals as follows :

the sheriffs of Kildare, Louth, Meath, Carlow, Wexford, Waterford, Limerick, Cork ; the seneschal of the Liberty of Kilkenny and the sheriff of the Crosses of the same ; the seneschal of the Liberty of Meath ; the seneschal of the Liberty of Ulster and the sheriff of the Crosses of the same ; the seneschal of the Liberty of Tipperary and the sheriff of the Crosses of the same ; the seneschal of the Liberty of Kerry, and the sheriff of the Crosses of the same.

' The King to the mayor and baillifs of his city of Dublin. Whereas for certain urgent reasons etc. (as above): We firmly enjoin and order you that by common assent of the commons of the said city you make to be chosen two of the most worthy and lawful of the citizens of the same, having obtained full power to act for themselves and the same commons, whom you shall make to come etc. (as above). And you shall have there their names and this writ.' Witness the said Lord Lieutenant (as above).

Similar writs addressed as follows :

To the mayor, seneschal and bailiffs of the town of Drogheda on both sides of the river.

The mayor and bailiffs of the city of Cork.

The mayor and bailiffs of the city of Waterford.

The mayor and bailiffs of the city of Limerick.

The sovereign and reeve of the town of Kilkenny.

The sovereign and reeve of the town of Ross.

The sovereign and reeve of the town of Wexford.

The sovereign and reeve of the town of Youghal.

The reeve and bailiffs of the town of Galway.

The reeve and bailiffs of the town of Athenry.

[From Lynch, *Legal Institutions, etc., in Ireland*, 1830, pp. 328–31 (in the original Latin). This Parliament met on 3 November, 1380, and voted to the King ' certain new small customs ' to be levied and taken for three years next to come, at the ports of the land as granted in the 43rd year of the reign of Edward III, viz. so much on herrings, salmon and other fish, on every tun or pipe of wine, on killed meat, on wheat, malt, pease, barley, salt, wool, etc. (See Berry, *Early Statutes*, p. 479.)]

21. KING RICHARD II IN IRELAND, 1395

Treaties with Irish chiefs

(1) With Niall Oge O'Neill.

On the 16th day of March, 1395, in a room of the Friars Preachers in Drogheda, in the presence of King Richard, Nellanus *juvenis* O Nel [Niall Oge O'Neill] in person, captain of his nation, removing his girdle, dagger and cap, and on bended knee, fell at the feet of our said lord the King and, raising his two hands with the palms together and hold them between the hands of the King, took these words in the Irish language, which were rendered into English by Thomas O Locheran, interpreter, in the presence of many well understanding the Irish language, viz.

I, Niall junior O'Neill, captain of my nation, swear to be faithful liegeman of my Lord Richard, King of England and France and Lord of Ireland, my sovereign lord, and of his heirs and successors, being kings of England, from this day henceforth in life, limb, and earthly honour, so that he and they shall have over me power of life and death, and I will be faithful to the same and his heirs for ever in all things and will help to defend him and his heirs against all worldly enemies whatsoever, and will be obedient to the laws, commands, and ordinances of the same or any of them according to my power and that of all mine : and I will come to the said lord my King and his heirs, being kings of England, and to his or their parliament and council or otherwise whensoever he or they shall send for me or whenever I shall be required, called, or summoned on his or their part or the part of their lieutenants : and I will well and faithfully come to the said Lord King, his heirs and their lieutenants, or to any of them, to give counsel, and I will do in all and singular that which a good and faithful liegeman ought to do and is bound to do to his natural liege lord, so help me God and these God's holy Gospels.

For the observing of which allegiance and fealty to the Lord our King etc., he bound himself if he should violate the said oath in whole or part that he would pay to the Papal Curia 20,000 marks of English money. Whereupon the King admitted him to the kiss of peace as his liege, and Niall requested the notary to make a public instrument thereof.

Witnesses being, Thomas, archbishop of York, John of Armagh, Primate of all Ireland, the bishops of London, Chichester and Llandaff, Thomas Mowbray, Earl of Nottingham, Thomas Percy, Marshal of the Household, and William Scrope, the King's Chamberlain.

(2) With Art Oge MacMurrough Kavanagh.
This indenture, made on Thursday the 7th day of January, in the 18th year of King Richard (1395), in a field between Tullow and Newcastle, between the noble lord Thomas, Earl of Nottingham and Marshal of England, etc., on one part, and Art MacMurrough, born liege Irishman of our said lord the King, for himself and his men on the other, witnessses : that at the instance and supplication of the said Art our lord the King received the said Art to his grace and peace under the form which follows, viz. that the said Art has sworn by the holy Cross and on the holy Gospels, touched by him, to keep fealty for ever to our lord the King, his heirs, and successors, being kings of England, and that he will deliver to our lord the King, or any of his deputies, or any whom he shall depute, full possession of all lands, tenements, castles, fortresses, woods, and pastures with all their appurtenances, which have been of late occupied by the said Art or his allies, men, or adherents within the land of Leinster, without any reservation to himself made or to be made in any manner and without fraud or guile ; and that the said Art has sworn and promised as for himself and all his, that all his

subjects and tenants of any condition whatsoever in the lands and places aforesaid shall likewise swear to keep fealty for ever to the Lord King and his successors and deputies, or those whom he shall depute, as above, and that they will stand to and obey the laws, commands, and ordinances of the King and his successors ; and that the said Art has likewise sworn that by the first Sunday of Lent next (28 February), he will leave the whole country of Leinster to the true obedience, use, and disposition of the King, his heirs, and successors, as above, saving and excepting always to him (Art) all his movable goods, and that for greater security of observance of the above fealty the said Art shall deliver to the said Lord our King and to his deputies or those whom he shall depute the son of Thomas Carragh Kavanagh his brother, as a true hostage within the next fortnight following after the date of these presents and sooner, if he can, without fraud or guile, and that, the said hostage thus received, our Lord the King shall of special grace kindly treat the said Art as his true liege, and that he will grant to the said Art to go and return well and peacefully in security ; and that the Lord our King after these things are done shall generously make provision for the said Art and will grant to him and his heirs eighty marks yearly for ever, together with the heritage of the said Art's wife in the barony of Norragh with its appurtenances ; and that all the armed men, warriors, or fighting men of the following, household, or nation of the said Art shall quit the whole land of Leinster aforesaid and shall go with him and shall have fitting wages from the King, for the time being, to go and conquer other parts occupied by rebels of the said Lord King, and that Art and all his men aforesaid shall have all lands which they may thus acquire and hold them of the said Lord King, his heirs, and successors as above, and as his true lieges and obedient and subject to his laws, by liege homage and befitting duty done therefor as above to the King, his heirs, and successors, and that they shall enjoy them in perpetuity and by hereditary descent.   Also subsequently by the above indenture it was understood and agreed between the Earl Marshal on one hand and O'Byrne, O'More, O'Nolan, O'Morchoe, MacEochaidh [Keogh], O'Dunn, Mackerelt, David More MacManus, and all those of Hy Kinsella on the other, that all the aforesaid O'Byrne, etc., and all of Hy Kinsella have sworn by the holy Cross and on the holy Gospels that they and all their armed men, warriors, and fighting men shall deliver all their possessions in Leinster to the said Lord King, his heirs, and successors, his deputies and those whom he may depute, and quit that country, saving however their movable goods always to themselves.   And that when that is done the Lord King shall maintain those captains at expense of his Household at good and fitting wages, fees, or salaries, payable yearly from the King's Treasury to all and sundry these captains for the term of their lives, and that the Lord King will give to them and their fighting men aforesaid fitting wages to go, attack, and conquer other parts occupied by rebels of the King.   And he will give to them all lands which they shall so acquire and they shall hold them of our Lord the King, his heirs and successors, by liege homage and befitting duty, as his true lieges, obedient and subject to his laws. And that they shall deliver hostages to the said King, his deputies and those whom he shall depute, for the fulfilment on their part of all the above as they have sworn it. And that the peace of all the aforesaid shall be publicly proclaimed in the said field by the said Earl in the name of the King, and that likewise it is understood that all the aforesaid Irishmen, so sworn, shall abide in peace in their places even to the first Sunday of Lent above-named, nor shall they permit any rebels of our Lord the King or evil-doers to be received in their localities, but shall expel them to the best of their power from their borders. And in case, which God forbid, that any mischance shall happen between the date of these presents and the first Sunday of Lent aforesaid against these conventions through any of the aforesaid parties or their adherents, the peace shall not on account of that be broken, but within a fortnight after due notice made it shall be amended and fittingly restored without guile or fraud. And that the said Art has sworn and promised that if any of the aforesaid who have thus sworn shall rashly presume to go against the said conventions, he will make war on them according to his power as his deadly and capital enemies. And so that all these conventions shall be faithfully observed by the aforesaid parties, the said Earl Marshal of England swore by the holy Cross on the holy Gospels and likewise the said Art and all the others for their part swore by the holy Cross and on the holy Gospels.

In witness whereof for his part of the indenture the said Earl affixed his seal in presence of the said Art MacMurrough, and for their part of the indenture the said Art and O'Byrne affixed their seals, in presence of the said Earl Marshal.

Witnesses : John Griffin, bishop of Leighlin, John Golafre, Lawrence Verkerell, lord of Coytyf, John Greyly of Gascony, etc., Brother Edmund Vale, Master of the Hospital of Kyllergy, and many others.

Which indenture, sealed with two seals in red wax, the notary saw, read, and has faithfully turned into a public deed. Whereupon the said Irishmen requested him to make them public instruments.

Witnesses : John Golafre and other knights.

(1395.)

[These submissions and treaties are taken from Curtis, *Richard II in Ireland*, 1394–5, pp. 159–60 and 169–73. In this work for the first time are published the documents which may be called 'Submissions of Irish Chiefs,' viz. the surrenders and treaties made by this King of England with almost all the ruling chiefs and local kings of the Gaelic race of the time, recorded in Latin by public notaries attendant on the King. They are classed in the Public Record Office, London, as Exchequer K.R. Mem. Roll (18 R. II).

Niall Oge O'Neill was acting for his aged father Niall More (senior), who is officially described as 'Princeps Hibernicorum Ultonie,' while the famous Art MacMurrough Kavanagh, king of Leinster in Irish eyes, is taken merely as the paramount chief of the Leinster Irish.]

22. REPORT OF THE KING'S COUNCIL IN IRELAND, 1399

Credentials for the Message sent to England by the Guardian of the land of Ireland, and by the Council there

Firstly, McMurghe [Art MacMurrough] began the war before the coming of the King, and continued it after his departure, until conference for a treaty was made between the Guardian and the Council of the land and the said McMurrough, whereat he demanded restitution of the barony of Norragh, and payment of his annuity of four-score marks per annum, with the arrears, otherwise he would not keep the peace ; and the Council, considering the trouble and the danger of greater mischief, agreed to pay him a sum of money for the said barony of Norragh and the said annuity, until the King shall have declared his will whether he shall have restitution or not, and they promised to send messengers to England to learn the will of the King thereupon ; and McMurrough assured his wife that he will not ever be at peace unless he have restitution of her lands, and especially if he have not restitution of her lands and the annuity after Michaelmas. The said McMurrough is at open war, and he is now gone to Desmond to aid the Earl of Desmond to destroy the Earl of Ormond, if they can ; and afterwards to return, with all the power that they can get from the parts of Munster, to destroy the country.

Item, inasmuch as the Anelle [O'Neill] has assembled a very great host of people without number to make war upon and to destroy the whole country, unless he have delivered to him his son and his cousins and other hostages that are in the castle of Dublin, as was according to his statement promised to him. Let some remedy be ordained for this.

Item, whereas the soldiers which were with Lord Surrey, Lieutenant of Ireland,[1] are now out of pay, and discharged, and thus there are no soldiers remaining for the defence of the land, no money in hand to pay any soldiers, nor to afford any relief against the enemies, because the money which was there in the hands of the said Lieutenant for the defence of the land is carried into England by Maudeleyn and the esquires who were sent for it ; and although they were often required by the Council there to pay and deliver part of the said money to find soldiers for the defence and safeguard of the said land, nevertheless they excused themselves, on the ground that they had power to receive, and no power to pay or deliver anything ; and thus the land is in danger of final destruction if it be not quickly relieved and succoured ; for which let a remedy be ordained.

Item, as regards other matters touching the state of the said land, be it known that the Irish enemies are strong and arrogant and of great power, and there is neither rule nor power to resist

---

[1] Thomas Holland, Duke of Surrey, was appointed Lord Lieutenant on 26 July, 1398, and arrived in Dublin on 7 October of the same year.

them, for the English marchers are not able, nor are they willing to ride against them without stronger paramount power.

Item, the English families in all parts of the land which are rebels, as the Butyllers, Powers, Gerardyns, Bermynghames, Daltons, Barretts, Dillons and others, who will not obey the law nor submit to justice, but destroy the poor liege people of the land, and take their living from them and rob them, will needs be called gentlemen of blood and idlemen, whereas they are sturdy robbers and not amenable to the law, and will make prisoners of the English and put them to greater duress than do the Irish enemies, and this from default of the execution of justice.

Item, in addition to this the said English rebels are accomplices of the Irish enemies, and will not displease them, and thus between the one and the other the loyal English are destroyed and injured.

Item, by the rebellion and falseness of the English rebels on the one side, and by the war of the Irish enemies on the other, the King has no profit of the revenues of the land, because the law cannot be executed, nor any officer dare put it, nor go to put it, in execution.

Item, many counties which are obedient to the law are not in the hands of the King, except the county of Dublin and part of the county of Kildare ; for the county of Uriel [Louth], with the office of sheriff and escheator and the feefarm of Drogheda, and all other profits, forfeitures, fees, wards, marriages, feefarms, custom, cocket and all other things, is given to others.

Item, the county of Meath is a Liberty of an Earl palatine, and given to others, and the King has nothing.

Item, the county of Ulster is a Liberty, and given to others, and the King has nothing.

Item, the county of Wexford is a Liberty of the Lord de Grey, and the King has nothing.

Item, many other counties are Liberties of an Earl palatine, which is a prejudice and destruction to the Crown and to the land.

Item, the county of Cork with every thing is given to others along with the Liberties of an Earl palatine.

Item, the county of Tipperary is a Liberty of the Earl of Ormond and the King has nothing.

Item, from the counties of Carlow, Kilkenny, Waterford, Kerry, Limerick, Connaught, Roscommon, the King has nothing, through default of obedience and execution of the law, and by the rebellion and the war of enemies as above.

Item, the coket and custom and the feefarm of Waterford is given for twenty years to the mayor and bailiffs of Waterford to enclose the town, and little is done.

Item, all the profits of the land, as well manors as lands, rents and other things, which are clear or of any value, are asked for and given to others, so that no profit comes to the Exchequer to pay the fees and charges and other things, whereas the revenues, in times past used to pay a great part of the expenses of the war.

Item, notwithstanding that the revenues are thus reduced, many fees and annuities are given as well to Irish as to English, which amount to a very great sum, to the very great and insupportable charge of the Exchequer ; and thus the revenues and profits are all reduced and the charges increased, which cannot possibly be paid.

Item, as regards the officers of the Exchequer, be it known that no baron [of that Court] there is learned in the law, as great need should be.

Item, the other offices of the Exchequer are ill filled by those who are neither learned nor lettered, nor have any knowledge of their duties, but have purchased patents of their said offices from covetousness of the fees, and also have in their absence [deputies] who have no care if only they have their profits and gain. That is to say, the offices of Remembrancer and Chief Engrosser and the office of Second Engrosser, and others, of whom the greater part do not know a letter, [whereas] it is requisite that they should be persons very well skilled in their duty ; and thus there is great mischief in this behalf.

Item, as regards the office of Escheator, the Escheators used to give a hundred marks yearly to have and serve the said office, and besides this there was a remainder to the King of the profits and issues thereof ; and now the Escheator takes yearly of the King's gift forty-two pounds to serve the said office, and in effect [no] profit rendered to the King.

Item, the customs and cokets of Ireland used to be a great part of the substance of the revenues there, and now little comes to the King because sundry of them are due to others, and the Customer has the office of Collector for term of his life, and takes yearly fifty pounds, and little comes to the King.

[From *A Roll of the Proceedings of the King's Council in Ireland* A.D. 1392–3, *etc., with an appendix*, ed. Rev. James Graves (1877), pp. 261–9. This portion is taken from Cotton MS. Titus B. XI, fol. 3 and refers to the period immediately after Richard II's second visit to Ireland, 1 June to 13 August, 1399. It is in French. The Guardian or Viceroy of Ireland referred to was Alexander de Balscot, and the King to whom the message of Council is addressed seems to be the new monarch, Henry IV.]

23. COMMISSION OF A LORD LIEUTENANT, 1429

(1) Letters patent of Henry VI, in Latin, appointing James, Earl of Ormond, Lieutenant of Ireland

Know that we, trusting in the fidelity and wisdom of our dear cousin James, Earl of Ormond, have appointed him our Lieutenant of Ireland from the first day on which he shall land there to the end of two years from this present date. Giving and granting him power to guard our peace and the laws and customs of that land and to do all and sundry to bring into our peace both English and Irish of that land and to punish them according to the laws and customs of that land or according as may seem best to him for our profit in the rule of our said land and of our lieges and subjects there.   And to summon and convoke parliaments and councils in said land as often as shall seem necessary in places where it seems best to hold them, summoning before him to parliament, prelates, magnates and others who ought to come to such parliaments to make statutes and ordinances there for the good rule of the land, according to the custom of the same, by assent of prelates, magnates and others aforesaid.

Also to proclaim in the said land by our writs of the same our royal services and all such services according to the due custom of the same and to punish those who are delinquent.   Also to proclaim as often as shall be necessary that all and sundry who have any annuities or fees of our gift or of our predecessors shall be prepared to set forth to ride and to labour with the said lieutenant within the said land for receiving and admitting to our peace both English and Irish who are rebels to our said land and customs.   And to make and grant full pardon for all or each of such persons seeking for our peace, both generally and particularly for treasons, homicides, robberies, felonies, murders, rapes, thefts, false allegations, adhesions, outlawries, transgressions, contempts, conspiracies and other rebellions, etc., etc., perpetrated by them in our said land of Ireland, according to the laws and customs of the same.   Otherwise to punish such refusal to come to justice with royal power if necessary.   Also to grant all lands and tenements of rebels confiscated or to be confiscated to us to suitable persons who shall faithfully stand to our allegiance and obedience at farm or by reasonable rent to be paid to us by advice of our council for ever or for a term of years.   Also full power to supervise all ministers or officers in Ireland, to remove those who are useless and to put others who are useful and suitable in their places—excepting our Chancellor and Treasurer there. And granting sufficient victuals for the expenses of his soldiers and household in any place within the said land by purveyors of his household and others his minsters together with sufficient carriage both within liberties as without—the fee of the church excepted— payable at reasonable prices according to the form of divers statutes made with regard to purveyors before this time.   Also to do and ordain all and sundry what is meet for the salvation of our land and people there.

In witness whereof we have had these our letters patent made.

Teste Humfrey, Duke of Gloucester, Guardian of England, at (*faded*) on the 10th day of February in the 7th year of our reign.

February 10, 1429.

(2) Indenture in French made between the King and James, Earl of Ormond, on taking office as King's lieutenant.

The tenour is as follows :

The King by his letters patent has appointed the Earl his Lieutenant in Ireland on certain conditions agreed upon therein.

The Earl shall occupy the said office for two years commencing on the day that he shall leave port to pass over into Ireland. He shall safely guard the land of Ireland according to his loyal power, taking as fee 2500 marks yearly to be paid in the following manner. In the first year 1250 marks paid on the day of the making of these indentures from the Treasurer of England or his deputy; and 416*l*. 13*s*. 4*d*. at Easter next and 416*l*. 13*s*. 4*d*. at Michaelmas after that, from the revenues of Ireland. For the second year, 1250 marks at Easter next after that Michaelmas, 1250 marks at Michaelmas next following, and further as much as the King of his special grace wishes to grant him for the defence of Ireland by the hands of the King's Treasurer of Ireland for the time being from the revenues of the same as those revenues beyond the charges may provide.

And if the revenues of Ireland do not suffice, then on this being certified in the King's Chancery of England before his Chancellor there under the Great seal of Ireland, the Earl shall be paid what is wanting by the hands of the Treasurer of England or his deputy. For the payments the Earl shall have out of the Chancery of England or that of Ireland at his own choice as many and such writs as shall seem good and reasonable to him for the said payments. And if the revenues of Ireland do not suffice then he shall have out of the Chancery of England as many and such writs as shall seem good and reasonable to him for the above payments. The Earl shall be at the port of Bristuit [Bristol] to pass over to Ireland on the 20th day of March next to exercise the above office, and for his passage shall have taken at that port sufficient and reasonable shipping for him and his soldiers at the King's costs. The Earl at the end of the said two years shall be freely discharged of that office towards the King or his heirs.

In witness whereof to the part of this indenture remaining with the Earl the King has had affixed his Privy seal.

Given at Westminster on the 15th day of February in the 7th year of our Lord the King.

February 15, 1429.

[From *Cal. Ormond Deeds*, III, pp. 67–9.]

24. DECLARATION OF INDEPENDENCE OF THE IRISH PARLIAMENT, 1460

Statutes, ordinances and acts published in a parliament of the Lord King at Drogheda on Friday next after the feast of St. Blaise in the 38th year of King Henry VI [February 7, 1460], held before Richard, Duke of York, Lieutenant of the Lord King, and thence adjourned to Dublin on Saturday next before the feast of St. Matthias, Apostle, next following [February 22], until Monday next after the feast of St. David next following; and there on Friday next after the feat of St. David until Monday next before the feast of the apostles Philip and James next following prorogued. And from that Monday to Monday next after the feast of Holy Trinity next following prorogued. And on Wednesday next before the feast of Corpus Christi next following to Monday next after the feast of St. Margaret, Virgin [July 21, 1460] next following prorogued, and there ended and terminated in the form which follows :

I. Firstly it is ordained and agreed that Holy Church be free and have and enjoy all her franchises, liberties, and free usages without any infringement, as it has been used heretofore.

II. Also it is ordained and agreed that the land of Ireland have and enjoy all its franchises, good usages and customs as it has been used heretofore.

III. Also it is ordained and established that the cities of Dublin Waterford and the town of Drogheda and all the other cities and good towns in the said land of Ireland have and enjoy all their good customs, liberties, franchises, privileges and usages as they have had and used heretofore.

IV. Also at the request of the Commons : That whereas the King our sovereign lord by his latters patent given at Coventry the 6th day of March in the 35th year of his reign [1457] ordained and constituted his well-beloved cousin Richard, duke of York, his lieutenant of his land of Ireland to have and to hold [the same] office from the 8th day of December next following, in manner and form as is more fully specified and declared in the said letters patent enrolled of record in the rolls of the Chancery of the said land that it may be ordained, established and enacted in the said Parliament that by authority of the said Parliament the said letters patent be confirmed ratified and approved and that the said Duke may have occupy and enjoy the office and all things contained in the said letters patent according to the tenor form and effect thereof from the said eighth day to the end of the said ten years. Whereupon the premises considered : It is ordained established and enacted in the said Parliament by authority of the said Parliament that the said letters patent be confirmed ratified and approved and that the said Duke may have occupy and enjoy the said office and all things contained in the said letters patent, according to the tenor form and effect thereof from the said 8th day to the end of the said ten years.

V. Also at the request of the Commons : That, whereas the King our sovereign lord has constituted and appointed his well-beloved cousin Richard duke of York lieutenant and governor of his land of Ireland, wherein he represents in the absence of our said sovereign lord out of the same land his right noble person and estate ; and that to the said lieutenant and governor in the said absence such reverence, obedience and fear ought to be given in the said land as to our sovereign lord whose estate is thereby honoured feared and obeyed. Whereupon, the premises considered, it is ordained, established and enacted in the said Parliament and by authority of the same that if any person or persons imagine, compass, excite or provoke the destruction or death of the said lieutenant and governor, or to that intent confederate or assent with the Irish enemies of our said sovereign lord or with any other persons, or provoke any rebellion or disobedience towards the said lieutenant

and governor or by any statute made in the said parliament be
proved a rebel to our said sovereign lord, that the said person or
persons upon whom such imagining, compassing, excitement or
provocation, confederacy, assent or rebellion is lawfully proved be
and stand as attainted of high treason committed against the high
person of our said sovereign lord. And it is ordained established
and enacted in the said Parliament . . . that if any person or
persons shall hereafter listen to the said imagining, compassing, etc.
and assent to them, they be attainted of rebellion. And that thereupon the King shall send his writ to any sheriff of any county of
the said land, any mayor, bailiff and commonalty, any mayor, sheriff
and commonalty, any mayor and commonalty, or any sovereign
portreeve and commonalty of any city or town or any other his
subject of his said land to assist his said lieutenant and governor in
resistance to the said person or persons in their said intention ; and
to chastise, punish, and subdue them as law requires, and that
every of the said mayor, bailiff, sheriff, sovereign, portreeve, commonalty and subject shall put himself with all his force and power
into due and immediate [readiness] for obedience to the said writ.
And if any mayor, bailiff and commonalty, etc. [as before] herein
disobey or harbour, receive, aid or favour the person or persons in
the said writ specified, that they shall forfeit all such profits and
commodities or other things as they have of the grant of the King
or of any of his noble progenitors and moreover a thousand pounds
to the King. And if any of the sheriffs of any county of the said land
or any of the said subjects do contrary [to this Act] that then they so
doing shall forfeit one thousand pounds, one moiety to the King for
the defence of the said land and the other moiety to the party who
in that case will sue a writ of ' scire facias ' upon this act. Provided
that this act be not prejudicial to the franchises of any city or town
of the said land granted to the same city or town by our said sovereign lord or any of his progenitors. This to continue so long as the
said lieutenant and governor shall be resident in his own person in
the said land.

VI. Also at the request of the Commons : That, whereas the
land of Ireland is, and at all times has been, corporate of itself by
the ancient laws and customs used in the same, freed of the burthen
of any special law of the realm of England save only such laws as
by the lords spiritual and temporal and the commons of the said
land had been in Great Council or Parliament there held, admitted,
accepted, affirmed and proclaimed, according to sundry ancient
statutes thereof made. And whereas also of ancient custom, privilege, and franchise of the said land there is, and at all times has been,
the seal of the King current by which the laws there and also the
King's subjects of the same land are guided and directed, which seal
is called the seal of the said land to which all the said subjects ought
to do lawful obedience. And it has not been seen or heard that any
person or persons inhabiting or resident in any other Christian land
so corporate of itself ought to obey any mandate within the same

land given or made under any other seal than the proper seal of the same by which any person should be had or compelled to go by any such mandate out of the said land. And if such mandate were obeyed in the said land of Ireland very great prejudice and derogation and very perilous inconveniences would result to the same contrary to the franchises, liberties and ancient customs thereof and to the very great and immeasurable vexations of the said subjects of the same, of which many instances have been in late days seen and experienced. And moreover, whereas in no realm or land which has within itself a Constable and Marshal of the same ought any person of that realm or land to sue or prosecute any appeal or other matter determinable before the said Constable and Marshal, before the Constable and Marshal of any other land where such appeal or matter took [can take] no foundation or effect. And this notwithstanding, that although there are in the said land, and of ancient custom have been, a Constable and Marshal, yet divers persons of the same land have oftentimes heretofore sued and procured of great malice many of the King's subjects of the same to be sent for to come into England by colour of such appeals in great derogation and prejudice of the said liberty and franchise. Whereupon, the premises considered : It is ordained, enacted and established in the said Parliament and by authority thereof that henceforth no person or persons being in the said land of Ireland shall be, by any command given or made under any other seal than the said seal of the same land, compelled to answer to any appeal or any other matter out of the said land. And that no officer or minister of the same land to whom any such command comes shall put that command or any proclamation or any other thing contrary or prejudicial to the said ancient, custom, privilege or franchise in execution, on pain of the forfeiture of all the lands and goods which he or any other to his use has in the said land, as well as [a fine] of a thousand marks, the one moiety to the King, and the other moiety to the party who will sue in this case against the said officer or minister by writ of ' scire facias ' or by any other action at the law proper in this behalf. It is also ordained by the said authority that any appeal of treason taken in this land shall be determined before the Constable and the Marshal of the said land for the time being and within the said land and in no other place. And if any person shall hereafter appeal any other person in the said land, and the matter of said appeal shall be found and proved not true, that then such person taking or commencing such appeal for the same shall be adjudged to death, and that no pardon shall serve him in such case.

VII. Also at the request of the Commons : That, whereas the defence of the English nation of this land from the danger and malice of the Irish enemies of the same land rests and depends on English bows, which give to the said enemies the greatest resistance and terror of any weapon of war used in the said land [which is] now very nearly destitute of any great number of the said bows which are not in these days employed in exercise of the occupation of archery, whereby the said enemies have grown into such great hardihood and audacity as to ride upon the King's subjects of the said land by night, so that they suffer from the said enemies very great and hard rebuke, spoliations and robberies, to their outrageous injury and loss. Whereupon, the premises considered : It is ordained in the said Parliament and by authority thereof that every of the said subjects, for and upon every twenty pounds of lands, tenements, rents, fees, annuities or other livelihood and possessions with their appurtenances which he has in the said land of yearly rent, shall provide in his house one archer mounted and arrayed defensively with bow and arrows fit for the war according to the English fashion, to be ready at all times upon warning for the defence of the said land in manner and form as heretofore it has been accustomed, so long as the most high puissant prince the Duke of York may remain in the said land. And that in every county of the said land the archers, mounted and arrayed as above with the said bows and arrows according to the assessment of their said yearly possessions, shall every quarter make their musters in the same county before the justices or wardens of the peace having authority and power to enquire in their sessions by those to whom [the power] is given. And that by this act the same justices or wardens shall have power and authority to enquire in their sessions from time to time the value of the possession of every man within the same, and also to amerce in the same sessions according to their discretions such person and persons as ought to find the said archers and who therein make default contrary to the intent and tenor of the said act, Holy Church excepted.

[This famous ' Home Rule ' declaration of the Irish Parliament, summoned by Richard, Duke of York, who was then an attainted traitor, is printed in Berry, *Statute Rolls, Ireland, Henry VI*, pp. 639–49. Sixty-three chapters or acts in all were passed in this Parliament, of which XI (' for the regulation of the coinage of Ireland ') is important, but we have selected only the seven which are of political importance.]

SECTION II. THE TUDOR PERIOD

THE ROYAL STYLE, 1541

From the end of the twelfth century the king of England had used the title lord of Ireland (*Dominus Hiberniae*). In 1540 the Irish council advised Henry VIII to style himself king of Ireland, since ' the Irishmen of long continuance, hath supposed the regal estate of this land to consist in the bishop of Rome for the time being and the lordship of the kings of England here to be but a governance under the obedience of the same.' [1]

I. AN ACT THAT THE KING AND HIS SUCCESSORS BE KINGS OF IRELAND

An act that the king of England, his heirs and his successors be kings of Ireland

Forasmuch as the king our most gracious dread sovereign lord, and his grace's most noble progenitors, kings of England, have been lords of this land of Ireland, having all manner kingly jurisdiction, power, pre-eminence, and authority royal, belonging or appertaining to the royal estate and majesty of a king, by the name of lords of Ireland, where the king's majesty, and his most noble progenitors, justly and rightfully were, and of right ought to be kings of Ireland, and so to be reputed, taken, named and called, and for lack of naming the king's majesty and his noble progenitors kings of Ireland, according to their said true and just title, style and name therein, hath been great occasion that the Irish men and inhabitants within this realm of Ireland have not been so obedient to the king's highness and his most noble progenitors, and to their laws, as they of right, and according to their allegiance and bounden duties ought to have been. Wherefore, at the humble pursuit, petition, and request of the lords spiritual and temporal, and other the king's loving, faithful and obedient subjects of this his land of Ireland, and by their full assents, be it enacted, ordained, and established by authority of this present parliament, that the king's highness, his heirs and successors, kings of England, be always kings of this land of Ireland, and that his majesty, his heirs and successors, have the name, style, title, and honour of king of this land of Ireland, with all manner honours, pre-eminences, prerogatives, dignities, and other things whatsoever they be, to the estate and majesty of a king imperial appertaining or belonging ; and that his majesty, his heirs and successors, be from henceforth named, called, accepted, reputed, and taken to be kings of this land of Ireland, to have, hold, and enjoy the said style, title, majesty, and honours of king of Ireland, with all manner pre-eminences, prerogatives, dignities and all other the premises, unto the king's highness, his heirs and successors for ever, as united and knit to the imperial crown of the realm of England.

[1] *S.P. Henry VIII*, ii. 480, iii. 278, 304.

II. And be it further enacted by authority aforesaid, that on this side the first day of July next coming, proclamation shall be made in all shires within this land of Ireland, of the tenor and sentences of this act. And if any person or persons, of what estate, dignity, or condition soever they or he be, subject or resident within this land of Ireland, after the said first day of July, by writing or imprinting, or by any exterior act or deed, maliciously procure or do, or cause to be procured or done, any thing or things to the peril of the king's majesty's most royal person, or maliciously give occasion by writing, deed, print, or act, whereby the king's majesty, his heirs or successors, or any of them might be disturbed or interrupted of the crown of this realm of Ireland, or of the name, style, or title thereof, or by writing, deed, print, or act, procure or do, or cause to be procured or done, any thing or things, to the prejudice, slander, disturbance, or derogation of the king's majesty, his heirs or successors, in, of or for the crown of this realm of Ireland, or in, of or for the name, title or style thereof, whereby his majesty, his heirs or successors, or any of them might be disturbed or interrupted in body, name, style, or title of inheritance, of, in or to the crown of this land of Ireland, or of the name, style, title, or dignity of the same, that then every such person and persons, of what estate, degree or condition they be, subject or residents within the said land of Ireland, and their aiders, counsellors, maintainers, and abettors therein, and every of them, for every such offence, shall be adjudged high traitors, and . . . shall suffer pains of death, as in cases of high treason ; and also shall lose and forfeit unto the king's highness, and to his heirs, kings of this realm of Ireland, all such his manors, lands, tenements, rents, reversions, annuities, and hereditaments, which they had in possession as owner, and were sole seised in their own right, of, by, or in any title or means. . . .

Ir. Stat., i. 176–7.

THE VICEROY[1]

2. A DEPUTY'S INSTRUCTIONS, 1530

Instructions, given by the king's highness to his trusty councillor, Sir William Skeffington, knight, master of the ordnance, whom his grace hath constituted and ordained to be deputy unto his right trusty and right entirely well-beloved cousin, the Duke of Richmond and of Somerset, lieutenant of his land of Ireland, as followeth.

First, the said Sir William Skeffington, taking with him the king's letters credentials directed to the chancellor, and other the king's councillors, of his said land of Ireland, shall at his repair thither, assemble them together, delivering unto them the king's said letters and showing unto them the cause of his coming and repair thither at this time ; which is, to serve the king's highness in the office and

---

[1] For the powers of the king's representative in Ireland (who might be termed lieutenant, deputy or justicer) see H. Wood, ' The office of chief governor of Ireland, 1172–1509 ' in *Proc. RIA*, xxxvi, section C, pp. 206–38.

room aforesaid, according to the effect of the letters patent made unto him upon the same, which the said deputy shall there exhibit and show, taking thereupon his admission to the same room, in such manner as in that case is accustomed. Which done, the said deputy shall consult, common, and devise with the said council, at good length and deliberation, upon all such points and matters, as by them shall be thought good now to proceed unto, for the surety weal, and defence of that land ; so as, by their discreet and politic orders and endeavours, the same may be preserved in as good tranquillity, obedience, order of justice, and quiet, as may be, the king's lands there well defended, and the king's rebellious subjects of the wild Irishry resisted in their attempts and invasions, the best they can. For the better accomplishment whereof, the king's highness sendeth now with the said deputy, for his more strength and assistance, not only the number of 200 horsemen, there to reside and demur upon the tuition and defence of the king's said land and good subjects of the same, but also money for contentation and payment of their wages ; whom, the king's trust is, the said deputy will employ to such good purpose, as may surely serve to the defence aforesaid ; whereunto nothing shall more confer, than to conserve and keep the king's said good subjects in good unity, love and concord, repressing and reforming all particular grudges and displeasures, which be, or may grow, among any of them, and chiefly and principally, between the king's right well-beloved cousins, the earls of Kildare, Desmond, and Ossory, who be the persons most able there, with their powers and assistance effectually (from time to time) given to the said deputy, to resist the malice of the enemies and to preserve the king's said land from invasion and annoyance. And therefore the said deputy, with the rest of the said council, must have special regard thereunto, so that all rancours and displeasures between the said earls, and any of them, may be clearly removed ; . . .

And albeit that the king's highness, minding and intending graciously to assist the noblemen and other his good subjects, of the said land, for their weal, surety, and defence, doth, as is aforesaid, now send the said number of persons to reside and demur, as is before mentioned ; yet, nevertheless, it is not the mind nor intention of his highness, that the said deputy, or any other, shall employ them, nor any other of the king's subjects in the said land, upon making of any hosting, or main invasion, upon the wild Irishry at such charges of the country, as in such main hostings is used, without the express consent, knowledge and agreement of the whole council, or the more part of them ; but that they intend to the sure preservation and defence of the said land, resisting the enemies with all such policies and advantages as be to be taken against them, as far as shall be thought convenient to the said deputy ; not taking any such hosting, charging the country otherwise than for victual as they pass, like as in such other journies hath been accustomed. Nevertheless whensoever, and as often as it shall be fully agreed and

determined, with the advice and consent of the whole council of the
said land, or the more part of them, for any great cause or benefit,
to make a hosting and main invasion, charging the country for exploits
to be done against the enemies, the said Sir William Skeffington
shall now, in that case, else not, use and employ his said number
to that purpose, as by the said council shall be agreed and thought
expedient, and otherwise in no manner, either with them or without,
make any such host, at the charge of the country, but by the advice
of the council, or the most part of them, otherwise than is aforesaid.

The said deputy shall also take with him the letters patent, under
the king's seal of Ireland, devised upon all such articles and points,
as there were thought good to be enacted and passed by authority
of the parliament of his said land ; which parliament the said
deputy shall call and convoke with as good diligence as he shall see
to be necessary and requisite, endeavouring him, with the assistance of the residue of the said council, to the establishment, enacting,
and passing of such acts, by the authority aforesaid, as by the
king's highness shall be devised, and to the due certificate to be made
unto the king's highness thereof, as is accustomed, and semblably to
the execution and performance of the same, after such sort and
manner, as may be to the weal of the king's said people and land,
and after such form as the said articles do purport. The discreet
ordering whereof, for attaining them to pass, the king's highness
committeth to the wisdom and endeavour of the said deputy, with
the assistance of the residue of the council as is aforesaid.

Among other things to be treated and communed of at the
assembly of the said council, upon the first arrival in Ireland of the
said deputy, it is specially to be remembered, that he, with the same
council, devise and consult together for the immediate conducing
and attaining of a subsidy within the said land, towards the sup-
portation and alleviation of the king's charges ; endeavouring them,
to the best of their powers, to have the same subsidy payable for one
year to be ended at Michaelmas next, and that failing, for half a year
ending the same day, if they can so conduce it, and also to induce
for as many years as they can attain the same. Which thing is not
to be tracted or retracted till the parliament, forasmuch as perchance
the same shall not be assembled till Michaelmas next, but is, with
all convenient diligence, to be practised and brought to pass before
the said parliament, if it may be, as both the said deputy, and
also the council aforesaid, can and do well consider. And the
sums rising out of the same subsidy, and of all other the king's
revenues and profits in that land, the said deputy shall cause and
suffer to be answered and payed to the hands of the prior of Kilmainham, under-treasurer there, without intermeddling or taking any
part thereof to himself, but to see the king duly answered thereof, as
to reason doth appertain.

And whereas the earl of Kildare hath made faithful promise unto
the king's highness to employ and endeavour himself, to the uttermost of his power, for the annoyance of the king's said rebellious

subjects of the wild Irishry, as well by making excourses upon them, as otherwise ; forasmuch as the men of war, now sent out of this realm with the said deputy, shall now, in such case, do right good stead to the said earl, in such exploits as he shall make, when the said deputy shall not fortune to proceed thereunto himself [he] shall, at the requisition of the said earl, send unto him the said men of war, or as many of them as he shall require for making of such exploits, reserving a convenient number of them to remain and attend upon himself ; and the profits of such impositions, that is to say, of beasts, or other things, that at an entry or exploit shall be imponed or had by way of patisement or agreement, upon the enemies, to be always the half answered to the king's highness, to the hands of the said under-treasurer, and the other half to render to the earl of Kildare, if he shall make the exploits and put the imposition, and to his company not having the king's wages, to be ordered and divided by his discretion, as hath been accustomed.

Finally, the said deputy shall from time to time as well by his letters apart, as also jointly with the residue of the king's said council, advertise the king's highness of the state and successes of the affairs in the said land of Ireland ; endeavouring himself always with diligence to those things, which, by common advice of the said council, shall be thought good, both for administration of justice, punishment of transgressors and malefactors, good order, quiet, and rule to be observed in the said land, with the dimission and letting of the farms, wards, marriages, and other the king's profits there, by common advice, as well of the king's said deputy, as of the council aforesaid, and also for the resistance of the malice and temerity of the king's said rebellious subjects ; using all politic provisions, as well by appointments to be taken with them, when the case shall require, as by force and other good and discreet ways as shall be thought convenient ; and, generally, shall do, observe, and accomplish all such things, as to the office, authority, and trust, which the king's highness, of special confidence, hath and doth put him in, shall appertain ; whereby he shall more and more deserve the king's special favour and thanks, to be hereafter remembered to his weal accordingly.

S.P. Henry VIII, ii. 147–50.

3. AN ACT FOR THE ELECTION OF A LORD JUSTICE, 1541

Repealed 1787

An act for the election of the lord justice

Forasmuch as continually since the conquest of this realm of Ireland it hath been used in this same realm of Ireland, that at every such time as it hath chanced the same realm to be destitute of a lieutenant, deputy, justice, or other head governor, by death, surrender, or departure out of the same realm, or otherwise, the council of this realm of Ireland, for the time being, have used by the laws and usages of the same to assemble themselves together to choose and elect a justice to be the ruler and governor of this realm, till the king's highness hath deputed and ordained a lieutenant, deputy, or other governor, for the same realm ; . . . notwithstanding at a parliament holden the Monday next before the feast of Saint Andrew the apostle, the tenth year of the reign of the most noble prince of famous memory King Henry VII, amongst other things it was ordained and enacted, as it should seem for some private affection, that immediately after such avoidance of any of the said lieutenants, deputy, governor, or justice within this realm of Ireland, the king's highness' lord treasurer of this his realm for the time being should be justice and governor of this his said realm, until such time that his highness had ordained, made, and sent his lieutenant or deputy into this his said realm of Ireland, . . . which act, at another parliament then after holden at Dublin in the xiii year of the reign of the said late King Henry VII, for divers considerations, mischiefs, and inconveniences then appearing, was by authority of the same parliament annihilated, repealed, made void and of none effect, the rule of record of which parliament by some sinister means was embezzled, and by no means now can be found ; by reason whereof divers ambiguities and doubts upon the election of the justice of this realm upon every such avoidance, and upon his authority, hath, and yet doth daily arise and groweth in this realm. For the remedy whereof, and establishment of a certain order to be had for the election of the justice within this realm . . . be it enacted . . . that immediately upon the avoidance of every the king's lieutenants, deputy, or justice of this realm, by death, surrender of their letters patent or office, departure of out this realm, or for any other cause the king's chancellor of this realm or keeper of his grace's great seal for the time being, shall by the king's writ or writs call and assemble together, at such place as the said chancellor or keeper of the great seal shall think convenient, the king's councillors being inhabiting or dwelling in the shires of Dublin, Meath, Louth, Kildare, Kilkenny, Tipperary, Wexford, Waterford, Cork, Kerry, and Limerick, for the assembly of the said councillors, which of them so assembled, shall by authority aforesaid have full power and authority by virtue of this act to elect and choose one such person, as shall be an Englishman, and born within the realm of England, being no spiritual person, to be justice and governor of this realm of Ireland during the king's highness's pleasure, if there shall be at that time any such person within this realm, that shall be able, meet, and convenient for the same room or office, and for the use and exercise thereof. And if there be no such person then within this realm, then they to elect and choose two persons of the said council of English blood and surname, being no spiritual persons, whom they shall think meet, able, and convenient to be justice and governor of this realm of Ireland, during the king's highness's pleasure ; upon which elections so by them or the more part of them had and made, as is aforesaid, the chancellor or keeper of the

great seal of this realm for the time being, shall by authority aforesaid according to the ancient usage make letters patent to the person
or persons so elected under the king's great seal of Ireland, of, for
and concerning the room of justice of this realm of Ireland ; which
person or persons being so elected as is aforesaid, after he or they
be solemnly sworn according to the ancient usage in this realm,
shall have, use and enjoy like authority, pre-eminence, and dignity
to every purpose and respect, as the king's lieutenant or deputy
there next before him, being made by the king's most gracious letters
patent, lawfully had and used to have, [and] hold, possess, exercise,
and enjoy the said office of justice or governor, with the said authority, preheminence, or dignity, unto such time as the king's highness,
his heirs or successors, do admit and authorize one to be his lieutenant, justice, deputy, or governor of this realm, and until such
time as the said lieutenant, justice, deputy or governor so authorized,
do take and receive his oath, as hath been before accustomed, or the
king's highness farther pleasure therein [be] known by writing. . . .

Ir. Stat., i. 207–9.

PARLIAMENT

4. POYNINGS' LAW (10 HENRY VII)[1]

Henry VII was determined that the legislative authority of parliament
should not be used by any over mighty viceroy for his own aggrandisement.
So when Sir Edward Poynings was deputy the following act was passed.

An act that no parliament be holden in this land until the acts be
certified into England

Item, at the request of the commons of the land of Ireland, be
it ordained, enacted and established, that at the next parliament
that there shall be holden by the king's commandment and licence,
wherein amongst other, the king's grace intendeth to have a general
resumption of his whole revenues since the last day of the reign of
King Edward the second, no parliament be holden hereafter in
the said land, but at such season as the king's lieutenant and council
there first do certify the king, under the great seal of that land, the
causes and considerations, and all such acts as them seemeth should
pass in the same parliament, and such causes, considerations, and
acts, affirmed by the king and his council to be good and expedient
for that land, and his licence thereupon, as well in affirmation of
the said causes and acts, as to summon the said parliament, under his
great seal of England had and obtained ; that done, a parliament to be
had and holden after the form and effect afore rehearsed : and if any
parliament be holden in that land hereafter, contrary to the form
and provision aforesaid, it be deemed void and of none effect in law.

Ir. Stat., i. 44.

[1] On Poynings' law see ' The History of Poynings' Law, Part I,' by R. Dudley
Edwards and T. W. Moody in *Irish Historical Studies*, ii. 414–24, and the authorities
quoted therein.

5. THE SUSPENSION OF POYNINGS' LAW, 1537

During the sixteenth century the Irish administration (after 1534 readily responsive to English control) found the procedure prescribed by Poynings' law a nuisance when complicated and contentious legislation, such as that required by the ecclesiastical changes, had to be passed. And on several occasions amongst the bills presented to parliament was one for the suspension of the law. But a section of the commons had come to consider it a safeguard against over-vigorous administrative action, and resisted its repeal. In 1569, when consenting to a suspension, parliament secured the concession that in future no suspension bill would be transmitted into England without its consent (document 7).

For the great trust and confidence that the king's highness hath in his deputy and council of this his land of Ireland, and in the nobles spiritual and temporal, and the commons his loving subjects of the same, his majesty is pleased and contented that it be enacted by authority of this present parliament, that this present parliament summoned, begun and holden, and every act, ordinance, provision, thing or things of what nature, name, condition, or quality it be of, had, made or established, or hereafter to be had, done, made or established, by authority thereof, shall be good and effectual to all intents and purposes according to the tenor and effect of the said acts, ordinances, and provisions ; the act made at Drogheda in the parliament there holden the Monday next after the feast of Saint Andrew, in the tenth year of the most noble king of famous memory, King Henry the seventh, before Sir Edward Poynings knight, then being deputy of this land, or any other act or acts, use or custom, heretofore had, done or made within this land to the contrary of this present parliament, or any thing made or established by authority of the same, in any wise notwithstanding.

II. Provided always and be it enacted, that by force and virtue of this present act or any thing therein contained, no act, ordinance, provision, thing or things, of what nature, name, condition, or quality soever it be, for any manors, lordships, lands, tenements, advowsons, abbeys, priories, cells, or any other hereditaments, whatsoever they be, for or between any person or persons, body or bodies politic or incorporate, or any other particular act, ordinance, or provision, that shall be prejudicial or hurtful, or in derogation of any grants, liberties, franchises, usages, customs or any other commodities or privileges, given or granted by our sovereign lord the king or his most noble progenitors to any city or borough towns within this land of Ireland, be enacted or established by virtue or authority of this present parliament, but only such acts, ordinances, and provisions, thing or things, as shall be thought expedient for our sovereign lord the king's honour, the increase of his grace's revenues and profits, and the common weal of this his land and dominions of Ireland.

Ir. Stat., i. 89–90.

6. THE AMENDMENT OF POYNINGS' LAW, 1557

From the start the government do not seem to have interpreted the law over strictly, for the English privy council did not hesitate to alter bills sent over from Ireland, and occasionally after parliament had met, to send to Ireland further bills in addition to those transmitted with the licence. Also draft bills were sometimes sent over from Ireland after the session had begun. These practices were sanctioned by the act of Philip and Mary given below.

An act declaring how Poynings' act shall be expounded and taken

Where at a parliament holden at Drogheda the Monday next after the feast of Saint Andrew the apostle, in the tenth year of the reign of the late king of famous memory, Henry VII, grandfather unto our sovereign lady the queen, before Sir Edward Poynings, knight, then lord deputy of this realm of Ireland, an act, among other things, was enacted and made, for and concerning the order, manner and forms of parliament to be from henceforth holden and kept in this realm of Ireland . . . [and] for as much as since the making of the said act divers and sundry ambiguities and doubts have been made and risen, upon the true understanding and meaning of the same ; for the avoiding of the which doubts and ambiguities, and for a full and plain declaration of the true meaning and understanding of the said act, be it ordained, enacted and established . . . that the said act . . . be expounded, understanded, and taken as hereafter followeth, that is to say, that no parliament be summoned or holden within this realm of Ireland, until such time as the lieutenant, lord deputy, lord justice, lords justices, chief governor or governors, or any of them, and the council, of this said realm of Ireland, for the time being, shall have certified the king and queen's majesties, her heirs and successors, under the great seal of this said realm of Ireland, the considerations, causes, and articles of such acts, provisions, and ordinances, as by them shall then thought meet and necessary to be enacted and passed here by parliament, and shall have also received again their majesties' answer, under their great seal of England, declaring their pleasure, either for the passing of the said acts, provisions, and ordinances, in such form and tenor as they should be sent into England, or else for the change or alterations of them, or any part of the same.

II. And it be further enacted . . . that after such return made, and after licence and authority to summon a parliament within the said realm of Ireland granted under the great seal of England unto the said lieutenant or lord deputy, or other lord justices, chief governor or governors of the same realm of Ireland, for the time being, and not before, the same lieutenant, lord deputy, lord justice, lords justices, chief governor or governors, shall and may summon and hold a parliament within this realm of Ireland, for passing and agreeing upon such acts, and no other, as shall be so returned under the said great seal of England.

III. And forasmuch as many events and occasions may happen during the time of the parliament, the which shall be thought meet and necessary to be provided for, and yet at or before the time of the summoning of the parliament, was not thought nor agreed upon, therefore be it further enacted and established . . . that as well after every such authority and licence sent into this realm of Ireland, as also at all times after the summons, and during the time of every parliament to be hereafter holden within the said realm of Ireland, according to the tenor and form of this act, the lieutenant, lord deputy, lord justice, lords justices, chief governor or chief governors and council of the same realm of Ireland for the time being, shall and may certify all such other considerations, causes, tenors, provisions and ordinances, as they shall further then think good to be enacted and established, at and in the same parliament within the same realm of Ireland, to the king and queen's majesties, her heirs and successors, under the great seal of this said realm of Ireland, and such considerations, causes, tenors, provisions, and ordinances, or any of them, as shall be thereupon certified and returned into the said realm, under the great seal of England, and no others, shall and may pass and be enacted here in every such parliament within this said realm of Ireland, in case the same considerations, causes, tenors, provisions, and ordinances, or any of them, be agreed and resolved upon by the three estates of the said parliament, any thing contained in this present act, or in the foresaid act made at Drogheda to the contrary notwithstanding.

Ir. Stat., i. 246–8.

7. THE SUSPENSION OF POYNINGS' LAW, 1569

An act that there be no bill certified into England, for the repeal or suspending of the statute, passed in Poynings' time, before the same bill be first agreed on, in a session of a parliament holden in this realm, by the greater number of the lords and commons

Where upon experiment of the Right Honourable Sir Henry Sidney, knight of the noble order of the garter, lord president of Wales, and lord deputy of this your majesty's realm of Ireland, his great travail and care for the advancement of the glory of God, your majesty's honour, and the utility of the commonwealth of this your highness' realm, and an undoubted hope, that his lordship would not seek the passing of any act, but such as should tend to the furtherance of your majesty's service, and benefit of your highness' realm, we your majesty's subjects assembled in parliament, assented to the repeal of a statute, passed before Sir Edward Poynings, lord deputy of Ireland, prohibiting either any parliament to be summoned, or any act to be treated of in parliament, before the acts were certified under the great seal of this your majesty's realm, and returned hither under the broad seal of England ; before which statute, when liberty was given to the governors under your majesty's progenitors, to call parliament at their pleasure, acts passed as well

to the dishonour of the prince, as to the hindrance of their subjects, the remembrance whereof would indeed have stayed us from
condescending to the repeal of the said statute, were it not that
the government of your majesty's deputy, hath been always, and
continueth such as to all your highness' subjects giveth just cause
to reckon what proceedeth through his motion to your highness,
to be meant only for the honour of your majesty, and the common
benefit of this your realm, and therefore as we might safely, so did
we willingly agree to the repeal of the said statute.   But most
gracious sovereign, fearing that some governor hereafter should
hap not to make answer unto the expectation of your majesty,
or your highness' heirs and successors, by whom he should be
appointed governor, and not following the example of your highness'
deputy at these presents, will upon affection, or some other respect,
abuse the like liberty given him, we your majesty's subjects now
assembled in parliament, do most humbly beseech your highness,
that it may please the same, that it may be enacted . . . that hereafter in the government of any other deputy or governor, of this your
majesty's realm, there be no bill certified into England for the
repeal, or suspending of the said statute, passed when Sir Edward
Poynings was lord deputy of Ireland, before the same bill be first
agreed on in a session of parliament to be holden within this realm,
by the more number of the lords assembled in parliament, and the
greater number of the common house.   And if there be that any act
passed or to be passed thereupon, touching the repeal, or suspending
of the said statute, passed in Sir Edward Poynings' government, [it is]
to be utterly void, and of no effect, to all purposes and intents.

Ir. Stat., i. 346–7.

8. A TRANSMISS, 1515

Henry by the grace of God king of England and France and
lord of Ireland to our dear cousin Gerald earl of Kildare greeting.
Know that we, on account of certain urgent and important matters
concerning the public weal of our aforesaid land of Ireland have
decided and decreed, by and with the advise and consent of our
council, that a parliament shall be held in our said land of Ireland.
Hence we, having full confidence in your loyalty, wisdom, zeal and
foresight, have constituted, appointed and designated you our
deputy in that place, and give and grant unto you full power and
authority to hold the aforesaid parliament in our land within a
year from the day following the date of these presents, summoning
and convening to the said parliament which is to be held there
according to custom, all and singular, lords spiritual and temporal,
proctors, knights, citizens and burgesses for our cities and towns,
and all others who have been accustomed to attend parliament in
our aforesaid land, to treat with them concerning the handling,
discussing, and debating the following articles inserted in these our
present letters, and no others, and to give our assent and authority
to the said articles thus discussed and agreed on ; and to proroge,

adjourn and prolong the said parliament as may be required. Provided however that the same parliament be fully concluded and dissolved within a year from the day immediately after it commences, so that the aforesaid parliament shall in no manner of means last, continue, or be prorogued beyond a year; and to perform and execute all the duties which pertain to the office of lord lieutenant of our aforesaid land in this matter.

The tenor of the aforesaid articles is as follows :

[Text of eight bills in English each beginning with the formula ' Pray the commons.']

Therefore we command you to strive diligently as regards the foregoing, and to perform and execute them in accordance with the form entrusted to you and inserted above and no otherwise. And we firmly command to all and singular, archbishops, bishops, abbots, priors, archdeacons, deans, and other ecclesiastical persons, also earls, barons, justices, knights, gentlemen, sheriffs, mayors, bailiffs, constables, governors of towns and places, and all other our officers, ministers, faithful lieges and subjects, whatsoever, both within liberties as without, by the tenor of these presents, that they be intendant, assistant and obedient to you in doing and performing the above said in all things as is fitting.

In witness whereof we have had these our letters patent made. Witness ourself at Westminster the seventh day of October in the seventh year of our reign. By writ of privy seal of the said date and by authority of parliament

Hist. MSS. Comm. Ninth Rep., App. 2, pp. 271–3.

9. THE EXPULSION OF THE PROCTORS FROM PARLIAMENT, 1537

Parliament was summoned in 1536 for the purpose of passing the bills which embodied the government's ecclesiastical policy. The clerical proctors who still had a right to attend parliament, displayed ' forwardness and obstinacy.' It seemed clear to the deputy that unless a remedy was found ' few things would pass to the king's profit.' So when parliament reassembled in 1537 the measure printed below was forced through.

An act against proctors to be any member of the parliament

Forasmuch as at every parliament begun and holden within this land, two proctors of every diocese within the same land have been used and accustomed to be summoned and warned to be at the same parliament, which were never by the order of the law, usage, custom, or otherwise any member or parcel of the whole body of the parliament, nor have had of right any voice or suffrage in the same, but only to be there as councillors and assistants to the same, and upon such things of learning, as should happen in controversy to declare their opinions, much like as the convocation within the realm of England, is commonly at every parliament begun and holden by the king's highness special licence, as his majesty's judges of his said realm of England, and divers other substantial and learned men, having groundly enquired and examined the root and first establishment of the same, do clearly determine, and yet by reason of this sufferance, and by the continuance of time, and for that most commonly the said proctors have been made privy to such matters as within this land at any time have been enacted and established, and their advices desired and taken to the same, they now of their ambitious minds and presumption inordinately desiring to have authority, and to intermeddle with every cause or matter without any just ground or cause reasonable to the same, do temerariously presume, and usurpedly take upon themselves to be parcel of the body, in manner claiming that without their assents nothing can be enacted at any parliament within this land, which as it is thought, cometh not without the procurement and maintenance of some of their superiors, to the only intent that the said proctors for the more part being now their chaplains and of mean degree, should be the stop and let that the devilish abuses, and usurped authority and jurisdiction of the bishop of Rome (by some men called the pope) nor of themselves should not come to light or knowledge, that some good and godly reformation thereof might be had and provided. Wherefore be it enacted . . . that the said proctors nor any of them so summoned or warned to any parliament begun or holden, or to be begun and holden within this land, is nor shall be any member nor parcel of the body of the same parliament, nor shall give nor have any voice, opinion, assent, or agreement to any act, provision, or ordinance to be regarded nor enacted in any parliament within this land, nor yet their voices, assents, or agreements, or opinions, shall not be requisite nor necessary to any such act, provision, or ordinance. . . .

Ir. Stat., i. 102–3.

10. AN ACCOUNT OF THE SESSION OF 1569 [1]

The author of this account, John Hooker, sat for Athenry

The lord deputy after this journey returned to Dublin, and there, when by the advice of the council he had disposed all things in good order concerning the government, he caused the writs for summons of the parliament to be awarded out unto every nobleman for his appearance, and to every sheriff for choosing of knights and burgesses for their like appearance at Dublin the seventeenth of January, in the eleventh year of her majesty's reign, at which time and day appearance was there and then made accordingly.

On the first day of which parliament, the lord deputy, representing her majesty's person, was conducted and attended in most honourable manner unto Christ Church, and from thence unto the parliament house, where he sat under the cloth of estate, being apparelled in the princely robes of crimson velvet doubled or lined with ermine. And then and there the lord chancellor made a very

---

[1] For a study of the Irish parliament in the sixteenth century see T. W. Moody, ' The Irish parliament under Elizabeth and James I : a general survey ' in *Proc. RIA*, xlv, section C, pp. 41–81.

eloquent oration, declaring what law was, of what great effect and value, how the common society of men was thereby maintained, and each man in his degree conserved, as well the inferior as the superior, the subject as the prince . . . And likewise, how the queen's most excellent majesty, as a most natural mother over her children, and as a most vigilant prince over her subjects, hath been always, and now presently is very careful, studious, and diligent in this behalf, having caused this present parliament to be assembled, that by the counsel and advice of you her nobility and you her knights and burgesses, such good laws, orders, and ordinances may be decreed, as may be to the honour of Almighty God, the preservation of her majesty, and of her imperial crown of this realm, and the safety of the commonwealth of the whole realm, for which they were not only to be most thankful, but also most careful to do their duties on this behalf. And then he the lord speaker directing his speeches to the knights and burgesses, who were there in the behalf of the whole commons of the realm, willed them that for the avoiding of confusion, and for an orderly proceeding in this action, they should assemble themselves at and in the house appointed for that assembly, and there to make choice of some wise and sufficient man to be their mouth and speaker. And then concluding with an exhortation of obedience and dutifulness, he ended, and the court adjourned until Thursday next, the twentieth of January. In the meantime, the knights and burgesses met in the lower house, and appointed for their speaker one Stanihurst, recorder of the city of Dublin, a very grave, wise, and learned man, who upon Thursday aforesaid was presented to the lord deputy, and to the lords of the higher house, and then he having done most humbly his obedience and duty, made his oration and speech ; first abasing himself, being not a man sufficiently adorned and furnished with such gifts of knowledge and learning as to such an office and calling doth appertain, wherein he was so much the more unfit, as the cause he had in hand was of great weight and importance. And therefore he wished, if it might so seem good to his lordship, some man of more gravity, and of better experience, knowledge and learning might supply the place. Nevertheless for as much as he might not refuse it, he was the more willing, because he did well hope that his service being done with his best good will and in all dutifulness, it would be accepted. And again his comfort was the more, because he had to deal in such a cause as was for the establishing of some good and wholesome laws, whereof he was a professor. And hereupon he took an occasion, according to the argument that was before handled by the lord chancellor, speaker in the higher house, to discourse of the nature and good effect of laws, and what good success there ensueth to all such realms, countries, and commonwealths as by laws are well ruled and governed. . . . When he had at large discoursed of this matter, then he concluded with a humble petition, that it might please her majesty to grant unto them their liberties and freedoms of old belonging unto every assembly of a parliament.

The first was, that every man being a member of the lower house, should and might have free coming and going to and from the parliament, and during their abode at the same without molestation or impeachment of any person or persons, or for any matter then to be laid against any of them. The second, that they and every of them might have liberty to speak their minds freely to any bill to be read, and matter to be proposed in that parliament. Thirdly, that if any of the said house should misorder and misbehave himself in any indecent manner, or if any other person should evil entreat or abuse any of the said house, that the correction and punishment of every such offendor should rest and remain in the order of the said house. When he had ended his speech, and in most humble manner done his obeisance, the lord deputy having paused upon the matter, made answer to every particular point in most eloquent and effectual manner, which consisted in these points : nothing misliking with the speaker for so much abasing of himself, because he knew him to be both grave, wise, and learned, and very sufficient for that place, doubting nothing but that he would perform the same in all dutifulness as to him appertained. And concerning the benefit which groweth to all nations and commonwealths by the use of the laws, besides that daily experience did confirm the same generally, so no one nation particularly could better avouch it than this realm of Ireland, and therefore he did well hope that they would accordingly frame themselves to live accordingly, and also to pray for her majesty's safety and long life, whereby under her they might enjoy a peaceable and a quiet life in all prosperity. And concerning the privileges, which they requested to be allowed, forsomuch as the same at the first were granted to the end that they might the better and more quietly serve her highness in that assembly, to her honour, and to the benefit of the commonwealth, it pleased her majesty so long as she were not impeached, nor her imperial state derogated that they should enjoy the same. And so after a long time spent in this oration the court was adjourned.

The next day following being Friday the lower house met, and contrary to the order of that house and duty of that company, in stead of unity there began a division, and for concord discord was received. For all, or most part of the knights and burgesses of the English pale, especially they who dwelled within the counties of Meath and Dublin, who seeing a great number of Englishmen to have place in that house began to except against that assembly as not good nor warranted by law. Their *vant parler* was Sir Christopher Barnwell, knight, who being somewhat learned, his credit was so much the more, and by them thought most meetest and worthy to have been the speaker for that house. And he being the spokesman alleged three special causes, why he and his accomplices would not yield their consents. The first was because there were certain burgesses returned for sundry towns, which were not corporate, and had no voice in the parliament. The second was that certain sheriffs and certain mayors of towns corporate had returned themselves. The third and chiefest was that a number of English-men were returned to be burgesses of such towns and corporations, as which some of them never knew, and none at all were resident and dwelling in the same, according as by the laws is required.

These matters were questioned among themselves in the lower house for four days together, and no agreement, but the more words the more choler, and the more speeches, the greater broiles, until in the end for appeasing the matter, the same was referred to the lord deputy and judges of the realm, unto whom the said speaker was sent to declare the whole matter, and to know their resolutions. And they having at large discoursed and conferred of this matter, returned their answer, that concerning the first and second exceptions, that the burgesses returned for towns not corporate, and for such sheriffs, mayors and sovereigns as have returned themselves, shall be dismissed out of the same ; but as for such others as the sheriffs and mayors had returned, they should remain, and the penalty to rest upon the sheriffs for their wrong returns. The messenger of this answer, howsoever he were liked, his message could not be received nor allowed, which being advertised unto the lord deputy and the judges, then Lucas Dillon her majesty's attorney-general was sent unto them to ratify and con-firm their resolutions, and yet could not he be credited, neither would they be satisfied, unless the judges themselves would come in person and set down this to be their resolutions. Upon this answer the speaker commanded a bill to be read, but the foresaid persons would not suffer nor abide the reading thereof, but rose up in very dis-ordered manner, far differing from their duties in that place, and contrary to that gravity and wisdom, which was or should be in them. Wherefore, for pacifying of the same, the chief justices of the queen's bench, and the chief justice of the common pleas, the queen's serjeant, attorney-general, and solicitor, the next day following came to the lower house, and there did affirm their former resolutions, which thought it might have sufficed. Yet certain lawyers who had place in that house did not altogether like thereof.

And albeit this matter were orderly compassed and sufficient to have contented every man, yet the same was so stomached, that the placeing of the Englishmen to be knights and burgesses could not be digested, and did appear in the sequel of that assembly, where every bill furthered by the English gentlemen was stopped and hindered by them. And especially Sir Edmund Butler, who in all things which tended to the queen's majesty's profit or common-wealth, he was a principal against it, fearing that their captainries should be taken away, and coynye and livery be abolished, and such other like disorders redressed, which he and his complices misliking, it did even open itself of a rebellion then abrewing and towards which indeed followed. For immediately after the parliament, he returned home with a discontented mind, and gathered his forces and followed his purpose.

But to the purpose. There were two bills put in of moment

and great consequence. The one was concerning the repeal of an act for that session only made in the time of Sir Edward Poynings lord deputy, in the tenth year of king Henry the seventh, which though it were meant most for their own benefit and commonwealth of that realm, yet so jealous they were, that they would not in long time enter into the consideration thereof. The other was for the granting of the impost for wines then first read. And in this matter they showed themselves very forward and so unquiet, that it was more like a bearbaiting of disordered persons, than a parliament of wise and grave men. Wherewith a certain English gentleman (the writer hereof) being a burgess of the town of Athenry, in Connaught, who had before kept silent, and still more meant to have done, when he saw these foul misorders and overthwarting, being grieved, stood up and prayed liberty to speak to the bill. . . .

[And when he had finished his speech] he sat down, the most part of the house very well liking and allowing both of the person and of the matter, saving the persons before named, who did not hear the same so attentively as they did digest it most unquietly, supposing themselves to be touched herein. And therefore some one of them rose up and would have answered the party, but the time and day was so far spent above the ordinary hour, being well near two of the clock in the afternoon, that the speaker and the court rose up and departed. Howbeit such was the present murmurings and threatenings breathed out, that the said gentleman for his safety was by some of the best of that assembly conducted to the house of Sir Peter Carew, where the said gentleman then lay and resided. The lord deputy in the meantime, hearing the lower house were so close, and continued together for so long above the ordinary time, he doubted that it had been concerning the questions before proposed, and therefore did secretly send to the house to learn and know the cause of their long sitting. But by commandement of the speaker, order was given to the doorkeepers that the doors should be close kept, and none to be suffered to come in or out, so long as the gentleman was in delivery of his speeches and after the court was ended, it was advertised to the said lord deputy, who thanked God that had raised up unknown friends unto him in that place.

The next day following being Friday, as soon as the court of the lower house was set, Sir Christopher Barnewell, and the lawyers of the English pale, who had conferred together of the former day's speeches, stood up and desired hearing, who leaving the matter in question, did in most disorderly manner inveigh against the said gentleman, affirming, avouching, and protesting, that if the words spoken had been spoken in any other place than in the said house they would rather have died than have born withal. Whereupon the speaker by consent of the residue of the house commanded them to silence, and willed that if they had any matter against the said gentlemen, they should present and bring it in writing against Monday next following. And forsomuch as their dealings then

7

were altogether disordered, being more like to a bearbaiting of loose persons than an assembly of wise and grave men in parliament ; motion and request was made to the speaker, that he should reform those abuses and disordered behaviours, who not only promised so to do, but also prayed assistance, advise, and counsel for his doings therein, of such as were acquainted with the orders of the parliament in England. Which was promised unto him and performed, and also promised that a book of the orders of the parliaments held in England should in time be set forth in print. . . .

The Monday following Sir Christopher Barnewell and his complices, having better considered of themselves, were quiet and contented, and the parliament begun with some troubles had its continuance and end with better success.

Holinshed: *Chronicles* (1586–7), ii. 119–29.

THE KING'S COUNCIL IN IRELAND

The Irish council of this period was composed of a group of leading officials. For certain purposes such as levying a cess, or electing a lord justice, it would be reinforced by the presence of prelates and nobles from the loyal shires. Together with the viceroy it settled questions of general policy, legislated by proclamation, and negotiated with the semi-independent magnates.

11. THE COMPOSITION OF THE IRISH COUNCIL

Order from the English council, 1 April, 1547

We have thought good also to signify unto you that in respect of the faithful and diligent service heretofore done unto our said father and us & upon special trust of the continuance of the same, we have appointed you our deputy, our chancellor, the archbishop of Dublin, the bishop of Meath, Sir William Brabazon our vice-treasurer, Sir Gerald Aylmer chief justice of our bench, Sir Thomas Luttrell chief justice of our common pleas, James Bathe chief baron of our exchequer, Sir Thomas Cusack master of our rolls & Thomas Hothe one of our justices there & every of you to be our privy council for all matters and affairs of that our realm.

B. M. Add. MSS., 4801, f. 222 v.

12. THE IRISH COUNCIL OATH

(1) The form of the oath ministered to such as be admitted to be of the king and queen's majesties' council

Ye shall swear to be true and faithful to our sovereign lord and lady, the king and queen's majesties, and their counsel to conceal and keep secret from time to time. And for the better furtherance of their majesties' service to give your best advice and counsel. And in all things concerning their highnesses' honour and profit to use such diligence and circumspection as to a true councillor shall appertain. And that ye shall by no means consent to their dishersion or hinderances, but shall make declaration thereof to the lord deputy for the time being if you have time thereto, or otherwise to such of their majesties' council as are next to you, as well of that as all other matters that may touch their majesties' service or be prejudicial in any condition to their persons, or to the person of their deputy for the time being. So help you God, in Christ Jesus, and all saints.

Acts privy council, Ire., 1556–71, p. 256.

13. ACTS OF THE COUNCIL

1. Apud Dubliniam, ix die Novembris, anno predicto [1556]:

T. FitzWalter.—It is condescended, concluded and agreed by us, the lord deputy, the lords and nobles of this realm, with the rest of the king and queen's majesties' council whose names are hereunto subscribed, that for the furniture and victualling as well of their majesties' forts in Leix and Offaly, as other their highnesses' holds and garrisons both in the north and elsewhere, that there shall be a universal cess of corn and beeves, that is to say, four thousand pecks wheat, and four thousand pecks of malt, whereof the third part beare [barley] malt, and the other two parts oaten malt ; the peck of wheat and beare malt at three shillings iv. d. sterling, and the peck of oaten malt at two shillings iv. d. sterling.

The whole to be cessed and levied within the counties of Meath, Westmeath, Kildare, Dublin and Uriell, and to be divided in sort as followeth, that is to say, in Meath and Westmeath four thousand pecks whereof three thousand in Meath and one thousand in Westmeath, the one half wheat the other malt ; in Kildare xv hundred pecks wheat and malt ; in Dublin, other xv hundred pecks wheat and malt ; and in the county of Uriell one thousand after like rate.

The counties of Wexford, Waterford, Kilkenny and Tipperary to be likewise cessed at the discretion of the said lord deputy and as his lordship by his letters shall appoint, to serve for the furniture of the manor of Leighlin and other the queen's majesty's garrisons that shall upon occasion reside on those borders. And further, it is concluded that for the furniture aforesaid there shall be cessed within the said five shires of Meath, Westmeath, Kildare, Dublin and Uriell, one thousand beeves ; whereof, in Meath and Westmeath, six hundred, in Kildare seven score, in Uriell seven score, and in the county of Dublin six score ; the rate of the said beef at xii s. sterling.

All which proportion of corn to be brought in as followeth, that is to say, one part by Christmas next, the second part by Candlemas and the third part by Saint Patrick's tide next following, with sufficient carriage appointed by the country for conveying of the same, after the rate of iv. d. the garran and vi. d. the man by the day, to be delivered at such places as in the mean time by the said lord deputy shall be appointed unto you, where they shall receive ready money after the rates aforesaid as well for the said grain as also for the beeves, which beeves we will shall be brought all in betwixt this and Christmas next, to the intent they may for store be put in salt, considering that after time they will fall and abate their flesh.

H. Dublin, canc.—Ronald Baltinglass.—Willelmus Midensis.— H. Sydney.—Richard Delvin.—John Travers.—John Plunket.

Ibid., pp. 22-3.

2. By the lord lieutenant and council

T. Sussex.—Where upon the fall of the base coins in England there seemeth to arise some doubt for paying and receiving within this realm of those kinds of coins and how they should be current here in this realm, it is for the deciding thereof thought fit to us the lord lieutenant and council to give notice to all the queen's majesty's subjects by this our proclamation that all those kinds of base coins be and ought to be current within this realm of Ireland, in such sort and at such rates as heretofore by proclamation was appointed, that is to say, every testen that was the fourth of October in the first year of the queen's majesty's reign current in England at sixpence should be from henceforth and so still is current within this realm of Ireland for and at eightpence sterling ; and that all other the base coins of England should be from henceforth and so still be current within this realm after like value in such sort and form as in the said proclamation for the rating of those coins is specified and declared.

Wherefore we straightly charge and command all the queen's majesty's subjects within this realm that no man presume to pay or receive any kind of those foresaid base coins, now proclaimed down in England, at other rates than by the said former proclamation was appointed and in this is rehearsed, upon pain by the laws in such cases provided.

And for the avoiding of the greediness of sundry persons that would take occasion hereby to raise and enhance the prices of all things to the great discommodity of the whole body of the realm, we will and command all mayors, justices of the peace, bailiffs, sheriffs, constables and all other the queen's majesty's officers that they according to the vocations and trust committed to them be careful and diligent as well in seeing of the markets furnished with all victuals and other things necessary as also to see that the same be sold at prices reasonable, that by the insatiable greediness of a few the whole commonweal of this realm be not hindered.

Dated at Dublin, this xxix[th] of October, in the second year of the queen's majesty's most prosperous reign [1560].

The true copy of this proclamation for the continuance of the base coin of England to be current here at vii*d.* sterling, le pence.

Signed by the lord lieutenant and council, videlicet :

Hugh Dublin, canc., G. Kildare, Rowland Baltinglass, Christopher Howth, W. Fitzwilliams, G. Stanley, H. Radecliffe, J. Plunkett, R. Dillon, James Bathe, J. Wingfield, T. Cusacke, F. Agarde, Mr. Deane, F. Harbarde, H. Warren, J. Challoner.

Ibid., pp. 112-13.

3. Apud Dubliniam, ix die Novembris, anno supradicto [1556] :

T. FitzWalter.—Memorandum : Where sundry variances and controversies have heretofore been moved and are yet depending between the right honourable the earl of Ormonde, on the one party, and the baron of Upper Ossory on the other, for diverse stelthes, bodderages, and other enormities done by them and their tenants, servants and followers, upon their several countries, to the great unquietness of themselves and much to the loss and hinderance of their majesties' subjects abiding under their several rules, it is ordered, condescended and agreed by us that Robert Dillon esquire, second justice of their majesties' bench here, and John Plunket, of Donshagley, esquire, as commissioners, indifferently elected and chosen, shall with as much speed as they may make their repair into the said earl's and baron's countries, and there travelling from place to place as occasion shall serve, learn and understand, by all the lawful ways and means they may, either by deposition of witnesses or otherwise, what hurts and damages have been done by the said earl and baron against another, or by any of their tenants, servants and followers or any the inhabitants within their several countries ; and the same so known shall immediately put in writing under their hands and seals and send it to us, the lord deputy, with convenient speed, to the end that we thereupon may take such order betwixt the said earl and baron for a friendly concord and quietness to be had between them, and for the better stay and quietness of the countries from henceforth as upon due consideration of the matter shall be thought consonant and agreeable to justice.

And hereupon it is further ordered and agreed that not only the costs and charges of the said commissioners to be sustained in this behalf shall be indifferently borne by the said earl and baron, but also that they shall give unto the said commissioners by way of reward for their pains taking in the premises twenty marks sterling apiece, to be paid in hand before their departure out of the countries aforesaid.

H. Dublin, canc.—John Travers.—H. Sydney.

Ibid., p. 23.

4. At Christ's church, the vth of June, 1569, anno regni
regine Elizabeth undecimo :

Memorandum : That the vth of June, being Trinity Sunday, Michael Bee, then mayor of the city of Dublin, was committed to her majesty's castle there, for his disobedience and arrogant contempt of a commandment addressed unto him from the lord deputy, and ordered and adjudged to pay so many pecks of corn as by his means and wilfulness in resisting and disobeying of the said lord deputy's commandment should be sufficiently and duly proved the garrison was appointed and unfurnished of.

And moreover, a fine of one hundred pounds, current money

of this realm, to be levied of his goods and chattels to the queen's majesty's use was imposed upon him for that his contempt.

And upon the seventh day of the said month then next following the council being assembled at the castle of Dublin, the mayor submitted himself upon his knees to the said lord deputy and the whole board, humbly acknowledging and confessing his fault and disobedience.

Where upon and likewise at the earnest suit and petition of the recorder, aldermen, and the rest of the co-brethren of the said city, being likewise upon their knees, and the rather to gratify the whole corporation in restoring unto them again their head and chief officer, it was thought good the said mayor should be enlarged and set at liberty.

Ibid., pp. 227-8.

THE COURT OF CASTLE CHAMBER

About 1562 the court of castle chamber was created to exercise some of the council's judicial powers. Composed of the judges often assisted by non-legal councillors, its methods were summary. It dealt mainly with cases of riot and sedition, and was particularly useful for handling disputes in which a powerful individual was concerned.[1]

14. WRIT ESTABLISHING THE COURT OF CASTLE CHAMBER IN IRELAND, 1581 [2]

(I) Elizabeth by the grace of God, etc. To our right trusty and well-beloved the lord deputy, lieutenant, justice, or justices of our realm of Ireland, lord chancellor or keeper of our great seal there, now being or that hereafter shall be, our lord treasurer of the same realm now being or [etc.], the chief justice of our high bench in that our realm that now is or [etc.], the chief justice of our common pleas in the same realm that now is or [etc.], the chief baron of our exchequer there that now is or [etc.], and the master of the rolls of our chancery in the same realm that now is or [etc.], greeting.

(II) Forasmuch as by unlawful maintenance, embraceries, confederacies, alliances, false bondings and taking of money by the common jurors of that our realm, and also by untrue demeaning of sheriffs in making of panels and other untrue returns, and by riots, routs, unlawful assemblies, forcible entries and other like hateful disorders . . . and offences the policy and good rule of that our realm is well near subverted, and for not punishing of these inconveniences and by occasion of the premises nothing or little is or may be found by inquiry, whereby the laws of that our realm in execution do and must take little or no effect, to the increase of murders, perjuries and unsureties of our subjects and loss of their lands and goods, to the great hindrance of our service and to the displeasure of Almighty God ; for the better remedy whereof and

[1] Herbert Wood, ' The court of castle chamber or star chamber of Ireland,' in *Proc. RIA*, xxxii, section C, pp. 152-69.
[2] This is the first commission of which an enrolment can be found.

to the intent that such execrable and pernicious evils . . . shall not escape without just due correction and punishment, we have thought meet to appoint that a particular court for the hearing and determination of these detestable enormities . . . shall be holden within our castle at our city of Dublin in that our realm of Ireland or in such other place where the ordinary term shall be kept in that our realm, and that the same our court shall be called the castle chamber of our said realm of Ireland.

(III) And having good experiment of your truth, circumspection, integrity and knowledge and like good hope of such as shall by our appointment succeed you in your office, we do by these presents appoint and constitute you and such as shall in your offices for the time execute, or any three of you, whereof the said lord deputy, lieutenant, justice or justices, lord chancellor or keeper of our said great seal, or lord treasurer to be one, our commissioners and justices of our said court of our castle chamber, together with such as by authority hereof shall be to you associate in the times of the four ordinary terms to be holden within that our realm from time to time, two days every week of the said term (that is to say) Wednesday and Friday or any other days and times when you or any two of you [quorum as before] shall think meet.

(IV) And further, we do give full power to the lord deputy, lieutenant, justice or justices, lord chancellor and keeper of our said great seal, and lord treasurer of our said realm and to every one of them for the time being, and which shall be present at any time of sitting in the said court, to call as associate unto him or them such and so many of the lords spiritual and temporal and such of our privy council or justices of any our benches in our said realm of Ireland as they or any of them . . . shall think meet to sit and join with him or them in the hearing and determining of such causes and matters as in our said court shall be heard or determined.

(V) And further, we give unto you or any three of you [quorum as before] together with such of the said lords, councillors and justices, or such a competent number of them or any of them as then shall be called and present to sit with you as aforesaid, full power to receive, hear and determine all bills, complaints, supplications and informations to be made . . . into our said court concerning any riots, routs, forcible entries, unlawful assemblies, deceits, perjuries, forgeries, defaults, falsities, misdemeanours of sheriffs and other officers, contempts, disorders, misdemeanours and offences committed . . . within our said realm of Ireland, and [the] dependents and incidents upon the same, in such like manner . . . as such like offences are or heretofore have been used to be received, heard, ordered and determined in the court of star chamber within our realm of England.

(VI) And [we] do also authorize and give full power unto you or three of you [quorum as before] to award all ordinary process as well upon all the said bills which be exhibited for any the causes or offences aforesaid as also upon all contempts to be committed in any of the said matters in like manner as is used in our court of star chamber within our realm of England, the manner and form whereof we have hereunto caused to be annexed.

(VII) And we do also give unto you or any three of you [quorum as before] full power together with any such your associates as afore is said or the more number of them, to call and command before you into the said court by all means and ways that you shall see to be expedient, all misdoers and offenders that shall so be complained upon, and to proceed to the examination, discussion and determination of the said disorders (etc.) in the same manner and order as in our said court of the star chamber here in England is used, and such as you shall find to be in fault to punish by fines to our use, imprisonment and otherwise after their demerits and according to your discretions ; and also to tax and cess to our use amercements, fines and penalties for defaults to be made by non-appearance, departures from the court without licence or other defaults or disobedience of the sheriffs, whatsoever to be committed within that court or against the authority of the same, and for the levying thereof to award process in like manner as is used for the having or obtaining of any of our debts or duties within our said realm of England, and the same to be to the use of us, our heirs and successors, and to be accounted for in such manner as other the perquisites or forfeitures of other our courts within our said realm of Ireland be or shall be accounted for.

(IX) And also we do will and order that the lord deputy, lieutenant, justice or justices of our said realm of Ireland for the time being shall from time to time at his or their will and pleasure come . . . into our said court of castle chamber and during his or their presence in the same shall have in our behalf the full power of chief head and principal justiciar and determiner, and shall be the chief head and principal judge in and of all of such matters and causes as shall be in the same court proponed, debated or controversed. . . .

(XI) And we do also give in strait charge and commandment to all our faithful subjects to whom it shall appertain, of what estate . . . so ever they shall be . . . that they shall be obedient . . . unto you and to such final orders and judgments as touching the premises shall be from time to time had and taken by you as shall appertain, as they will eschew our high indignation and will answer for the contrary at their extreme perils.

Witness our self at Westminster the fifteenth day of April in the [blank] year of our reign.

G. W. Prothero, *Select statutes and other constitutional documents* (Oxford 1913), pp. 150–3.

15. CASES DECIDED BY THE COURT

1. Mem. that her majesty's attorney-general at the relation of Theobald Dillon gent. exhibited an information against Henry Ealand esquire late sheriff of the county of Roscommon, for many extortions, wrong forces, briberies, oppressions and injuries against

many of her majesty's subjects within the said county during the time of his sheriffalty. Which misdemeanours were contained in the said information in 27 articles. And upon hearing of this cause upon the 24 November 1586 the greatest part of the said articles were sufficiently proved against the said Ealand. The court therefore conferred and decreed that the first and second articles in the information wherein the defendant is impeached for murdering of some of good credit unlawfully by colour of martial law, shall be dismissed out of this court, and prosecuted in her majesty's court of chief place, where it properly belongeth to be determined. And for the rest of the offences the court conferred and declared that the said Henry Ealand shall pay unto her majesty by way of fine the sum of five hundred pounds sterling, and be imprisoned by the space of one whole year and until he receives trial in the king's bench for the offences committed to that court. And until he shall make restitution of all gifts and bribes and extortions given this day against him to be by him, his officers and servants unlawfully extorted or taken from any of her majesty's good subjects. And shall stand in some market place in market time in the county of Roscommon with a paper upon his head declaring the quality of his offences.

T. C. D. MS. 852.

2. Mem. that Sir Thomas Fleming knight, lord baron of Slane exhibited against Christopher Preston, Lord Viscount Gormanstown, Christopher Plunkett, William Fitzwilliams and divers others, thereby setting so forth that the said lord baron of Slane being sent for by the lord chancellor and others her majesty's commissioners to make his presence and repair to Dublin to be examined before the said commissioners upon causes greatly importing her majesty's service, and the said lord baron of Slane going through the High Street in Dublin with five or six of his ordinary servants towards St Patrick's church where the said commissioners were, the said Viscount Gormanstown with the number of thirty followers or thereabout did meet the said lord baron of Slane and gave him divers blows and in the said assault Bartholomew Langan one of the said lord baron of Slane's servants was sore wounded and in great peril of his life. And upon full showing of this cause it manifestly appeared unto the court that the said Lord Viscount Gormanstown as well for himself as the rest of his company defendants, should pay unto her majesty for a fine the sum of one hundred pounds and be restrained of his liberty during the lord deputy's pleasure.

Ibid.

3. Mem. that her majesty's learned council *ore tenus* informed against Nicholas White of Moynan in the county of Kildare that the said Nicholas had traitorously published that there was a prophecy in Ireland that O'Donnell should be king of Ireland, and that there was an old crown of the kings of Ireland in Rome, and that the catholic bishops of this land did write to Rome for that

crown and to advance their religion, of which his disloyal speeches he could not bring forth the pretended author, which words he confessed before the lord deputy and council. The court therefore upon the 28 November 1593 conferred and decreed that the said Nicholas White shall stand upon the pillory in the city of Dublin three market days with a paper on his head declaring his disloyal and undutiful speeches, the first day to have [one] of his ears nailed to the pillory and cut off, the second time to have the other ear nailed to the pillory and cut off, and after he had been upon the pillory the third time to be whipped through the city, and then to be committed during the lord deputy's pleasure.

Ibid.

4. Mem. that her majesty's solicitor general *ore tenus* informed the court against John FitzEdmund of Clone in the county of Cork esquire, one of her majesty's commissioners of the peace for the said county, that the said John FitzEdmund having intelligence that one Walter Coppinger under-sheriff of the said county had taken a distress from one Thomas Grangogh brother-in-law to the said John, the said John FitzEdmund being in his house at Clone accompanied with some of his men sent for the said Walter Coppinger to come to him to shew him by what authority he took the said distress, the said Coppinger presently repaired to the said John and delivered unto him a green wax book under the seal of her majesty's court of exchequer. The said John FitzEdmund having the said green wax book in his hand, in great choler and fury did swear with grievous oaths that there was nothing in that book but knavery, packing and shifting contained in the said book, and called the said Coppinger knave, villain and many other vile names for taking the said distress, and caused his servant to take the said Coppinger's dagger from him, and did grievously assault and beat him and kept from him the said green wax book to the great hinderance of her majesty's service. All which appearing to be true, the court upon the 7 February 1592 [i.e. 1593], conferred and decreed that the said John FitzEdmund shall pay unto her majesty by way of fine for his offence the sum of twenty pounds sterling and be committed during the lord deputy's pleasure.

Ibid.

THE ENGLISH PRIVY COUNCIL AND IRISH AFFAIRS

Throughout the century the English government kept up an increasingly close supervision over Irish affairs. A steady correspondence went on between the officials and councils on either side of the channel, and the English privy council appointed special sub-committees for Irish affairs.

16. ACTS OF THE PRIVY COUNCIL

1. At St. James', the day 28 March 1554
The appearance of the day before

It was this day agreed by the lords and others of the council that the Lord Treasurer, Lord Steward, Mr. Secretary Bourne,

Sir Richard Southwell, being appointed as commissioners for the examination of the state and accounts of Ireland, should call before them Sir Edmond Rouse and Valentine Browne, who are now repaired out of Ireland, and as well by examination of such accounts, reports and declarations as they bring with them, as by such other means as they can, to understand in what terms the account of Andrew Wise, late treasurer of that realm, standeth in, and to make report unto the board of that they shall find in that behalf, to the end that thereupon such further order may be taken herein as to equity and justice shall appertain.

Acts privy council, 1554–6, pp. 4–5.

2. At Greenwich, the 24 April 1587

Lord Treasurer	Lord Admiral
Earl of Shrewsbury	Lord Chamberlain
Earl of Derby	Mr. Treasurer
Earl of Leicester	Mr. Secretary Walsingham
	Mr. Wolley

A letter to the lord deputy of Ireland. That although their lordships are persuaded that his lordship of himself will have such consideration toward Jaques Wingfield esquire, master of the ordnance there, as a man of his quality, in respect also of his long and good service, deserveth in all his reasonable causes and requests there, yet their lordships themselves have been very willing to accompany him at this time of his return thither with their letters unto his lordship, and specially to recommend him, to this end that his lordship will not lay any check upon him either in fee or in other his allowance for any of his charges there for the time of his absence from thence, which their lordships are to let his lordship know hath been the longer in respect of his travail about sundry things tending to her majesty's better service in that realm . . . in respect of which his honest and dutiful care, their lordships are further to pray his lordship on his behalf, to take order that he may enjoy his office of constable of the castle of Dublin in such ample manner as he hath had the same now thirty years past, the rather for that, his lordship having displaced his vice-constable, their lordships are to remember unto him her majesty's express order and commandment given by her letters in March, 1582, that no officers should be removed upon pretence of abuse of his office, but that first the abuse should be proved by the governor and council there, and by them certified hither to be considered of by their lordships of her majesty's privy council, and by them to be judged sufficient for the removing and displacing of such officer, which order her majesty willed by her said letters to be recorded there for observation of the same from time to time, which remaining in force, their lordships doubt not but at the least his lordship will cause to be allowed by the vice-constable, whom he hath placed in the absence of the said Jaques

Wingfield, all such profits as he hath had of the other whom his lordship hath displaced.

Acts privy council, 1587–8, p. 34.

3. Last of September (1598)

Lord Keeper	Lord Chamberlain
Earl of Essex	Lord North
Lord Admiral	Lord Buckhurst

Mr. Secretary

A letter to the lords justices of Ireland. Though we doubt not but you will without any motion from us have good regard for the appointing of meet and serviceable persons to be sheriffs in the several counties, which is a matter of great importance, especially at this time when all parts of the realm are touched with the infection of the rebellion, yet we think it not amiss sometimes to commend unto you such men as we hold to be fit for that office, among whom we may justly reckon Edmund Spenser, a gentleman dwelling in the county of Cork, who is so well known unto your lordships for his good and commendable parts, being a man endowered with good knowledge in learning and not unskilful or without experience in the service of the wars, as we need not use many words in his behalf. And therefore as we are of opinion that you will favour him for himself and of your own accord, so we do pray you that this our letter may increase his credit so far forth with you as that he may not fail to be appointed sheriff of the county of Cork, unless there be to you known some important cause to the contrary. We are persuaded he will so behave himself in the place as you shall have just cause to allow of our commendation and his good service. And so, etc.

Acts privy council, 1598–9, p. 204.

4. 23 November 1579, Greenwich

The Lord Treasurer	The Earl of Leicester
The Lord Admiral	Mr. Comptroller
The Lord Chamberlain	Mr. Secretary Wilson

Appointed by her majesty's special commandment to consult of the affairs of Ireland.

Acts privy council, 1578–80, p. 313.

5. Last September (1600)

Lord Treasurer	Lord Chamberlain
Lord Admiral	Mr. Secretary Cecil

A letter to Sir George Carew, knight, lord president of Munster. Though we do well enough know the evil disposition of the Irish people in most places of that kingdom and especially of the in- habitants of Waterford in matter of religion, and her majesty has been pleased in that behalf to hold a very remiss and favourable hand over them because they should not serve themselves with pretence of any matter of conscience to fall from their duty and obedience to her majesty, yet we have had no doubt or distrust of any such presumption and insolence as by the archbishop of Cashel and others we are informed they are grown into, who avoweth unto us that in Waterford there are certain buildings erected under colour and pretence of alms-houses or hospitals, but that the same are in very deed intended and publicly professed to be used for monasteries and such like houses of religion, and that friars and popish priests are openly received and maintained in them, even such as do not deny to have recourse unto Spain and unto the chief rebel Tyrone ordinarily, insomuch, as they publicly seek to seduce her majesty's subjects from their allegiance, and exercise their service of the mass openly and usually in many places as if they were in no awe or fear of any exception to be taken thereunto. Of which things (if we have been well informed) we cannot but think it very necessary that a more watchful eye and a straighter hand of authority be kept over them, for as we do well consider that it is as yet inconvenient to take any sudden or sharp course for reformation (in such sort as were to be wished) of their blind superstition, being with strong head so generally carried away with opinion of conscience, so we must put a great difference betwixt the secret exercise of their religion and practise of treason under colour of religion. And therefore, though we do not think it convenient that any extraordinary course be taken or any disturbance made to enquire after or to punish them for their masses or any other their popish superstitions (unless they show thereby openly to the world an insolent contempt of her majesty's authority), yet on the other side it is not to be suffered that such persons should go unpunished as are known to be practicers for the kings of Spain or for the rebel to withdraw the subjects from their obedience to her majesty, or to adhere unto the traitors, or give them aid and assistance either open or secret, who being guilty thereby of treason ought by the law both of this and that realm to have punishment due for the same.

Acts privy council, 1599–1600, p. 703.

6. At Richmond, the first of February, 1590

A letter to the lord deputy and council of Ireland signifying that their lordships have referred the examination of the controversies in law depending between the queen's majesty's marshal of that realm and the city of Dublin to the judges and her majesty's learned counsel here, who have certified their opinions upon consideration of both the letters patent that the city of Dublin ought by their letters patent to have the trial of the prisoner in the case sent unto us, and that the marshal by virtue of his letters patent can not try the said offence done within their liberties of that city. Wherefore they pray your lordship and the rest to give order therein accordingly that the city may have the benefit of their charter, for her majesty's pleasure is that all offences punished by death may be tried according to the due course of her common laws, unless the necessity of service, where the common law can not have course, require the proceeding and punishment of marshal law, which ought not to be erected but in times of necessity.

Acts privy council, 1590–1, p. 252.

THE EXTENSION OF ENGLISH AUTHORITY

17. AGREEMENT BETWEEN THE GOVERNMENT AND MACGILPATRICK, 1543 [1]

Certain articles and conditions, which MacGilpatrick did promise duly to observe and perform, at such time as he made his submission to the king's majesty.

First, the said MacGilpatrick doth utterly forsake and refuse the name of MacGilpatrick, and all claims which he might pretend by the same ; and promiseth to name himself, for ever hereafter, by such name as it shall please the king's majesty to give unto him.

Item, the said MacGilpatrick, his heirs and assigns and every other the inhabiters of such lands as it shall please the king's majesty to give unto him, shall use the English habits and manner, and, to their knowledge, the English language, and they, and every of them, shall, to their power, bring up their children after the English manner, and the use of the English tongue.

Item, the said MacGilpatrick, his heirs and assigns, shall keep and put such of the said lands as shall be meet for tillage, in manurance and tillage of husbandry, and cause houses to be made and built for such persons as shall be necessary for the manurance thereof, within such time as he conveniently may.

Item, the said MacGilpatrick, his heirs and assigns, nor any of them, shall take, put, or cess, or cause to be taken, put, or cessed, any manner imposition or charge upon the king's subjects, in-habiters of the said lands, other than their yearly rent or custom, but such as the deputy shall be content withal ; and that they, nor none of them, shall have any galloglass or kern, but such, so many, and after such manner, sort, and time, as shall stand with the contentation of the said deputy and council.

Item, that the said MacGilpatrick, his heirs and assigns, and every of them, shall be obedient to the kings majesty's laws, and answer to his highnesses' writs, precepts and commandments, in his majesty's castle of Dublin, or in any other place where his court shall be kept, and his grace's laws ministered, and do what in them is, to cause all the inhabitants of the same to do the semblable, or else they shall bring them, if they may, to justice.

Item, the said MacGilpatrick, his heirs and assigns, and every of them, for the time being, shall answer and go with the king's lieutenant or deputy to all such hostings, rides, journeys, whereunto

---

[1] For the date see *Calendar of State Papers relating to Ireland*, 1509–1573 (London 1860), p. 66.

they shall be warned and assigned, and that after such manner, and with such number of company, as the marchers of the county of Dublin do.

Item, that the said MacGilpatrick, his heirs and assigns, nor any of them, shall maintain or succour, receive or take to sojourn, any of the king's enemies, rebels, or traitors.

Item, the said MacGilpatrick shall hold his lands by one whole knight's fee.

S.P. Henry VIII, iii. 291–2.

18. CONDITIONS OF SUBMISSION OFFERED TO CONN BACACH O'NEILL, 1541

Towards the close of 1541 the deputy, St. Leger, led three punitive expeditions against O'Neill, who was 'reputed amongst the Irishry a man of great power, and having a country under his rule no less.'[1] As a result at the end of the year O'Neill submitted. The king seems to have accepted the terms of submision, though he was greatly annoyed by the suggestion that O'Neill should be created earl of Ulster, 'one of the greatest earldoms in Christendom and our own proper inheritance.' In the middle of 1542 O'Neill went over to England, and in October was created earl of Tyrone.[2]

Articles by which I, Conn O'Neill, am bound

I. I recognize his royal majesty to be my most serene lord and king, and I swear to be a faithful, loyal and obedient subject to him and his heirs and successors, kings of England, France and Ireland.

II. I openly renounce obedience to the pope of Rome, and forsake his usurped authority, and I recognize my most serene lord as supreme head under Christ of the church of England and Ireland, and in future as far as I am able, I will compel all who live under my rule to do likewise. And if it happen that any provisors shall obtain any faculties for bulls from the aforesaid usurped authority I will compel them to surrender the said bulls and faculties, and submit themselves to the ordinances of his majesty, and if any who have such bulls or provisions shall wish to surrender them and receive them of the royal gift then I will humbly implore his majesty to mercifully restore them to their former dignities.

III. I, the aforesaid Conn O'Neill, confess myself to have offended his majesty and so implore his grace and mercy, and beg him to grant me his pardon for my offences.

IV. I humbly implore that on this account it may please his excellence to accept, regard and reckon me as one of his most faithful subjects, and that order be given to all his subjects of this kingdom to accept, regard and reckon me as such and in the same fashion.

V. I offer and pledge myself to live under the laws of my most

[1] *S.P. Henry VIII*, iii. 342.
[2] For an account of the circumstances of O'Neill's submission see P. Wilson, *The beginnings of modern Ireland* (Dublin 1912), pp. 251–5.

serene lord, even as the earls of Ormond and Desmond and other nobles and subjects of this realm live, and I beg that it may please his serenity to grant the name of earl of Ulster to me and my heirs, paying to his majesty yearly from each plow land in the name of subsidy [1]; and that all, each and all those who live under my lordship may have their lands in the same fashion; and those who stubbornly refuse to do this may it please his majesty to grant their lands as forfeited to me and my heirs, by his gift to hold the same of his majesty, and also to pay such rent annually for the same as shall seem meet to his highness to assign.

VI. I submit myself to the ordinances and judgement of my most serene lord and will stand to such peace and terms as his majesty shall ordain for me; and I humbly implore that it may please him to grant me my lands as aforesaid, together with the command of all those whom his majesty will assign to me and they to be under my rule as often as I am required to serve his majesty or his deputy, in the same manner and fashion as the noble earls of Ormond and Desmond use under his majesty in his counties of which they have the care and rule.

VII. I will attend the great councils called parliaments, which are held in any parts of this realm. Nevertheless I implore his majesty that he will not compel me, on account of the perils of the ways, to attend any parliaments which are held in the western parts beyond the river Barrow, lest on account of the dangers of the ways I should be at too great expence.

VIII. I swear and promise that Felim ' Ruffus,' Neill Connelagh and Hugh O'Neill shall have all lands which rightly and lawfully belong to them and that I will treat them as shall please his majesty.

IX. I openly renounce for the future all and sundry rents which formerly I was wont to levy upon the king's subjects of Oriel and elsewhere; humbly imploring his majesty to grant and give me some stipend or salary during my lifetime only by which I may be made all the more able to serve his excellency; and in return I bind myself to do such service as shall seem befitting to his majesty, his lieutenant and deputy.

X. I promise to serve his royal majesty, lieutenant or deputy in all great expeditions commonly called ' hostings ' with such a number of horsemen, Scots, and footmen in certain areas as shall seem befitting to the said deputy; and this I will do from time to time at my own costs and those of my people who shall be under my rule, in the same manner and fashion as the said earls of Ormond and Desmond do in the lands subject to their lordships.

XI. I promise that until the royal pleasure be known, that all who were under his majesty's peace according to the form of indentures formerly made [2] shall remain in the same, and also I implore that all who were under my peace may remain in the same until the royal pleasure be known.

---

[1] Blank in the original.
[2] 21 July 1535 (*S.P. Henry VIII*, ii. 257).

XII. I promise that all and sundry woods, thickets and groves which are between my country and the borders of English shall be cut down and levelled, so that the lieutenant or deputy of his majesty may freely come and go to me and I to him as often as shall be required.

XIII. I promise to rebuild or have rebuilt all parish churches which are now in ruins in my said lordship ; and this with all convenient speed, so that the divine offices may be celebrated and ignorant people taught and instructed to admit and to perform their bounden duty to God and the king.

(Translated from the Latin) *S.P. Henry VIII*, iii. 353–5.

19. AN ACT TO CONVERT WASTE GROUNDS INTO SHIRE GROUNDS, 1557

A similar act was passed in 1569.

An act to convert and turn divers and sundry waste grounds into shire grounds

Where divers and sundry robberies, murders and felonies be daily committed and done within sundry towns, villages, and other waste grounds of this realm, being no shire grounds, to the great loss of divers and sundry true subjects of this realm, to the great boldness and encouraging of all other like offenders, by reason that the same towns, villages and waste grounds, be not made shire grounds, for remedy whereof, be it enacted by authority of this present parliament, that immediately upon the prorogation or dissolution of the same, the lord chancellor of this realm for the time being, shall have full power and authority by virtue of this act to award and direct the king and queen's majesties' commission under their graces' great seal of this realm to such number of persons, as shall by warrant under the lord deputy's hand and seal for the time being be thought most convenient and meet ; giving thereby full power and authority to the same commissioners by authority of the same commission, to view, survey, and make inquiry of all the towns, villages, and waste grounds of this realm, now being no shire grounds, and upon the said view, inquiry, and survey, to limit, make, nominate, and divide by certain limits and bounds, all such towns, villages, and waste grounds within this realm, being presently no shire ground nor county, into such and as many several counties, shires, and hundreds, as to the said commissioners shall be thought most meetest and convenient, and after they have made such survey, inquiry, and division . . . the said commissioners shall certify the same unto the lord deputy for the time being ; who, liking the said certificate, shall under his hand and seal and the hands and seals of the said commissioners return and certify the doing together with the said commission into the high court of chancery, before such feast or time as by the said commission shall be to them limited and appointed, to the intent the same may there remain

8

of record ; and the same certificate so made shall be of the same force and effect, as it were done and made by act of parliament ; and that the said shires, countries, and hundreds, after the said certificate so made shall be used and taken as other counties, shires, and hundreds be in every other shire within this realm of Ireland.

II. Provided always . . . that the king and queen's majesties, her heirs and successors, shall and may have full power and authority for the term of seven years next after the end and dissolution of this present parliament, for such time as shall please their majesties, her heirs and successors, to suspend or utterly to repeal, revoke, and abrogate this whole act, together with all other things done by force of the same or any part thereof from time to time, as shall stand with their majesties' most gracious pleasure, so that every such suspending, repeal, and revocation, from time to time as often as any such case shall happen, shall be made in writing under the great seal of Ireland, and that proclamations of every such suspending, repeal, and revocation shall be made in such and as many shires of this realm of Ireland, as to their majesties, her heirs, and successors, shall be thought meet and convenient ; and thereupon the said commission to be enrolled in the rolls of this present parliament, wherein this act shall be enrolled. . . .

Ir. Stat., i. 244–6.

20. INSTRUCTIONS FOR THE PRESIDENT AND COUNCIL OF MUNSTER, 1570

As the government's control spread over the island a president and council were appointed for Munster (1568) and Connaught (1569). These bodies were subordinate to the viceroy and council, and performed similar duties in the provincial sphere.

A formular of instructions and orders, for the establishing of a council in Munster, with a lord president to govern the same

The lord deputy and council of the realm, having such care as becometh them, for the universal good government of this her majesty's realm, and finding that the remote parts thereof have of long time, by lack of justice and administration of laws, continued in great disorders, and that upon good consultation herein of long time had, no means can be found more meet, to reduce the same to order, for the honour and service of Almighty God, for obedience to the queen's majesty, for the recovery and conservation of common peace and tranquillity, and finally, for to breed and establish all good civility, than to have justice indifferently applied and administered to all states and sorts of people, have, for that purpose, certified the same to the queen's most excellent majesty ; who having no less princely and natural regard to her said universal realm, and to the people thereof, than ever to her realm of England, and being desirous, that the knowledge of Almighty God and the good fruits of justice, should be equally distributed through all parts of her said realm, hath (without regard had to any charge of expence of yearly sums of money) given commandment to her said lord deputy and council of her realm, according to their advice, to erect and establish by her commission, special councils in sundry remote parts of her said realm, with honourable stipends and entertainments. Whereupon, by her majesty's authority and gracious consent, the lord deputy and council have, in her name, devised, ordered, and established, in the portion of the realm which is commonly called Munster, a council of a convenient number of persons of the three estates, in the same parts. And because the same councillors shall have an ordinary continuance, for resort of her subjects, suits, and complaints, her majesty hath, by advice of her said deputy and council, determined to have one special person, being known meet, not only for wisdom and love of justice, but also by birth indifferent and free from all partiality towards the people of the same country, to be the chief and head of the same council, and to be named the lord president of her majesty's council established in Munster. . . . And for the further instruction of the said lord president and council, in the execution of the said commission, the said lord deputy and council, by authority which they have from her majesty, will and command the said lord president and council so established by her majesty's commission, to direct their doings, in all manner of things, to the best of their power, according to these instructions following.

1. First the said lord president shall, at all times, when he shall think meet, for the service of the queen's majesty, call together all such as be, or that hereafter shall be appointed to be of that council and shall, with the advice of such of the council as shall be by their instructions appointed to assist him with counsel, by letters, and precepts, command all and every person of the said council, at all convenient times, to do such things as shall be meet for the service of the queen's majesty, in administration of justice and maintenance of the same amongst all her subjects, residing, or coming into the parts of the jurisdiction of the said commission. . . .

6. And the said lord deputy and council have thought fit, by the assent of the queen's majesty, that the said lord president shall have, in consideration of his continual attendance and great pains to be taken in that office, the wages and entertainment of one hundred and thirty three pounds, five shillings, eight pence, sterling, by the year for himself ; and for that the countries aforesaid being in such disorder, and the people in the same, in such disobedience, as presently they are, whereby it shall be needful for him to have continually about him some competent number of soldiers, whereby his decrees and orders justly taken and made, the more effectually may be executed, it is considered and ordered by the lord deputy and council, that, the said lord president shall have the choice, leading and entertainment of xxx persons, being horsemen, at nine pence Irish by the day, xx footmen at eight pence Irish by the day, and two shillings by the day for a petty captain, and for

a trumpeter and guidon, it shall be allowed as the lord deputy of the realm shall think fit. . . .

8. Item, for the further reputation and honour of the same office, the said lord president shall appoint some one discreet and comely personage, which shall continually attend upon him as sergeant at arms . . . which sergeant may, at all times, be sent by the said lord president and council, for the apprehending and bringing in of any disobedient or contemptuous person. . . .

10. Item, the said lord president and council shall (if opportunity may serve) monthly advertise us, the lord deputy and council here, of the state of the country within their commission, or oftener, if they shall see cause.

11. And where the said lord president and council shall have, by their commission, sufficient authority to hear and determine, by their discretions, all manner of complaints, within any part of the province of Munster, as well yieldable as franchise, yet, they shall have good regard that, except great necessity, or other matter of conscience, conceived upon the complaint, shall move them, they shall not hinder nor impeach the good court and usage of the common laws of the realm, but shall to their power further the execution thereof ; nor shall, without evident and necessary cause, interrupt such liberties and franchises, as have lawful commencement and continuance by the warrants of the law, otherwise than where any special complaint shall be made unto them of any manifest wrong or delay of justice, done or used by the owners, officers, or ministers of the said franchises or liberties ; in which cases the said lord president and council shall examine the said defaults so alleged by way of complaint to be committed in the said franchises, and shall send for the officers against whom complaint shall be made. And, finding the same to be true, they shall not only hear and determine the particular and principal causes of the parties' complaints, but shall also reform and punish, according to their discretion, the defaults of the said owners or ministers of the said liberties. And if the matter shall so serve, they shall cause due information to be made to the lord deputy of this realm, of the abuses of the said franchises and liberties, so as the same may be, by our order, according to the laws tried, and upon just causes the liberties resumed into the queen's majesty's hands. . . .

12. Item, where the said president and council, together with such other commissioners as the lord deputy and council shall appoint, shall have commission, power and authority, by letters patent under the great seal of this realm of Ireland, of oyer, determiner, and gaol delivery, in as large and ample manner as any such commission or authority is granted to any commissioners for that purpose within the realms of England or Ireland the said lord deputy and council do strictly require and charge the said lord president and council that he and they do often and diligently . . . determine . . . such causes as shall be brought before them. . . .

13. Item, where also the said lord president and council, or two of them at the least, whereof the lord president to be one, hath full power and authority, by letters patent under the great seal of this realm, to execute the martial law, when necessity shall require, in as large and ample manner as to any other it hath been accustomed to be granted within this realm of Ireland, the said lord president and council shall have good regard thereto, that no use be of the martial law, but where mere necessity shall require, for the exercise thereof is only to be allowed where other ordinary administration of justice by law cannot assume place ; foreseeing always, that no party having five pounds of freehold, or goods to the value of forty pounds, shall be tried by the order of the martial law, but by order of the common law, and yet, if necessity, for service and terror to others, shall at any time require to execute the martial law upon any one person or more, being of greater value in lands or goods than above is expressed, the president, in such special cases, may use his discretion, and thereof and of the causes that moved him, shall make us the lord deputy of the realm privy.

14. Item, it is and shall be lawful for the lord president and council, or to any two of them whereof the lord president to be one, to prosecute and oppress any rebel or rebels with swords and with fire ; and for the doing of the same, to levy in warlike manner and array, and with the same to march such and so many of the queen's highness's subjects, as to his discretion shall seem convenient ; and if that any castle, pile, or house, be with force kept against them, it shall be lawful for the said lord president and council, or two of them, whereof the lord president to be one, to bring before any such castle, pile, or house, so to be kept against them, any of the queen's majesty's ordnance and great artillery. . . .

15. And it is ordered by the said lord deputy and council, that if any person complain to the said lord president and council, and that they shall think their complaints worthy the hearing, that the persons so complained upon, shall be sent for by a letter missive under the queen's signet, to appear before the lord president and council at a day and place by them to be appointed, there to answer to such things as shall be laid to their charge. . . .

17. And the said lord president and council, according to their commission, shall have power and authority by these presents, diligently to hear, determine and try all and all manner of extortions, maintenance, embraceries, and oppressions, conspiracies, rescues, escapes, corruptions, falsehoods, and all other evil doings, defaults and misdemeanours of all sheriffs, justices of peace, mayors, sovereigns, portreeves, bailiffs, stewards, lieutenants, escheators, coroners, gaolers, clerks, and other officers and ministers of justice, and their deputies, as well in all the counties and countries within the province of Munster aforesaid, and within the supposed liberties of Tipperary and Kerry, as in all cities and other towns corporate within the limits of their said commission, of what degree soever they be, and punish the same according to the quality and

quantity of their offence, by their discretions, leaving nevertheless to the lords and owners of all lawful liberties such profits as they may lawfully claim.

18. And it shall be lawful for the said lord president and council, or any three of them, whereof the lord president to be one, to conceive, make and cause to be proclaimed in her highnesses' name, and as they shall think good, any thing or matter tending to the better order of her majesty's subjects, within the precincts of their commission, and the repressing of malefactors and misdoers, after such tenor and form as they shall think convenient and to punish the offenders there by their discretions, so the same be not repugnant to the common laws and statutes of the realm.

19. And also the said lord deputy and council have thought meet that the said lord president and council or any three of them, whereof the said lord president to be one, shall and may compound, upon reasonable causes by their discretions, with any person, for all forfeitures. . . .

20. And also the said lord president, shall cause, as much as in him lieth, all writs or processes, or letters missive, sent, or to be sent, to any person or persons inhabiting or being within the precinct of his commission, from the lord deputy, out of the king's bench, chancery, or exchequer, or any other court of record, diligently to be observed and effectually to be obeyed. . . .

21. And it shall be lawful for the said lord president and council, or any three of them, whereof the lord president to be one, after examination in the causes necessary, upon vehement suspicion and presumption of any great offence in any party committed against the queen's majesty, to put the same party so suspected to tortures, as they shall think convenient, and as the cause shall require. And also to respite judgment of death upon any person convicted or attainted before him and the council. . . .

23. Also the said lord deputy and council earnestly requireth, and straightly chargeth the said lord president and council, that they, at all times and in all places, where any great assembly shall be made before them, shall persuade the people by all good means and ways to them seeming good, and especially by their own examples in observing all orders for divine service, and other things appertaining to Christian religion, and to embrace, follow, and devoutly to observe the order and service of the church established in the realm by parliament. . . .

24. Also, the lord president and council shall examine the decay of all parish churches, and through whose default the same be decayed, and to proceed to the procuring or enforcing of such as ought to repair any church or churches. . . .

28. And the said lord president and council shall, immediately upon their repair to some convenient place, where they mean to reside within the limits of their commission, appoint three or four honest and sufficient men to be clerks or attorneys to that council, for the making of bills, answers, and processes, for all manner of

suitors, and, therein, not to multiply such officers, least also they be occasion to multiply unnecessary suits, and some trusty wise persons, to examine witnesses between party and party, which, of necessity, would be chosen with good advice. Foreseeing expressly and charitably, that no excessive fees be by any of them taken of the subjects, but that their fees be assessed by the lord president and council, and the same written upon a table, and fixed up in some public place where the same may be seen and understood of all suitors, and that in the beginning, the same fees may appear, and be mean and reasonable ; so as in no wise, the prosecution of relief by way of justice, be not so chargeable, as the poor oppressed sort of subjects be thereby discouraged to make their complaints.

29. And because it shall be convenient that a register be duly kept for all the doings, orders, decrees, and proceedings, which from time to time shall pass by the said lord president and council, . . . that the clerk of the said council, for the time being . . . shall diligently execute and perform this charge. . . .

31. Also, the said lord deputy and council have thought good, that there be a signet graven with the queen's majesty's arms under a crown imperial, which always shall remain in the custody of the clerk of the council, who shall sign with the same, all processes, which shall be sent from the said lord president and council. . . .

A. Collins, *Letters and memorials of state* (London 1746), i. 48–59.

21. AGREEMENT BETWEEN THE GOVERNMENT AND BRIEN McCAHIR McART CAVANAGH, 1571

An indenture betwixt the queen's majesty and Brien McCahir McArt Cavanagh

This indenture made betwixt the Right Honourable Sir Henry Sidney, knight of the noble order of the garter, lord president of the council of Wales and lord deputy general of Ireland, for and in the behalf of the queen's most excellent majesty of the one part, and Brien McCahir McArt Cavanagh of Ballyian, in the county of Wexford, gentleman, chief of his name and sept called Slaght Dermod lawdarage, for and in the behalf of himself and all the rest of the gentlemen and freeholders of the said sept in the baronies of Ballyian, St. Molinge and Clanhauricke and Fassaghesleabuy, in the county aforesaid, and in the county of Carlow, as authorized by the said gentlemen and freeholders under this deed and seal, of the other party, witnesseth.

That the said Brien McCahir McArt Cavanagh do for himself and all the rest of the said gentlemen and freeholders of the baronies and places aforesaid, for them, their heirs and assigns, covenant promise, grant, agree, and condescend to and with the said right honourable the lord deputy to surrender and give up in the queen's majesty's most honourable court of chancery within this realm of Ireland, to the use of the queen's majesty, her heirs and successors when he thereunto shall be required, all such manors, castles, lands, tenements, rents, reversions and all other hereditaments that they and every of them have within either in use or possession, and that the said Brien McCahir and the rest aforesaid shall receive and take the same back by letters patent from her majesty to have and to hold to them and their heirs for ever, yielding and paying unto her majesty, her heirs and successors such yearly rents, services and reservations as shall be expressed, mentioned and contained in the said letters patent.

And the said right honourable the lord deputy, for and in the behalf of the queen's most excellent majesty, doth promise and grant to and with the said Brien McCahir that the said Brien and the said gentlemen and freeholders, their heirs and assigns, shall not only have letters patent made unto them of the said lands tenements and hereditaments according as before is expressed, but also shall from and after the date hereof be free and wholly discharged, acquitted and exonerated for ever of and from the bonnacht, accustomed to be paid out of the said baronies and places aforesaid and by the sept aforesaid to the queen's galloglasses, and of all cesses, charges, exactions and impositions of soldiers, horse, horseboy and all other manner cesses, charges, duties and exactions whatsoever they be, other than the rents, reversions and charges hereafter specified.

In consideration of the discharge of which bonnacht and other charges aforesaid, the said Brien McCahir, for and in the behalf of himself and all the rest aforesaid, have given and granted like as hereby he doth give and grant to the said right honourable the lord deputy to the use of the queen's majesty, her heirs and successors, for ever, one yearly rent-charge of fifty-two marks of good and lawful money of Ireland, payable at the feasts of St. Michael and Easter by even portions, the first payment to begin at the feast of Easter which shall be in the year of our Lord God 1572, and so yearly for ever at the several feasts aforesaid, at her highness's exchequer within the said realm of Ireland, or to the hands of the vice-treasurer or general receiver of the same realm for the time being.

And if it fortune the said rent of fifty-two marks to be behind in part or in the whole by the space of six months next after any of the said feasts, that then it shall be lawful unto the said right honourable the lord deputy or other governor or governors of this realm for the time being, to enter and distrain in all and singular the lands tenements and hereditaments within the said country, baronies and places aforesaid, and the distresses so taken to detain and keep till the said yearly rent be fully and wholly satisfied and paid.

And further the said Brien McCahir doth for himself and the rest aforesaid, their heirs and assigns, covenant, promise and grant to and with the said right honourable the lord deputy for and in the behalf of the queen's majesty, her heirs and successors, not only to bear yearly for ever to all and general rides, hostings, journies a rising out of three horsemen six kern, as they have been accustomed, but also to pay and yield yearly to the queen's majesty her heirs and successors for ever such ancient rent, custom and duties as they have usually yielded heretofore, that is to say, xii marks lawful money of Ireland and thirteen bushels oats, at such terms, times, and places, as they have been accustomed.

And the said right honourable the lord deputy doth promise and grant for and in the behalf of the queen's most excellent majesty, that the said Brien McCahir and the rest of the gentlemen and freeholders aforesaid, nor none of their lands, tenements and hereditaments aforesaid, nor no part parcel or member thereof, shall from henceforth be charged, cessed, imposed or be contributory with the counties of Wexford or Carlow in any manner cess, charge, exaction, rising out or otherwise. . . .

And the said right honourable the lord deputy, for and in the behalf of the queen's most excellent majesty, doth promise and grant to and with the said Brien McCahir and the rest of the gentlemen and freeholders of the baronies and places aforesaid, that if it fortune at any time hereafter any part and parcel the lands, tenements and hereditaments chargeable with the said yearly rent of fifty-two marks to be evicted, recovered and taken out of the hands and possession of the said Brien or any of the rest of the gentlemen and freeholders of the places aforesaid, by due order and ceremony of the queen's majesty's laws, that then and for so much of the yearly rent charges of fifty-two marks as the same lands tenements and hereditaments was charged with to be defaulked and allowed in the said yearly rent-charge of fifty-two marks, any thing herein contained to the contrary notwithstanding.

In witness whereof to this part of this indenture remaining in the custody of the said Brien McCahir for him and the rest aforesaid, the said right honourable the lord deputy, for and in the behalf of the queen's most excellent majesty, have hereunto put his seal, 15 March in anno 1570 [71] and in the thirteenth year of the reign of our sovereign lady Elizabeth, by the grace of God, queen of England, France and Ireland, defender of the faith, etc.—H. Sydney.

Acts privy council, Ire., 1556–71, pp. 220–2.

22. COMMISSION FOR THE COMPOSITION OF CONNAUGHT, 1585

In 1585, acting under the commission printed below, the government made a series of agreements with the land-owners of Connaught similar in type to those already made with Gaelic lords in other parts of Ireland (*e.g.* document 21). But fifty years later Wentworth declared these Connaught agreements invalid, arguing that the commissioners were only authorized to commute the various taxes on land for a fixed charge and had no power to settle questions of tenure.

Elizabeth by the grace of God queen of England, France and Ireland, defender of the faith, etc. to our trusty and right well beloved Sir Richard Bingham knight, chief commissioner in our province of Connaught and Thomond, the most reverend father in God the archbishop of Tuam, our right trusty and right well-beloved cousins the earls of Thomond and Clanricard, the reverend fathers the bishops of Clonfert and Elphin, our right trusty and well beloved the lord Bermingham lord baron of Athenry, Sir Nicholas White knight, master of our rolls in our realm of Ireland, Sir Edward Waterhouse one of our privy council in our said realm, Sir Thomas Le Strange knight, one of our privy council in our said realm, our trusty and well beloved Thomas Dillon esquire, chief justice of our said province, Charles Calthorp, our attorney-general, Gerald Quemerford esquire, our attorney in our said province, Sir Tirrelaugh O'Brien knight, Sir Donell O'Connor Sligo knight, Sir Brien O'Rorck knight, Sir Richard Berwick knight, Sir Morogh NeDoe O'Flaherty knight, Francis Barkely provost-marshal in our said province, Nicholas Fitzsimons of the city of Dublin alderman, John Marbury, Robert Fowle and John Browne gent.—greeting. Where our province of Connaught and Thomond aforesaid through the continual dissentions of the lords and chieftains dwelling within the same, each whereof challenging to themselves in the time of justice its declination, authorities, cuttings and cessings uncertain, unlawful and unprofitable, under pretext of defending the people under their several rules, have run into all errors of forgetting their duties to us and contemning the ways of justice, by which their own estates (both for life, living, and manners) might be made equal with the best subjects of this our realm of Ireland, we having tender consideration thereof, and understanding likewise the inclination of these our subjects through the good ministry of our right trusty and well-beloved Sir John Perrot knight, our deputy general of this our realm of Ireland, to embrace all good ways and means that may be desired, to conserve them in their loving obedience to us, whereby our prerogatives may be known, and their rights and titles reduced from the uncertainty wherein it stood, to continue certain forever hereafter, delivering by equal distribution to each subject in his degree, that which may be wisely and quietly drawn from the pretence of each party's claims, as also of the approved fidelity, trust, and confidence which we conceive of your wisdoms and circumspections, do by and with the assent of said deputy general, give unto you . . . or three of you, whereof the said Sir Richard Bingham or Sir Nicholas White, or Sir Edward Waterhouse knight always be one, full power and authority to call before you or any three of you, at such days, times, and places as to you or any three of you as is aforesaid shall seem most convenient, all the nobility spiritual or temporal and all the chieftains and lords of the countries and all other in every several barony of that province, as unto you or any three of you in manner before expressed shall seem most convenient, and thereupon in lieu of the uncertain cess accustomed to be born to us for the martial government of that country, and of the uncertain cutting and spendings of the lords aforesaid upon our subjects under their rules, to compound after your best discretion between us and the said lords, ours and their freeholders, customary holders and tenants, and the lords and their tenants, for a charge and a rent certain to us upon every quarter or quantity of land within that province. And further these are to authorize you . . . or any three of you whereof the said Sir Richard Bingham or the said Sir Nicholas White, or the said Sir Edward Waterhouse knights always to be one, to do in all things as to your discretions shall seem best, as well in the said composition as in the division of the baronies into manors, and to do, devise and lay down all and singular other thing and things that shall tend to the general good and quiet of that country and the good subjects of the same, which after the passage of the same by indenture tripartite is meant to be ratified by act of parliament, and of your doings and proceedings in and about the premises, to make relation and certificate in writing under your hands and seals unto our highness' court of chancery of this our said realm of Ireland at and by the last of the next Easter term, to the end the same may then remain of record, wherefore we will and command you and every of you to be diligent and careful in and about the due execution of the premises in form aforesaid. And we do likewise give in straight commandment to all mayors, sheriffs, bailiffs, constables, officers, ministers, and other our loving and obedient subjects to whom in this case it shall or may appertain to be obedient and attendant unto you and every of you in and about the due execution of the premises, as they will answer for the contrary at their perils. In witness whereof we have caused these our letters to be made patent, witness our said lord deputy general, at Dublin, the 15 July in the XXVII year of our reign.

A. M. Freeman, *The compossicion booke of Connought* (1936), pp. 3–5.

23. HUGH O'NEILL'S WAR AIMS, 1599

Articles intended to be stood upon by Tyrone [1]

1. That the catholic, apostolic, and Roman religion be openly preached and taught throughout all Ireland, as well in cities as borough towns, by bishops, seminary priests, jesuits, and all other religious men.

2. That the Church of Ireland be wholly governed by the pope.

3. That all cathedrals and parish churches, abbeys, and all other religious houses, with all tithes and church lands, now in the hands of the English, be presently restored to the catholic churchmen.

4. That all Irish priests and religious men, now prisoners in England or Ireland, be presently set at liberty, with all temporal Irishmen, that are troubled for their conscience, and to go where they will, without further trouble.

5. That all Irish priests and religious men may freely pass and repass, by sea and land, to and from foreign countries.

6. That no Englishman may be a churchman in Ireland.

[1] Endorsed by Sir Robert Cecil with the word ' Ewtopia.'

7. That there be erected an university upon the crown rents of Ireland, wherein all sciences shall be taught according to the manner of the catholic Roman church.

8. That the governor of Ireland be at least an earl, and of the privy council of England, bearing the name of viceroy.

9. That the lord chancellor, lord treasurer, lord admiral, the council of state, the justices of the laws, queen's attorney, queen's serjeant, and all other officers appertaining to the council and law of Ireland, be Irishmen.

10. That all principal governments of Ireland, as Connaught, Munster, etc., be governed by Irish noblemen.

11. That the master of ordnance, and half the soldiers with their officers resident in Ireland, be Irishmen.

12. That no Irishman's heirs shall lose their lands for the faults of their ancestors.

13. That no Irishman's heir under age shall fall in the queen's or her successors' hands, as a ward, but that the living be put to the heir's profit, and the advancement of his younger brethren, and marriages of his sisters, if he have any.

14. That no children nor any other friends be taken as pledges for the good abearing of their parents, and, if there be any such pledges now in the hands of the English, they must presently be released.

15. That all statutes made against the preferment of Irishmen as well in their own country as abroad, be presently recalled.

16. That the queen nor her successors may in no sort press an Irishman to serve them against his will.

17. That O'Neill, O'Donnell, the Earl of Desmond, with all their partakers may peacable enjoy all lands and privileges that did appertain to their predecessors 200 years past.

18. That all Irishmen, of what quality they be, may freely travel in foreign countries, for their better experience, without making any of the queen's officers acquainted withal.

19. That all Irishmen may freely travel and traffic all merchandises in England as Englishmen, paying the same rights and tributes as the English do.

20. That all Irishmen may freely traffic with all merchandises, that shall be thought necessary by the council of state of Ireland for the profit of their republic, with foreigners or in foreign countries, and that no Irishman shall be troubled for the passage of priests or other religious men.

21. That all Irishmen that will may learn, and use all occupations and arts whatsoever.

22. That all Irishmen may freely build ships of what burden they will, furnishing the same with artillery and all munition at their pleasure.—[1599, November].

Calendar of State Papers relating to Ireland, 1599–1600 (London, 1899), pp. 279–81.

THE ECCLESIASTICAL CHANGES

In 1537 the Irish parliament passed a series of measures dealing with ecclesiastical affairs which were almost literally copied from the legislation of the English reformation parliament. These measures were repealed *en bloc* in 1557. The death of Mary was followed by a reversal in policy reflected in Ireland by the enactment of the measures given below (documents 24, 25).

24. THE ACT OF SUPREMACY, 1560 [1]

An act restoring to the crown the ancient jurisdiction over the state ecclesiastical and spiritual, and abolishing all foreign power repugnant to the same

Most humbly beseech your most excellent majesty, your faithful and obedient subjects the lords spiritual and temporal and the commons in this present parliament assembled, that where in the time of the reign of your dear father of worthy memory, King Henry VIII, divers good laws and statutes were made and established, as well for the utter extinguishment and putting away of all usurped and foreign powers and authorities out of this your realm, as also for the restoring and uniting to the imperial crown of this realm the ancient jurisdictions, authorities, superiorities, and pre-eminences to the same appertaining, by reason whereof we, your most humble and obedient subjects . . . were continually kept in good order, and were disburdened of divers great and intolerable charges and exactions before that time unlawfully taken and exacted by such foreign power and authority as before that was usurped, until such time as all the said good laws and statutes by one act of parliament made in the third and fourth years of the reigns of the late King Philip and Queen Mary, your highness's sister, entitled *An act repealing all statutes, articles, and provisions made against the see apostolic of Rome since the twentieth year of King Henry VIII, and also for the abolishment of spiritual and ecclesiastical possessions and hereditaments conveyed to the laity*, were clearly repealed and made void, . . . by reason of which act of repeal, your said humble subjects were eftsoons brought under an usurped foreign power and authority, and yet do remain in that bondage to the intolerable charges of your loving subjects. . . . may it therefore please your highness, for the repressing of the said usurped foreign power and the restoring of the rights, jurisdictions, and pre-eminences appertaining to the imperial crown of this your realm, that it may be enacted . . . that the said act made in the third and fourth years of the said late King Philip and Queen Mary . . . be repealed, and shall from thenceforth be utterly void and of none effect ; and also

[1] For the circumstances under which this act and the act of uniformity (document 25) were passed see R. Dudley Edwards, *Church and state in Tudor Ireland* (Dublin 1935), pp. 177–86. The English acts of supremacy and uniformity which the Irish statutes closely resemble are given by G. W. Prothero, *Select statutes and other constitutional documents* (Oxford 1913), pp. 1–20 and J. R. Tanner, *Tudor constitutional documents* (Cambridge 1930), pp. 130–9.

for the reviving of divers of the said good laws and statutes made in the time of your said dear father, it may also please your highness that one act and statute made in a parliament holden at Dublin the first of May in the eight and twentieth year of the said late King Henry VIII . . . entitled *An act of appeals,* and also one act made in the said parliament entitled *The act of faculties,* . . . at all times after the last day of this session of parliament shall be revived, and shall stand and be in full force and strength, to all intents, constructions, and purposes ; . . .

V. And to the intent that all usurped and foreign power and authority spiritual and temporal may be for ever clearly extinguished, and never to be used or obeyed within this realm, may it please your highness, that it may be further enacted . . . that no foreign prince, person, prelate, state or potentate, spiritual or temporal, shall at any time after the last day of this session of parliament, use, enjoy or exercise any manner of power, jurisdiction, superiority, authority, pre-eminence, or privilege, spiritual or ecclesiastical within this realm ; . . .

VI. And may it also please your highness that it may be established and enacted . . . that such jurisdiction, privileges, superiorities, and pre-eminences spiritual and ecclesisatical, as by any spiritual or ecclesiastical power or authority hath heretofore been or may lawfully be exercised or used for the visitation of the ecclesiastical state or persons, and for reformation, order and correction of the same, and of all manner errors, heresies, schisms, abuses, offences, contempts, and enormities, shall for ever by the authority of this present parliament be united and annexed to the imperial crown of this realm, and that your highness, your heirs and successors, kings and queens of this realm, shall have full power and authority by virtue of this act by letters patent under the great seal of England or of this realm, and the lord deputy and other governor or governors of this realm for the time being, shall have likewise have full power and authority by virtue of this act by letters patent to be made by his or their warrants under the great seal of this realm, to assign, name and authorize . . . such person or persons being natural born subjects to your highness, your heirs or successors, as your majesty, your heirs or successors, or the lord deputy, the governor or governors of this realm for the time being shall think meet, to exercise, use, occupy, and execute . . . all manner of jurisdiction, privileges, and pre-eminences, in any wise touching or concerning any spiritual or ecclesiastical jurisdiction within this your realm of Ireland. . . .

VII. And for the better observation and maintenance of this act, may it please your highness that it may be further enacted . . . that all and every archbishop, bishop, and all and every other ecclesiastical person, and other ecclesiastical officer and minister . . . and all and every temporal judge, justicer, mayor, and other lay or temporal officer and minister and every other person having your highness's fee or wages within this realm, shall make, take and receive a corporal oath upon the evangelists, before such person or persons as shall please your highness, your heirs or successors, under the great seal in England, or of this realm, or the lord deputy, or other governor or governors of this realm for the time being, by letters patent to be made by his or their warrant under the great seal of this realm, to assign or name, according to the tenor and effect hereafter following, that is to say : I. A.B. do utterly testify and declare in my conscience that the queen's highness is the only supreme governor of this realm, and of all other her highness's dominions and countries, as well as in all spiritual or ecclesiastical things or causes, as temporal, and that no foreign prince, person, prelate, state or potentate, hath or ought to have any jurisdiction, power, superiority, pre-eminence or authority, ecclesiastical or spiritual within this realm, and therefore I do utterly renounce and forsake all foreign jurisdictions, power, superiorities and authorities, and do promise that from henceforth I shall bear faith and true allegiance to the queen's highness, her heirs and successors, and to my power shall assist and defend all jurisdictions, privileges, pre-eminences and authorities granted or belonging to the queen's highness, her heirs or successors, or united and annexed to the imperial crown of this realm, so help me God, and by the contents of this book.

X. And may it be further enacted . . . that all and every person and persons temporal, suing livery or ouster-le-main out of the hands of your highness, your heirs or successors, before his or their livery or ouster-le-main sued forth and allowed, and every temporal person or persons, doing any homage to your highness, your heirs or successors, or who shall be received into service with your highness, your heirs or successors, shall make, take and receive the said corporal oath, . . . and that also all and every person or persons taking orders, and all and every other person or persons which shall be promoted or preferred to any degree of learning, in any university that hereafter shall be within this your realm, before he shall receive or take any such orders, or be preferred to any such degree of learning, shall make, take and receive the said oath, by this act set forth. . . .

Ir. Stat., i. 275–84.

25. THE ACT OF UNIFORMITY, 1560

An act for the uniformity of common prayer and service in the church, and the administration of the sacraments

Where at the death of our late sovereign lord King Edward VI there remained one uniform order of common service, prayer and the administration of sacraments, rites and ceremonies in the church of England, which was set forth in one book entitled ' The book of common prayer, and administration of sacraments, and other rites and ceremonies in the church of England ' authorized by act of parliament, holden in the said realm of England, in the fifth and sixth years of our late sovereign lord King Edward VI entitled, *An act for the uniformity of common prayer and the administration of the sacraments*, which was repealed and taken away by act of parliament in the said realm of England in the reign of our late sovereign lady Queen Mary, to the great decay of the true honour of God, and discomfort to the professors of the truth of Christ's religion, be it therefore enacted . . . that the said book with the order of service, and of the administration of sacraments, rites and ceremonies, with the alterations and additions therein added and appointed by this statute, shall stand and be from and after the feast of Pentecost next ensuing in full force and effect, . . .

II. And further be it enacted . . . that all and singular ministers in any cathedral or parish church, or other place within this realm of Ireland, shall from and after the feast of Saint John Baptist then next ensuing, be bounder to say and use the matins, evensong, celebration of the lord's supper, and administration of each of the sacraments, in all their common and open prayer, in such order and form as is mentioned in the said book . . . with one alteration or addition of certain lessons to be used every Sunday in the year, and the form of the litany altered and corrected, and two sentences only added in the delivery of the sacrament to the communicants, and none other or otherwise, and that if any manner of parson, vicar or other whatsoever minister . . . refuse to use the said common prayers, or to minister the sacraments in such cathedral or parish church, or other places as he should use to minister the same, in such order and form as they be mentioned and set forth in the said book . . . and shall be lawfully convicted according to the laws of this realm, by verdict of twelve men or by his own confession, or by notorious evidence of the fact, [he] shall lose and forfeit to the queen's highness, her heirs and successors, for his first offence the profits of all his spiritual benefices or promotions, coming or arising in one whole year next after his conviction, and also the person so convicted shall for the first offence suffer imprisonment for the space of six months without bail or mainprise, and . . . the same person shall for his second offence suffer imprisonment for the space of one whole year, and shall therefore be deprived (*ipso facto*) of all his spiritual promotions. . . .

III. . . . from and after the said feast of Saint John Baptist all and every person and persons inhabiting within this realm shall diligently and faithfully, having no lawful or reasonable excuse to be absent, endeavour themselves to resort to their parish church or chapel accustomed, or upon reasonable let thereof to some usual place, where common prayer and such service of God shall be used in such time of let, upon every Sunday and other days ordained and used to be kept as holy days, and then and there to abide orderly and soberly during the time of common prayer, preachings or other service of God, there to be used and ministered, upon pain of punishment by the censures of the church, and also upon pain that every person so offending shall forfeit for every such offence twelve pence to be levied by the churchwarden of the parish where such offence shall be done to the use of the poor of the same parish, of the goods, lands, and tenements of such offender by way of distress ; and for the due execution thereof the queen's most excellent majesty, the lords temporal, and all the commons in this present parliament assembled, do in God's name earnestly require and charge all archbishops, bishops, and other ordinaries, that they shall endeavour themselves to the uttermost of their knowledge that the due execution hereof may be had throughout their dioceses and charges. . . .

XV. And foreasmuch as in most places of this realm, there cannot be found English ministers to serve in the churches or places appointed for common prayer or to minister the sacraments to the people, and that if some good mean were provided, that they might use the prayer, service and administration of sacraments set out and established by this act in such language as they might best understand, the due honour of God should be thereby much advanced, and for that also that the same may not be in their native language, as well as for the difficulty to get it printed, as that few in the whole realm can read the Irish letters . . . [be it enacted] that in every such church or place, where the common minister or priest hath not the use or knowledge of the English tongue, it shall be lawful for the same common minister or priest to say and use the matins, evensong, celebration of the Lord's supper and administration of each of the sacraments, and all their common and open prayer in the Latin tongue, in such order and form as they be mentioned and set forth in the said book established by this act, . . .

Ir. Stat., i. 284–90.

SECTION III. THE SEVENTEENTH CENTURY

THE CONDEMNATION OF IRISH LAW

The Gaelic system of land owning was based on gavelkind and tanistry. The former was condemned by the judgment given below, the latter by a decision of the king's bench (1608).

I. THE DECISION OF THE JUDGES ON GAVELKIND, 1606

Hilary 3rd year of King James

The judges' decision regarding the Irish custom of gavelkind. Firstly it should be known that the lands possessed by the mere Irish in this realm were divided into several territories or countries, and the inhabitants of each Irish county were divided into several septs or lineages.

Secondly, in each Irish territory there was a seigneur or chief, and a tanist who was his heir apparent. And in each Irish sept or lineage there was also a chief termed the canfinny [*ceanne fine*] or *caput cognationis*.

Thirdly, all possessions in these Irish territories (before the common law of England was established through all the realm as it now is) went always either by tanistry or gavelkind. Each seigniory or chieftaincy and the share of land which accompanied it, went undivided to the tanist, who always succeeded to his office by election or *fort main*, never by descent. But all the inferior tenancies were partible between the males in gavelkind. Again the estate which the seigneur had in the chieftaincy, or which the inferior tenants held in gavelkind, was not an estate of inheritance, but a temporary or transitory possession. For the nearest heir to the seigneur or chief did not inherit, but the eldest and most worthy of the sept (as was shown before in the case of tanistry) was often removed and expelled by another who was more active or strong than he ; and the lands held in gavelkind were not divided between the nearest heirs male of him who died seised of them, but between all the males of his sept, in this manner. The canfinny or chief of the sept (who was commonly the oldest of the sept) made the partitions at his discretion. This canfinny after the death of the holder of a competent portion of land assembled all the sept, and having put their possessions in hotch-potch, made a new partition of all. In that partition he did not assign to the sons of the deceased the portions which their father held, but he allotted to each of the sept according to his age the better or the poorer share. These portions or shares so allotted were possessed and enjoyed accordingly, until a new partition was made, which at the discretion or will of the canfinny might be done at the death of each inferior tenant. So on account of these frequent partitions, removals and translations of the tenants from one portion to another, all possessions were uncertain, and the uncertainty of possessions was the true cause why no civil habitations were erected and no enclosures or improvements made on the land in the Irish counties where this custom of gavelkind was used, particularly in Ulster, which seemed in very truth a wilderness before the new plantation made by the English undertakers there. And these were the fruits of Irish gavelkind.

By this Irish custom of gavelkind bastards had shares along with the legitimate, women were utterly excluded from dower, daughters could not inherit if their fathers died without male issue. Thus this custom differed from the custom of gavelkind in Kent in 4 points. For (1) by the custom of Kent the land held in gavelkind was divisible between male heirs and such co-parteners after partition had a certain estate of inheritance in their shares.

(2) The bastards were not admitted along with the legitimate male issue.

(3) The wife of a tenant in gavelkind was endowered with half the land.

(4) In default of male heirs females inherited. Vide Lambert in the *Peramb. de Kent* fol. 570.

And so the Kentish custom of gavelkind was always allowed and approved as a good and legal custom by the law of England.

But the Irish custom of gavelkind was agreeable in many respects to the custom of gavelkind followed in North Wales. . . . Vide the statute of 34 Henry VIII cap 28 [1] (Rastall, Wales, 32),[2] where the gavelkind of Wales is totally abolished with divers other usages resembling other customs of the Irish.

For these reasons and since all the said Irish counties and their inhabitants were to be governed by the rules of English common law, it was resolved and declared by all the judges, that the said Irish custom of gavelkind was void in law, not only because it was inconvenient and unreasonable, but because it was a mere personal custom and could not alter the descent of inheritance.

So it was adjudged that the lands in the Irish counties were to descend according to the course of common law, and that women would be endowed, and daughters would inherit, notwithstanding Irish usage or custom.

And where the wives of Irish seigneurs or chieftains claimed to have sole property in a certain share of goods during coverture with power of disposing of such goods without the assent of their husbands, it was resolved and declared by all the justices, that the ownership of such goods was adjudged to be in the husband and never in the wife, as is the common law in such case.

These resolutions of the justices by a special order of the lord

---

[1] See *Statutes of the realm* (1817), iii. 926.
[2] The reference is to W. Rastall, *A collection in English of the statutes now in force* (London 1583).

deputy, were registered amongst the acts of the council but this provision was added to them, that if one of the mere Irish possessed and enjoyed a portion of land by this custom of Irish gavelkind, before the beginning of the reign of our sovereign lord the king who now is, he would not be disturbed in his possession but might continue established in it. But that after the beginning of his majesty's reign all such lands shall be adjudged to descend to the heirs by common law, and shall be possessed and enjoyed accordingly.

(Translated from the Norman-French.) John Davies, *Le premier report des cases et matters en ley resolues et adiudges en les courts del roy en Ireland* (Dublin 1615), p. 49.

THE PLANTATION IN ULSTER, 1610

The first 'Orders and conditions to be observed by the undertakers' were issued in 1609. These terms were severely criticised, and new conditions were drafted. Those for the British undertakers were published early in 1610 (document 2). Revised conditions for the servitors and natives were formulated at the same time (document 3) but apparently not published. It was on these new conditions that grants to all three classes were made.

2. CONDITIONS TO BE OBSERVED BY THE BRITISH UNDERTAKERS, 1610

Conditions to be observed by the British undertakers of the escheated lands in Ulster, etc.

1. What the British undertakers shall have.

First, the lands to be undertaken by them, are divided into sundry precincts of different quantities.

Every precinct is subdivided into proportions of three sorts, great, middle, and small.

The great proportion containeth 2000 English acres at the least.

The middle proportion containeth 1500 acres at the least.

The small proportion containeth 1000 acres at the least.

Unto every of which proportions such bog and wood shall be allowed, as lieth within the same, for which no rent shall be reserved.

The precincts are by name distinguished, part for the English, and part for the Scottish, as appeareth by the table of distribution of the precincts.

Every precinct shall be assigned to one principal undertaker and his consort, as will appear by the table of assignation of the precincts.

The chief undertakers shall be allowed two middle proportions if they desire the same ; otherwise no one undertaker is to be allowed above one great proportion.

They shall have an estate in fee simple to them and their heirs.

They shall have power to create manors, to hold courts baron twice every year and not oftener, and power to create tenures in socage to hold of themselves.

They, their heirs and assigns, for the space of 7 years next ensuing, shall have liberty to export out of Ireland all commodities growing or arising upon their own land undertaken, without paying custom or imposition.

They, their heirs and assigns, for the space of 5 years next ensuing, shall have freedom to import into Ireland out of Great Britain, victual and utensils for their households, materials and tools for their buildings and husbandry, and cattle to stock and manure the lands undertaken, without paying any custom or imposition ; which shall not extend to any commodities transported by way of merchandise.

They shall have allowance of timber for their buildings to be erected upon their proportions, the same to be taken in any of the precincts, by the assignment of the commissioners, without paying anything for the same for the space of two years ; and after that time expired every undertaker to hold to his own use the timber and woods remaining upon his own proportion.

The principal undertaker shall have one advowson within his precinct to him and his heirs.

2. What the said undertakers shall for their parts perform.

They shall yearly yield unto his majesty for every proportion of 1000 acres, five pound six shillings eight pence English, and so rateably for the great proportions ; the first half year's payment to begin at Michaelmas 1614.

Every of the said undertakers shall hold the lands so undertaken in free and common socage, as of the castle of Dublin, and by no greater service.

Every of the said undertakers of a great proportion, shall within 3 years to be accounted from Easter next, build thereupon a stone house, with a strong court or bawn about it ; and every undertaker of a middle proportion shall within the same time build a stone or brick house thereupon, with a strong court or bawn about it ; and every undertaker of a small proportion, shall within the same time make thereupon a strong court or bawn at least.

Every undertaker shall within three years, to be accounted from Easter next, plant or place upon a small proportion, the number of 24 able men of the age of 18 years or upwards, being English or inland Scottish ; and so rateably upon the other proportions ; which numbers shall be reduced into 10 families at least, to be settled upon every small proportion, and rateably upon the other pro-proportions, in this manner, viz. the principal undertaker and his family to be settled upon a demesne of 300 acres, two fee-farmers upon 120 acres a piece, three leaseholders for three lives or 21 years upon 100 acres a piece, and upon the residue being 160 acres, four families or more of husbandmen, artificers or cottagers, their portions of land to be assigned by the principal undertaker at his discretion.

Every of the said undertakers shall draw their tenants to build houses for themselves and their families, not scattering, but together, near the principal house or bawn, as well for their mutual defence and strength, as for the making of villages and townships.

The said undertakers, their heirs and assigns, shall have ready in the houses at all times, a convenient store of arms which may be viewed and mustered every half year according to the manner of England.

Every of the said undertakers before he be received to be an undertaker, shall take the oath of supremacy, either in the chancery of England or Scotland, or before the commissioners to be appointed for the establishment of the plantation, and shall also conform themselves in religion according to his majesty's laws ; and every of their undertenants being chief of a family, shall take the like oath before the said commissioners or the justices of assize coming into the county, wherein the said tenants shall be placed, at the next assizes, after they shall sit down and inhabit in the said several counties. And they and their families shall be also conformable in religion, as aforesaid.

Every of the said undertakers for the space of five years, to be accounted from Michaelmas next, shall be resident himself in person upon his portion, or place some such other person thereupon, as shall be allowed by the state of England or Ireland, and shall take the oath of supremacy, and likewise be himself with his family conformable in religion as aforesaid, who shall be resident during the said five years, unless by reason of sickness or other important cause, he be licensed by the lord deputy and council of Ireland to absent himself for a time.

The said undertakers, their heirs and assigns, shall not alien or demise their portions or any part thereof to the mere Irish, or to such persons as will not take the said oath of supremacy, and to that end a proviso shall be insert in their letters patent, that the parcel of land so aliened shall be forfeited.

The said undertakers shall not alien their portions during five years to be accounted from Michaelmas next, but unto their under tenants in the form before expressed in the fourth article. The said undertakers shall not reserve any uncertain rent but the same shall be expressly set down without reference to the custom of the country.

3. In what manner the said performance shall be.

The said undertakers either in person or by such agents as shall be allowed by the councils of estate of England or Scotland respectively, shall before midsummer day next, repair unto the realm of Ireland, and offer themselves to the lord deputy and the commissioners for the plantation, who shall take order with the said undertakers for the distribution of the proportions in their every precinct, either by agreement or lot, so as every undertaker shall know his portion if the same be not distributed here in England before.

The said undertakers by themselves or their said agents, shall take possession of their several portions, and sit upon down the same before Michaelmas next.

The said undertakers shall bring over into Ireland, and plant and place upon their several proportions, the several numbers of men and families aforesaid, viz. one third part before the feast of All Saints next, and the third part before the first day of May then next ensuing, and the other third part before the feast of All Saints in the year of our Lord God 1611.

The said undertakers shall take out their letters patent either in England or in Ireland at their election, before midsummer day next.

The said undertakers shall before the feast of All Saints next make their several courts or bawns upon their proportions, and erect habitants for one third part of the men and families which they are to plant thereupon ; before the first day of May then next ensuing they shall erect habitations for the other third part, and provide and bring in place all the materials for building of their stone houses ; and before the feast of All Saints 1611 following, they shall erect habitations for the residue of their men and families, and in the meantime proceed in the building of their stone houses, so as they may be fully finished within three years as aforesaid.

Every undertaker before the ensealing of their letters patent, shall enter into bond or recognizance with good sureties to his majesty's use, in the office of his majesty's chief remembrancer in England or Ireland, or his majesty's exchequer or chancery in Scotland, to perform the aforesaid articles according to the several distinctions of building, planting, residence, alienation within five years, and making of certain estates to their tenants, viz. the undertakers of the greatest proportion to become bound in four hundred pounds, of the middle, in three hundred pounds, of the least, in two hundred pounds, which bonds or recognizances shall be delivered up after five years upon certificate of the L. deputy and the council, that the true meaning of the conditions thereof hath been performed.

Bulletin of the Institute of Historical Research, xii. 178–83.

3. CONDITIONS TO BE OBSERVED BY THE SERVITORS AND NATIVES, 1610

7 April 1610. Conditions to be observed by the servitors and natives, undertakers of the escheated land in Ulster, consisting in three principal points, viz. :
1. What they shall have of his majesty's gift.
2. What they shall for their parts perform.
3. In what manner the same performance shall be.

The conditions of the servitors

What the servitors shall have of his majesty's gift

First the lands to be undertaken by them are contained in sundry precincts, alloted unto them and the natives to be planted mixtly and together, being of different quantities and in several counties, viz. :

Counties.			Precincts.
Armagh	..	..	Orior
Tyrone	..	..	Dungannon
Donegal	..	..	Doe & Fawnett
In : Fermanagh	..	..	Clankelly
			Coole & Tirkennedy
Cavan ..	..	..	Tullyhaw
			Castlerahan
			Clanmahon

Every of the said precincts is subdivided into proportions of 3 sorts, great, middle, small, the great containing 2,000 acres, the middle 1,500, the small 1,000 or thereabouts; with allowance of such bog and wood as the British undertakers are to have by the printed conditions.

No servitor is to undertake above one great proportion or after that rate, except the lord deputy, who is to have two middle proportions or after that rate.

They shall have estates in fee simple, power to create manors and to hold courts baron, to create tenures, liberty of exportation and importation, allowance of timber as the British undertakers.

What the said servitors shall for their parts perform

They shall yearly yield unto his majesty, eight pounds English for every portion of 1,000 acres, which they shall not plant as the British undertakers, and so rateably, for the greater proportions, the first half year's payment to begin at Michaelmas 1614. But if they shall plant and perform the conditions, which the British undertakers are to observe, they shall pay no greater rent than the British undertakers.

They shall hold in socage, build houses of stone or brick, make courts or bawns, draw their undertenants to build houses together, have a convenient store of arms in their houses, take the oath of supremacy, conform themselves in religion, be resident upon their proportions, be estrained from all such alienations and from reservation of uncertain rents, as the British undertakers.

In what manner the said performance shall be

1. They shall before midsummer next, present themselves to the lord deputy and commissioners, who shall take order for the distribution of the proportions to be undertaken by each of them, according to such direction as they shall receive from his majesty and wherein no direction shall be given, they shall have power to do the same, according to their good discretion so as the several quantities to be allotted to the servitors do amount to 40,000 acres or thereabouts.

2. They shall take possession and sit down upon their pro-

portions, erect their buildings, enter into bonds or recognizances as the British undertakers, and they shall take out their letters patent before the end of Michaelmas term next.

The conditions of the natives

The lord deputy and commissioners shall take order to allot unto the natives several proportions, as they shall be directed by his majesty, and where no special direction shall be, to allot unto them convenient portions at their good discretions, so as the lands to be distributed unto them do amount unto 58,000 acres or thereabouts.

The said natives shall have estates in fee farm. They shall yearly yield to his majesty for every proportion of 1,000 acres £10, 13s. 4d. and so rateably for greater or lesser quantities. They shall hold in socage, sit down upon their portions, build their houses and bawns, and have allowance of timber as the British undertakers and servitors.

They shall take out their letters patent before the end of Michaelmas term next, wherein there shall be a proviso of forfeiture of their estates, if they enter into actual rebellion.

They shall make certain estates to their undertenants with reservation of rents certain, and they shall take no Irish exactions.

They shall use tillage and husbandry after the manner of the English.

Signed by the Earl of Salisbury, the Earl of Northampton, the Earl of Nottingham, the Earl of Suffolk, the Earl of Shrewsbury, the Earl of Worcester.

Analecta Hib., vii. 220–2.

THE PARLIAMENT OF 1613–15

Chichester had in 1610 and 1611 invited the nobility at large to suggest legislation which might be considered in the coming parliament. But he flatly rejected the contention, that they formed part of the council referred to in Poynings' law. Six catholic lords then stated their grievances in a letter to the king (document 4). After parliament met the catholics again complained to the king. Their complaints were investigated and as a result the elections for eleven boroughs (eight of which had been created since parliament was summoned) were anulled.

4. A LETTER DIRECTED TO HIS MAJESTY, FROM SIX CATHOLIC LORDS OF THE PALE

Most renowned and dread sovereign, the respective care of your highness's honour, with the obligation that our bounden duty requireth from us, doth not permit, that we, your nobility of this part of your majesty's realm of Ireland commonly termed the English pale, should suppress and be silent in aught, which in the least measure might import the honour of your majesty's most royal person, the reputation of your happy government, or the good and quiet of your estates and countries, and therefore, are humbly bold to address these our submissive lines to your highness, and so much the rather, till that of late years it hath been a duty specially required the nobility of this kingdom to advertise their princes, your majesty's most noble progenitors, of all matters tending to their service, and to the utility of the commonwealth.

Your majesty's pleasure for calling a parliament in this kingdom hath been lately divulged, but the matters therein to be propounded not made known unto us and others of the nobility, we being, notwithstanding, of the grand council of the realm, and may well be conceived to be the council meant in the statute made in King Henry the seventh's time, who should join with the governor of this kingdom, in certifying thither, what acts should pass here in parliament, especially, it being hard to exclude those that in respect of their estates and residence, next your majesty, should most likely understand what were fittest to be enacted and ordained for the good of their prince and country.

Yet are we for our own parts well persuaded they be such as will comport with the good and relief of your majesty's subjects, and give hopeful expectation of restoration of this lately torn and rended estate, if your majesty have been rightly informed, they having (as it is said) passed the censure of your highness's most rare and matchless judgment. But the extern and public course held (whereof men of all sorts and qualities do take notice for the management thereof) hath generally bred so grievous an apprehension, as is not in our power to express, arising from a fearful suspicion that the project of erecting so many corporations in places that can scantly pass the rank of the poorest villages, in the poorest country of Christendom, do tend to nought else at this time, but that by the voices of a few selected for the purpose, under the name of burgesses, extreme penal laws should be imposed upon your subjects here, contrary to the natures, customs, and dispositions of them all in effect, and so the general scope and institution of parliaments frustrated, they being ordained for the assurance of the subjects not to be processed with any new edicts or laws, but such as should pass with their general consent and approbation.

Your majesty's subjects here in general do likewise very much distaste and exclaim against the deposing of so many magistrates, in the cities and boroughs of this kingdom, for not swearing the oath of supremacy in spiritual and ecclesiastical causes, they protesting a firm profession of loyalty, and an acknowledgment of all kingly jurisdiction and authority in your highness ; which course, for that it was so sparingly and mildly carried on in the time of your late sister of famous memory, Queen Elizabeth, and but now in your highness's happy reign first extended unto the remote parts of this country, doth so much the more affright, and disquiet the minds of your well-affected subjects here, especially, they conceiving that by this means, those that are most sufficient and fit to exercise and execute those offices and places, are secluded and removed, and they driven to make choice of others conformable in that point, but otherwise very unfit and uncapable to undertake the charges, being generally of the meaner sort. Now, whether it conduceth to the good of your estate, hereby to suffer the secret, home, evil affected subjects (of whom we wish there were none) to be transported with hope and expectation of the effects which a general discontentment might in time produce, and to give scope to the rebels discontented of this nation abroad, to calumniate and cast an aspersion upon the honour and integrity of your highness's government, by displaying in all countries, kingdoms, and estates, and inculcating into the ears of foreign kings and princes, the foulness (as they will term it) of such practices, we humbly leave to your majesty's most sacred, high, and princely consideration. And so, upon the knees of our loyal hearts, do humbly pray that your highness will be graciously pleased not to give way to courses, in the general opinion of your subjects here, so hard and exorbitant, as to erect towns and corporations of places consisting of some few poor and beggarly cottages, but that your highness will give direction that there be no more erected, till time, or traffic and commerce, do make places in the remote and unsettled countries here fit to be incorporated, and that your majesty will benignly content yourself with the service of understanding men to come as knights of the shires out of the chief countries to the parliament. And to the end to remove from your subjects' hearts those fears and discontents, that your highness further will be graciously pleased to give order that the proceedings of this parliament may be with the same moderation and indifferency as your most royal predecessors have used in like cases heretofore, wherein, moreover, if your highness shall be pleased, out of your gracious clemency, to withdraw such laws as may tend to the forcing of your subjects' consciences here in matters concerning religion, you shall settle their minds in a most firm and faithful subjection.

The honour which your majesty, in all your actions and proceedings, hath hitherto so well maintained, the renown of your highness' transcendent understanding in matters of estate and government, and in particular the exemplary precedent of your majesty's never-to-be-forgotten moderation in not descending to such extraordinary courses for effecting the union of both kingdoms so much desired, doth give us full hope and assurance, that your highness will duly weigh and take in good worth these considerations by us laid down, and most graciously grant this our humble submissive suit, in which hope we do, and will always remain,

Your majesty's most humble and dutiful subjects, Gormanston, Chr. Slane, Kileen, Rob. Trimblestown, Pat. Dunsany, Ma. Louth.

Dublin, 25 November 1612.

T. Leland, *History of Ireland* (Dublin 1773), ii. 443–6.

THE GRACES, 1628

At the beginning of the reign of Charles I the government wanted to increase the revenue with the object of enlarging the army, and the king intimated his willingness to make certain reforms in return for a grant. However, an assembly of notables and a gathering of representatives from the provinces both refused to give anything. In August 1627 delegates from the provinces went over to England, and in May 1628 it was settled that in return for £120,000 the king would sponsor a series of reforms which would gratify the various sections of Irish public opinion. But since parliament was not summoned, the ' graces ' remained unimplemented, and the parliaments of 1634 and 1640 demanded legislation based on them.

5. INSTRUCTIONS FROM THE KING TO THE DEPUTY AND COUNCIL OF IRELAND, 1628

Instructions from your majesty to be observed by your deputy and council of Ireland, brought over by the agents in the year 1628.

4. That the laying of any burden upon our subjects for payment of soldiers be forborn, except in cases of inevitable necessity.

8. For reforming of the barbarous abuse of the short ploughs, we are pleased that the penalty now imposed thereon shall be presently taken away, and that hereafter an act of parliament shall pass for the restraining of the said abuse upon such a penalty as shall be thought fit.

10. And for the furtherance of traffic and bringing in of coin into that our kingdom, we are graciously pleased that corn may be transported without licence into any of our dominions and other countries in amity with us, when wheat shall not exceed the price of ten shillings English a Bristol band barrel, and likewise that living cattle may be brought into our dominions without restraint or licence, and that wool also may be transported, provided that it be into our kingdom of England only, and paying the ordinary customs and duties, in which three last particulars we require you to take order by act of state, or otherwise as shall be most expedient.

15. That subjects of that our realm are to be admitted to sue their liveries, ouster-le-mains, and other grants depending on our court of wards, taking only the oath hereunder expressed, and any other oath to be forborn in that case, and the natives of that kingdom being lawyers, and who were heretofore practised there, shall be admitted to practice again, and all other natives of that nation that have been or shall be students at the Inns of Court in England for the space of five years, and shall bring any attestation sufficient to prove the same, are also to be freely admitted by the judges there to practice the laws, taking the said oath, viz. I A. B. do truely acknowledge, profess, testify and declare in my conscience, before God and the world, that our sovereign lord King Charles is lawful and rightful king of this realm, and other his majesty's dominions and countries. And I will bear faithful and true allegiance to his majesty, his heirs and successors, and him and them will defend to the uttermost of my power against all conspiracies and attempts whatsoever,

which shall be made against his or their crown or dignity, and to do my best endeavour to disclose and make known unto his majesty, his heirs and successors, or to the lord deputy or other governors for the time being, all treasons and traiterous conspiracies, which I shall know or hear to be intended against his majesty or any of them. And I do make this recognition and acknowledgement, heartily, willing and truely upon the true faith of a Christian. So help me God.

17. Our court of wards is not to make any inquiry further than to the last deceased ancestor, except it be by special direction from us.

24. For the better settling of our subjects estates in that kingdom, we are pleased that the like act of grace shall pass in the next parliament there touching the limitation of our titles not to extend above three score years, as did pass here the 21 James, wherein are to be excepted the lands whereunto we are entitled by offices already taken, and those already disposed of by our directions. And we are further graciously pleased for a more ample testimony of our goodness to our subjects of that kingdom, to direct hereby that from henceforth no advantage be taken for any title accrued to us three score years past, and above, except only to such lands in the King's county and the Queen's county whereunto we are entitled by offices already taken within the said term of three score years, and which are not yet granted nor lawfully conveyed from us and our crown.

25. And we are also graciously pleased, and accordingly do hereby require you that you give present order for the inhabitants of Connaught, and county of Thormond, and county of Clare, to have their surrenders made in the time of our late most dear father enrolled in our chancery there as of the time of our said father, according to the date of the said surrenders, allowing what fees were formerly paid for the same, and that such of them that please to make new surrenders of their lands and hereditaments may have the same accepted of them, and enrolled in the said court, and thereupon new letters patent passed unto them and their heirs, according to the true intenent of our father's letters in that behalf, paying half fees, and that they and every one of them may have such further assurances for securing of their several estates from all ancient titles accrued unto our crown before three score years last past as shall be requisite and reasonably devised by their counsel. And we are pleased for their further security, that their several estates shall be confirmed unto them and their heirs against us and our heirs and successors etc. by an act to be passed in the next parliament to be holden in Ireland, to the end the same may never hereafter be brought into any further question by us, our heirs and successors. . . .

26. The undertakers of Ulster are to have their estates confirmed upon the payment of a fine of £30 sterling upon every thousand acres in two half year's time by equal portions, and upon doubling their rents to be charged only from the date of their patents. And

for your further directions and more ample authority therein, a commission shall be directed to you and others, together with instructions for passing patents unto them accordingly and for declaring our royal intention and purpose in the same.

27. The planters of Leitrim, Longford, and Ossory, the King's County, the Queen's county and the county of Westmeath are to have two years time for performing their conditions of plantation, and if by that time they perform them not, they are to forfeit their recognizances. In the meantime no process to issue upon their recognizances or bonds.

40. All Scotish men undertakers in Ulster, and in other places there, are to be made free denizens of that our kindom, and no advantage for want of denization to be taken against the heirs or assigns of those that be dead.

The earl of Strafford's letters and despatches. Ed. W. Knowler
(London, 1739), i. pp. 312–27.

PARLIAMENT AND POYNINGS' LAW

During the seventeenth century the Irish parliament had a limited initiatory power, either by co-operating with the council in preparing draft bills, or by submitting the 'heads' of bills to the council for transmission. From about 1660, in spite of Stafford's rebuke to the lords (document 7), the latter method alone was used. The 'heads' passed— in which ever house they originated—through the stages of a bill before going to the council. That body of course could drastically alter them or refuse to transmit them. At the end of the century the commons attempted unsuccessfully to claim the sole right of originating money bills (document 8).

6. COMMITTEES SET UP BY THE HOUSE OF COMMONS TO DRAFT BILLS,
1614 AND 1640

1. Die Martiis, 29 Novembris, 1614

It is thought fit by the house, that the speaker shall move the lord deputy to be pleased to appoint these following viz. :

Mr. Treasurer, Sir Adam Loftus, senior, Mr. Justice Silthorp, Sir John Everard, Sir Christopher Plunkett, Mr. Francis Annesley, Mr. Dr. Reeves, Mr. Bolton, Mr. Talbot, Mr. Barnwell and Mr. Fernham, to join with such others as his lordship shall think fit, in drawing up those acts, as are to be transmitted into England, to be propounded in the next session of parliament.

Commons journ., Ire., i. 27.

2. 1 Die Aprilis, 1640

It is thought fit, and ordered upon question by the house, that the select committee under-named shall meet in this house, at two of the clock this afternoon, to consider and advise of what laws have been propounded in the house this session of parliament, and also of what other laws and ordinances they do conceive are wanting, and not yet thought on, that may be useful, and tend to the better settling of this commonwealth, and the remedying of such abuses and inconveniences, for redress whereof laws have not heretofore been ordained ; and that the said committee shall draw and prepare bills for the same, to be presented to the lords, and others of the committee of the council-board, and there to become suitors for the transmission of the same, that they may be further passed as shall be thought fit. And it is also ordered, that this committee shall have further power to call to their advice and assistance any lawyers, either of the common law or civil law, that be in or near the town, and likewise any merchant or merchants, or other persons, though not members of the house, as they shall have occasion to confer with, from time to time. It is further ordered, that, for the more ease of the committee and dispatch of the business, this committee shall have power to divide themselves into several sub-committees, and to adjourn themselves, from time to time as they shall see cause, at which committee every other member of the house may be present, if they please and give their advice and assistance.

Commons journ., Ire., i. 142–2.

7. WENTWORTH'S REBUKE TO THE HOUSE OF LORDS, 2 AUGUST 1634

Protestation of the lord deputy

Whereas at a parliament holden . . . in the tenth year of King Henry VII . . . an act was made for and concerning the order, manner and form of parliaments to be holden and kept in this realm of Ireland . . . and whereas at a parliament holden . . . in the third and fourth years of the reign of King Philip and Queen Mary . . . it was ordained, enacted, and established that the said act should be expounded, understood and taken, as in the said act of the third and fourth of King Philip and Queen Mary was declared . . . and whereas in this present session of parliament the lords spiritual and temporal being assembled, did the 24 July now last past, appoint and select a committee of eighteen lords for grievances and for taking into consideration of such acts as are fit to be propounded to be passed, and such statutes as are in force, which are fit to be repealed, which committee met accordingly and gave order unto his majesty's learned counsel for drawing of several acts to be passed, . . . and lastly, on the first day of this instant month, another committee of the lords, appointed for privileges, gave like order to his majesty's attorney-general, with advice to some of the judges, to draw an act for making such noblemen as are resident in England liable to all public charges and payments taxed by parliament in this kingdom, whence their titles of honour are derived, . . . and whereas also the said committee of privileges directed the lord chancellor to move us the lord deputy, that divers acts, drawn up by his majesty's judges of the several courts, and considered of and allowed by their lordships, might be further proceeded in, as apperaineth, which the lord chancellor did accordingly. All which former proceedings of their lordships, we the lord deputy, taking into due consideration, and weighing the same with the said statutes, although we do not conceive, that the said lords advisedly or purposely intended to violate or to innovate in any thing, otherwise than by the statutes are provided, yet for avoiding any misinterpretation, which, by reason of that manner of proceeding, may in after-times be made to the entrenchment on the said acts of parliament, or his majesty's royal power, whereof we are and will be always, most tender, in discharge of the duty we owe to the preservation of his majesty's honour, and that the like mistake in their lordships' proceedings may futurely be avoided, we have therefore thought fit, this day in full parliament, to protest against that course held by their lordships, as not any ways belonging to their lordships to give order to the king's learned counsel, or any other, for the framing or drawing up any acts to pass in parliament, but that the same solely belongs to us the lord deputy and council. We the lord deputy do hereby further declare, that their lordships have power only by remonstrance or petition to represent to the lord deputy and council for the time being, such public considerations as they shall think fit and good for the commonwealth, and so submit them to be drawn into acts, and transmitted into England, or otherwise altered or rejected, according as the lord deputy and council, in their wisdoms, shall judge and hold expedient, and that in such wise as the said acts of parliament, in these cases, have limited and appointed. And we the said lord deputy do trust, their lordships will take this as a reasonable and necessary admonishment from us, and forbear the like course hereafter.

Lords journ., Ire., i. 22–3.

8. SIDNEY'S REBUKE TO THE HOUSE OF COMMONS, 3 NOVEMBER 1692

His excellency makes a speech, wherein he declares a dislike to some proceedings of the house of commons, against which he makes protestation in writing, as an assertion of their majesties' prerogative and then delivers the said protestation to the lord chancellor, who making a sign to the clerk to come to him gave him the same to be read, which was accordingly done at the clerk's table, in *haec verba* :

Sidney. Whereas at a parliament held at Drogheda in the tenth year of the reign of King Henry VII an act was made for and concerning the order, manner and form of parliaments, to be holden and kept in this realm of Ireland, and by another act made at a parliament holden at Dublin in the third and fourth year of King Philip and Queen Mary, it was ordained, enacted and established that no parliament should be summoned or holden within this realm of Ireland, until such time as the lieutenant, lord deputy, lord justice or lords justices, chief governor or governors, or any of them, and the council of the realm for the time being, should have certified the king and queen's majesties, their heirs and successors under the great seal of this realm of Ireland, the considerations, causes, and articles of such acts, provisions and ordinances as by them should be thought meet and necessary to be enacted. . . .

And whereas in this present session of parliament, a bill, entitled, *An act for granting unto their majesties an additional duty on beer, ale, and other liquors*, which had been certified by us the lord lieutenant of this kingdom and the council unto the king and queen's majesties, under the great seal of this kingdom, and by their majesties approved of and returned under the great seal of England and by us sent to the house of commons to be considered of in this present parliament, the said commons having the said bill lying upon their table, on the 27th day of the month of October last, did come to a vote thereupon and resolve, that it is the sole and undoubted right of the said commons to prepare heads of bills for raising money. And further, on the 28th day of the same October, a motion being made in the said house, and the question put, that a bill then on the table, which had likewise been regularly transmitted in the same form, entitled, *An Act for granting to their majesties certain duties for one year*, might be read, it passed in the negative, and the said house of commons resolved, that the said bill be rejected by that house, and further resolved, that it be entered in the journals of that house, that the reason why the said bill was rejected, is, that the same had not its rise in that house. All which resolutions and proceedings, appear in the journals of the house of commons, printed by their order and authority, by which votes and resolutions, the said house of commons do exclude their majesties and the crown of England from the right of transmitting any bills for granting of money or other aids to their majesties, and their successors. Which recited votes, resolutions and proceedings of the house of commons, being contrary to the said recited acts of parliament, and the continued usage and practice ever since the making thereof, and a great invasion upon their majesties' prerogative, and the rights of the crown of England, we the lord lieutenant, as well to assert the rights of their majesties, and the rights of the crown of England (whereof we are and ever will be most tender) in transmitting such bills under the great seal of England, to be considered of in parliament, as to discharge the trust reposed in us, and prevent the inconveniences which may hereafter happen in case these votes and resolutions of the house of commons should be made public, or remain in their journals, without any contradiction or animadversion, have thought it necessary this day, in full parliament, to protest. And we do accordingly protest against the aforesaid votes and resolutions made by the house of commons, and entered in their journals, and do assert, protest and declare, that it is their majesties' prerogative and the undoubted right of the crown of England, observing the forms in the said several acts prescribed, to transmit bills under the great seal of England for granting of aids to their majesties, their heirs and successors, which said bills, so transmitted, ought to be read and considered of by the house of commons in this kingdom, and therefore, the said recited votes and proceedings of the house of commons, are contrary to the acts of parliament above mentioned, and the constant practice and usage in all parliaments

10

since the making thereof, and also highly derogatory to their majesties' royal authority, and the rights of the crown of England.

Lords journ., Ire., i. 477–8.

THE PARLIAMENT OF 1640

The second Irish parliament of Charles I met in March 1640 and voted four subsidies. In April Strafford left Ireland, and in September the king was compelled by the successes of the Scots to summon a parliament for England. In October the Irish parliament reassembled after a three months' recess. The commons voted a remonstrance (document 9), appointed a committee to look after their interests in England (documents 10, 11) and protested against the methods used in collecting the subsidies. Wandesford, the deputy, tore the protest from the journals and prorogued parliament. When it met again in January the king surrendered. The protest was reinserted in the journals and other concessions granted. Meanwhile the commons voted the ' queries,' impeached several officials, and joined with the peers in asserting the jurisdiction of the Irish house of lords. In August parliament adjourned and did not meet again until after the rebellion had broken out. The commons had shown surprising determination both in demanding constitutional concessions and in trying to correct administrative defects.

9. THE REMONSTRANCE OF THE HOUSE OF COMMONS, 1640

Voted by the house of commons 7th November 1640

To the Right Honourable the lord deputy

The humble and just remonstrance of the knights, citizens, and burgesses, in parliament assembled

Shewing, that in all ages past, since the happy subjection of this kingdom to the imperial crown of England, it was, and is a principal study and princely care of his majesty, and his most noble progenitors, kings and queens of England and Ireland, to the vast expence of treasure and blood, that their loyal and dutiful people of this land of Ireland, being now for the most part derived from British ancestors, should be governed according to the municipal and fundamental laws of England, that the statute of Magna Charta or the great charter for the liberties of England, and other laudable laws and statutes, were in several parliaments here enacted and declared, that by means thereof, and of the most prudent and benign government of his majesty and his royal progenitors, this kingdom was, until of late, in its growth to a flourishing estate ; whereby the said people were heretofore enabled to answer their humble and natural desires to comply with his majesty's royal and princely occasions, by their free gift of one hundred and fifty thousand pounds sterling, and likewise by another gift of one hundred and twenty thousand pounds more, during the government of the Lord Viscount Falkland, and after, by the gift of forty thousand pounds, and their free and cheerful gift of six entire subsidies in the tenth year of his majesty's reign, which, to comply with his majesty's then occasions, signified to the then house of commons, they did allow should amount in the collections unto two hundred and fifty thousand pounds, although, as they confidently believe, if the said subsidies had been levied in a moderate parliamentary way,[1] they would not have amounted to much more than half the said sum, besides the four entire subsidies granted in this present parliament. So it is, may it please your lordship, that, by occasion of ensuing and other grievances and innovations, though to his majesty no considerable profit, this kingdom is reduced to that extreme and universal poverty, that the same is now less able to pay two subsidies, than it was heretofore to satisfy all the before recited great payments, and his majesty's most faithful people of the same do conceive great fears, that the said grievances and consequences thereof may hereafter be drawn into precedents, and be perpetuated upon their posterity, which, in their great hopes and strong belief, they are persuaded is contrary to his majesty's royal and princely intention towards his said people. Some of which said grievances are as followeth.

1. The general and apparent decay of trades, occasioned by the new and illegal raising of the book of rates and impositions, as twelve-pence a-piece custom for hides bought for four or five shillings, and other heavy impositions upon native and other commodities, exported and imported, by reason whereof, and of extreme usage and censures merchants are beggared, and both disenabled and discouraged to trade, and some of the honourable persons who gain thereby are often judges and parties, and that in the conclusion his majesty's profit thereby is not considerably advanced.

2. The arbitary decision of all civil causes and controversies by paper petitions before the lord lieutenant and lord deputy, and infinite other judicatories upon references from them derived, in the nature of all actions determinable at the common law, not limited unto certain time, season, cause, or thing whatsoever, and the consequences of such proceedings by receiving immoderate and unlawful fees by secretaries, clerks, pursuivants, serjeants-at-arms, and otherwise, by which kind of proceedings his majesty loseth a considerable part of his revenue upon original writs and otherwise, and the subject loseth the benefit of his writ of error, bill of reversal, vouchers, and other legal and just advantages, and the ordinary course and courts of justice declined.

3. The proceedings in civil causes at the council board, contrary to the law and great charter, and not limited to any certain time or season.

4. That the subject is, in all the material parts thereof, denied the benefit of princely graces, and more especially of the statute of limitations of 21 Jacobi, granted by his majesty in the fourth year of his reign, upon great advice of the council of England and Ireland, and for great consideration, and then published in all the courts at Dublin, and in all the counties of this kingdom, in open assizes,

---

[1] That a subsidy should be levied in a ' parliamentary way ' apparently implied that the taxpayer should be assessed on only a fixed proportion of his property and income (*Commons journ., Ire.*, i. 170).

whereby all persons do take notice, that, contrary to his majesty's pious intention, his subjects of this kingdom have not enjoyed the benefit of his majesty's princely promise thereby made.

5. The extrajudicial avoiding of letters patent of estates of a very great part of his majesty's subjects under the great seal, the public faith of the kingdom, by private opinions delivered at the council-board, without legal evictions of their estates, contrary to the law, and without precedents or example of any former age.

6. The proclamation for the sole emption and uttering of tobacco, which is bought at very low rates, and uttered at high and excessive rates, by means whereof, thousands of families within this kingdom, and of his majesty's subjects in several islands and other parts of the West Indies, as your petitioners are informed, are destroyed, and the most part of the coin of this kingdom is engrossed into particular hands, insomuch as the petitioners do conceive, that the profit arising and engrossed thereby, doth surmount, his majesty's revenue, certain or casual, within this kingdom, and yet his majesty receiveth but very little profit by the same.

7. The unusual and unlawful increasing of monopolies, to the advantage of a few, to the disprofit of his majesty, and the impoverishment of his people.

8. The extreme and cruel usage of certain late commissioners and others, the inhabitants of the city and county of Londonderry, by means whereof, the worthy plantation of that county is almost destroyed, and the said inhabitants are reduced to great poverty, and many of them forced to forsake the country, the same being the first and most useful plantation in the large province of Ulster, to the great weakening of the kingdom in this time of danger, the said plantation being the principal strength of those parts.

9. The late erection of the court of high commission for causes ecclesiastical in those necessitous times ; the proceedings of the said court in many causes, without legal warrant ; and yet so supported, as prohibitions have not been obtained, though legally sought for ; and the excessive fees exacted by the ministers thereof ; and the encroaching of the same upon the jurisdiction of other ecclesiastical courts of this kingdom.

10. The exorbitant and barbarous fees and pretended customs exacted by the clergy against the law, some of which have been formerly represented to your lordship.

11. The petitioners do most heartily bemoan, that his majesty's service and profit are much more impaired than advanced by the grievances aforesaid, and the subsidies granted in the last parliament having much increased his majesty's revenue, by the buying in of grants and otherwise, and that all his majesty's debts, then due in this kingdom, were satisfied out of the said subsidies, and yet his majesty is of late, as the petitioners have been informed in the house of commons, become indebted in this kingdom in great sums, and they do therefore humbly beseech that an exact account may be sent to his majesty, how, and in what manner, his treasure issued.

12. The petitioners do humbly conceive great and just fears at a proclamation, published in this kingdom in Anno Domini 1635, prohibiting men of quality or estates for to depart this kingdom into England, without the lord deputy's licence, whereby the subjects of this kingdom are hindered and interrupted from free access and address to his sacred majesty and privy council of England, to declare their just grievances, or to obtain remedies for them, in sort as their ancestors have done, in all ages, since the reign of King Henry II ; and great fees exacted for every of the said licences.

13. That of late his majesty's late attorney-general hath exhibited informations against many antient boroughs of this kingdom, into his majesty's court of exchequer, to shew cause, by what warrant the said boroughs, who heretofore sent burgesses to the parliament, should send the said burgesses to parliament, and thereupon, for want of an answer, the said privilege of sending burgesses was seized by the said court, which proceedings were altogether *coram non judice*, and contrary to the laws and privileges of the house of parliament, and, if way should be given thereunto, might tend to the subversion of parliaments, and, by consequence, to the ruin and destruction of the commonwealth, and that the house of commons hath hitherto, in this present parliament, been deprived of the advice and counsel of many profitable and good members by means thereof.

14. That, by the powerfulness of some ministers of state in this kingdom, the parliament in its members and actions, hath not its natural freedom.

15. That the fees taken in all the courts of justice in this kingdom, both ecclesiastical and civil, and by other inferior officers and ministers, are so immoderately high, that it is an unspeakable burden to all his majesty's subjects of this kingdom, who are not able to subsist, except the same be speedily remedied, and reduced to such a moderation, as may stand with the condition of this realm.

And lastly, that the gentry, merchants, and others his majesty's subjects of the kingdom, are of late, by the grievances and pressures aforesaid, and other the like, very near to ruin and destruction ; and farmers of customs, customers, waiters, searchers, clerks of unwarrantable proceedings, pursuivants, and gaolers, and sundry others, very much enriched, whereby, and by the slow redress of the petitioners' grievances, his majesty's most faithful and dutiful people of this kingdom do conceive great fears, that their readiness approved upon all occasions hath not been of late rightly represented to his sacred majesty, for remedy whereof, the said petitioners do humbly, and of right, beseech your lordship, that the said grievances and pressures may be speedily redressed. And if your lordship shall not think fit to afford present relief therein, that your lordship may admit a select committee of this house, of persons uninterested in the benefit arising of the aforesaid grievances, to be licensed by your lordship to repair to his sacred majesty in England, for to pursue the same, and to obtain fitting remedies for their aforesaid and other just grievances, and oppressions, and upon all just and honourable occasions they will, without respect of particular interest or profit to be raised thereby, most humbly and readily in parliament extend their utmost endeavours to serve his majesty, and to comply with his royal and princely occasions, and shall pray, etc.

Commons journ., Ire., i. 162–3.

10. THE APPOINTMENTS OF AGENTS TO ENGLAND, 11 NOVEMBER 1640

It is ordered upon question, that a select committee of this house shall be nominated to repair into England, with a remonstrance of the grievances of this kingdom, some whereof have been voted in this session of parliament, and to present the same to his most excellent majesty for redress therein, and to do all other matters and things therein, as to the said committee shall seem meet or necessary for obtaining fitting remedy of the said grievances, and that the said committee shall stand, and be agents for, and in the name of the commons, or commonality, of this kingdom, in case this house be dissolved, prorogued or adjourned, before such redress shall be obtained, and the said committee or agents, not to proceed, if speedy and satisfactory redress be had in this kingdom, before prorogation or adjournment of this house.[1]

Commons journ., Ire., i. 165.

11. INSTRUCTIONS FOR THE AGENTS IN ENGLAND

Voted 30 January 1641

Instructions for the committee, or agents, employed by this house in England

1. To move his majesty for the passing of a bill, for the further explanation of Poynings' act, in such parts thereof, whereon any doubt may be raised for the manner of certifying of bills from hence into England, and returning them again hither, or any other matter concerning the further explanation of the said act, which they shall think fit.

2. That the house of commons, during the parliament, may draw up bills by their own committee, and transmit them.

3. For that the kingdom hath heretofore, and still doth suffer much inconvenience, by the farming of his majesty's customs in such hands as they have been of late rented, that they may humbly move his majesty for transmitting of a bill, to prevent such inconveniences for time to come.

4. Also, for that the kingdom hath heretofore, and still doth suffer great detriment, by making of gain of licences obtained for

---

[1] The following were nominated members of the committee: Sir Donogh MacCarty, Sir Hardress Waller, John Walsh, merchant, Nicholas Plunkett, Nicholas Barnewall, Richard FitzGerald, Simon Digby, Thomas Bourke, Sir Robuck Lynch, Geoffrey Browne, Sir James Montgomery, Sir William Cole, Edward Rowley.

the exportation of commodities prohibited by statute, that likewise they would humbly move his majesty for transmitting of a bill, to prevent that inconvenience, and in case the governor, or governors, for the time being, and the council of this kingdom shall think it necessary at any time to license the exportation of any such commodities, that they may license the same without making any gain thereof.

5. That where great inconvenience hath happened to many of his majesty's subjects in this kingdom, by reason of an act of state for the cessing of the kindred with soldiers, when any of their sept do shun the course of law, until he be brought in, that they would humbly move his majesty for abolishing thereof.

6. That the printed instructions for regulating the courts of justice may be established by act of parliament, in such parts thereof as the house of commons shall conceive to be for the good of the kingdom.

Commons journ., Ire., i. 167.

12. THE JUDICIAL POWERS OF THE IRISH HOUSE OF LORDS, 1641

It is ordered upon question, that the declaration and protestation of the lords spiritual and temporal and commons in parliament, having been three times read this day in this house, shall pass, and be entered among the acts, orders, and ordinances of this house, and to be presented to his majesty by the committee in England.

The second instrument [1]

The declaration and protestation of the lords spiritual and temporal and commons in parliament assembled. . . . For the avoiding of any doubt or ambiguity, which might be moved or stirred against the power of judicature of the high court of parliament of this realm, and to manifest and declare a most clear, undoubted, and undeniable truth to all posterity, the lords spiritual and temporal and commons, in parliament assembled, do hereby declare and protest, that the said court of parliament of this kingdom hath always had and ought to have, full power and authority to hear and determine all treasons and other offences, crimes, causes, and things whatsoever, as well capital and criminal as civil, contrived, perpetrated, done, or happened within this realm, and likewise to inflict condign punishment upon all offenders, and to administer equal justice unto all persons whatsoever in the said realm according to the ancient course and rights of parliament, in all times and ages used and exercised within the said realm of England, and that all other the courts of justice, and all magistrates, judges, offices, and subjects of any estate, degree, quality, or condition whatsoever, of the said realm of Ireland, are liable to the resolutions, orders, and

---

[1] Three ' instruments ' were enacted on the same day (24 May 1641). The first thanked the king for his letter concerning the ' graces,' the third emphasized that the Irish parliament had the power of impeachment.

judgments of the said court of parliament of this realm, and that the said court of parliament is the supreme judicatory in the said realm.

Commons journ., Ire., i. 212–3.

THE REBELLION OF 1641

13. THE CONFEDERATION OF KILKENNY

In May 1642 the catholic prelates, nobles, gentry and clergy met at Kilkenny and set up a supreme council. Summons ' in nature of writs ' were sent to the lords spiritual and temporal and to the counties and boroughs. When the persons so summoned met, they issued the orders given below, ' to be observed as the model of their government.' [1]

Orders made and established by the lords spiritual and temporal, and the rest of the general assembly for the kingdom of Ireland, met at the city of Kilkenny, the 24th day of October, Anno Domini 1642, and in the eighteenth year of the reign of our sovereign lord, King Charles, by the grace of God, of Great Britain, France and Ireland, etc.

I. Imprimis that the Roman catholic church in Ireland shall and may have and enjoy the privileges and immunities according to the great charter, made and declared within the realm of England, in the ninth year of King Henry III, sometime king of England, and the lord of Ireland, and afterwards enacted and confirmed in this realm of Ireland. And that the common law of England, and all the statutes of force in this kingdom, which are not against the Roman catholic religion, or the liberties of the natives, and other liberties of this kingdom, shall be observed throughout the whole kingdom, and that all proceedings in civil and criminal cases shall be according to the same laws.

II. Item, that all and every person and persons within this kingdom shall bear faith and true allegiance unto our sovereign lord King Charles . . . his heirs and lawful successors, and shall uphold and maintain his and their rights and lawful prerogatives, . . .

III. Item, that the common laws of England and Ireland, and the said statutes, called the great charter, and every clause, branch and article thereof, and all other statutes confirming, expounding or declaring the same, shall be punctually observed within this kingdom, so far forth as the condition of the present times, during these times, can by possibilities give way thereunto, and after the war is ended the same to be observed without any limitations, or restriction whatsoever.

IV. Inasmuch as the city of Dublin is the usual and principal seat of justice of this kingdom, where the parliament and ordinary courts were held, and some other places where principal councils were kept sometimes, are as yet possessed and commanded by the malignant party who are enemies to God and their king and his majesty's well-affected subjects, this assembly is necessitated during

---

[1] J. T. Gilbert, *History of the Irish confederation and the war in Ireland* (Dublin 1882–9), i. 87, 112.

this war in some formalities and circumstances to deviate from the proceedings prescribed by the said laws and statutes ; . . . For the exaltation therefore of the holy Roman catholic church, for the advancement of his majesty's service, and the preservation of the lives, estates, and liberties of his majesty's true subjects of this kingdom against the injustice, murders, massacres, rapes, depredations, robberies, burnings, frequent breaches of public faith and quarters, and destruction daily perpetrated and acted upon his majesty's said subjects, and advised, contrived, and daily executed by the malignant party, some of them managing the government and affairs of state in Dublin, and some other parts of this kingdom, to his majesty's greatest disservice, and complying with their confederates, the malignant party in England and elsewhere, who (as it is manifest to all the world) do complot, and practise to dishonour and destroy his majesty, his royal consort the queen, their issue, and the monarchial government, which is of most dangerous consequence to all the monarchs and princes of Christendom, the said assembly doth order and establish a council by name of a supreme council of the confederate catholics of Ireland, who are to consist of the number of four and twenty to be forthwith named, whereof twelve at the least, to be forthwith named, shall reside in this kingdom, or where else they shall think expedient, and the members of the said council shall have equal votes, and two parts of three or more concurring present votes, to conclude, and not fewer to sit in council than nine, whereof seven at least are to concur ; and of the four and twenty a president shall be named by the assembly, to be one of the said twelve resident . . . And the said council shall have the power and pre-eminence following, viz. the lords general and all other commanders of armies, and civil magistrates and officers in the several provinces shall observe their orders and decrees, and shall do nothing contrary to their directions, and shall give them speedy advertisement and account of their proceedings. . . .

That the said council shall have power to order and determine all such matters as by this assembly shall be left undetermined, and shall be recommended unto them, and their orders therein to be of force until the next assembly, and after, until the same be revoked.

That the said council shall have power and authority to do and execute all manner of acts and things conducing to the advancement of the catholic cause, and good of this kingdom, and concerning the war, as if done by the assembly, and shall have power to hear and determine all matters capital, criminal or civil, excepting the right or title of land. . . .

V. Item, it is further ordered and established, that in every province of this kingdom there shall be a provincial council, and in every county a county council. The provincial council to be composed of the number of two of each county, and the said provincial council shall choose a president for themselves.

That the provincial council shall sit four times a year, and oftener if there be cause for it. That they shall have power and authority to review or reverse the judgment of the county council, the party complaining, entering security *de adjudicate solvendi*. And shall (during the troubles) have power to hear and determine all matters of the crown, as judges of oyer and terminer and gaol delivery were wont to do, so that no spiritual person be present at the determing matters of blood. And shall have power to hear and determine all civil causes, and to establish rents and possessions, so they meddle not with the title of lands, other than in case of dower and jointure.

VI. And the sheriffs, provincial generals, and all commanders of the armies in case of disobedience, are respectively required to execute the decrees and orders . . .

VII. Item, in every county there shall be a county council, consisting of one or two of each barony at the election of the county, and where there are no baronies, the council of such county to consist of the number of twelve.

And the said county council shall have power and authority in all points as justices of the peace. . . .

IX. Item, in every county there shall be coroners, high-sheriffs, high-constables, and petty-constables and gaolers, who are to do their respective offices as accustomed. The high-sheriff to be confirmed or nominated by the supreme council, and the high-sheriff is required to execute the commands, orders, and decrees of the provincial and county council.

XII. Item, it is further ordered, that whosoever hath entered since the first day of October, 1641, or shall hereafter during the continuance of the war in this kingdom, enter into the lands, tenements, or hereditaments, at or immediately before the first day of October . . . shall immediately restore upon demand, the said possession to the party or parties so put out . . . provided, and so it is meant, that if any of the parties so put out, be declared a neuter or enemy by the supreme or provincial council, then the party who gained the possession as aforesaid shall give up the possession to such person or persons, as shall be named either by the said council provincial, or supreme council, to be disposed of towards the maintenance of the general cause, . . .

XIV. Item, for the avoiding of national distinction between the subjects of his Majesty's dominions, which this assembly doth utterly detest and abhor, and which ought not to be endured in a well-governed commonwealth, it is ordered and established, that, upon pain of the highest punishment, which may be inflicted by authority of this assembly, that every Roman catholic, as well English, Welsh, as Scotch, who was of that profession before the troubles, and who will come and please to reside in this kingdom and join in the present union, shall be preserved and cherished in his life, goods, and estates, by the power, authority, and force (if need require it) of all the catholics of Ireland, as fully and as freely as any native born therein, and shall be acquitted and eased of one third part (in three parts to be divided) of public charges or levies raised or to be raised for the maintenance of this holy war.

XV. Item, and it is further ordered and established, that there shall be no distinction or comparison made betwixt Old Irish, and Old and New English or betwixt septs or families, or betwixt citizens and townsmen and countrymen, joining in union, upon pain of the highest punishment that can be inflicted by any of the councils aforesaid, according to the nature and quality of the offences, and division like to spring thence.

XVI. Item, it is further ordered and established, that all new converts born in any of his majesty's dominions or elsewhere, without manifest occasion given by the persons converted to the contrary, and joining in this cause, shall be accounted catholics and natives to all intents and purposes.

XVII. Item, it is further ordered and established, that all artificers, artizans, navigators, and mariners, not being denizens, who shall please to reside in this kingdom, after such time as they and their families shall be here settled, have and enjoy the free liberties and privileges of natives in all respects.

XVIII. Item, it is further ordered and established, that as in regard of the present estate and condition of this kingdom, no Irishman especially if he be a catholic, or any other catholic, is admitted of or permitted to continue in the Inns of Court, and to the end the laudable laws of England and Ireland may not die amidst the disasters of these times, one Inns of Court shall be erected in such a place of this kingdom as to the supreme council shall be thought fit, for the training of the gentry of this kingdom to the knowledge of these laws.

XIX. Item, it is further ordered and established, that no lord, gentleman, or any other person, shall raise or keep any company of soldiers, but such as shall be authorized by the supreme council, provincial council, or county council, or magistrate within their own corporate towns ; and that the statute against cesses, and coynye or livery be duly put in execution. And that no company or soldiers whatsoever shall be paid or relieved by the country, excepting such as are or shall be enrolled in the marshals' lists, and none shall be billeted but by the constable.

XX. Item, it is further ordered and established for the advancement of learning, that in every province of this kingdom free-schools shall be erected and maintained, and in such places, and in such manner and form as by the metropolitan of the diocese in their respective provinces shall be thought fit.

XXI. Item, it is further ordered and established, that the king's customs, rents, revenues, arrears and dues, and the rents, estates and profits of the lands, hereditaments, goods and chattels of the enemies, which are or shall be declared by the provincial or supreme council, or by the general council, be received and collected, and be disposed for his majesty's use and service.

XXII. Item, it is further ordered and established, that church lands and tithes impropriate in the catholic owners before those troubles, and joining in this cause may be left to them according to their several estates, until the same be disposed of by the parliament. . . .

XXVI. Item, it is ordered and established, that the possession of protestant archbishops, bishops, deans, dignitaries, and parsons, in right of their respective churches, or their tenements in the beginning of these troubles, shall be deemed, taken, and construed as the possession of the catholic archbishops, bishops, deans, dignitaries, pastors and their tenements respectively, . . .

XXXIII. Item, it is ordered and established, that to prevent the springing up of all national distinctions, the oath of association or union be taken solemnly, after confession and receiving the sacrament in the parish churches, throughout the kingdom, and the names of all the persons of rank and quality in every parish that must take the same to be enrolled in parchment. . . .

Gilbert MSS, 219 (Pearse Street Public Library).

14. THE CATHOLICS' DEMANDS,[1] 1644

After the cessation of 1643 the confederate catholics sent agents to Oxford to lay their demands before the king. The propositions first presented were regarded by the council as unreasonable. But the agents proved ' councellable,' and presented new propositions, ' which though in many things unreasonable for the king to grant, yet are not very scandalous for them to ask.' [2]

The demands of the Roman catholics of Ireland humbly presented to his sacred majesty in pursuance of their remonstrance of grievances,[3] and to be annexed to the said remonstrance.

1. That all acts made against the professors of the Roman catholic faith, whereby any restraint, penalty, mulct, or incapacity may be laid upon any Roman catholic within the kingdom of Ireland may be repealed, and the said catholics to be allowed the freedom of the Roman catholic religion.

2. That your majesty be pleased to call a free parliament in the said kingdom, to be held and continued as in the said remonstrance is expressed, and the statute of the tenth year of the reign of King Henry VII, called Poynings' act, and all acts explaining or enlarging the same, be suspended during that parliament, for the speedy settlement of the present affairs, and the repeal thereof to be there further considered of.

3. That all acts and ordinances made and passed in the now pretended parliament in that kingdom, since the seventh day of August 1641, be clearly annulled, declared void, and taken off the file.

4. That all indictments, attainders, outlawries in the king's

---

[1] The text given here is that of the first demands. Matter omitted in the revised propositions is placed in square brackets.

[2] Digby to Ormond, 2 April 1644 (T. Carte, *Life of James, duke of Ormond* (London 1736), iii. 277).

[3] For text of remonstrance see J. T. Gilbert *History of the Irish confederation and the war in Ireland* (Dublin 1882–9), ii. 226–42.

bench, or elsewhere, since the said seventh day of August 1641, and all letters patent, grants, leases, custodiums, bonds, recognizances, and all other records, act or acts depending thereupon, or in prejudice of the said catholics, of any of them, be taken off the files, annulled, and declared void, first by your majesty's public proclamation and after by act to be passed in the said free parliament.

5. That inasmuch as under colour of such outlawries, and attainders, debts due to the said catholics have been granted, levied and disposed of, and of the other side, that debts due upon the said catholics to those of the other party have been levied and disposed to public uses, that therefore all debts be by act of parliament mutually released or all to stand in *statu quo*, notwithstanding any grant or disposition.

6. [That whereas your majesty's subjects of that kingdom have and do suffer extremely by the offices found since the first year of Queen Elizabeth, of many countries and territories, upon no real title, or upon feigned or old titles of two hundred, three hundred, four hundred years, and by many illegal, and unjust attainders, by acts of parliament or otherwise, since the time aforesaid, unto which hitherto no traverse, monstrans de droit, or petition of right could be admitted, it is therefore humbly desired that the said offices, and attainders, and all grants, leases, and estates thereupon derived from the crown be reviewed in free parliament according to justice and conscience, still reserving to your majesty the rents and profits thereout answered before the late commission of defective titles, and special care to be therein likewise had of purchases made for valuable consideration by your majesty's faithful subjects. And] That the late offices, taken or found upon feigned or old titles since the year 1634, to entitle your majesty to several countries in Connaught, Thomond, and in the counties of Tipperary, Limerick, and Wicklow, be vacated and taken off the file, the possessors settled and secured in their ancient estates by act of parliament, and that the like act of limitation of your majesty's titles for the security of the estates of your subjects of that kingdom be passed in the said parliament, as was enacted in the 21st year of his late majesty's reign in this kingdom.

7. That all marks of incapacity imposed upon the natives of that kingdom to purchase or acquire leases, offices, lands, or hereditaments, be taken away by act of parliament, and the same to extend to the securing of purchases, leases, or grants already made, and that for the education of youth, an act be passed in the next parliament for the erecting of one or more inns of court, universities, free and common schools.

8. That the offices and places of command, honour, profit and trust within that kingdom be conferred upon Roman catholics natives of that kingdom, in equality and indifference with your majesty's other subjects.

9. That the insupportable oppression of your majesty's subjects

by reason of the court of wards, and respite of homage be taken away, and a certain revenue in lieu thereof settled upon your majesty without diminution of your majesty's profit.

10. That no lord not estated in that kingdom, or estated and not resident, shall have vote in the said parliament by proxy or otherwise, and none admitted to the house of commons but such as shall be estated and resident within the kingdom.

11. That an act shall be passed in the next parliament, declaratory that the parliament of Ireland is a free parliament of itself, independent of, and not subordinate to, the parliament of England, and that the subjects of Ireland are immediately subject to your majesty as in right of your crown, and that the members of the said parliament of Ireland, and all other the subjects of Ireland are independent, and in no way to be ordered or concluded by the parliament of England, and are only to be ordered and governed within that kingdom by your majesty and such governors as are or shall be there appointed, and by the parliament of that kingdom according to the laws of the land.

12. [That two acts passed in the parliament of this kingdom of England, the one entitled *An act for the speedy and effectual reducing of the rebels in his majesty's kingdom of Ireland to their due obedience to his majesty and the crown of England*, and another act entitled *An act for adding unto and explaining the same*, shall be declared void ; and that all grants and assignments, under such grants or any other acts or estates whatsoever made in pursuance of them, or otherwise, or in pursuance of the act or acts of subscriptions, or any other act or proclamation, and all other acts and ordinances made in the parliament of England in prejudice of the said catholics, shall be declared void.]

13. That the assumed power or jurisdiction in the council board, of determining all manner of causes, be limited to matters of state, and all patents, estates, and grants illegally and extra-judicially avoided, there or elsewhere, be left in state as before, and the parties grieved, their heirs or assigns, till legal eviction.

14. That the statutes of the eleventh, twelfth, and thirteenth years of the reign of Queen Elizabeth concerning staple commodities be repealed, reserving to his majesty lawful and just poundage, and a book of rates to be settled by an indifferent committee of both houses for all commodities.

15. That in as much as the long continuance of the chief governor or governors of that kingdom in that place of so great eminence and power, hath been a principal occasion that much tyranny and oppression hath been exercised upon the subjects of that kingdom, that your majesty will be pleased to continue such governor hereafter but for three years, and that none once employed therein be appointed for the same again until the expiration of six years next after the end of the said three years ; and that an act pass to disable such governor, or governors, during their government, directly or indirectly, in use, trust, or otherwise, to make any

manner of purchase, or acquisition of any manors, lands, tenements, or hereditaments within that kingdom, other than from your majesty, your heirs, or successors.

16. [That, whereas your majesty's standing army formerly in that kingdom, was of so small and inconsiderable a number, that they rather appeared a mark of suspicion and jealousy on the nation, and rendered them to all other nations as a people not to be trusted, than any strength for the defence of the kingdom, and yet exhausted a great part of your majesty's revenue, which the several officers converted to their private use, having few or no soldiers, but such as they collected of their tenants and servants, at days of musters and pay ; to remove therefore that badge of distrust from your said subjects, it is humbly desired that no such army be any longer maintained in that kingdom, whereby much of your majesty's revenue will be hereafter saved for better uses, and your subjects there, with your majesty's consent, will take such course for the safety of that kingdom, by way of trained bands, or otherwise as shall be most serviceable to your majesty, and satisfactory to your said subjects.] [1]

17. [That the present government of the said catholics may continue within their quarters and jurisdictions until the parliament, and after until their grievances be redressed by acts of parliament, and for a convenient time for the execution thereof.]

18. [That an act of oblivion be passed in the next free parliament, to extend to all your majesty's said catholic subjects of that kingdom, for all manner of offences, capital, criminal, and personal, with a saving and reservation to both houses within six months next after the passing of the said act, to question any person or persons of any side for any notorious murders, cruelties, rapines, and robberies against public faith, and such persons as have privately or publicly in their councils or actions joined against your majesty with the rebels at Westminster, and the same to hear and determine according to law, honour, and justice, and the said act to extend to all goods and chattels, customs, mesne profits, and prizes, arrears of rents, received or incurred since these troubles.] [2]

Forasmuch, dread sovereign, as the ways of our address unto

---

[1] In the revised propositions this clause was replaced by ' That an act be passed in the next parliament, for the raising and settling of trained bands within the several counties of that kingdom, as well to prevent foreign invasions as to render them the more serviceable and ready for your majesty's occasions, as causes shall require.'

[2] In the revised propositions this clause is replaced by ' That an act of oblivion be passed in the next free parliament to extend to all your majesty's catholic subjects, and their adherents, for all manner of offences, capital, criminal, and personal, and the said act to extend to all goods, and chattels, customs, mesne profits, prises, arrears of rents taken, received, or incurred since the troubles.

' Forasmuch as your majesty's said catholic subjects have been taxed with many inhumane cruelties which they never committed, your majesty's said supplicants, therefore, for their vindication, and to manifest to all the world their desire to have such heinous offences punished, and the offenders brought to justice, do desire that in the next parliament all notorious murders, breaches of quarter, and inhumane cruelties, committed of either side, may be questioned in the said parliament (if your majesty so think fit), and such as shall appear to be guilty to be excepted out of the act of oblivion, and punished according to their deserts.'

your majesty for apt remedies unto our grievances was hitherto debarred us, but now at length through your benign grace and favour laid open, we therefore, in pursuance of our remonstrance formerly presented, do humbly offer these, which granted, your said subjects will readily contribute the ten thousand men, as in the said remonstrance is specified, towards[1] the suppressing the unnatural rebellion now in this kingdom, and will further expose their lives and fortunes to serve your majesty as occasion shall require.

> J. T. Gilbert, *History of the Irish confederation and the war in Ireland* (1882–91), iii. 128–33.

15. THE PROTESTANTS' DEMANDS, 1644

As soon as it was known that a catholic mission was going to Oxford, a group of protestants secured permission from the lord lieutenant to send over a delegation. It presented its propositions in April 1644.

1. We most humbly desire the establishment of the true protestant religion in Ireland, according to the laws and statutes in the said kingdom now in force.

2. That the popish titular archbishops, bishops, jesuits, friars, and priests, and all others of the Roman clergy be banished out of Ireland, because they have ever been the stirrers up of all rebellion, and while they continue there, there can be no hope of safety for your majesty's protestant subjects ; and that all the laws and statutes established in that kingdom against popery and popish recusants may continue of force, and be put in due execution.

3. That restitution may be made of all our churches and church rights and revenues, and all our churches and chapels re-edified, and put in as good estate as they were at the breaking out of the rebellion, and as they ought to be, at the charge of the confederate Roman catholics (as they call themselves) who have been the occasion of the destruction of the said churches, and possessed themselves of the profits and revenues thereof.

4. That the parliament now sitting in Ireland, may be continued there for the better settlement of the kingdom, and that all persons duly indicted in the said kingdom, of treason, felony, or other heinous crimes, may be duly and legally proceeded against, outlawed, tried, and adjudged according to law, and that all persons lawfully convicted and attainted, or so to be convicted or attainted for the same, may receive due punishment accordingly.

5. That no man may take upon him, or execute the office of a mayor or magistrate in any corporation, or the office of a sheriff, or justice of peace, in any city or county in the said kingdom, until he hath first taken the oaths of supremacy and allegiance.

6. That all popish lawyers who refuse to take the oath of supre-

---

[1] In the revised propositions ' we do humbly present these in pursuance of the said remonstrance, which granted, your said subjects are willing to contribute the 10,000 men (as in their remonstrance is specified) towards.'

macy and allegiance, may be suppressed and restrained from practice in that kingdom, the rather because the lawyers in England do not here practise until they take the oath of supremacy, and it hath been found by woeful experience, that the advice of the popish lawyers to the people of Ireland hath been a great cause of their continued disobedience.

7. That there may be a present absolute suppression and dissolution of all the assumed arbitrary and tyrannical power, which the said confederates exercise over your majesty's subjects, both in causes ecclesiastical and temporal.

8. That all the arms and ammunition of the said confederates, be speedily brought into your majesty's stores.

9. That your majesty's protestant subjects, ruined and destroyed by the said confederates, may be repaired for their great losses, out of the estates of the said confederates, not formerly by any acts of this present parliament in England otherwise disposed of, whereby they may the better be enabled to reinhabit and defend the said kingdom of Ireland.

12. That the said confederates may give satisfaction to the army of the great arrears due unto them since the rebellion, and that such commanders as have raised forces at their own charges, and laid forth great sums of ready money out of their own purses, and engaged themselves for money and provisions, to keep themselves, their holds, and soldiers under their commands, in the due and necessary defence of your majesty's rights and laws, may be in due sort satisfied, to the encouragement of others in like times and cases which may happen.

13. That touching such parts of the confederate estates as being forfeited for their treasons, are come, or shall duly come into your majesty's hands and possession by that title, your majesty, after due satisfaction first made to such as claim by former acts of parliament, would be pleased to take the same into your own hands and possession, and for the necessary increase of your majesty's revenue, and better security of the said kingdom of Ireland, and the protestant subjects living under your gracious government there, to plant the same with British and protestants upon reasonable and honourable terms.

14. That one good walled town may be built and kept repaired in every county of the said kingdom of Ireland and endowed and furnished with necessary and sufficient means of legal and just government and defence, for the better security of your majesty's laws and rights, more especially the true protestant religion, in times of danger, in any of which towns no papist may be permitted to dwell or inhabit.

16. That all your majesty's towns, forts, and places of strength destroyed by the said confederates since the said rebellion, may be by them, and at their charges, re-edified and delivered up into your majesty's hands, to be duly put into the government under your majesty and your laws of good protestants, and that all strengths and

II

fortifications made and set up by the said confederates since the said rebellion, may be slighted and thrown down, or else delivered up and disposed of for protestant government and security, as aforesaid.

20. That the establishment and maintenance of a complete protestant army, and sufficient protestant soldiers and forces, for the time to come, be speedily taken into your majesty's prudent, just and gracious consideration, and such course laid down and continued therein, according to the rules of good government, that your majesty's right and laws, and the protestant religion and peace of that kingdom be no more endangered by the like rebellions in time to come.

21. That whereas it appeareth in print that the said confederates amongst other things aim at the repeal of Poynings' law, thereby to open an easy and ready way for the passing of acts of parliament in Ireland, without having them first well considered of in England, which may produce many dangerous consequences both to that kingdom, and to your majesty's other dominions, your majesty would be pleased to resent and reject all propositions tending to introduce so great a diminution of your royal and necessary power for the confirmation of your royal estate and protection of your good protestant subjects both there and elsewhere.

22. That your majesty, out of your grace and favour to your protestant subjects of Ireland, will be pleased to consider effectually of answering them, that you will not give order for, or allow of the transmitting into Ireland any act of general oblivion, release or discharge of actions or suits whereby your majesty's said protestant subjects there may be barred or deprived of any of their legal remedies which by your majesty's laws and statutes of that kingdom, they may have against the said confederates or any of them, or any of their party, for, or in respect of any wrongs done unto them or any of their ancestors or predecessors, in or concerning their lives, liberties, persons, goods, or estates, since the contriving or breaking forth of the said rebellion.

23. That some fit course may be considered of to prevent the filling or overlaying of the commons house of parliament in Ireland, with popish recusants, being ill affected members, and that provision may be duly made that none shall vote or sit therein, but such as shall first take the oaths of allegiance and supremacy.

Cox, *Hibernia Anglicana* (1689), appendix, pp. 75–8.

THE RESTORATION LAND SETTLEMENT

16. THE ACT OF SETTLEMENT, 1662

After the Commonwealth forces conquered Ireland, the policy of confiscation and plantation initiated by the act of 1641 (document 20) was implemented. By an Act for the settling of Ireland (1652), many protestant and nearly all the catholic landowners, graded according to their guilt in the eyes of parliament, had lost all or a portion of their estates. By the Act for satisfaction (1653), the lands so secured, were divided amongst the soldiers and adventurers.[1] The restoration of 1660 was welcomed by all the Irish parties, each of which could claim that it had at some period supported the royal authority or the British cause. The new government's land policy was embodied in the act of settlement (document 16). This measure was soon found to be unworkable since there was not sufficient land to satisfy all the claims based on it. In consequence it was amended three years later by the Act of explanation (1665). By the provisions of this latter act the various protestant interests lost one third of their claims, while all unheard catholic petitioners were debarred from bringing their cases before the court of claims.[2]

An act for the better execution of his majesty's gracious declaration for the settlement of his kingdom of Ireland, and satisfaction of the several interests of adventurers, soldiers, and other his subjects, there

Whereas an unnatural insurrection did break forth against your majesty's royal father of ever blessed memory, his crown and dignity, in this your majesty's kingdom of Ireland upon the 23 October in the year of our Lord God 1641, and manifest itself by the murder and destructions of many thousands of your said majesty's good and loyal subjects, which afterwards universally spreading and diffusing itself over the whole kingdom, settled into, and became a formed and almost national rebellion of the Irish papists, against your royal father of blessed memory, his crown and dignity, to the destruction of the English and protestants inhabiting in Ireland, the which Irish papists being represented in a general assembly chosen by themselves, and acting by a council called by them, ' The supreme council of the confederate Roman catholics of Ireland,' did first assume, usurp and exercise the power of life and death, make peace and war, levy and coin money, and many other acts of sovereign authority, treating with foreign princes and potentates for their government and protection, and afterwards acted under a foreign authority, by all the said ways disowing and rejecting your royal father, and your majesty's undoubted right to this kingdom, even whilst they treacherously used his and your majesty's names in the outward forms of their proceedings . . . and whereas several of your majesty's subjects, by whom, as instruments, the said rebels were totally subdued, did in the time of your majesty's absence beyond the seas, for supply of the then pressing necessities, and to prevent the further desolation of this your majesty's kingdom, enquire into the authors, contrivers, and abettors of the said rebellion and war, and after much deliberation among themselves . . . did dispossess such of the said popish Irish rebels of their lands, tenements and hereditaments, as they found guilty of, and to have been engaged in, the said rebellion or war aforementioned, and did withal distribute and set out the said lands to be possessed by sundry persons, their agents and tenants,

[1] For the text of these two ordinances see C. H. Firth and R. S. Rait, *Acts and ordinances of the interregum* (1642–60), ii. 598–603, 722–53.
[2] For an account of the land policy of the Commonwealth and the Restoration see R. Dunlop, *Ireland under the Commonwealth* (Manchester 1913), i, preface, and W. F. T. Butler, *Confiscation in Irish history* (London 1918), chapters V and VI.

who by advancing of their monies and goods, or by hazarding of their lives, had contributed into the said conquest, or who had been otherwise useful, as having served or suffered in the suppression of the said rebellion and war ; and whereas several of your majesty's protestant subjects as soon as with much difficulty and hazard they had gotten the power of this kingdom into their hands, did according to their bounden duty, with all humility and cheerfulness, invite your majesty into this your kingdom, . . . and afterwards when your sacred majesty, their sovereign lord and king, by your gracious letters from Breda, bearing date the $\frac{4}{14}$ day of April in the twelfth year of your majesty's reign, intimated your royal intentions of returning to the exercise of your regal authority, they, with others of your majesty's protestant subjects, did readily and dutifully yield up themselves and the said subdued people with this your kingdom of Ireland, unto your majesty's absolute obedience and disposition, who thereupon after many months consideration, and the public hearing of all parties concerned in, and pretending to lands and estates in this your majesty's kingdom ; . . . did . . . set forth a declaration bearing the date the 30 November, in the twelfth year of your majesty's reign, with several explanations and instructions relating thereunto, expressing your royal pleasure concerning the people and territories of this your majesty's said kingdom, declaring it likewise to be your pleasure, that all the particulars in the said declaration mentioned should be effectually recommended unto your majesty's chief governor or governors, privy council and parliament in this kingdom, for the establishing the same, by law. Now we the lords spiritual and temporal, and the commons in this present parliament assembled . . . do most thankfully acknowledge, accept and admire your sacred majesty's wisdom, grace and justice towards all interests in that your majesty's said gracious declaration and instructions expressed. . . . It is therefore enacted . . . that all honours, manors, castles, houses, places, lands, tenements, and hereditaments, right, title, service, chiefry, use, trust, condition, fee, rent-charge, chattels real, mortage, right of redemption of any mortgages, recognizance, judgments, forfeitures, extent, right of action, right of entry, stature or any other estate of what nature or kind soever, in all and every the counties, baronies, cities, towns, corporate and walled towns in this kingdom, which at any time from and after the said 23 October, in the year of our Lord 1641, were seized or sequestered into the hands, or to the use of his late majesty King Charles I, or of your most gracious majesty that now is, or otherwise disposed of, distributed, set out, or set apart, by reason of, or upon account of the said rebellion or war, or which were allotted, assigned, given, granted, ordered, disposed, distributed, demised, set out, or set apart to or for any person or persons, use or uses, for adventures, arrears, reprisals or otherwise, or whereof his late majesty, or your majesty that now is, or any adventurer, soldier, reprisable person, or others respectively had and received the rent, issue or profits, by reason or upon account of the said rebellion or war, or whereof the adventurers, officers or soldiers now or formerly of the English army in this kingdom, or transplanted or transplantable persons, or any of them, or their or any of their heir, heirs or assigns, or any other person or persons whatsoever, upon account of the said rebellion or war, were in seizin, possession or occupation . . . on 7 May 1659, or which were assigned, given, set apart, or reserved for or towards the satisfaction of any the said adventurers, soldiers or other persons for or in consideration of any money or provisions advanced, lent or furnished, or for arrears of pay, or in compensation of any service or reputed services, or other account whatsoever, or reserved or mentioned to be reserved, for or in order to a reprisal or reprisals for such incumbrances as then were, now are, or shall be adjudged due to any person or persons . . . or unto which your royal father, or your majesty that now is, are any ways entitled by reason of, or upon account of the said rebellion or war, or which are wrongfully detained or concealed by any person or persons whatever ; as also all chantries, and all manors, lands, tenements, rents, tithes . . . of any persons or persons, who by the qualifications in this act shall not be adjudged innocent persons, as also all lands, tenements, and hereditaments belonging to any ecclesiastical person or persons, in his or their politic capacity, and that have formerly by them or any of them been let in fee-farm, the right whereof, or title thereunto, or interest therein, was in any person or persons, his or their heirs or assigns, who by the qualifications in this act expressed, shall not be adjudged innocent persons, as also all leases that have been made by any ecclesiastical persons, of any lands, tenements or hereditaments belonging to them in their politic capacity, to any person or persons, their executors, administrators, or assigns, who by the qualifications in this act expressed shall not be adjudged innocent persons, as also all impropriations or appropriate tithes belonging to any person or persons, his or their heirs, executors, administrators or assigns, who by the qualifications in this present act expressed shall not be adjudged innocent, are and shall be, and are hereby declared, deemed and adjudged, as from the said 23 October, 1641, forfeited, and to have been forfeited to your majesty, your heirs and successors ; . . .

IV. Provided likewise, that this act . . . shall not vest . . . in your majesty, your heirs or successors, or otherwise be prejudicial unto or take away any estate, right, title, interest, service, chiefry, use, trust, condition, fee, rent-charge, chattel, real, mortgage, right of redemption of mortgages, recognizance, judgment, forfeiture, extent, right of action, right of entry, stature, or any other estate, of what nature or kind soever, from any protestant or protestants, their heirs, executors, administrators or assigns, who did not join with the said rebels before 15 September, 1643, . . . nor to the vesting any of the lands, tenements, hereditaments, or chattels real, right title, service, chiefry, use, trust, condition, fee, rent-charge, chattel-real, mortgage, right of redemption of mortage, recognizance, judgment, forfeiture, extent, right of action, right of entry, statute, or any other estate, of what nature or kind soever, of any innocent papist, or their innocent heirs, executors, administrators or assigns.

V. And be it further enacted . . . that all and every such person or persons . . . to whom any lands, tenements, or hereditaments belonging unto such protestant or innocent papist have been assigned . . . shall forthwith, and before any other reprisals whatsoever to be set out, be reprized ; . . .

VII. And whereas your sacred majesty hath by your said gracious declaration and instructions declared your royal pleasure and intentions, how the said honours, manors, castles, houses, lands, tenements, and hereditaments, and all other the estates and interests hereby forfeited unto, and vested in your majesty, your heirs, and successors, should be disposed of, and also by commission under your great seal of this your kingdom, bearing date 30 April in the 13th year of your majesty's reign, appointed certain commissioners for putting in execution all the matters and things in the said declaration and instructions contained, be it enacted . . . that all the said honours, manors, lands, castles, houses, tenements, hereditaments, and all other the estates and interests hereby vested and settled in your majesty, your heirs and successors . . . shall be and remain in your most sacred majesty, your heirs and successors, to the intent to be settled, confirmed, restored, or disposed to and for such use and uses, and in such manner, as in and by the said declaration and instructions hereafter following, and by this present act, and true intent and meaning thereof, is declared, limited, meant, intended or appointed.

His Majesty's gracious declaration for the settlement of his kingdom of Ireland, and satisfaction of the several interests of adventurers, soldiers, and other his subjects there.

Charles the second, by the grace of God, King of England, Scotland, France and Ireland, defender of the faith, etc. To all our loving subjects of our kingdom of Ireland, of what degree or quality soever, greeting. It having pleased Almighty God out of His great mercy and compassion towards us, and all our subjects, to restore us in so wonderful a manner to each other, and with so wonderful circumstances of affection and confidence in each other as must for ever fill our hearts (if we are in any degree sensible of such blessings) with an humble and grateful acknowledgment of the obligation we owe to His Divine Providence, that He would vouchsafe to work that miracle for us Himself, which no endeavours of our own could bring to pass. We think it agreeable to the just sense we have, and ought to have of the good affection of all our good subjects, who have contributed so much in bringing this unspeakable blessing upon us and themselves, that we acknowledge that our good subjects in our kingdom of Ireland have born a very good part in procuring this happiness, . . . however it was not easy for us to make any public declaration with reference to that our kingdom, there being many difficulties in the providing for, and complying with the several interests and pretences there, which we were bound in honour and justice in some degree to take care of, and which were different from the difficulties we were to contend within this kingdom ; we well knew the acts of parliament which had formerly past for the security of the adventurers in that kingdom, and had heard of the proceedings which had been thereupon, by which very many officers, soldiers, and others, as well of this, as that our kingdom were in possession of a great part of the lands of that our kingdom, and of whose interests we resolve to be very careful.

II. We well remember the cessation, and the peace which our royal father of blessed memory had been forced, during the late troubles, to make with the Irish subjects of that our kingdom,[1] by which he was compelled to give them a full pardon for what they had before done amiss upon their return to their duties, and their promise of giving his majesty a vigorous assistance, and that from that time divers persons of honour and quality had not (that we know or have heard of) swerved from their allegiance towards him or us. We could not forget the peace that ourself was afterwards necessitated to make with our said subjects,[2] in the time when they who wickedly usurped the authority in this kingdom, had erected that odious court for the taking away of the life of our dear father ; and then no body can wonder that we were desirous, though upon difficult conditions, to get such an united power of our own subjects, as might have been able, with God's blessing, to have prevented that infamous and horrible parricide.

III. And therefore we could not but hold ourself obliged to perform what we owe by that peace, to those who had honestly and faithfully performed what they had promised to us, though we and they were miserably disappointed of the effect of those promises, by an unhappy part of them which foolishly forfeited all the grace which they might have expected from us.

IV. And in the last place, we did and must always remember the great affection a considerable part of that nation expressed to us, during the time of our being beyond the seas, when with all cheerfulness and obedience, they received and submitted to our orders, and betook themselves to that service which we directed as most convenient and behooveful at that time to us, though attended with inconvenience enough to themselves ; . . . and yet all these important considerations and obligations appeared so many contradictions to the present interest of our good subjects in that kingdom, who had at this time likewise merited very much from us, and for whose security and advantage we held ourself obliged to provide as well as for their indemnity, and so the good settlement of that our kingdom appeared much the more difficult unto us, and even lessened and abated much of that joy of heart we found ourself possessed with, for the great blessings we enjoy in the peace and quiet of this our kingdom of England.

[1] Refers to the agreement made between Charles I and the confederates in March 1646.   [2] Refers to the agreement made in January 1649.

V. But we raised our spirits again with the comfortable assurance that God who had wrought so much for us in England would graciously bring His work to the same perfection in Ireland, and not suffer our good subjects to weep in the one kingdom, whilest they rejoiced in the other, and our satisfaction was much increased when upon conference with several of our good subjects of that nation of quality and interest, who were concerned both as soldiers and adventurers, we found that they had a due sense of the obligations which lay upon our honour and justice; and were very willing, that we should comply with both, . . .

VI. And therefore in the first place, in order to a settlement of that interest claimed by the adventurers, although the present estates and possessions they enjoy, if they were examined by the strict letter of the law, would prove very defective and invalid, as being no ways pursuant to those acts of parliament upon which they pretend to be founded, but rather seem to be a structure upon their subsequent assent, both to different mediums and ends than the observance of those, yet we being always more ready to consult (where the prejudice can only reflect upon ourself) with our natural inclinations to mercy (we praise God we can say so) than with the positive reason of law, we do hereby declare, that all the lands, tenements and hereditaments, of which all or any of the adventurers were possessed [on] 7 May 1659 having been allotted or set out to them or enjoyed by them as adventurers in satisfaction of and for their adventures, shall be confirmed and made good to them, their heirs and assigns for ever, with allowance or correction of the admeasurement, according to the tenor and directions of the respective acts of parliament of 17 and 18 Caroli, as to English or plantation measure, except as is hereafter excepted; and that the deficient adventurer, either in part or in whole, shall be satisfied out of the moiety of the counties of Limerick, Tipperary, and Waterford, in the province of Munster, the King's county, the Queen's county, and the counties of East-Meath and West-Meath, in the province of Leinster, and the counties of Down, Antrim, and Armagh, in the province of Ulster, yet not set out to the said adventurers, as also the forfeited lands in the county of Louth, (except the barony of Atherdee in the said county) and said province of Leinster ; . . .

VII. And whereas the officers and soldiers now of our army in Ireland, and that have been formerly of the army in Ireland, have had also lands set out to them respectively in satisfaction of their arrears of pay for their service in that our kingdom, and are accordingly possessed of the same by former pretended orders and powers then in being ; and although the incompetency of such powers may justly render such possessions and estates liable to question, . . . yet in regard to our letter to General Monk from Breda, in the twelfth year of our reign, and of our several declarations and proclamations concerning the army, and of the full assurance of the forwardness and readiness of the said army and loving subjects in Ireland to contribute, as in duty bound, all that in them lay for our restoration, we are pleased of our special grace and favour to declare, and do hereby declare, that all officers and soldiers, their heirs and assigns, who have been, and are of the said army in Ireland, and to whom lands have been given out in satisfaction of their arrears for their service in that our kingdom, and have by the general convention of Ireland, or by any other public act declared submission and obedience to us . . . shall enjoy their respective estates. . . .

IX. Being sensible, that several officers, who were engaged in our service in Ireland, and eminently acted and suffered therein, have by the partiality and injustice of the powers then in being received no satisfaction for the same, we are therefore further pleased graciously to declare, that all commissioned officers, their heirs or assigns, who . . . served our royal father or ourself in the wars in Ireland, at any time before 5 June 1649, other than those who have received lands or money, for their pay due unto them since the 5 June 1649 shall be satisfied their respective personal arrears out of the particulars following, viz. out of the forfeited lands, tenements, and hereditaments, undisposed of to adventurers or soldiers, in the counties of Wicklow, Longford, Leitrim, and Donegal, out of all the forfeited lands tenements and hereditaments, undisposed of in the province of Connaught and county of Clare, lying within one mile of the river Shannon or of the sea, commonly called the Mile line, out of all the houses and tenements, forfeited in Ireland, in the several walled towns and corporations, and lands thereunto belonging, not already set out to the adventurers or soldiers . . . out of the benefit arising from the redemption of mortgages, statutes-staples, and judgments, where the lands are not already disposed of to adventurers or soldiers, . . . out of one year's rent and profits of the lands set out to the officers and soldiers for their arrears in the year 1653, and likewise of the army now in being, . . . as also out of one year and a half's rent, and profits arising out of the lands for the arrears of those officers and soldiers who were ordered, or received satisfaction for their said arrears, in the years 1655, 1656, and 1657, . . .

XI. That such protestants, whose estates have been given out for satisfaction of adventurers or soldiers, or otherwise disposed of to any other persons, shall be forthwith restored to their former estates, and a reprisal of equal value, worth, and purchase forthwith assigned to such adventurers or soldiers, as shall be removed out of their said estates.

XII. Provided no person or persons shall have benefit hereof, who were in the rebellion before 15 September 1643, and have taken out decrees for lands in the province of Connaught or county of Clare in recompence of their former estates ; . . .

XVI. And whereas we understand, that by the late usurped powers, during the distempers, of these times, several Irish proprietors of the popish religion, have been dispossessed of their estates merely for being papists, and have sued out decrees, and are possessed of lands in the province of Connaught, and county of Clare, in compensation of their former estates, . . . we declare, that all innocent papists, being such as shall prove themselves to have been faithful and loyal unto, and never acted against our royal father or ourself since 22 October, 1641, though they have sued out decrees, and are possessed of lands in the province of Connaught, or county of Clare, in lieu of their former estates, shall notwithstanding be restored to their said estates by 2 May 1661. . . .

XVII. Provided also, that whatsoever adventurer or soldier that shall be removed from his present possession, to make room for any such papist, shall forthwith have a reprise of equal value . . . in other forfeited lands.

XVIII. Provided always, that whereas the corporations of Ireland are now planted with English, who have considerably improved at their own charges, and brought trade and manufacture into that our kingdom and by their settlement there do not a little contribute to the peace and settlement of that country, the disturbing or removal of which English would in many respects be very prejudicial, that all such of the popish religion, of any corporations in Ireland, who have been for public security dispossessed of their estates within any corporation, shall be forthwith reprised in forfeited lands, tenements and hereditaments, near the said corporations, . . .

XXII. And as we cannot but with extraordinary sadness of heart remember, and even at present behold the desolate and distracted condition that our kingdom of Ireland hath been, and is reduced unto, by the unnatural insurrection begun in the year 1641, and consequently abhor and detest the contrivers and obstinate promotors of the same against us, our crown and dignity, so we cannot, upon the considerations formerly expressed in this our declaration, deny all just and reasonable provision that may stand with the present juncture of our affairs into such of the Irish nation, who not only gave early evidences of their repentance for their crimes, but also persevered in their loyalty to us and our commands, and that as near as we can, our justice and our mercy, in accommodating this interest might not jostle each other, we are in a different manner to consider of such of them as are justly entitled to the benefit of those articles of peace formerly mentioned, and such who did not submit unto the same, or after a submission made a departure from the same, which two latter sorts have justly forfeited that favour which otherwise they might have received. We are also further to consider of those who embraced the said articles, and submitted to the said peace without any apostasy, in a different notion, as of those who remained in that our kingdom, who sued out decrees and received lands in satisfaction of their ancient estates, and those who being transported into foreign parts, through many difficulties united, rendevouzed, and served under our obedience ; so that upon these consideration, we think fit and declare . . . that as to those who embraced the said articles, and submitted to the said peace and constantly adhered thereunto, and remaining at home sued out decrees and obtained possession of lands in the province of Connaught, or county of Clare, that they are to stand bound by them, and not to be relieved against their own act, . . . and yet if the conditions of those seem hard, they can no more reasonably expect that we should further relieve them, than our friends in England and Ireland can expect we should pay back to them all the moneys they were compelled in the evil times to pay for their compositions which they would have avoided had it been in their power.

XXIII. And in case any justly entitled to the said peace, have obtained decrees for the lands in the province of Connaught or county of Clare, in lieu of their estates, and have not been possessed of lands according to such their respective decrees, we further declare, that if by 1 November 1661 they shall not be possessed of such decreed lands, they shall immediately after the said day be otherwise satisfied for the same.

XXIV. And as for those who continued with us, or served faithfully under our ensigns beyond the seas, we think fit and accordingly declare, that they shall be restored to their former estates, if they . . . have not prosecuted and obtained decrees and lands in the province of Connaught or county of Clare, in compensation of their former estates, a reprise being first assigned and legally set out of the remaining forfeited lands undisposed of, to such adventurer or soldier, or other person before named, of equal value . . . to the estate, out of which such adventurer or soldier or other person aforesaid shall be so removed, . . .

XXVIII. And though some, not sensible of the great perplexities we have laboured under to reconcile these jarring interests, may infer that we judge persons fitting to be restored to their estates, yet the limitation of a previous reprisal may eclipse much of our grace, to this we say, that the laying of the foundations is not now before us, when we might design the model of the structure answerable to our own thoughts ; and how hard it would be, that the English after so many expensive difficulties in suits of law, and finding several officers in order to get the present possession they enjoy, and that after so many thousands of families, who have sold their interests in England, have transported and settled themselves in Ireland, and have made great improvements in buildings and otherwise, should in the interval of those accommodations (reprisal not being first provided for) be dispossessed of their houses and their flocks (the sole subsistence of them and their families) exposed to certainty of loss (though greater inconveniences we pretermit) may easily be judged ; to this we might add, that since the persons of the Irish for whom we do hereby intend satisfaction, are such who have been abroad with us, who probably being not furnished with stock and other provisions, may with less inconveniences wait for a reprisal, than to dispossess others, especially since we are fully assured that a very short time may and will assign them their respective reprisals, there being so good and large a proportion of undisposed forfeited lands in our power reserved for this purpose, and we doubt not but the persons most concerned in this supposed prejudice, thoroughly weighing these inconveniences, and that they will be but of a short duration, and how great and reasonable a dissatisfaction a contrary acting in us will produce, will acquiesce therein, and by such a forbearance lay the foundation of a good understanding between themselves and those other their fellow-subjects who are to be settled with them in that our kingdom. And least any ambiguity or controversy might arise for precedency in restitution to their former rights, we do declare, that first all innocent protestants, and those persons termed innocent papists (who never took out any decree, or had lands assigned to them in Connaught or Clare) be first restored. In the next place, that those innocent protestants and papists, who took out decrees, and had lands allotted to them in pursuance thereof, in Connaught or Clare, shall be restored, and that such transplanted persons as shall be dispossessed of their decreed estates in Connaught or Clare, by virtue of this our declaration, shall be reprised out of other forfeited lands of equal value, worth, and purchase . . . before they be dispossessed of their said estates, and that then such of the Irish papists who constantly served under our ensigns abroad, having right to the articles of peace, are to be restored, . . .

[Clause XI of the Instructions] Whereas by our said declaration, several innocent protestants and papists are to be restored to their estates, and a reprise of equal value, worth, and purchase, is to be assigned to such adventurers and soldiers, and other persons as do possess the same, in the doing thereof, you are to observe these following directions, viz. Not to restore any as an innocent papist, that at, or before the cessation which was made upon 15 September 1643 were of the rebels' party, nor any, who being of full age and sound memory, enjoyed their estates real or personal in the rebels quarters, . . . nor such as entered into the Roman catholic confederacy, at any time before the articles of peace concluded 1648, nor such as at any time adhered to the nuncio's or clergy's party, or papal power, in opposition to the king's authority ; nor such as have been excommunicated for adhering to the king's authority, and afterwards owned their offences for so doing, and were relaxed thereupon from their excommunication, nor such who derived their titles to their estates from any who died guilty of any the aforementioned crimes, nor such as pleaded the articles of peace for their estates, nor such as being in the quarters which were under the authority of our royal father, or ourself, held correspondence with, or gave intelligence to such as were then in opposition against our said royal father, or ourself, in Ireland, nor such as before any of the peaces in 1646 or 1648, sat in any of the confederate Roman catholic assemblies or councils, or acted upon any commissions or powers derived from them, or any of them ; nor such as empowered agents or commissioners to treat with any foreign papal power beyond the seas, for bringing into Ireland foreign forces, or were persons which acted in such negociations, nor such persons as have been wood-kerns or tories, before the marquess of Clanrickarde's leaving the government of that kingdom.

Ir. Stat., ii. 239–348.

THE IRISH PARLIAMENT OF JAMES II

17. THE DECLARATORY ACT, 1689

James II summoned a parliament the day after his arrival in Dublin. It met on 7 May and sat until 20 July. Its legislation included a declaratory act (document 17), a navigation act, the repeal of the acts of settlement and explanation, and a measure which would have transferred a considerable proportion of the tithes from the protestant to the catholic clergy.

An act declaring, that the parliament of England cannot bind Ireland [and] against writs of error and appeals, to be brought for removing judgments, decrees and sentences given in Ireland, into England

Whereas his majesty's realm of Ireland is, and hath been always a distinct kingdom from that of his majesty's realm of England, always governed by his majesty and his predecessors, according to the ancient customs, laws and statutes thereof, and as the people of this kingdom did never send members to any parliament ever held in England, but had their laws continually made and established by their own parliaments, so no acts passed in any parliament held in England were ever binding here, excepting such of them as by acts of parliament passed in this kingdom were made into laws here, yet of late times (especially in the times of distractions) some have pretended, that acts of parliament passed in England, mentioning Ireland, were binding in Ireland ; and as these late opinions are against justice and natural equity, and so they tend to the great oppression of the people here, and to the overthrow of the fundamental constitutions of this realm, and to the end, that by these modern and late opinions no person may be further deluded, be it therefore enacted . . . that no act of parliament passed, or to be passed in the parliament of England, though Ireland should be therein mentioned, can be, or shall be any way binding in Ireland ; excepting such acts passed, or to be passed in England, as are or shall be made into law by the parliament of Ireland. And whereas several writs of error were formerly sued out and returnable into the king's bench in England, in order to reverse judgments given in his majesty's court of king's bench in Ireland, and whereas most of the said writs of error have been brought for delay, and thereby many of his majesty's subjects of this realm were greatly hindered from recovering their just rights, and put to vast charges in attending such suits in England, for the prevention whereof, be it hereby enacted by the authority aforesaid, that no writ of error shall be hereafter brought out of England, in order to remove any record, or transcript of record, out of his majesty's court of king's bench in Ireland, or out of any other court of record here into England, in order to reverse any such judgments, But in regard judgments to be given in his majesty's court of king's bench in Ireland may happen sometimes to be erroneous, be it enacted . . . that where any judgment shall at any time hereafter be given in the said court of king's bench in Ireland, in any suit or action of debt, detinue, covenant, account, action upon the case, *ejectione firmae*, or trespass, first commenced, or to be first commenced there, other than where the king's majesty shall be party, plaintiff or defendant or other person or persons against whom any such judgment shall be given may at his election sue forth out of the high court of chancery in Ireland, a special writ of error to be devised in the said court of chancery, directed to the chief justice of the said court of king's bench in Ireland for the time being, commanding him to cause the said record, and all things concerning the said judgments, to be brought before the justices of the common pleas, and barons of the exchequer here, into the exchequer chamber in Ireland, there to be examined by the said justices of the common pleas and barons of the exchequer. Which said justices of the common pleas and barons of the exchequer, or any four or more of them by virtue of this present act, shall thereupon have full power and authority to examine all such errors as shall be assigned or found in or upon any such judgment as the law shall require . . . And, that any one or more of the said justices and barons, in the absence of the rest, shall have power to adjourn the said court, and continue the proceedings of the said writ of error from time to time ; and that after the said judgment shall be affirmed or reversed, the said record, and all things concerning the same, shall be removed and brought back into the said court of king's bench, that such further proceedings may be thereupon, as well for execution as otherwise, as shall appertain. And be it further enacted . . . that such reversal or affirmation of any such former judgment shall not be so final, but that the party who findeth himself grieved therewith, shall and may sue in the high court of parliament in Ireland, for the further and due examination of the said judgment, anything herein contained to the contrary notwithstanding. . . .

And whereas of late times several persons have brought appeals before the house of lords in England, in order to reverse decrees granted in the high court of chancery in Ireland, which tend to the great trouble, charge and vexation of such of his majesty's subjects as have obtained such decrees, and is an apparent new encroachment upon the fundamental constitutions of this realm, and also appeal before delegates in England, be it further enacted . . . that no person or persons whatsoever, do hereafter presume to sue out any such appeals, or to tender or produce any such appeal to the lord chancellor, or lord keeper of Ireland, or to any of the officers of the said court of chancery, and that such appeals shall be void, and that no appeal whatsoever (to reverse any decree or sentence passed, or to be passed in Ireland) shall be brought into England either before the house of lords there, or any commissioner or delegates of appeal, and, that all such appeals shall be disallowed. And for rendering this present act the more effectual, be it hereby enacted . . . that it shall be a high misdemeanour in any person or persons whatsoever, that shall in drawing of pleadings either in law or equity, or in any bill of exception to be filed in any court of Ireland, or that at any trial, before any court within this realm, shall deliberately insist, that any act of parliament made, or to be made, in England, wherein Ireland is or shall be mentioned, is or can be binding in Ireland, though it should not be made into a law here by any act made or to be made, in a parliament held or to be held here. And also, it shall be a high misdemeanour in any person or persons whatsoever, who within this realm shall tender or produce any writ or writs of error out of England in his majesty's court of king's bench in Ireland, or to all or any of the judges of the said court for the time being, returnable to the court of king's bench in England, or that shall tender or produce any appeal to the lord chancellor or lord keeper of Ireland for the time being, or to any of the officers of the said court of chancery, or to the chancellor, treasurer and barons of the exchequer, from the house of lords in England, or that shall tender any appeal out of England to any spiritual judge or spiritual court, or delegates within this realm, in order to reverse any sentence given in Ireland, by any court of delegates in England. And, that if any person or persons shall offend herein, he shall be fined and imprisoned, according to the discretion of the court where he shall be prosecuted for the same.

A list of the names of the nobility, gentry and commonalty of England and Ireland . . . who are by an act of a pretended parliament . . . attainted . . . together with the true and authentic copies of the acts of the said pretended parliament . . . (London, 1690), pp. 5–8.

THE TREATY OF LIMERICK

On 3 October 1691 two treaties were signed at Limerick. The military one made arrangements for transporting to the continent those who wished to leave Ireland. The civil one is given below. In 1697 an act (9 William III c. 2) of the Irish parliament ratified ' so much ' of the articles, ' as may consist with the safety and welfare of your majesty's subjects of this kingdom.'

18. THE CIVIL ARTICLES OF LIMERICK, 1691

Articles agreed upon the third day of October 1691 between the Right Honourable Sir Charles Porter knight and Thomas Conningsby Esq., lords justices of Ireland, and his excellency the Baron De Ginckle, lieutenant-general, and commander-in-chief of the English army, on the one part, and the Right Honourable Patrick earl of Lucan, Piercy Viscount Gallmoy, Colonel Nicholas Purcel, Colonel Nicholas Cusack, Sir Toby Butler, Colonel Garret Dillon, and Colonel John Brown, on the other part, in the behalf of the Irish inhabitants in the city and county of Limerick, the counties of Clare, Kerry, Cork, Sligo, and Mayo.

In consideration of the surrender of the city of Limerick and other agreements made between the said Lieutenant-General Ginckle, the governor of the city of Limerick, and the generals of the Irish army, bearing date with these presents, for the surrender of the said city, and submission of the said army, it is agreed, that :

1. The Roman catholics of this kingdom, shall enjoy such privileges in the exercise of their religion, as are consistent with the laws of Ireland, or as they did enjoy in the reign of King Charles II, and their majesties, as soon as their affairs will permit them to summon a parliament in this kingdom, will endeavour to procure the said Roman catholics such farther security in that particular, as may preserve them from any disturbance upon the account of their said religion.

2. All the inhabitants or residents of Limerick, or any other garrison now in the possession of the Irish, and all officers and soldiers, now in arms, under any commission of King James, or those authorized by him to grant the same in the several counties of Limerick, Clare, Kerry, Cork, and Mayo, or any of them, and all the commissioned officers in their majesties' quarters, that belong to the Irish regiments, now in being, that are treated with, and who are not prisoners of war or have taken protection, and who shall return and submit to their majesties' obedience, and their and every of their heirs, shall hold, possess and enjoy all and every their estates of free-hold, and inheritance, and all the rights, titles, and interests, privileges and immunities, which they, and every, or any of them held, enjoyed, or were rightfully and lawfully entitled to in the reign of King Charles II, or at any time since, by the laws and statutes that were in force in the said reign of King Charles II, and shall be put in possession, by order of the government, of such of them as are in the king's hands or the hands of his tenants, without being put to any suit or trouble therein ; and all such estates shall be freed and discharged from all arrears of crown-rents, quit-rents, and other public charges incurred and become due since Michaelmas 1688, to the day of the date hereof. And all persons comprehended in this article, shall have, hold, and enjoy all their goods and chattels, real and personal, to them, or any of them belonging, and remaining either in their own hands, or the hands of any persons whatsoever, in trust for or for the use of them, or any of them ; and all, and every the said persons, of what profession, trade, or calling soever they be, shall and may use, exercise and practise their several and respective professions, trades and callings, as freely as they did use, exercise and enjoy the same in the reign of King Charles II, provided, that nothing in this article contained, be construed to extend to or restore any forfeiting person now out of the kingdom, except what are hereafter comprised. Provided also, that no person whatsoever shall have or

enjoy the benefit of this article, that shall neglect or refuse to take the oath of allegiance made by act of parliament in England, in the first year of the reign of their present majesties, when thereunto required.[1]

3. All merchants, or reputed merchants of the city of Limerick, or of any other garrison, now possessed by the Irish, or of any town or place in the counties of Clare, or Kerry, who are absent beyond the seas, that have not bore arms since their majesties' declaration in February 1688, shall have the benefit of the second article, in the same manner as if they were present, provided such merchants, and reputed merchants, do repair into this kingdom within the space of eight months from the date hereof.[2]

4. The following officers, viz. Colonel Simon Lutterel, Captain Rowland White, Maurice Eustace of Yermanstown, Chievers of Maystown, commonly called Mount-Leinster, now belonging to the regiments in the aforesaid garrisons and quarters of the Irish army, who were beyond the seas, and sent thither upon affairs of their respective regiments, or the army in general, shall have the benefit and advantage of the second article, provided they return hither within the space of eight months from the date of these presents, and submit to their majesties' government, and take the above-mentioned oath.[3]

5. That all and singular, the said persons comprised in the second and third articles, shall have a general pardon of all attainders, outlawries, treasons, misprisions of treason, praemunires, felonies, trespasses, and other crimes and misdemeanours whatsoever, by them or any of them committed since the beginning of the reign of King James II ; and if any of them are attainted by parliament, the lords justices and general, will use their best endeavours to get the same repealed by parliament, and the outlawries to be reversed gratis, all but writing-clerks' fees.[4]

6. And whereas these present wars have drawn on great violences on both parts, and that if leave were given to the bringing all sorts of private actions, the animosities would probably continue, that have been too long on foot, and the public disturbances last ; for the quieting and settling therefore of this kingdom, and avoiding those inconveniences which would be the necessary consequence of the contrary, no person or persons whatsoever, comprised in the foregoing articles, shall be sued, molested, or impleaded at the suit of any party or parties whatsoever, for any trespasses by them committed, or for any arms, horses, money, goods, chattels, merchandises, or provisions whatsoever, by them seized or taken, during the time of the war. And no person or persons whatsoever, in the second or third articles comprised, shall be sued, impleaded, or made accountable for the rents or mean rates of any lands, tenements, or houses

---

[1] This article was in the main confirmed by 9 William III c. 2. But it should be noticed that the phrase dealing with the right to exercise professions and trades is not referred to in the act.

[2] Confirmed by 9 William III c. 2.   [3] *Ibid*.   [4] *Ibid*.

12

by him or them received or enjoyed in this kingdom, since the beginning of the present war, to the day of the date hereof, nor for any waste or trespass by him or them committed in any such lands, tenements, or houses ; and it is also agreed, that this article shall be mutual, and reciprocal, on both sides.[1]

7. Every nobleman and gentleman, comprised in the said second and third article, shall have liberty to ride with a sword, and case of pistols, if they think fit, and keep a gun in their houses, for the defence of the same or for fowling.

8. The inhabitants and residents in the city of Limerick, and other garrisons, shall be permitted to remove their goods, chattels, and provisions, out of the same, without being viewed and searched, or paying any manner of duties, and shall not be compelled to leave the houses or lodgings they now have, for the space of six weeks next ensuing the date hereof.

9. The oath to be administered to such Roman catholics as submit to their majesties' government, shall be the oath abovesaid, and no other.

10. No person or persons, who shall at any time hereafter break these articles, or any of them, shall thereby make, or cause any other person or persons to forfeit or lose the benefit of the same.

11. The lords justices and general do promise to use their utmost endeavours, that all the persons comprehended in the above-mentioned articles, shall be protected and defended from all arrests and executions for debt or damage, for the space of eight months, next ensuing the date hereof.

12. Lastly, the lords justices and general do undertake, that their majesties will ratify these articles within the space of eight months, or sooner, and use their utmost endeavours, that the same shall be ratified and confirmed in parliament.

13. And whereas Colonel John Brown stood indebted to several protestants, by judgments of record, which appearing to the late government, the Lord Tyrconnel, and Lord Lucan, took away the effects the said John Brown had to answer the said debts, and promised to clear the said John Brown of the said debts, which effects were taken for the public use of the Irish and their army, for freeing the said Lord Lucan of his said engagement, passed on their public account, for payment of the said protestants, and for preventing the ruin of the said John Brown and for satisfaction of his creditors, at the instance of the Lord Lucan, and the rest of the persons aforesaid, it is agreed, that the said lords justices, and the said baron de Ginckle, shall intercede with the king and parliament, to have the estates secured to Roman catholics, by articles and capitulation in this kingdom, charged with, and equally liable to the payment of so much of the said debts, as the said Lord Lucan, upon stating accounts with the said John Brown, shall certify under his hand, that the effects taken from the said Brown

[1] Confirmed by 9 Will. III c. 2.

amount unto ; which account is to be, stated, and the balance certified by the said Lord Lucan in one and twenty days after the date hereof :

For the true performance hereof, we have hereunto set our hands, Char. Porter, Tho. Coningsby, Bar. De Ginckle. Present, Scravenmore, H. Maccay, T. Talmash.

And whereas the said city of Limerick hath been since, in pursuance of the said articles, surrendered unto us. Now know ye, that we having considered of the said articles are graciously pleased hereby to declare, that we do for us, our heirs and successors, as far as in us lies, ratify and confirm the same, and every clause, matter and thing therein contained. And as to such parts thereof, for which an act of parliament shall be found to be necessary, we shall recommend the same to be made good by parliament, and shall give our royal assent to any bill or bills that shall be passed by our two houses of parliament to that purpose. And whereas it appears unto us, that it was agreed between the parties to the said articles, that after the words, ' Limerick, Clare, Kerry, Cork, Mayo,' or any of them in the second of such articles, the words following ; viz. ' And all such as are under their protection in the said counties,' should be inserted, and be part of the said articles. Which words having been casually omitted by the writer, the omission was not discovered till after the said articles were signed, but was taken notice of before the second town was surrendered ; and that our said justices, and general or one of them, did promise that the said clause should be made good, it being within the intention of the capitulation, and inserted in the foul draught thereof. Our further will and pleasure is, and we do hereby ratify and confirm the said omitted words, viz. ' and all such as are under their protection in the said counties ' hereby for us, our heirs and successors, ordaining and declaring, that all and every person and persons therein concerned, shall and may have, receive, and enjoy the benefit thereof, in such and the same manner, as if the said words had been inserted in their proper place, in the said second article, any omission, defect, or mistake in the said second article, in any wise notwithstanding.[1] Provided always, and our will and pleasure is, that these our letters patents shall be enrolled in our court of chancery in our said kingdom of Ireland, within the space of one year next ensuing. In witness, etc. Witness Ourself at Westminster, the twenty-fourth day of February, Anno Regni Regis and Reginae Guilielmi and Mariae Quarto per breve de privato sigillo. . . .

The civil articles of Limerick exactly printed from the letters patent (Dublin, 1692).

---

[1] In the parliamentary ratification of the treaty the royal intention to restore the omitted words is ignored.

THE ENGLISH PARLIAMENT AND IRELAND

19. APPOINTMENT OF A COMMITTEE OF BOTH HOUSES FOR IRISH AFFAIRS, 1641

On the 1 November 1641 the two houses set up the first of several joint committees through which they attempted to handle Irish affairs during the period 1641–9.

Die Lunae, primo Novembris, 1641

Memorandum. This day the lord keeper, lord privy seal, lord high chamberlain, earl marshal, lord admiral, lord chamberlain, earl of Bath, earl of Dorset, earl of Leicester, earl of Warwick, earl of Holland, earl of Berks, earl of Bristol, Lord Viscount Say and Seale, Lord Mandevile, Lord Goring, Lord Wilmot, all lords of his majesty's most honourable privy council, came into this house, and informed it of certain intelligences, that were lately come, of a great treason, and a general rebellion, of the Irish papists in Ireland, and a design of cutting off all the protestants in Ireland ; and seizing all the king's forts there.

The letters and examinations, that express the nature of these treasons, and the manner of the discovery, were all read publicly here, by the clerk, in the presence of the lords of the council, who had chairs set them purposely, and, after they had been here a little while, Mr. Speaker desired them to sit, and be covered.

Ordered, that the house be forthwith resolved into a committee, to take into consideration the matter this day offered, concerning the rebellion in Ireland, and likewise, to provide for the safety of both kingdoms. . . .

Sir John Clotworthy is appointed to go to the lords, to desire a conference, by a committee of both houses, so soon as may stand with their lordships' occasions, concerning the troubles now risen in Ireland.

Mr. Whitlock reports from the grand committee, the heads resolved by the committee to be the heads of the conference desired with the lords.

The heads were particularly put to the question, and assented unto, to be heads of the conference, as followeth :

Resolved, upon the question, that fifty thousand pounds shall be forthwith provided.

Resolved, upon the question, that a conference be desired with the lords, to move them, that a select committee of the members of both houses may be appointed to go to the city of London, and make a declaration unto them of the state of the business in Ireland, and to acquaint them, that the lending of monies at this time will be an acceptable service to the commonwealth, and that they propose unto them the loan of fifty thousand pounds, and to assure them that they shall be secured, both for the principal and interest, by act of parliament.

Resolved, upon the question, that another head of this conference shall be, to desire the lords, that a select committee may be named of both houses, to consider of the affairs of Ireland, and of the raising and sending of men and ammunition from hence into Ireland, and of the repairing of the lord lieutenant of Ireland thither, and of a declaration of both houses of parliament, to be sent into Ireland, and that this committee may have power to open such packets as come out of Ireland, or go from hence thither.

Resolved, upon the question, that Owen Connelles, who discovered this great treason in Ireland, shall have five hundred pounds presently paid to him, and two hundred pounds per annum pension, until provision be made of inheritance of a greater value, and to be recommended to the lord lieutenant general of Ireland, for some preferment there.

Resolved, upon the question, to desire the lords, that a committee of their house may be nominated, to take the further examination of Owen Connelles [Connelly], upon oath, upon such interrogatories as shall be offered unto them by a committee of this house, and in the presence of that committee.

Resolved, upon the question, that the custody of the Isle of Wight, for the present, may be sequestered into another hand.

Resolved, upon the question, that the persons of papists of quality, in the several counties of this kingdom where they reside, may be secured ; and that such English papists as have, within one year last past, removed themselves into Ireland, except the Lord of St. Albans, and such other persons as have an ancient estate and habitation there, may, by proclamation, be commanded to return hither, within one month after the proclamation there published, or else some course be taken, by act of parliament, for confiscation of their estates.

Commons journ., ii. 300.

20. AN ACT FOR THE REDUCTION OF THE REBELS, 1642

During the first few months of the rebellion parliament found it hard to raise funds for the war. On 11 February 1642 ' divers worthy and well affected persons ' offered to raise a war loan on the security of Irish land. Their offer was accepted, and the act incorporating it received the royal assent 24 February. This act was amended in minor detail by three further acts passed in the following three months.

An act for the speedy and effectual reducing of the rebels in his majesty's kingdom of Ireland to their due obedience to his majesty and the crown of England

Whereas the lords and commons taking into their serious considerations as well the necessity of a speedy reducing of the rebels of Ireland to their due obedience as also the great sums of money that the commons of this realm have of late paid for the public and necessary affairs of this kingdom, whereof the lords and commons are very sensible, and desirous to embrace all good and honourable ways tending to his majesty's greatness and profit, the settling of that realm and the ease of his majesty's subjects of England, and whereas diverse worthy and well affected persons perceiving that many millions of acres of the rebels' lands of that kingdom which go under the name of profitable lands, will be confiscate and to be disposed of, and that in case two millions and an half of those acres, to be equally taken out of the four provinces of that kingdom, may be allotted for the satisfaction of such persons as shall disburse any sums of money for the reducing of the rebels there, [it] would effectually accomplish the same, have made these propositions ensuing :

1. That two millions and a half of those acres may be assigned allotted and divided amongst them after this proportion, viz. for each adventure of two hundred pounds one thousand acres in Ulster, for three hundred pounds one thousand acres in Connaught, for four hundred and fifty pounds one thousand acres in Munster, for six hundred pounds one thousand acres in Leinster. All according to the English measure and consisting of meadow, arable and profitable pasture the bogs woods and barren mountains being cast in over and above these two millions and a half of acres, to be holden in free and common socage of the king as of his castle of Dublin.

2. That out of these two millions and a half of acres a constant yearly rent shall be reserved to the crown of England after this proportion, viz. out of each acre thereof in Ulster one penny, out of each acre in Connaught three half pence, out of each acre in Munster two pence farthing, and out of each acre in Leinster three pence, whereby his majesty's revenues out of those lands will be much improved, besides the advantages that he will have by the coming to his hands of all other the lands of the rebels and their personal estates without any charge unto his majesty.

3. That for the erecting of manors, settling of wastes and commons, maintaining of preaching ministers, creating of corporations and regulating of the several plantations, one or more commissions be hereafter granted by authority of parliament.

4. That moneys for this great occasion may be the more speedily advanced all the undertakers in the city of London and within twenty miles distant thereof shall underwrite their several sums before the twentieth day of March 1641 and all within sixty miles of London before the first day of April 1642 and the rest of the kingdom before the first day of May 1642.

5. That the several sums to be underwritten shall be paid in at four payments, viz. one fourth part within ten days after such underwriting and the other three parts at three months and three months, all to be paid into the chamber of London. . . .

And whereas as well our sovereign lord the king as the lords and commons have approved of the said propositions . . . be it therefore enacted . . . that all and every of the said propositions and every clause therein contained are and shall be according to the tenor and purport thereof hereby ratified established and confirmed with such explanations alterations and additions as in this act are expressed.

II. And be it further enacted that all and every person and persons which upon the three and twentieth day of October in the year 1641 or at any time after shall be in rebellion or levy war against the king's majesty within his realm of Ireland, or shall willingly aid, assist, or countenance any person or persons in rebellion against the king's majesty, shall lose and forfeit unto the king's majesty, his heirs and successors, all such right, title, interest, use, and possession which they or any of them, or any other person or persons in trust for them, or any of them, on the said three and twentieth day of October or at any time after shall have of in or unto any honours, castles, manors, messuages, lands, tenements, rents, annuities, reversions, remainders, uses, possessions, offices, rights, conditions, or any other hereditaments, of what name nature or quality soever they be, and that all such right, title, interest, use, and possession, which they or any of them, or any other person or persons in trust for them, or any of them, on the said three and twentieth day of October or at any time after shall have, or of right ought to have, of, in, or to the same honours, castles, manors, messuages, rents, annuities, reversions, remainders, uses, possessions, offices, rights, conditions, or any other hereditaments, shall by the authority aforesaid, be deemed vested, adjudged, and taken to be in the actual and real possesion of our sovereign lord the king, his heirs and successors, without any office or inquisition thereof. . . .

IV. And be it further enacted that John Warner, John Towse and Thomas Andrewes aldermen and Lawrence Halsted Esquire are and shall be hereby appointed and authorized to give their daily attendance at the said chamber of London to receive all such subscriptions and sums of money and to give receipts for the same. . . . .

Stat. of realm, v. 168–72.

21. THE CATTLE ACT, 1666

In 1663 an act was passed laying prohibitive duties on the importation of Irish cattle into England between 1 July and 20 December. In 1665 a bill completely forbidding importation was passed by the commons and rejected by the lords. In the following year this measure was enacted (document 21). The phrase ' public and common nuisance ' was introduced as a bar to the use of the royal dispensing power.

An act against importing cattle from Ireland and other parts beyond the seas and fish taken by foreigners

Whereas by an act of this present parliament entitled *An act for the encouragement of trade,* amongst other things some provision was made for the preventing of coming in of vast numbers of cattle, whereby the rents and values of the land of this kingdom were much fallen and like daily to fall more, to the great prejudice, detriment and impoverishment of this kingdom, which nevertheless hath by experience been found to be ineffectual, and the continuance of any importation either of the lean or fat cattle dead or alive herein after specified not only unnecessary but very destructive to the welfare of this kingdom, be it therefore enacted . . . that such importation from and after the second day of February in this present year 1666 is a public and common nuisance, and shall be so adjudged, deemed and taken to be, to all intents and purposes whatsoever. And that if any great cattle, sheep or swine, or any beef, pork or bacon (except for the necessary provision of the respective ships or vessels in which the same shall be brought, not exposing the same or any part thereof to sale) shall, from and after the said second day of February, by any wise whatsoever be imported or brought from beyond seas into this kingdom of England, dominion of Wales or town of Berwick upon Tweed, that then it shall and may be lawful for any constable, tithingman, headborough, churchwarders, or overseers of the poor or any of them, within their respective liberties, parishes, or places, to take and seize the same, and keep the same, during the space of eight and forty hours in some public and convenient place where such seizure shall be made, within which time if the owner or owners or any for them or him shall make it appear unto some justice of the peace of the same county, where the same shall be so seized, by the oath of two credible witnesses, which oath the said justice of peace is hereby empowered and required to administer, that the same were not imported from Ireland, or from any other place beyond the seas not herein after excepted after the second day of February, then the same upon the warrant of such justice of peace shall be delivered without delay. But in default of such proof and warrant, then the same to be forfeited, one half thereof to be disposed to the use of the poor of the parish where the same shall be so found or seized, the other half to be to his or their own use that shall so seize the same.

Stat. of realm, v. 597.

22. AN ACT FOR THE ABROGATING OF THE OATH OF SUPREMACY, 1691

When the Irish parliament met in 1692 each house required its members to take the oath and subscribe to the declaration prescribed in the act.

An act for the abrogating the oath of supremacy in Ireland, and appointing other oaths

Whereas by a statute made in Ireland in the second year of the reign of our late sovereign lady Queen Elizabeth, entitled, *An act restoring to the crown the ancient jurisdiction over the estate ecclesiastical and spiritual, and abolishing all foreign power repugnant to the same*, the persons therein mentioned are thereby obliged to take the oath in the said act expressed, be it enacted . . . that from henceforth no person whatsoever residing in Ireland shall be obliged to take the said oath by force or virtue of the said recited statute. . . .

II. And be it further enacted, that the oaths appointed, intended,

or required by this act to be taken, from and after the first day of
January next in the year of our Lord 1691, be taken by the persons
herein and hereafter mentioned, and by every such other person
and persons as were appointed and required by the said recited
act, or any other statute whatsoever made in Ireland, to take the
said abrogated oath, before such person or persons, and in such
court as hereafter in this act is expressed (that is to say) all and
every archbishop and bishop of the realm of Ireland, that now is,
and all and every person of or above the degree of a baron of parliament there, and all and every person and persons inhabitants of or
residing within the said realm of Ireland, now having any promotion, office or employment ecclesiastical, civil or military, or receiving
any pay, salary, fee, or wages, by reason of any patent or grant of
their majesties, or any of their predecessors, or being master,
governor, head, or fellow of the college or university of Dublin,
or master of any hospital, or school, or barrister-at-law, clerk in
chancery, attorney, or professor of law, physic, or other science,
that shall inhabit, be, or reside within the city of Dublin, or within
thirty miles of the same, on the first day of Hilary term next, or at
any time during the said term, in their majesties' high court of
chancery in that kingdom, or in the court of king's bench there, . . .
and all the said persons which inhabit at greater distance from the
said city, at the general quarter sessions to be holden for that county,
barony, or place in Ireland aforesaid, where he or they shall be or
reside, . . . at any time before the five and twentieth day of July
next; and shall likewise make and subscribe, and audibly repeat,
the declaration herein and thereafter mentioned, and expressed. . . .
And if any archbishop or bishop, or any other person having any
ecclesiastical dignity or promotion, . . . shall neglect or refuse to
take the said oaths, and make and subscribe to the said declaration,
as aforesaid, then he or they shall be *ipso facto* deprived, . . . and
all and every other person having any office, or receiving any pay,
salary, fee, or wages, by reason as aforesaid, or being master,
governor, head, or fellow of the said university or college, or master
of any hospital, or school, barrister-at-law, clerk in chancery, attorney,
or professor of law, physic, or other science as aforesaid, that
shall neglect or refuse to take the said oaths, and make and subscribe the said declaration, within the time, and in the manner
aforesaid respectively, shall be *ipso facto* thenceforth adjudged
uncapable and disabled . . . to have, occupy, or enjoy such office,
pay, salary, fee, wages, mastership, governor's place, headship,
fellowship, employment or employments, . . .

III. And be it further enacted, . . . that every person that shall
become a barrister-at-law, attorney, clerk, or officer in chancery,
or any other court, their deputy or deputies . . . is hereby required
to take the said oaths, and make and subscribe the said declaration,
in the court of king's bench . . . and that all persons that shall
after the first day of March next be admitted into any office or
employment, ecclesiastical or civil, or come into any capacity, in

respect or by reason whereof they should have been obliged to take the said abrogated oath in the said recited act mentioned, shall take the said oaths, and make and subscribe the said declaration . . .

IV. And forasmuch as great disquiet and many dangerous attempts have been made, to deprive their majesties and their royal predecessors of the said realm of Ireland, by the liberty which the popish recusants there have had and taken to sit and vote in parliament, be it enacted . . . that from and after the last day of January next, no person that now is, or shall be hereafter a peer of that realm, or member of the house of peers there, shall vote or make his proxy in the said house of peers or sit there during any debate in the said house nor any person that after the said last day of January shall be a member of the house of commons, shall be capable to vote in the said house, or sit there during any debate in the same, after their speaker is chosen, until he first take the oaths herein and hereafter mentioned and expressed, and make, subscribe, and audibly repeat this declaration following :

I A.B. do solemnly and sincerely in the presence of God profess, testify, and declare, that I do believe, that in the sacrament of the Lord's supper there is not any transubstantiation of the elements of bread and wine into the body and blood of Christ, at or after the consecration thereof by any person whatsoever, and that the invocation or adoration of the Virgin Mary, or any other saint, and the sacrifice of the mass, as they are now used in the church of Rome, are superstitious and idolatrous. And I do solemnly in the presence of God, profess, testify, and declare, that I do make this declaration, and every part thereof, in the plain and ordinary sense of the words read unto me, as they are commonly understood by protestants, without any evasion, equivocation, or mental reservation whatsoever, and without any dispensation already granted me for this purpose by the pope, or any other authority or person whatsoever, or without any hope of any such dispensation from any person or authority whatsoever, or without believing that I am or can be acquitted before God or man, or absolved of this declaration or any part thereof, although the pope, or any person or persons, or power whatsoever, should dispense with or annul the same, or declare that it was null and void from the beginning.

V. And be it further enacted . . that if any person that now is, or hereafter shall be, a peer of Ireland, or member of the house of peers, or member of the house of commons there, or that shall become a barrister-at-law, attorney, clerk, or officer in chancery, or any other court, and all and every deputy and deputies in any office whatsoever, shall presume to offend, contrary to this act, that then every such peer and member, and such other person and persons so offending, shall be thenceforth disabled to hold or execute any office or place of profit or trust, ecclesiastical, civil or military, in any of their majesties realms of Ireland or England, or dominion of Wales, or town of Berwick-upon-Tweed, or in any of their majesty's islands or foreign plantations, to the said realms belonging ; and shall be disabled from thenceforth to sit or vote in either house of parliament of the said realm of Ireland, or make a proxy in the house of peers there, or to sue or use any action, bill, plaint, or information in course of law, or to prosecute any suit in any court of equity, or to be guardian of any child, or executor or administrator of any person, or capable of any legacy or deed of gift, and shall forfeit, for every wilful offence against this act, the sum of five hundred pounds. . . .

VIII. And be it further enacted, that the oaths that are intended and required to be taken by this act, are the oaths in these express words hereafter following :

I A.B. do sincerely promise and swear, that I will be faithful and bear true allegiance, to their majesties King William and Queen Mary : So help me God, etc.

I A.B. do swear, that I do from my heart abhor, detest, and abjure, as impious and heretical, that damnable doctrine and position, that princes excommunicated or deprived by the pope, or any authority of the see of Rome, may be deposed or murdered by their subjects, or any other whatsoever.

And I do declare, that no foreign prince, person, prelate, state, or potentate, hath or ought to have any jurisdiction, power, superiority, pre-eminence or authority, ecclesiastical or spiritual, within this realm : So help me God, etc.

Stat. of realm, vi. 254–7.

23. ADDRESSES OF THE HOUSE OF COMMONS ON MOLYNEUX'S BOOK AND THE IRISH WOOLLEN TRADE, 1698

Voted on 30 June 1698

Mr. Boscawen reported from the committee to whom it was referred to examine into the printed pamphlet, entitled, *The case of Ireland's being bound by acts of parliament in England stated*, that they had drawn up an humble address, to be presented to his majesty, relating to the matters in the resolutions in the house, upon the report from the said committee, which they had directed him to report to the house, which he read in his place, and afterwards delivered in at the clerk's table, where the same was twice read, and is as follows :

Most gracious sovereign, we, your majesty's most dutiful and loyal subjects, the commons in parliament assembled, conceive ourselves in duty bound to represent to your majesty the dangerous attempts, that have been of late made, by some of your subjects of Ireland, to shake off their subjection to, and dependence on, this kingdom, which has manifestly appeared to us, not only by the bold and pernicious assertions in a book, published, and dedicated to your most excellent majesty, entitled, *The case of Ireland's being bound by acts of parliament in England stated*, which book we examined and considered, upon its being brought to us, by your majesty's leave, but, more fully and authentically, by the votes and proceedings of the house of commons in Ireland, in their late sessions, and by a bill sent hither, under the great seal of Ireland, entitled, *An act for the better security of his majesty's royal person and government*, whereby, they would have an act passed in the parliament of England, expressly binding Ireland, to be re-enacted there, and alterations therein made, some of which amount to a repeal of what is required by the said act, made in England, and in other of the said alterations, pretending to give authority to, and oblige, the courts of justice, and great seal, here in England.

This we cannot but look on, as an occasion and encouragement to the forming and publishing, the dangerous positions contained in the said book, and an open and explicit act of disobedience to the legislative authority of this your kingdom of England.

The consequence of such positions and proceedings will be so fatal to this kingdom, and even Ireland itself, that they need not be enlarged on or aggravated.

Therefore we, your dutiful subjects, rest satisfied, that your majesty by your royal prudence, will prevent their being drawn into example.

And we, with all duty and humility, assure your majesty of our ready concurrence and assistance, in a parliamentary way, to preserve and maintain the dependence and subordination of Ireland to the imperial crown of this realm.

And we humbly beseech your majesty, that you would be graciously pleased to give effectual orders, to prevent any thing of the like nature for the future, and the pernicious consequences of what is past, by punishing and discountenancing those that have been guilty thereof.

And we beseech your majesty to take all necessary care, that the laws which direct and restrain the parliament of Ireland in their actings, be not evaded, but strictly observed.

And that your majesty would be pleased to order copies of the journals of the last parliament, and so, from time to time, of all succeeding parliaments of Ireland, to be transmitted into England, in order to be laid before the parliament here ; and to discourage all things, which may, in any degree tend to lessen the dependence of Ireland upon England.

And several amendments being proposed to be made therein, viz. to leave out ' and an open an explicit act of disobedience, to the legislative authority of this your kingdom of England ' ; and ' to order copies of the journals of the last parliament, and so, from time to time, of all succeeding parliaments of Ireland, to be transmitted into England, in order to be laid before the parliament here ; and ' ;

The same were, upon the question severally put thereupon, agreed unto by the house.

Resolved, that the house doth agree to the said address. . . .

Resolved, that the said address be presented to his majesty by the whole house. . . .

Mr. Boscawen also reported from the said committee, that they had drawn up an humble address, to be presented to his majesty, for the discouraging the making the woollen manufactures in Ireland, and encouraging the making the linen manufactures there, which they had directed him to report to the house, which he read in his place, and afterwards delivered in at the clerk's table, where the same was twice read, and is as follows, viz.

Most gracious sovereign, we, your majesty's most dutiful and loyal subjects, the commons in parliament assembled, being very sensible that the wealth and power of this kingdom do in great measure depend on the preserving the woollen manufacture, as much as possible it may be, entire to this realm, think it becomes us, like our ancestors, to be jealous of the establishment and the increase thereof elsewhere, and to use our utmost endeavours to prevent it.

And, therefore, we cannot without trouble observe, that Ireland, which is dependent on, and protected by, England, in the enjoyment of all they have, and which is so proper for the linen manufacture, the establishment and growth of which there, would be so enriching to themselves, and so profitable to England, should, of late, apply itself to the woollen manufacture, to the great prejudice to the trade of this kingdom ; and so unwillingly promote the linen trade, which would benefit both them and us.

The consequence whereof will necessitate your parliament of England to interpose, to prevent the mischief that threatens us, unless your majesty by your authority and great wisdom, shall find means to secure the trade of England, by making your subjects of Ireland to pursue the joint interest of both kingdoms.

And we do most humbly implore your majesty's protection and favour in this matter, and that you will make it your royal care, and enjoin all those you employ in Ireland to make it their care, and use their utmost diligence, to hinder the exportation of wool from Ireland, except to be imported hither ; and for the discouraging the woollen manufactures, and encouraging the linen manufactures, in Ireland, to which we shall always be ready to give our utmost assistance.

And an amendment being proposed, to leave out ' it may be ' ;

The same was, upon the question put thereupon, agreed unto by the house.

Resolved, That the house doth agree to the said address so amended. . . .

Resolved, That the said address be presented to his majesty by the whole house.

Commons journ., xii. 336–8.

SECTION IV. THE EIGHTEENTH CENTURY

BRITISH ACTS RELATING TO IRELAND

I. THE DECLARATORY ACT,[1] 1719

During the seventeenth century the English parliament had legislated for Ireland (Section III, 20, 22), though its right to do so had been challenged (Section III, 14). In 1717 in the case of Sherlock *v.* Annesley the Irish house of lords reversed a decree of the court of exchequer in favour of the respondent. Annesley appealed to the British house of lords, complaining ' of the want of jurisdiction in the house of lords in Ireland to hear appeals.' And the British house ordered the court of exchequer to restore him to his estate. When the Irish parliament met in 1719 the Irish peers committed the barons of the exchequer, who had obeyed the British decision, and voted an address to the king (document 13) asserting their right to be the final court of appeal for Ireland. The British parliament promptly and brusquely retorted by passing the declaratory act.

An act for the better securing the dependency of the kingdom of Ireland on the crown of Great Britain

Whereas the house of lords of Ireland have of late, against law, assumed to themselves a power and jurisdiction to examine, correct and amend the judgments and decrees of the courts of justice in the kingdom of Ireland ; . . . be it declared . . . that the said kingdom of Ireland hath been, is and of right ought to be, subordinate unto and dependent upon the imperial crown of Great Britain, as being inseparably united and annexed thereunto, and that the king's majesty, by and with the advice and consent of the lords spiritual and temporal, and commons of Great Britain in parliament assembled, had, hath, and of right ought to have full power and authority to make laws and statutes of sufficient force and validity to bind the kingdom and the people of Ireland.

II. And be it further declared and enacted . . . that the house of lords of Ireland have not, nor of right ought to have, any jurisdiction to judge of, affirm or reverse any judgment, sentence or decree, given or made in any court within the said kingdom, and that all proceedings before the said house of lords, upon any such judgment, sentence or decree, are, and are hereby declared to be utterly null and void to all intents and purposes whatsoever.

Stat. at large, iv. 481.

2. THE REPEAL OF THE DECLARATORY ACT, 1782

Towards the end of the American war public opinion in Ireland vehemently attacked the declaratory act and criticized the working of Poynings' law. Lord North's whig successors yielded to the Irish demands. The declaratory act was repealed, and at the same time measures drastically

---

[1] Often referred to as the 6 Geo. I. 65.

amending Poynings' law, limiting the duration of the mutiny act and establishing the independence of the Irish judges and the right of the Irish peers to form the final court of appeal for Ireland, were passed by the Irish parliament (documents 9, 10, 11).

An act to repeal an act, made in the sixth year of his late majesty King George the first, entitled, an act for better securing the dependency of the kingdom of Ireland upon the crown of Great Britain

Whereas an act was passed in the sixth year of his late majesty King George the first, entitled, *An act for the better securing the dependency of the kingdom of Ireland upon the crown of Great Britain*, . . . be it enacted . . . that from and after the passing of this act, the above mentioned act, and the several matters and things therein contained, shall be, and is, and are hereby repealed.

Public general statutes, 22 Geo. III, pp. 859–60.

3. THE RENUNCIATION ACT, 1783

To satisfy a section of Irish opinion led by Flood which contended that by repealing the declaratory act, England had not surrendered, but merely ceased to affirm her claims, the renunciation act was passed early in 1783.

An act for preventing and removing all doubts which have arisen or might arise, concerning the exclusive rights of the parliament and courts of Ireland, in matters of legislation and judicature, and for preventing any writ of error or appeal from any of his majesty's courts in that kingdom from being received, heard and adjudged, in any of his majesty's courts in the kingdom of Great Britain

Whereas, by an act of the last session of the present parliament, (entitled, *An act to repeal an act made in the sixth year of his late majesty King George the first, entitled, An act for the better securing the dependency of the kingdom of Ireland upon the crown of Great Britain*), it was enacted that the last mentioned act, and all the matters and things therein contained, should be repealed :

And whereas doubts have arisen whether the provisions of the said act are sufficient to secure to the people of Ireland the rights claimed by them to be bound only by the laws enacted by his majesty and the parliament of that kingdom, in all cases whatever, and to have all actions or suits at law or in equity, which may be instituted in that kingdom, decided in his majesty's courts there finally and without appeal from thence, therefore for removing all doubts respecting the same, . . . be it declared and enacted, that the said right claimed by the people of Ireland to be bound only by laws enacted by his majesty and the parliament of that kingdom in all cases whatever, and to have all actions and suits at law or in equity, which may be instituted in that kingdom, decided in his majesty's courts therein finally and without appeal from thence, shall be and is hereby declared to be established and ascertained for ever, and shall be at no time hereafter be questioned or questionable.

II. And be it further enacted . . . that no writ of error or appeal shall be received or adjudged, or any other proceeding be had by or in any of his majesty's courts in this kingdom, in any action or suit at law or in equity, instituted in any of his majesty's courts in the kingdom of Ireland, and all such writs, appeals and proceedings, shall be, and are hereby declared, null and void to all intents and purposes, and that all records, transcripts of records or proceedings, which have been transmitted from Ireland to Great Britain, by virtue of any writ of error or appeal, and upon which no judgment has been given or decree pronounced, before the first day of June 1782, shall, upon application made by or in behalf of the party in whose favour judgment was given or decree pronounced in Ireland, be delivered to such party, or any person by him authorized to apply for and receive the same.

Public general statutes, 23 Geo. III, pp. 487–8.

ACTS OF THE IRISH PARLIAMENT

4. AN ACT TO PREVENT THE GROWTH OF POPERY, 1704

At the committee stage of the bill in each house, the catholics and 'persons comprised in the articles of Limerick' appeared by counsel and opposed it. On the other hand clause xviii provoked opposition from the friends of the protestant dissenters.[1]

An act to prevent the further growth of popery

I. Whereas divers emissaries of the church of Rome, popish priests, and other persons of that persuasion, taking advantage of the weakness and ignorance of some of her majesty's subjects, or of the extreme sickness and decay of their reason and senses, in the absence of friends and spiritual guides, do daily endeavour to persuade and pervert them from the protestant religion, to the great dishonour of Almighty God, the weakening of the true religion, by His blessing so happily established in this realm, to the disquieting the peace and settlement, and discomfort of many particular families thereof ; and in further manifestation of their hatred and aversion to the said true religion, many of the said persons so professing the popish religion in this kingdom, have refused to make provision for their own children for no other reason but their being of the protestant religion ; and also by cunning devices and contrivances found out ways to avoid and elude the intents of an act of parliament, made in the ninth year of the reign of the late King William the Third for preventing protestants intermarrying with papists, and of several other laws made for the security of the protestant religion ; and whereas many persons so professing the popish religion have it in their power to raise division among protestants, by voting in elections for members of parliament, and also have it in their power to use other ways and means tending to the destruction of the protestant interest in this kingdom ; for remedy of which great mischiefs, and to prevent the like evil practices for the future be it enacted . . .

[1] For an account of this act see Froude, *English in Ireland* (1872), i. 303–17.

that if any person or persons from and after the twenty-fourth day of March, in this present year of our Lord 1703, shall seduce, persuade or pervert any person or persons professing, or that shall profess, the protestant religion, to renounce, forsake, or adjure the same, and to profess the popish religion, or reconcile him or them to the church of Rome, then and in such case every such person or persons so seducing, as also every such protestant or protestants who shall be so seduced, perverted and reconciled to popery, shall for the said offences, being thereof lawfully convicted, incur the danger and penalty of praemunire, mentioned in the statute of praemunire made in England in the sixteenth year of the reign of King Richard the Second ; and if any person or persons professing the popish religion, shall from and after the said twenty-fourth day of March send, or cause, or willingly suffer, to be sent or conveyed any child under the age of one and twenty years, except sailors, ship-boys, or the apprentice or factor of some merchant in trade of merchandise, into France or any other parts beyond the seas, out of her majesty's dominions, without the special licence of her majesty, her heirs or successors or of her or their chief governor or governors of this kingdom . . . he, she or they shall incur the pains, penalties and forfeitures mentioned in act made in the seventh year of his late majesty King William, entitled, *An act to restrain foreign education.*

III. And to the end that no child or children of popish parent or parents who have professed or embraced the protestant religion, or who shall profess and embrace, or are or shall be desirous or willing to be instructed and educated therein, may in the life time of such popish parent or parents, for fear of being cast off or disinherited by them, or for want of fitting maintenance or further provision, be compelled and necessitated to embrace the popish religion, be it further enacted . . . that from and after the twenty-fourth day of March 1703, upon complaint in the high court of chancery . . . it shall and may be lawful for the said court to make such order for the maintenance of every such protestant child, not maintained by such popish parent, suitable to the degree and ability of such parent, and to the age of such child, and also for the portion of every such protestant child, to be paid at the decrease of such popish parent, as the court shall adjudge fit, suitable to the degree and ability of such parent ; and in case the eldest son and heir of such popish parent shall be a protestant, that then from the time of enrollment in the high court of chancery of a certificate of the bishop of the diocese, in which he shall inhabit, testifying his being a protestant, and conforming himself to the church of Ireland as by law established, such popish parent shall become, and shall be, only tenant for life of all the real estate, whereof such popish parent shall then be seized in fee-tail or fee-simple, and the reversion in fee shall be vested in such eldest son being a protestant ; subject nevertheless to all such debts and real encumbrances at the time of the enrollment of such certificate charging such estate, and subject also to such maintenances and portions for the other children, as well protestants as papists of such popish parents then born, or after to be born, as the said court of chancery in manner aforesaid shall order . . .

IV. And that care may be taken for the education of children in the communion of the church of Ireland as by law established, be it enacted . . . that no person of the popish religion shall, or may be guardian unto, or have the tuition or custody of, any orphan child or children, under the age of twenty-one years ; but that the same, where the person having or entitled to the guardianship of such orphan child or children, is or shall be a papist, shall be disposed of by the high court of chancery to some near relation of such orphan child or children, being a protestant, and conforming himself to the church of Ireland as by law established, to whom the estate cannot descend, in case there shall be any such protestant relation fit to have the education of such child ; otherwise to some other protestant conforming himself as aforesaid, who is hereby required to use his utmost care to educate and bring up such child or minor in the protestant religion. . . .

VI. And be it further enacted . . . that every papist, or person professing the popish religion, shall from and after the said twenty-fourth day of March be disabled, and is hereby made incapable, to buy and purchase either in his or in their own name, or in the name of any other person or persons to his or her use, or in trust for him or her, any manors, lands, tenements, or hereditaments, or any rents or profits out of the same, or any leases or terms thereof, other than any term of years not exceeding thirty-one years, whereon a rent not less than two-thirds of the improved yearly value, at the time of the making such leases of the tenements leased, shall be reserved. . . .

VII. And be it further enacted . . . that from and after the first day of February, in this present year of our Lord 1703, no papist or person professing the popish religion, who shall not within six months after he or she shall have become entitled to enter, or to take or have the profits by descent, or by virtue of any devise or gift, or of any remainder already limited, or at any time hereafter to be limited, or by virtue of any trust, of any lands, tenements or hereditaments, whereof any protestant now is, or hereafter shall be seized in fee-simple absolute, or fee-tail, or in such manner that after his death, or the death of him and his wife, the freehold is to come immediately to his son or sons, or issue in tail, if then of the age of eighteen years, or if under within six months after he shall attain that age, until which time from his being so entitled he shall be under the care of such protestant relation or person conforming himself as aforesaid, as shall for that purpose be appointed by the high court of chancery, for his being educated in the protestant religion, become a protestant, and conform himself to the church now established in this kingdom, shall take any benefit by reason of such descent, devise, gift, remainder, or trust, but from thenceforth during the life of such person, or until he or she do become a protestant, and conform as aforesaid, the nearest protestant relation or relations, or other protestant or protestants, and his and their heirs, being and continuing protestants, who shall or would be entitled to the same in case such person professing the popish religion, and not conforming as aforesaid, and all other intermediate popish relations and popish persons were actually dead, and his and their heirs shall have and enjoy the said lands. . . .

X. And further be it enacted . . . that all lands tenements and hereditaments, whereof a papist now is, or hereafter shall be, seized in fee-simple or fee-tail, shall from henceforth, so long as any papist shall be seized of or entitled to the same in fee-simple or fee-tail, be of the nature of gavelkind ; and if not sold, aliened, or disposed of by such papist in his life time for good and valuable consideration of money really and *bona fide* paid for such estate, shall from such papist descend to, and be inherited by, all and every the sons of such papist any way inheritable to such estate, share and share alike, and not descend on or come to the eldest of such sons only, being a papist, as heir-at-law ; and shall in like manner from such respective sons, being papists, descend to and be inherited by all and every the sons of such sons, share and share alike, and not descend to the eldest of such sons, being a papist, as heir-at-law only ; and that for want of issue male of such papist, the same shall descend to all his daughters any way inheritable to such estate in equal proportions ; and for want of such issue, among the collateral kindred of such papist, of the kin of his father, any way inheritable to such estate in equal degree ; and for want of such kindred, to the collateral kindred of such papist of the kin of his mother, any way inheritable to such estate, and not otherwise ; . . .

XI. Provided nevertheless, it shall and may be lawful to and for such papist to charge such his estate with reasonable maintenances and portions for his daughters, to be raised and paid in such manner as he shall direct.

XII. Provided always, that if the eldest son or heir-at-law of such papist shall be a protestant at the time of the decease of such papist, . . . the lands whereof such papist shall be seized, shall descend to such eldest son or heir-at-law according to the rules of the common law of this realm, . . . and if the eldest son or heir-at-law of any such papist, who shall at the time of the decease of such papist, whose heir he is, be of the age of one and twenty years, shall become a protestant and conform himself to the church of Ireland, as by law established, within one year after such decease of such papist, or being then under the age of one and twenty years, shall within one year after he shall attain that age become a protestant, and conform himself as aforesaid, . . . he shall be entitled to, and shall have, and enjoy from thenceforth the whole real estate of such papist. . . .

XV. Provided always, that no person shall take benefit by this act as a protestant within the intent and meaning hereof, that shall not conform to the church of Ireland as by law established, and subscribe the declaration, and also take and subscribe the oath of adjuration following, viz. I A.B. do solemnly and sincerely, in the presence of God, profess, testify and declare, that I do believe, that in the sacrament of the Lord's-Supper, there is not any transubstantiation of the elements of bread and wine into the body and blood of Christ, at or after the consecration thereof by any person whatsoever, and that the adoration or invocation of the Virgin Mary, or any other saint, and the sacrifice of the mass, as they are now used in the church of Rome, are superstitious and idolatrous.   And I do solemnly, in the presence of God, profess, testify, and declare, that I do make this declaration, and every part thereof, in the plain and ordinary sense of the words read unto me, as they are commonly understood by protestants, without any evasion, equivocation or mental reservation whatsoever ; and without any dispensation already granted me for this purpose by the pope, or any other authority or person whatsoever, or without any hope of dispensation from any person or authority whatsoever, or without believing that I am, or can be acquitted before God or man, or absolved of this declaration, or any part thereof, although the pope, or any other person or persons, or power whatsoever should dispense with or annul the same, or declare that it was null and void from the beginning.

I A.B. do truly and sincerely acknowledge, profess, testify and declare in my conscience, before God and the world, that our sovereign lady Queen Anne is lawful and rightful queen of this realm, and of all other her majesty's dominions and countries thereunto belonging.   And I do solemnly and sincerely declare, that I do believe in my conscience, that the person pretending to be Prince of Wales, during the life of the late King James, and since his decease pretending to be, and taking upon himself the style and title of King of England by the name of James III, hath not any right or title whatsoever to the crown of this realm, or any other the dominions thereto belonging, and I do renounce, refuse and abjure any allegiance or obedience to him.   And I do swear that I will bear faith and true allegiance to her majesty Queen Anne, and her will defend to the utmost of my power against all traiterous conspiracies and attempts whatsoever, which shall be made against her person, crown, or dignity.   And I will do my best endeavour to disclose and make known to her majesty, and her successors, all treasons and traiterous conspiracies, which I shall know to be against her or any of them.   And I do faithfully promise to the utmost of my power to support, maintain and defend the limitation and succession of the crown against him the said James, and all other persons whatsoever, as the same is and stands limited by an act, entitled, *An act declaring the rights and liberties of the subject, and settling the succession of the crown,* to her present majesty, and the heirs of her body being protestants ; and as the same by one other act, entitled, *An act for the further limitation of the crown, and better securing the rights and liberties of the subject,* is and stands limited, after the decease of her majesty, and for default of issue of her majesty, to the Princess Sophia, electress and duchess dowager of Hanover, and the heirs of her body being protestants. And all these things I do plainly and sincerely acknowledge and swear, according to the express words by me spoken, and according to the plain and common sense and understanding of the same words, without any equivocation, mental evasion or secret reservation whatsoever. And I do make this recognition, acknowledgement, abjuration, renunciation and promise, heartily, willingly, and truly, upon the true faith of a Christian. So help me God.

XVII. And be it further enacted . . . that all and every such person and persons, that shall be admitted, entered, placed, or taken into any office or offices, civil or military, or that shall receive pay, salary, fee, or wages belonging to or by reason of any office or place of trust, by reason of any patent or grant from her majesty, or that shall have command or place of trust from or under her majesty, or any of her predecessors or successors, or by her or their authority, or by authority derived from her or them, within this realm of Ireland, after the first day of Easter-term aforesaid, shall take the said oaths and repeat the said declaration, and subscribe the said oaths and declaration, in one of the said respective courts in the next term, or at the general quarter-session for that county, barony, or place where he or they shall reside, next after his or their respective admittance or admittances into any such office . . . and all and every such person or persons so to be admitted as aforesaid, shall also receive the sacrament of the Lord's supper according to the usage of the Church of Ireland, within three months after his or their admittance in or receiving their said authority and employments in some public church, upon the Lord's-day commonly called Sunday, immediately after divine service and sermon, and every of the said respective persons, touching whom the said several provisions are herebefore made, in the respective court, where he or she takes the said oaths, shall first deliver a certificate of such his or her receiving the said sacrament as aforesaid, under the hands of the respective minister and church-wardens, and shall then make proof of the truth thereof by two credible witnesses at the least, upon oath, all which shall be required of and put upon record in their respective courts.

XVIII. And be it further enacted, that all and every the person or persons aforesaid, who do or shall refuse or neglect to take the said oath and sacrament, and to deliver such a certificate of his receiving the sacrament, as aforesaid, or to subscribe the said declaration as aforesaid in one of the said courts and places, and at the respective times aforesaid shall be *ipso facto* adjudged incapable and disabled in law to all intents and purposes whatsoever to have, occupy, or enjoy the said office or offices, . . .

XXIV. And for the preventing papists having it in their power to breed dissention amongst protestants by voting at elections of members of parliament ; be it further enacted . . . that from and after the twenty-fourth day of March 1703 no freeholder, burgess, freeman, or inhabitant of this kingdom, being a papist or professing the popish religion, shall at any time hereafter be capable of giving his or their vote for the electing of knights of any shires or counties within this kingdom, or citizens or burgesses to serve in any succeeding parliament, without first repairing to the general quarter sessions of the peace to be holden for the counties, cities, or boroughs wherein such papists do inhabit and dwell, and there voluntarily take the oath of allegiance in the words following, viz. I A.B. do sincerely promise and swear, that I will be faithful and bear true allegiance to her majesty Queen Anne. So help me God, etc.

And also the oath of abjuration aforesaid : [1] . . .

XXVI. And whereas the superstitions of popery are greatly increased and upheld by the pretended sanctity of places, especially of a place called Saint Patrick's purgatory in the county of Donegal, and of wells, to which pilgrimages are made by vast numbers at certain seasons, by which not only the peace of the public is greatly disturbed, but the safety of the government also hazarded, by the riotous and unlawful assembling together of many thousands of papists to the said wells and other places, be it further enacted, that all such meetings and assemblies shall be deemed and adjudged riots and unlawful assemblies, and punishable as such . . .

Ir. Stat., iv. 12–31.

5. THE CATHOLIC RELIEF ACT, 1778

Earlier acts releasing the stringency of the penal laws were passed in 1771 and 1774.[2]

An act for the relief of his majesty's subjects professing the popish religion

Whereas by an act made in this kingdom in the second year of her late majesty Queen Anne, entitled, *An act to prevent the further growth of popery*, and also by another act made in the eighth year of her said reign for explaining and amending the said act, the Roman catholics of Ireland are made subject to several disabilities and incapacities therein particularly mentioned ; and whereas for their uniform peaceful behaviour for a long series of years it appears reasonable and expedient to relax the same, and it must tend not only to the cultivation and improvement of this kingdom, but to the prosperity and strength of all his majesty's dominions, that his subjects of all denominations should enjoy the blessings of our free constitution, and should be bound to each other by mutual interest and mutual affection, therefore be it enacted . . . that from and after the first day of August 1778 it shall and may be lawful to and for any papist, or person professing the popish religion, subject

---

[1] By an act passed in 1727 (1 Geo. II. c. 9) papists were incapacitated from voting at parliamentary elections.
[2] For details of these acts see Lecky, *A history of Ireland in the eighteenth century* (1892), ii. 191–6.

to the proviso hereinafter contained as to the taking and subscribing the oath and declaration therein mentioned, to take, hold, and enjoy any lease or leases for any term or term of years, not exceeding nine hundred and ninety-nine years certain, or for any term of years determinable upon any number of lives, not exceeding five, provided always, that upon every such lease a rent *bona fide* to be paid in money shall be reserved and made payable during such terms with or without the liberty of committing waste, as fully and beneficially to all intents and purposes, as any other his majesty's subjects in this kingdom, and the same to dispose of by will or otherwise as he shall think fit; and all lands tenements, hereditaments, whereof any papist or person professing the popish religion is now seized or shall be seized by virtue of a title legally derived by, from, or under such person or persons, now seized in fee simple or fee tail, whether at law or in equity, shall from and after the time aforesaid be descendable, deviseable, and transferable, as fully, beneficially, and effectually, as if the same were in the seizin of any other of his majesty's subjects in this kingdom.

III. Provided, that no papist or person professing the popish religion shall take any benefit from this act, unless he or she shall on or before the first day of January 1779, or some time previous to any such lease made to or in trust for him, if he or she shall be in this kingdom, or within six months after any devise, descent, or limitation shall take effect in possession, if at that time within this kingdom, or if then abroad beyond the seas, or under the age of twenty-one years, or in prison, or of unsound mind, or under coverture, then within six months after his or her return from abroad, or attaining the age of twenty-one years, or discharge from prison, or becoming of sound mind, or after she shall become a *femme sole*, take and subscribe the oath of allegiance and the declaration prescribed by an act passed in this kingdom in the thirteenth and fourteenth years of his present majesty's reign,[1] . . .

V. And be it enacted . . . that no maintenance or portion shall be granted to any child of a popish parent, upon a bill filed against such parent . . . out of the personal property of such papist, except out of such leases which they may hereafter take under the powers granted in this act, . . .

VI. And whereas by an act made in this kingdom in the second year of the reign of her late majesty Queen Anne, entitled, *An act to prevent the further growth of popery*, it is amongst other things enacted to the effect following ; in case the eldest son and heir of a popish parent shall be a protestant, . . . such popish parent shall

---

[1] ' An act to enable his majesty's subjects of whatever persuasion to testify their allegiance to him ' permitted catholics to take an oath in which they promised allegiance to the king and his successors and repudiated the opinions that faith need not be kept with heretics, that it was lawful to murder heretics, that sovereigns excommunicated by the pope could be deposed or murdered by their subjects, and ' that the pope of Rome, or any other foreign prince, prelate, state or potentate hath or ought to have any temporal or civil jurisdiction, power, superiority or pre-eminence, directly or indirectly within this realm ' (*Ir. Stat.*, x. 589–90).

become and be only tenant for life of all the real estate, whereof such popish parent shall then be seized in fee tail or fee simple, and the reversion in fee shall be vested in such eldest son, being a protestant subject, . . . and whereas it is found inexpedient to continue any longer that part of the said recited act, be it enacted . . . that from and after the first day of November 1778 the conformity of the eldest son . . . shall not affect or alter the estate of any popish parent . . . but such popish parent shall remain seized and possessed of the same estate and interest in all and every his or her real estate, as he or she would have been, if such eldest son had not conformed, or the said act of the second year of Queen Anne had not been made.

X. Provided also that no person shall take benefit by this act who having been converted from the popish to the protestant religion shall afterwards relapse to popery, nor any person who being a protestant shall at any time become a papist, or shall educate or suffer to be educated, any of his children under the age of fourteen years in the popish religion.

Ir. Stat., xi. 298–301.

6. THE CATHOLIC RELIEF ACT, 1782

An act for the further relief of his majesty's subjects of this kingdom professing the popish religion

I. Whereas all such of his majesty's subjects in this kingdom, of whatever persuasion, as have heretofore taken and subscribed, or shall hereafter take and subscribe, the oath of allegiance and declaration prescribed by an act passed in the thirteenth and fourteenth years of his present majesty's reign, entitled, *An act to enable his majesty's subjects of whatever persuasion, to testify their allegiance to him*, ought to be considered as good and loyal subjects to his majesty, his crown and government ; and whereas a continuance of several of the laws formerly enacted, and still in force in this kingdom, against persons professing the popish religion, is therefore unnecessary, in respect to those who have taken or shall take the said oath, and is injurious to the real welfare and prosperity of Ireland ; therefore be it enacted . . . that from and after the first day of May 1782 it shall and may be lawful to and for any person or persons professing the popish religion, to purchase, or take by grant, limitation, descent, or devise, any lands, tenements, or hereditaments in this kingdom, or any interest therein (except advowsons, and also except any manor or borough, or any part of a manor or borough, the freeholders or inhabitants whereof are entitled to vote for burgesses to represent such borough or manor in parliament) and the same to dispose of as he, she, or they shall think fit, . . .

V. And be it enacted . . . that no popish ecclesiastic, who hath heretofore taken and subscribed, or who shall hereafter take and subscribe, the oath of allegiance and declaration, prescribed by an

act passed in the thirteenth and fourteenth years of his present
majesty's reign, entitled, *An act to enable his majesty's subjects of
whatever persuasion, to testify their allegiance to him,* in the manner
and form as hereinafter is particularly specified and set forth, and
who shall register his christian and surnames, place of abode, age,
and parish, if he have a parish, and the time and place of his receiving
his first, and every other popish orders, and from whom he received
them, with the register of the diocese where his place of abode is
(for every which registry the sum of one shilling and no more shall
be paid to the register) shall, after the passing of this act, be subject
to any of the penalties, incapacities, or disabilities, mentioned in an
act made in the ninth year of the reign of King William the third,
entitled, *An act for banishing all popish papists exercising any
ecclesiastical jurisdiction, and regulars of the popish clergy out of this
kingdom,* or in an act made in the second year of Queen Anne,
entitled, *An act for registering the popish clergy,* or in an act made in
the second year of Queen Anne, entitled, *An act to prevent the further
growth of popery,* or in an act made in the second year of Queen Anne,
entitled, *An act to prevent popish priests from coming into this kingdom,*
or in an act made in the fourth year of Queen Anne, entitled, *An act
to explain and amend an act, entitled, An act for registering popish
clergy* ; or in an act made in the eighth year of Queen Anne, entitled,
*An act for explaining and amending an act, entitled, An act to prevent
the further growth of popery.*

VI. Provided always, that no benefits in this act contained shall
extend, or be construed to extend, to any regular of the popish
clergy, who shall not be in this kingdom at the time of passing this
act, . . .

VIII. Provided always, that no benefits in this act contained shall
extend, or be construed to extend, to any popish ecclesiastic who
shall officiate in any church or chapel with a steeple or bell, or at any
funeral in any church or church-yard, or who shall exercise any of
the rites or ceremonies of the popish religion, or wear the habits of
their order, save within their usual places of worship, or in private
houses, or who shall use any symbol or mark of title whatsoever, . . .

IX. Provided also, that nothing in this act contained shall be
construed to extend to any person or persons who shall be perverted
from the protestant to the popish religion, but that all the pains
penalties and disabilities, which now subsist, according to the laws
now in being, shall remain in full force against such . . .

X. Provided also, that no benefits in this act contained shall be
construed to extend to any popish ecclesiastic, who shall procure,
incite, or persuade any protestant to become a papist ; . . .

XII. And be it enacted . . . that so much of an act passed in
the seventh year of King William III, entitled, *An act for the better
securing the government by disarming papists,* as subjects any papist,
who shall after the twentieth day of January 1695 have or keep in
his possession, or in the possession of any other person to his use
or at his disposal, any horse, gelding, or mare, which shall be of

the value of five pounds or more, to the penalties therein mentioned ; and also so much of an act passed in the eighth year of Queen Anne, entitled, *An act for explaining and amending an act, entitled, An act to prevent the further growth of popery*, as enables the lord lieutenant or other chief governors of this kingdom, to seize and secure any horse, mare or gelding belonging to any papist, or reputed papist, upon any invasion likely to happen, or in case of intestine war broke out, or likely to break out, shall be, and is, and are hereby repealed.

XIII. And be it enacted . . . that so much of an act passed in the ninth year of King George the second, entitled, *An act for continuing and amending several statutes now near expiring*, as enables the grand jury to present for the reimbursing such persons who have been robbed by privateers in time of war, for such losses as they shall respectively sustain thereby and for applotting and levying the fame on the lands, tenements and hereditaments, goods, and chattels of all the popish inhabitants of the county where such robbery shall be committed, shall be, and is hereby repealed.

XIV. And be it enacted . . . that so much of an act passed in the sixth year of King George the first, entitled, *An act for the better regulating the parish watches, and amending the highways in this kingdom, and for preventing the misapplication of public money*, as subjects such papist or papists who shall not provide a protestant watchman to watch in their turn, to the penalties therein mentioned, shall be, and is hereby repealed.

XVI. Provided also, that no benefit herein contained shall extend or be construed to extend, to any person who hath not heretofore, or who shall not hereafter before the accruing of such benefit to such persons or persons, being of the age of twenty-one years, or who being under the age of twenty-one years, shall not within six months after he or she shall attain the age of twenty-one years, or being of unsound mind, or in prison, or beyond the seas, or under coverture, then within six months, after such disability removed, take, and subscribe the oath of allegiance and declaration prescribed by an act passed in the thirteenth and fourteenth years of his present majesty's reign, entitled, *An act to enable his majesty's subjects of whatever persuasion, to testify their allegiance to him*, . . .

Ir. Stat., xii. 237–42.

7. THE CATHOLIC RELIEF ACT, 1793

A minor relief act was passed in 1792. When the house was going into committee on the act of 1793, George Knox moved that catholics be allowed to sit in parliament. The motion was defeated by 163 to 69.

An act for the relief of his majesty's popish, or Roman catholic subjects of Ireland

Whereas various acts of parliament have been passed, imposing on his majesty's subjects professing the popish or Roman catholic religion many restraints and disabilities, to which other subjects of this realm are not liable, and from the peaceful and loyal demeanour of his majesty's popish or Roman catholic subjects, it is fit that such restraints and disabilities shall be discontinued ; be it therefore enacted . . . that his majesty's subjects being papists, or persons professing the popish or Roman catholic religion, or married to papists, or persons professing the popish or Roman catholic religion, or educating any of their children in that religion, shall not be liable or subject to any penalties, forfeitures, disabilities, or incapacities, or to any laws for the limitation, charging, or discovering of their estates and property, real or personal, or touching the acquiring of property, or securities affecting property, save such as his majesty's subjects of the protestant religion are liable and subject to ; and that such parts of all oaths as are required to be taken by persons in order to qualify themselves for voting at elections for members to serve in parliament, as import to deny that the person taking the same is a papist or married to a papist, or educates his children in the popish religion, shall not hereafter be required to be taken by any voter, but shall be omitted by the person administering the same ; and that it shall not be necessary, in order to entitle a papist, or person professing the popish or Roman catholic religion to vote at an election of members to serve in parliament, that he should at, or previous to his voting, take the oaths of allegiance and abjuration, . . .

VI. Provided also, that nothing herein contained, shall extend to authorize any papist, or person professing the popish or Roman catholic religion, to have or keep in his hands or possession any arms . . . or to exempt such person from any forfeiture, or penalty inflicted by any act respecting arms, armour, or ammunition, in the hands or possession of any papist, or respecting papists having or keeping such warlike stores, save and except papists, or persons of the popish or Roman catholic religion seized of a freehold estate of one hundred pounds a year, or possessed of a personal estate of one thousand pounds or upwards, who are hereby authorized to keep arms and ammunition as protestants now by law may ; and also save and except papists or Roman catholics, possessing a freehold estate of ten pounds yearly value, and less than one hundred pounds, or a personal estate of three hundred, and less than one thousand pounds, who shall have at the session of the peace in the county in which they reside, taken the oath of allegiance prescribed to be taken by an act passed in the thirteenth and fourteenth years of his present majesty's reign, entitled, *An act to enable his majesty's subjects, of whatever persuasion, to testify their allegiance to him.* . . .

VII. And be it enacted, that it shall and may be lawful for papists, or persons professing the popish or Roman catholic religion, to hold, exercise, and enjoy all civil and military offices, or places of trust or profit under his majesty, his heirs and successors, in this kingdom ; and to hold or take degrees or any professorship in, or be masters, or fellows of any college, to be hereafter founded in this kingdom, provided that such college shall be a member of the university of Dublin, and shall not be founded exclusively for the education of papists or persons professing the popish or Roman catholic religion, nor consist exclusively of masters, fellows, or other persons to be named or elected on the foundation of such college, being persons professing the popish or Roman catholic religion, or to hold any office or place of trust, in, and to be a member of any lay-body corporate, except the college of the holy and undivided Trinity of Queen Elizabeth, near Dublin, without taking and subscribing the oaths of allegiance, supremacy, or abjuration, or making or subscribing the declaration required to be taken, made and subscribed, to enable any person to hold and enjoy any of such places, and without receiving the sacrament of the Lord's supper, according to the rites and ceremonies of the church of Ireland, any law, statute, or bye-law of any corporation to the contrary notwithstanding ; provided that every such person shall take and subscribe the oath appointed by the said act passed in the thirteenth and fourteenth years of his majesty's reign, entitled, *An act to enable his majesty's subjects of whatever persuasion to testify their allegiance to him*; and also the oath and declaration following, that is to say, I A.B. do hereby declare, that I do profess the Roman catholic religion. I A.B. do swear, that I do abjure, condemn, and detest, as unchristian and impious, the principle that it is lawful to murder, destroy, or any ways injure any person whatsoever, for or under the pretence of being a heretic ; and I do declare solemnly before God, that I believe, that no act in itself unjust, immoral, or wicked, can ever be justified or excused by or under pretence or colour, that it was done either for the good of the church, or in obedience to any ecclesiastical power whatsoever. I also declare, that it is not an article of the catholic faith, neither am I thereby required to believe or profess that the pope is infallible, or that I am bound to obey any order in its own nature immoral, though the pope or any ecclesiastical power should issue or direct such order, but on the contrary, I hold that it would be sinful in me to pay any respect or obedience thereto. I further declare, that I do not believe that any sin whatsoever, committed by me, can be forgiven at the mere will of any pope, or of any priest, or of any person or persons whatsoever, but that sincere sorrow for past sins, a firm and sincere resolution to avoid future guilt and to atone to God, are previous and indispensible requisites to establish a well-founded expectation of forgiveness, and that any person who receives absolution without these previous requisites, so far from obtaining thereby any remission of his sins, incurs the additional guilt of violating a sacrament ; and I do swear that I will defend to the utmost of my power the settlement and arrangement of property in this country, as established by the laws now in being ; I do hereby disclaim, disavow and solemnly abjure any intention to subvert the present church establishment for the purpose of substituting a catholic establishment in its stead ; and I do solemnly swear, that I will not exercise any privilege to which I am or may become entitled, to disturb and weaken the protestant religion and protestant government in this kingdom. So help me God !

IX. Provided always, and be it enacted, that nothing herein contained shall extend, or be construed to extend to enable any person to sit or vote in either house of parliament, or to hold, exercise, or enjoy the office of lord lieutenant, lord deputy, or other chief governor of this kingdom, lord high chancellor or keeper, or commissioner of the great seal of this kingdom, lord high treasurer, chancellor of the exchequer, chief justice of the court of king's bench, or common pleas, lord chief baron of the court of exchequer, judge of the high court of admiralty, master or keeper of the rolls, secretary, vice-treasurer, teller and cashier of the exchequer, or auditor-general, lieutenant or governor, or custos rotulorum of counties, secretary to the lord lieutenant, lord deputy, or other chief governor or governors of this kingdom, member of his majesty's most honourable privy council, prime serjeant, attorney-general, solicitor-general, second and third serjeants-at-law, or king's counsel, masters in chancery, provost, or fellow of the college of the Holy and Undivided Trinity of Queen Elizabeth, near Dublin, postmaster-general, master and lieutenant-general of his majesty's ordnance, commander-in-chief of his majesty's forces, generals on the staff, and sheriffs and sub-sheriffs of any county in this kingdom or any office contrary to the rules, orders and directions made and established by the lord lieutenant and council, in pursuance of the act passed in the seventeenth and eighteenth years of the reign of King Charles the Second, entitled, *An act for the explaining of some doubts arising upon an act, entitled, An act for the better execution of his majesty's gracious declaration for the settlement of his kingdom of Ireland*, . . . unless he shall have taken, made, and subscribed the oaths, and declaration, and performed the several requisites which by any law heretofore made, and now of force, are required to enable any person to sit or vote, or to hold, exercise, and enjoy the said offices respectively.

XII. Provided also, and be it enacted, that nothing herein contained, shall be construed to extend to authorize any popish priest, or reputed popish priest, to celebrate marriage between protestant and protestant, or between any person who hath been, or professes himself or herself to be a protestant at any time within twelve months before such celebration of marriage, and a papist, unless such protestant and papist shall have been first married by a clergyman of the protestant religion ; and that every popish priest, or reputed popish priest, who shall celebrate any marriage between two protestants, or between any such protestant and papist, unless such protestant and papist shall have been first married by a clergyman of the protestant religion, shall forfeit the sum of five hundred pounds to his majesty, upon conviction thereof.

XIII. And whereas it may be expedient, in case his majesty,

his heirs and successors, shall be so pleased so to alter the statutes
of the college of the Holy and Undivided Trinity near Dublin and of
the university of Dublin, as to enable persons professing the Roman
catholic religion to enter into, or to take degress in the said university,
to remove any obstacle which now exists by statute law ; be it
enacted, that from and after the first day of June 1793 it shall not be
necessary for any person upon taking any of the degrees usually
conferred by the said university, to make or subscribe any declaration, or to take any oath, save the oaths of allegiance and
abjuration, . . .

XIV. Provided always, that no papist or Roman catholic, or
person professing the Roman catholic or popish religion, shall take
any benefit by, or under this act, unless he shall have first taken and
subscribed the oath and declaration in this act contained and set
forth, and also the said oath appointed by the said act passed in the
thirteenth and fourteenth years of his majesty's reign, entitled, *An
act to enable his majesty's subjects of whatever persuasion to testify
their allegiance to him*, in some one of his majesty's four courts in
Dublin, or at the general sessions of the peace, or at any adjournment thereof to be holden for the county, city, or borough wherein
such papist or Roman catholic, or person professing the Roman
catholic or popish religion, doth inhabit or dwell, or before the going
judge or judges of assize, . . .

Ir. Stat., xvi. 685–92.

8. THE OCTENNIAL ACT, 1768

Until the passing of this act an Irish parliament was only necessarily
terminated by the death of the sovereign.

An act for limiting the duration of parliaments

That whereas a limitation of the duration of parliaments may
tend to strengthen the harmony and good agreement subsisting
between his majesty and his people of Ireland, and may be productive
of other good effects to his majesty's subjects there, we, your
majesty's most dutiful and loyal subjects the commons of Ireland in
parliament assembled, do most humbly beseech your majesty, that
it may be declared and enacted . . . that from henceforth no
parliament, which shall at any time hereafter be called, assembled,
or held, shall have any longer continuance than for eight years, to
be accounted from the day on which by the writs of summons the
said parliament shall be appointed to meet.

11. And be it further enacted . . . that this present parliament
shall cease and determine on the twenty-fourth day of June, which
shall be in the year of our Lord 1768 unless his majesty shall think
fit sooner to dissolve the same.

Ir. Stat., ix. 504.

9. YELVERTON'S ACT, 1782

See remarks on document 2. For the debate on the committee stage see document 19. For an interpretation of the act see document 20.

An act to regulate the manner of passing bills, and to prevent delays in summoning of parliaments

Whereas it be expedient to regulate the manner of passing bills in this kingdom, be it enacted . . . that the lord lieutenant, or other chief governor or governors and council of this kingdom for the time being, do and shall certify all such bills, and none other, as both houses of parliament shall judge expedient to be enacted in this kingdom, to his majesty his heirs and successors, under the great seal of this kingdom without addition, diminution, or alteration.

II. And be it further enacted . . . that all such bills as shall be so certified to his majesty, his heirs and successors, under the great seal of this kingdom, and returned into the same under the great seal of Great Britain, without addition, diminution, or alteration, and none other shall pass in the parliament of this kingdom ; any former law, statute, or usage to the contrary thereof in anywise notwithstanding.

III. And be it further enacted, that no bill shall be certified into Great Britain, as a cause or consideration for holding a parliament in this kingdom, but that parliaments may be holden in this kingdom, although no such bill shall have been certified previous to the meeting thereof.

IV. Provided always, that no parliament shall be holden in this kingdom until a licence for that purpose shall be first had and obtained from his majesty, his heirs and successors, under the great seal of Great Britain.

Ir. Stat., xii. 356.

10. AN ACT FOR THE REDRESS OF ERRONEOUS JUDGMENTS, 1782

See remarks on document 2.

An act for redress of erroneous judgments, orders and decrees

Whereas erroneous judgments, orders, and decrees ought only to be reformed finally in the high court of parliament in this kingdom, be it declared and enacted . . . that from henceforth all such judgments, orders, and decrees, shall be finally examined and reformed in the high court of parliament in this kingdom only, any law, statute, or practice to the contrary thereof, in anywise notwithstanding.

II. Provided always . . . that nothing herein contained shall invalidate or affect any judgment, order, or decree which has been given or made in Great Britain, previous to the first day of June 1782 but that the same shall remain in full force, any thing herein contained to the contrary thereof in anywise notwithstanding.

III. And be it enacted . . . that it shall and may be lawful to and for the lord lieutenant or other chief governor or chief governors of this kingdom for the time being, to grant warrants for sealing writs of error returnable into parliament. . . .

Irish Stat., xii. 358–9.

11. AN ACT FOR SECURING THE INDEPENDENCE OF THE JUDICIARY 1782

See remarks on document 2

An act for securing the independency of judges, and the impartial administration of justice

Whereas the independency of the judges of the land is essential to the impartial administration of justice, and highly conducive to the support of the honour of the crown, and the security of the rights and liberties of the people, be it enacted . . . that from and after the passing of this act, the present and all future commissions of judges for the time being shall continue and remain in full force during their good behaviour, and that the same shall continue and remain in full force during the term aforesaid notwithstanding the demise of the king (whom God long preserve) or of any of his heirs or successors, any law, usage, or practice to the contrary thereof in anywise notwithstanding.

II. And be it enacted . . . that all such salaries and appointments as have been or shall be granted by his majesty, his heirs and successors, to any judge or judges, shall in all time coming be paid and payable to every such judge and judges for the time being, so long as the patents or commissions of them, or any of them respectively, shall continue and remain in force.

III. Provided always, and be it enacted . . . that it shall and may be lawful to and for his majesty, his heirs and successors, to remove any judge or judges upon the address of both houses of parliament, any thing herein to the contrary thereof in anywise notwithstanding.

Ir. Stat., xii. 359,

12. THE INSURRECTION ACT, 1796

Introduced 22 February, received the royal assent 24 March 1796. Repealed and partly replaced in 1807 by an Act to suppress insurrections and prevent the disturbance of the public peace in Ireland.

An act more effectually to suppress insurrections, and prevent the disturbance of the public peace

Whereas traitorous insurrections have for some time past arisen in various parts of this kingdom, principally promoted and supported by persons associating under the pretended obligation of oaths unlawfully administered . . . be it enacted . . . that any person or persons who shall administer, or cause to be administered, or be present, aiding and assisting at the administering, or who shall by threats, promises, persuasions, or other undue means, cause, procure, or induce to be taken by any person or persons, upon a book, or otherwise any oath or engagement, importing to bind the person taking the same, to be of any association, brotherhood, society, or confederacy formed for seditious purposes, or to disturb the public peace, or to obey the orders or rules, or commands of any committee, or other body of men, not lawfully constituted, or the commands of any captain, leader, or commander (not appointed by his majesty, his heirs and successors) or to assemble at the desire or command of any such captain, leader, commander or committee, or of any person or persons not having lawful authority, or not to inform or give evidence against any brother, associate, confederate, or other person, or not to reveal or discover his having taken any illegal oath, or done any illegal act, or not to discover any illegal oath or engagement which may be tendered to him, or the import thereof, whether he shall take such oath, or enter into such engagement, or not, being by due course of law convicted thereof, shall be adjudged guilty of felony, and suffer death without benefit of clergy, and every person who shall take any such oath or engagement, not being thereto compelled by inevitable necessity, and being by due course of law thereof convicted, shall be adjudged guilty of felony and be transported for life.

VI. And be it further enacted, that all persons who shall have arms in their possession at any time after the passing of this act, shall on or before the first day of May 1796, or immediately after they shall have possession of such arms, deliver to the acting clerk of the peace in the county, town, or city in which he resides . . . a written notification, signed by him or her, specifying therein . . . the place or places where the same are usually kept, accompanied by an affidavit, sworn by the person signing such notification, that the notification is true, and that he believes he is by law entitled to keep arms. . . .

VIII. And be it enacted, that any person having arms, and not making such registry as aforesaid, shall upon being convicted thereof, on the testimony of two credible witnesses on oath before any magistrate, for the first offence forfeit the sum of ten pounds . . . or be imprisoned by such magistrate for the space of two months, and for the second and every other offence shall in like manner forfeit the sum of twenty pounds, or be imprisoned for the space of four months.

X. And be it further enacted, that it shall and may be lawful for any justice of the peace, or for any person authorized thereto by warrant under the hand of any justice of the peace, to search for arms in the houses or grounds of any person not having made such notification as aforesaid, and whom he shall have reasonable ground to suspect of having arms, and also in the houses or grounds of any person who having made such notification, shall refuse or neglect to deliver such list or inventory, or whom he shall have reasonable ground to suspect to have delivered a false list or inventory, and in case of refusal of admission, to break into such house and every part thereof

14

by force, and if any arms shall be found in the possession of any such person respectively, to seize and carry away the same for the use of his majesty.

XII. And whereas in several instances persons who have given information against persons accused of crime have been murdered before trial of the persons accused, in order to prevent their giving evidence and to effect the acquittal of the accused, and some magistrates have been assassinated for their exertions in bringing offenders to justice, be it declared and enacted, that if any person who hath given or shall give information or examinations upon oath against any person or persons for any offence against the laws, shall after the twentieth day of February 1796 and before the trial of the person or persons against whom such information or examination hath been or shall be given, be murdered or violently put to death, or so maimed or forcibly carried away and secreted as not to be able to give evidence on the trial of the person or persons against whom such information or examinations were given, the information or examination of such person so taken on oath, shall be admitted as evidence on the trial of the person or persons against whom such information or examination was given.

XV. And be it further enacted, that it shall and may be lawful for any justice of the peace to arrest and bring before him, or cause to be arrested or brought before him, any stranger sojourning or wandering, and to examine him on oath respecting his place of abode, the place from whence he came, his manner of livelihood, and his object or motive for remaining or coming into the county, town or city, in which he shall be found, and unless he shall answer to the satisfaction of such magistrate, such magistrate shall commit him to gaol or the house of correction, there to remain until he find surety for his good behaviour.

XVI. And in order to restore peace to such parts of the kingdom as are or may be disturbed by seditious persons, be it further enacted, that it shall and may be lawful to and for any two justices of the peace . . . to summon a special session of the peace . . . to consider the state of the county . . . and that the justices assembled in consequence, not being fewer than seven, or the major part of them, one of whom to be of the quorum, or if in a county of a town or city, not being fewer than three, shall and may if they see fit . . . signify by memorial signed by them to the lord lieutenant or other chief governor or governors of this kingdom, that they consider their county or any part thereof, to be in a state of disturbance or in immediate danger of becoming so, and praying that the lord lieutenant and council may proclaim such county, or part thereof, to be in a state of disturbance or in immediate danger of becoming so, and thereupon it shall and may be lawful to and for the lord lieutenant or other chief governor or governors of this kingdom, by and with the advice of his majesty's privy council by proclamation to declare such county, or any part of such county, to be in a state of disturbance or in immediate danger of becoming so, and also such parts of any adjoining county or counties as such chief governor or governors and council shall think fit, in order to prevent the continuance or extension of such disturbance.

XVII. And be it further enacted, that within three days after such proclamation made, or as soon after as may be, every clerk of the peace of every part of the district proclaimed, shall respectively in his county, give notice of holding within two days, or as soon after as may be, a petty session of the peace, and the justices of the peace shall pursuant to such notice assemble . . . and the said justices at said first meeting shall order and direct a notification signed by them to be made throughout the district so proclaimed, that such district has been so proclaimed, and commanding the inhabitants to keep within their dwellings at all unseasonable times between sun-set and sunrise, and warning them of the penalties to which a contrary conduct will expose them . . .

XVIII. And be it further enacted, that it shall and may be lawful to and for any magistrate or other peace officer within such district, after such notification shall be made as aforesaid, to arrest or cause to be arrested any person who shall within such district be found in the fields, streets, highways, or elsewhere out of his dwelling or place of abode, at any time from one hour after sun-set until sunrise and to bring him before two justices of the peace . . . and unless he can prove to their satisfaction that he was out of his house upon his lawful occasions, such person shall be deemed an idle and disorderly person, and shall be transmitted by the warrant of such justices to the officer at some port appointed to receive recruits for his majesty's navy, by which officer such person shall be received as a recruit for his majesty's navy, and transmitted to serve on board his majesty's navy.

XIX. Provided always, that it shall and may be lawful to and for every such person so arrested, to appeal to the next sessions of the peace . . .

XXII. And be it enacted . . . that persons who cannot upon examination prove themselves to exercise and industriously follow some lawful trade or employment as a labourer or otherwise, or to have some substance sufficient for their support or maintenance, shall be deemed idle and disorderly persons, and shall be dealt with according to what is herein before directed respecting persons out of their dwellings at unreasonable hours aforesaid.

XXIX. And be it further enacted, that it shall and may be lawful for any justice of the peace, or any person authorized by the warrant of such justice in any district so proclaimed and whilst such proclaimation shall remain in force, to call upon every person who has registered arms within such district to produce or account for the same, and to enter any house or place whatever, and search for arms and ammunition, and to take and carry away all arms and ammunition which they may think necessary to take possession of, in order to preserve or restore the public peace . . .

XXXI. And be it further enacted, that all persons found

assembled in any proclaimed district, in any house in which malt or spirituous liquors are sold, not being inmates thereof or travellers, whether licensed or unlicensed, after the hours of nine at night and before six in the morning, shall be liable to be deemed idle and disorderly persons within the meaning of this act . . .

XXXII. And be it further enacted, that if any man or boy shall, in any district so proclaimed, hawk or disperse any seditious hand-bill, paper or pamphlet, or paper by law required to be stamped and not duly stamped, such man or boy shall be deemed an idle and disorderly person, and dealt with accordingly, and as is herein before directed ; and if any woman shall hawk or disperse any seditious hand-bill, paper, or paper not duly stamped, such woman being convicted thereof by the oath of one witness before two justices of the peace, one of whom to be of the quorum, such woman shall by the warrant of such two justices be committed to the gaol of the county, there to remain for three months, unless she shall sooner discover the person or persons from whom she received or by whom she was employed to sell, hawk or disperse such papers or pamphlets, provided always, that such woman may appeal from such adjudication to the next sessions of the peace.

XXXVII. Provided always . . . that when a verdict shall be given for the plaintiff in any action to be brought against any justice of the peace, peace officer or other person, for taking or imprisoning or detaining any person, or for seizing arms or ammunition, or entering houses under colour of any authority given by this act, and it shall appear to the judge or judges before whom the same shall be tried, that there was a probable cause for doing the act complained of in such action, and the judge or court shall certify the same on record, then in that case the plaintiff shall not be entitled to more than sixpence damages, nor to any costs of suit.

XXXVIII. Provided also, that where a verdict shall be given for the plaintiff in any such action as aforesaid, and the judge or court before whom the cause shall be tried, shall certify on the record that the injury for which such action is brought was wilfully and maliciously committed, the plaintiff shall be entitled to double costs of suit.

Ir. Stat., xvii. 978–90.

13. THE ACT OF UNION, 1800

Resolutions in favour of a union were passed by the British parliament early in 1799. At the beginning of the Irish parliamentary session of 1799 a clause in the address referring to a union was defeated in the commons. But in March 1800 the Irish parliament agreed to resolutions similar to those passed by the British parliament in the previous year. The act of union was introduced into the Irish house of commons on 21 May 1800 and received the royal assent 1 August 1800.

An act for the union of Great Britain and Ireland

Whereas in pursuance of his majesty's most gracious recommendation to the two houses of parliament in Great Britain and Ireland respectively, to consider of such measures as might best tend to strengthen and consolidate the connexion between the two kingdoms, the two houses of the parliament of Great Britain, and the two houses of the parliament of Ireland have severally agreed and resolved, that in order to promote and secure the essential interests of Great Britain and Ireland, and to consolidate the strength, power, and resources of the British empire, it will be advisable to concur in such measures as may best tend to unite the two kingdoms of Great Britain and Ireland, into one kingdom, in such manner, and on such terms and conditions, as may be established by the acts of the respective parliaments of Great Britain and Ireland.

And whereas in furtherance of the said resolution, both houses of the said two parliaments respectively have likewise agreed upon certain articles for effectuating and establishing the said purposes in the tenor following :

1. That it be the first article of the union of the kingdoms of Great Britain and Ireland, that the said kingdom of Great Britain and Ireland shall, upon the first day of January, which shall be in the year of our Lord 1801, and for ever, be united into one kingdom, by the name of ' The United Kingdom of Great Britain and Ireland,' and that the royal style and titles appertaining to the imperial crown of the said united kingdom and its dependencies, and also the ensigns, armorial flags, and banners thereof, shall be such as his majesty by his royal proclamation under the great seal of the united kingdom shall be pleased to appoint.

2. That it be the second article of union, that the succession to the imperial crown of the said united kingdom, and of the dominions thereunto belonging, shall continue limited and settled in the same manner as the succession to the imperial crown of the said kindoms of Great Britain and Ireland now stands limited and settled, according to the existing laws, and to the terms of union between England and Scotland.

3. That it be the third article of union, that the said united kingdom be represented in one and the same parliament, to be styled ' The parliament of the United Kingdom of Great Britain and Ireland.'

4. That it be the fourth article of union that four lords spiritual of Ireland, by rotation of sessions, and twenty-eight lords temporal of Ireland, elected for life by the peers of Ireland, shall be the number to sit and vote on the part of Ireland in the house of lords of the parliament of the united kingdom, and one hundred commoners (two for each county of Ireland, two for the city of Dublin, two for the city of Cork, one for the university of Trinity college, and one for each of the thirty-one most considerable cities, towns, and boroughs) be the number to sit and vote on the part of Ireland in the house of commons of the parliament of the united kingdom. . . .

That any person holding any peerage of Ireland now subsisting, or hereafter to be created, shall not thereby be disqualified from being elected to serve, if he shall so think fit, or from serving, or continuing to serve, if he shall so think fit, for any county, city, or borough of Great Britain, in the house of commons of the united kingdom, unless he shall have been previously elected as above to sit in the house of lords of the united kingdom, but that so long as such peer of Ireland shall continue to be a member of the house of commons, he shall not be entitled to the privilege of peerage, nor be capable of béing elected to serve as a peer on the part of Ireland, or of voting at any such election, . . .

That it shall be lawful for his majesty, his heirs and successors, to create peers of that part of the united kingdom called Ireland, and to make promotions in the peerage thereof, after the union, provided that no new creation of any such peers shall take place after the union, until three of the peerages of Ireland, which shall have been existing at the time of the union, shall have become extinct, and upon such extinction of three peerages that it shall be lawful for his majesty, his heirs and successors, to create one peer of that part of the united kingdom called Ireland, and in like manner, so often as three peerages of that part of the united kingdom called Ireland, shall become extinct, it shall be lawful for his majesty, his heirs and successors, to create one other peer of the said part of the united kingdom ; and if it shall happen that the peers of that part of the united kingdom called Ireland, shall by extinction of peerages or otherwise, be reduced to the number of one hundred, exclusive of all such peers of that part of the united kingdom called Ireland as shall hold any peerage of Great Britain, subsisting at the time of the union, or of the united kingdom created since the union, by which such peers shall be entitled to an hereditary seat in the house of lords of the united kingdom, then and in that case it shall and may be lawful for his majesty, his heirs and successors, to create one peer of that part of the united kingdom called Ireland, as often as any one of such one hundred peerages shall fail by extinction, or as often as any one peer of that part of the united kingdom called Ireland shall become entitled by descent or creation to a hereditary seat in the house of lords of the united kingdom, it being the true intent and meaning of this article, that at all times after the union, it shall and may be lawful for his majesty, his heirs and successors, to keep up the peerage of that part of the united kingdom called Ireland, to the number of one hundred, over and above the number of such of the said peers as shall be entitled by descent or creation to an hereditary seat in the house of lords of the united kingdom. . . .

That if his majesty, on or before the first day of January 1801, on which day the union is to take place, shall declare, under the great seal of Great Britain, that it is expedient that the lords and commons of the present parliament of Great Britain should be the members of the respective houses of the first parliament of the united kingdom on the part of Great Britain then the said lords and commons shall accordingly be the members of the respective houses of the first parliament of the united kingdom on the part of Great Britain, and they, together with the lords spiritual and temporal, and commons so summoned and returned as above, on the part of Ireland, shall be the lords spiritual and temporal and commons for the first parliament of the united kingdom, and such first parliament may (in that case) if not sooner dissolved, continue to sit so long as the present parliament of Great Britain may now by law continue to sit, if not sooner dissolved : provided always, that until an act shall have passed in the parliament of the united kingdom, providing in what cases persons holding offices or places of profit under the crown in Ireland, shall be incapable of being members of the house of commons of the parliament of the united kingdom, no greater number of members than twenty holding such offices or places as aforesaid, shall be capable of sitting in the said house of commons of the parliament of the united kingdom. . . .

5. That it be the fifth article of union, that the churches of England and Ireland, as now by law established, be united into one protestant episcopal church, to be called ' The united church of England and Ireland,' and that the doctrine, worship, discipline and government of the said united church shall be, and shall remain in full force for ever, as the same are now by law established for the church of England ; and that the continuance and preservation of the said united church, as the established church of England and Ireland, shall be deemed and taken to be an essential and fundamental part of the union ; and that in like manner the doctrine, worship, discipline and government of the church of Scotland shall remain, and be preserved as the same are now established by law, and by the acts for the union of the two kingdoms of England and Scotland.[1]

6. That it be the sixth article of union, that his majesty's subjects of Great Britain and Ireland shall, from and after the first day of January 1801, be entitled to the same privileges, and be on the same footing as to encouragements and bounties on the like articles, being the growth, produce, or manufacture of either country respectively, and generally in respect of trade and navigation in all ports and places in the united kingdom and its dependencies ; and that in all treaties made by his majesty, his heirs and successors, with any foreign power, his majesty's subjects in Ireland shall have the same privileges and be on the same footing as his majesty's subjects of Great Britain. That from the first day of January 1801, all prohibitions and bounties on the export of articles the growth, produce, or manufacture of either country to the other shall cease and determine ; and that the said articles shall thenceforth be exported from one country to the other, without duty or bounty on such export.

That all articles, the growth, produce, or manufacture of either country (not herein-after enumerated as subject to specific duties) shall from thenceforth be imported into each country from the other free from duty . . . and that for the period of twenty years from the

[1] By the provisions of the Irish church act, 1869, on 1 January 1871 the union between the churches of England and Ireland was dissolved and the church of Ireland ceased to be established by law.

union, the articles enumerated in the schedule, No. II. hereunto annexed, shall be subject, on importation into each country from the other, to the duties specified. . . .

7. That it be the seventh article of union that the charge arising from the payment of the interest and the sinking fund for the reduction of the principal of the debt incurred in either kingdom before the union shall continue to be separately defrayed by Great Britain and Ireland respectively, except as herein-after provided.

That for the space of twenty years after the union shall take place, the contribution of Great Britain and Ireland respectively towards the expenditure of the united kingdom in each year shall be defrayed in the proportion of fifteen parts for Great Britain and two parts for Ireland, that at the expiration of the said twenty years the future expenditure of the united kingdom (other than the interest and charges of the debt to which either country shall be separately liable) shall be defrayed in each proportion as the parliament of the united kingdom shall deem just and reasonable, upon a comparison of the real value of the exports and imports of the respective countries upon an average of the three years next preceding the period of revision, or on a comparison of the value of the quantities of the following articles consumed within the respective countries on a similar average, viz. beer, spirits, sugar, wine, tea, tobacco and malt, or according to the aggregate proportion resulting from both these considerations combined, or on a comparison of the amount of income in each country estimated from the produce for the same period of a general tax, if such shall have been imposed on the same descriptions of income in both countries ; and that the parliament of the united kingdom shall afterwards proceed in like manner to revise and fix the said proportions according to the same rules or any of them at periods not more distant than twenty years, nor less than seven years from each other, unless previous to any such period the parliament of the united kingdom shall have declared as herein-after provided that the expenditure of the united kingdom shall be defrayed indiscriminately by equal taxes imposed on the like articles in both countries. . . .

That if at any future day the separate debt of each country respectively shall have been liquidated, or if the value of their respective debts . . . shall be to each other in the same proportion with the respective contributions of each country respectively, or if the amount by which the value of the larger of such debts shall vary from such proportion shall not exceed one hundredth part of the said value, and if it shall appear to the parliament of the united kingdom that the respective circumstances of the two countries will thenceforth admit of their contributing indiscriminately by equal taxes imposed on the same articles in each to the future expenditure of the united kingdom, it shall be competent to the parliament of the united kingdom to declare that all future expense thenceforth to be incurred, together with the interest and charges of all joint debts contracted previous to such declaration, shall be so defrayed indiscriminately by equal taxes imposed on the same articles in each country, and thenceforth from time to time as circumstances may require to impose and apply such taxes accordingly, subject only to such particular exemptions or abatements in Ireland, and in that part of Great Britain called Scotland, as circumstances may appear from time to time to demand.[1] . . .

8. That it be the eighth article of union, that all laws in force at the time of the union, and all the courts of civil and ecclesiastical jurisdiction within the respective kingdoms, shall remain as now by law established within the same, subject only to such alterations and regulations from time to time as circumstances may appear to the parliament of the united kingdom to require, provided that all writs of error and appeals depending at the time of the union, or hereafter to be brought, and which might now be finally decided by the house of lords of either kingdom, shall from and after the union be finally decided by the house of lords of the united kingdom, and provided that from and after the union there shall remain in Ireland an instance court of admiralty for the determination of causes civil and maritime only ; . . . and that all laws at present in force in either kingdom, which shall be contrary to any of the provisions which may be enacted by any act for carrying these articles into effect, be from and after the union repealed.

And whereas the said articles having by address of the respective houses of parliament in Great Britain and Ireland been humbly laid before his majesty, his majesty has been graciously pleased to approve the same, and to recommend it to his two houses of parliament in Great Britain and Ireland, to consider of such measures as may be necessary for giving effect to the said articles, in order to give full effect and validity to the same, be it enacted . . . that the said foregoing recited articles . . . be ratified, confirmed and approved, and be and they are hereby declared to be, the articles of the union of Great Britain and Ireland, and the same shall be in force and have effect for ever, from the first day of January, which shall be in the year of our Lord 1801, provided that before that period an act shall have been passed by the parliament of Great Britain for carrying into effect, in the like manner, the said foregoing recited articles.

10. And be it enacted, that the great seal of Ireland may, if his majesty shall so think fit, after the union be used in like manner as before the union, except where it is otherwise provided by the foregoing articles, within that part of the united kingdom called Ireland, and that his majesty may, so long as he shall think fit, continue the privy council of Ireland, to be his privy council for that part of the united kingdom called Ireland.

Ir. Stat., xx. 448–87.

---

[1] In 1811 the national debts of Great Britain and Ireland were in the same ratio to one another as the contributions. So from 1 January 1817 the exchequers and consolidated funds of Great Britain and Ireland were united.

PARLIAMENTARY PROCEEDINGS

14. REPRESENTATION OF THE IRISH HOUSE OF LORDS, 1719

See remarks on document 1

To the king's most excellent majesty

The humble representation of the lords spiritual and temporal in parliament assembled

Most gracious sovereign, it is with the greatest concern, that we your majesty's most dutiful and loyal subjects, the lords spiritual and temporal in parliament assembled, do find ourselves under a necessity of making this our humble representation to your majesty.

It evidently appears, by many ancient records, and sundry acts of parliament passed in this kingdom, and particularly by one in the 11th of Queen Elizabeth, entitled, *An act for attainder of Shane O'Neal*, etc., that the kings, with the princes and men of value of the land, did, of their own good-wills, and without any war, or chivalry, submit themselves to your majesty's royal ancestor King Henry II, took oaths of fidelity to him, and became his liege subjects ; who (as is asserted by the Lord Chief Justice Coke and others) did ordain and command at the instance of the Irish, ' that such laws as he had in England, should be of force and observed in Ireland.' By this agreement, the people of Ireland obtained the benefit of the English laws, and many privileges, particularly that of having a distinct parliament here, as in England, and of having weighty and momentous matters relating to this kingdom treated of, discussed and determined in the said parliament.

This concession and compact, thus made and afterwards by succeeding kings confirmed to the people of this land, in process of time, proved a great encouragement to many of the English to come over and settle themselves in Ireland, where they were to enjoy the same laws and liberties, and live under the like constitution, as they had formerly done in the kingdom of England. Which, through God's Good Providence, has proved a means of securing this kingdom to the crown of England, and we trust, will do so to all futurity. By this happy constitution, and these privileges, by us for so many years enjoyed, the English subjects of this kingdom have been enabled faithfully to discharge their duty to the crown of England, and vigorously set themselves, upon all occasions, to assert the rights thereof, against all the rebellions which have been raised by the Irish enemies. And therefore we your majesty's loyal subjects do, with all submission to your majesty, insist upon them, and hope, through your majesty's goodness, to have them preserved inviolable.

And we beg leave to represent to your majesty, that though th imperial crown of this realm was formerly inseparably annexed to the imperial crown of England, and is now to that of Great Britain, yet this kingdom, being of itself a distinct dominion, and no part of the kingdom of England, none can determine concerning the affairs thereof, unless authorized thereto by the known laws and customs of this kingdom, or by the express consent of the king.

And as your royal ancestors have always enjoyed the right and power of determining all matters, that related only to this kingdom, by their royal authority in their parliaments held here, so we humbly hope, your majesty will always look on this right as a most valuable jewel of your crown, which none should presume to touch without your majesty's consent; and that your majesty will graciously allow us to represent it as an invasion of your prerogative and a grievance to your loyal subjects in this kingdom, that any court of judicature should take upon them to declare that your majesty cannot determine all controversies between your subjects of this kingdom, and about matters relating wholly to the same, by your royal authority, in your parliament summoned to meet here; or that your subjects of Ireland, appealing to your majesty, in your parliament in Ireland in matters wholly relating to this kingdom, do bring their cause before an incompetent judicature.

We have (may it please your sacred majesty) endeavoured with our utmost care to inquire into the grounds of all such appeals or removals of causes from this kingdom, as have at any time been made into England ; and are persuaded that such usages have been introduced by slow degrees. At first, the judges here being to determine the causes that came before them by the common laws of England, and sometimes, not knowing well the usages there applied to Henry III their then king, for information, who gave them an account what the common law and custom of England in like cases was. And this undoubtedly, by the advice of the justices of the king's bench, who then were obliged to attend the king wherever he should be. And, in process of time, when his successors had settled the court of king's bench after another manner, and had forborn to sit there themselves in person, the application which formerly used to be made to the king who presided in that court, came of course to be brought before the justices of the court, although the king was not there personally present. And this, as we conceive, gave rise to that custom of removing causes by writs of error from the king's bench in Ireland, to the king's bench in England. But from thence to infer, that therefore appeals from the parliament of Ireland, may be brought before the house of peers in England or Great Britain, is a consequence for which there appears to be no manner of ground.

As for the practice of appealing from the high court of chancery in Ireland, to the lords of Great Britain, we can find but two precedents of such appeals, before the late happy revolution, one in 1670, and the other in 1679. And we can account for them no otherwise, than by observing that they happened at a juncture, when no opposition could be given them from this kingdom, because, through the prevalency of a popish interest, no parliament had been held here for some years before, nor were we then in any likelihood of having any called here for many years to come, nor can we find that any like subsequent appeals from that court have any other foundation, than those two precedents.

And such appeals (though they had been of longer standing and better founded) yet were never supposed to preclude the king's majesty from his right of giving redress to his subjects of Ireland, in his parliament when assembled here, any more than writs of error to the king's-bench in England, had hindered the like writs from being returnable in the parliament here.

And accordingly, when, by God's blessing on the late happy revolution, this kingdom came to have a parliament, after twenty-six years' intermission, complaints were heard, writs of error and appeals were received, and proper orders were made thereon, as formerly, nor were they, as far as we can find, ever questioned, or their validity doubted till the year 1699, when two appeals from the parliament here were carried before the lords in England, though no pleadings to the jurisdiction of the parliament of Ireland had been offered or mentioned, by either party, on hearing the said causes here.

And though the parliament of Ireland could not then interpose, or any ways assert their jurisdiction, because it was not fitting, yet the lords of England declared the said causes to be *coram non judice*; and, without hearing the merits of the causes, reversed the decrees that had been made here.

Upon which occasion, we cannot but observe, that the parliament of Ireland (as the constitution thereof has been for some hundreds of years) being convened by the same authority and writs of summons, and consisting of like members, and distinct houses of peers and commons, and the former having the same assistance and attendance from the judges of the several courts and masters of chancery, as in England or Great Britain, either some record, act of parliament or ancient usage must be shewn, whereby to make a difference (which has never yet been attempted) or else, from our very constitution, it must, as we conceive, appear, that whatever power of judicature is lodged in the English or British parliament, with respect to that kingdom and its inferior courts, the same must also be allowed to be in the parliament of Ireland, with like respect to the kingdom and courts thereof. And if it be looked upon as illegal for any inferior court in Great Britain to act in direct opposition to, or contempt of, the orders and decrees of the house of lords in parliament there assembled, the same must also be concluded upon the like opposition given or contempt shown, to such parliamentary orders and decrees, as are or shall be made within this kingdom. . . .

It is, under God, the great security of this your majestys' kingdom of Ireland, that by the laws and statutes thereof, the same is annexed and united to the imperial crown of England and declared to be depending upon, and for ever belonging to, the same. But if all judgments, decrees and determinations made in this your majesty's highest court within this kingdom, are subject to be nulled and reversed by the lords in Great Britain, the liberties and properties of all your subjects of Ireland, must thereby become finally dependent on the British peers, to the great diminution of that dependence, which, by law, we always ought to have immediately upon the crown itself.

That your majesty has, by the constitution of this your realm of Ireland, the full power of judging and determining all causes that belong to it alone in *pleno parliamento*, is what no man hitherto has ventured openly to deny or doubt of.

But, if in all cases that relate to this kingdom, the dernier resort (as some of late have affected to speak) ought to be to the house of lords in Great Britain, however this your majesty's power may still in words be acknowledged, the force and effect of it is in reality taken away and wholly vested in the British peers. . . .

It is notorious, that the lords of Great Britain have not in themselves, either by law or custom, any way of putting their decrees in execution within this kingdom, of which they have given most undoubted evidence by their late application to your majesty to cause such their decrees to be executed by an extraordinary interposition of your royal power. And should your majesty think fit to yield to this their desire, we humbly presume to think it would highly affect the liberty of your majesty's loyal subjects of this kingdom, . . .

And we further represent to your majesty, that these proceedings of the lords of England have greatly embarrassed your parliament and disquieted the generality of your most loyal protestant subjects of this your kingdom, and must of necessity bring all sheriffs and officers of justice under great hardships, by reason of the clashing of different jurisdictions. Nor can we but with grief observe, that whilst many of the peers and commons who sat in parliament were papists, their judicature was never questioned. But of late, since only protestants are qualified to have a share in the legislature, their power and the right of hearing causes in parliament hath been denied, to the great discouragement and weakening of the protestant interest in Ireland.

And having thus, with all humility, laid before your majesty, your undoubted power and prerogative within this your kingdom of Ireland, the immediate dependence of the same upon your majesty's crown, the right your majesty has to hold parliaments there as in Great Britain, and of finally determining therein all matters that wholly relate to this realm, together with the great encroachments that have of late been made upon your majesty's prerogative, and the rights of this your parliament, and the illegal unprecedented proceedings of the lord chief baron and the other barons of your majesty's court of exchequer, whereby they have endeavoured to support those encroachments, with the evil consequences of such proceedings, in case that a speedy and effectual stop be not thereunto put. We most humbly hope, that all these things being duly considered and weighted with your majesty's usual wisdom, will abundantly justify us in the methods we have taken, as well for the supporting of your majesty's royal prerogative as the preservation of the just rights and liberties of ourselves and our fellow-subjects, as the same are set forth in the several resolutions we have come to, a copy whereof we have hereunto annexed, with all humility, assuring your majesty, that no difficulties which we may be laid under shall hinder us from giving the utmost despatch to all your majesty's affairs, or from most cheerfully demonstrating that loyalty and affection to your majesty's person and attachment to your interest, which becomes your majesty's dutiful and obedient subjects. Whereof we again, from our hearts, make an humble tender to your most sacred majesty.

Lords journ., Ire., ii. 655–60.

15. ADDRESS OF THE HOUSE OF COMMONS ON WOOD'S HALFPENCE, 1723

In July 1722 a patent was issued granting Wood the right to coin copper halfpence and farthings for Ireland. When parliament met in 1723 the house of commons went into committee (20 September) and passed six resolutions on which the address given below was based. The lords voted a similar address. The patent was cancelled in August 1725.

To the king's most excellent majesty

The humble address of the knights, citizens, and burgesses in parliament assembled

Most gracious sovereign, it is with the utmost concern that we, your majesty's most dutiful and loyal subjects, the commons of Ireland in parliament assembled, find ourselves indispensably obliged humbly to represent to your majesty our unanimous opinion, that the importing and uttering of copper farthings and halfpence, by virtue of the patent lately granted to William Wood, Esq. under the great seal of Great Britain, will be highly prejudicial to your majesty's revenue, destructive of the trade and commerce of this nation, and of the most dangerous consequence to the properties of the subject.

We are fully convinced, from the tender regard your majesty has always expressed for our welfare and prosperity, that this patent could not have obtained, had not William Wood and his accomplices greatly misrepresented the state of this nation to your majesty, it having appeared to us by examinations taken in the most solemn manner, that though the terms thereof had been strictly complied with, there would have been a loss to this nation of at least £150 per cent by means of the said coinage, and a much greater in the manner the said halfpence have been coined.

We likewise beg leave to inform your majesty, that the said William Wood has been guilty of a most notorious fraud and deceit in coining the said halfpence, having, under colour of the powers granted unto him, imported, and endeavoured to utter great quantities of different impressions, and of much less weight than was required by the said patent.

Your faithful commons have found by experience, that the granting of the power or privilege of coining money or tokens to pass for money, to private persons, has been highly detrimental to your loyal subjects, and being apprehensive that the vesting of such power in any body politic or corporate, or any private person, or persons whatsoever, will be always of dangerous consequence to this kingdom, are encouraged by the repeated assurances your majesty hath given us of your royal favour and protection, humbly to entreat your majesty, that whenever you shall hereafter think it necessary to coin any farthings or halfpence, the same may be made as near the intrinsic value as possible, and that whatever profit shall accrue thereby may be applied to the public service.

And we do further humbly beseech your majesty, that you will be graciously pleased to give such directions as you in your great wisdom shall think proper, to prevent the fatal effects of uttering any farthings or halfpence, pursuant to the said patent.

As this inquiry has proceeded entirely from our love to our country, so we cannot omit this opportunity of repeating our unanimous resolution to stand by and support your majesty to the utmost of our power, against all your enemies both at home and abroad, and of assuring your majesty, that we will, upon every occasion, give your majesty and the world all possible demonstration of our zeal and inviolable duty and affection to your majesty's most sacred person and government, and to the succession as established in your royal house.

Commons journ., Ire., iii. 325.

16. THE MONEY BILL OF 1753

The court party asserted that the disposal of a surplus in the treasury belonged to the crown. A bill whose preamble expressed this view was passed in 1751. In 1753 the country party, strengthened by quarrels amongst the government's supporters, rejected a similar bill. Thereupon the government applied the surplus to debt reduction by a 'king's letter.' From this time the commons were careful to appropriate the portion of the revenue voted by parliament.

Extract from the lord lieutenant's speech, 9 October 1753

' I am commended by his majesty to acquaint you, that he will graciously consent, and recommends it to you, that so much of the money remaining in his treasury as shall be necessary, be applied to the discharge of the national debt, or of such part thereof as you shall think expedient.'

Extract from the reply of the house of commons

' That we are truly sensible of his majesty's royal care and goodness, in recommending to us the application of so much of the money remaining in the treasury as shall be necessary for the discharge of the national debt, or of such part thereof as shall be judged expedient.

Lunae, 17° Die Decembris, 1753

The house according to order, resolved itself into a committee of the whole house to take into consideration a bill, entitled, *An act for the payment of the sum of £77,500, or so much thereof as shall remain due on the twenty-fifth day of December, one thousand seven hundred and fifty-three, in discharge of the national debt, together with the interest for the same, at the rate of four pounds per centum, per annum, from* 25 *December* 1753 *until* 25 *March* 1754, and after some time spent therein, Mr. Speaker resumed the chair.

The right honourable the master of the rolls reported from the committee, that they had agreed to the enacting paragraphs of the bill, but disagreed to the preamble of the said bill.

Ordered, that the bill be rejected.

Commons journ., Ire., v. 167–8, 204.

17. TOWNSHEND'S REBUKE TO THE HOUSE OF COMMONS, 1769

Amongst the bills sent over from England before parliament met in 1769 was, as was customarily, a money bill. This was rejected by the house of commons.

Lord Townshend's speech at the proroguing of parliament, 26 December 1769

It is therefore with great concern that I have seen and observed in the votes and journals of the house of commons . . . the vote and resolution of the 21 day of November last, by which you gentlemen of the house of commons, declare, that a bill, entitled, *An act for granting his majesty the several duties, rates, impositions and taxes therein particularly expressed, to be applied to the payment of the sums therein provided for, and toward the discharge of the principal sums, in such manner as is therein directed* which had been duly certified from hence to his majesty, and by his majesty had been transmitted in due form, under the great seal of Great Britain, and which had been read a first time by you, and which was rejected by you on that day, was so rejected because it did not take to rise in your house. . . . This vote and resolution of your's . . . being contrary to the acts of parliament of this kingdom of the 10th Henry VII and the 3rd and 4th of Philip and Mary, and the usages and practices ever since, and intervening upon the just rights of his majesty and the crown of Great Britain to transmit such bills to be treated of and considered in parliament here, I am now to assert his majesty's just authority, and the rights of the crown of Great Britain in this respect and in such a manner as may be most public and permanent; and therefore I do here in full parliament, make my public protest against the said vote and

resolution of the house of commons, . . . and I do require the
clerk of the house, now to read my said protest, and to enter it in
the journals of this house, that it may there remain to future ages,
as a vindication of the undoubted right and authority of his majesty,
and of the rights of the crown of Great Britain, in this particular.

Lords journ., Ire., iv. 538–9.

PARLIAMENTARY SPEECHES ON ANGLO-IRISH RELATIONS, 1782–99

18. CHARLES JAMES FOX ON THE IRISH QUESTION, BRITISH HOUSE OF COMMONS, 17 MAY 1782

And first, on the 6th of George I it had always been his opinion
out of office, that it was downright tyranny to make laws for the
internal government of people who were not represented among
those by whom such laws were made. This was an opinion so
founded in justice, reason and equity, that in no situation had he,
or would he ever depart from it. It was true, nevertheless, that
he was not an enemy to the declaratory act, which had been passed
relative to America ; yet his scruples were not inconsistent or
incompatible with that act. He had always made a distinction
between internal and external legislation ; and though it would be
tyranny to enforce the former, in countries not represented in the
British parliament, yet he was clear that the latter was, in reason
and policy, annexed to the British legislature ; this right of prerogative or supremacy, he was convinced, would never have given
umbrage to any part of the British empire, if it had been used
solely for the general good of the empire, but when it was made an
instrument of tyranny and oppression, it was not to be thought
wonderful, that it should excite discontent, murmurings and opposition. When local legislatures were established in different parts
of the empire, it was clear that it was for this purpose, that they
might answer all municipal ends, and the great superintending
power of the state ought not to be called into action, but in aid of
the local legislature, and for the good of the empire at large ; but
when ministers, judging by what they had, of what they might have,
carried the principle of external to internal legislation, and attempted
to bind the internal government of its colonies by acts, in the passing
of which the colonies had no voice, that power, which, on proper
occasions, would have been cheerfully obeyed, created animosity
and hatred, and had produced the dismemberment of an empire,
which, if properly exerted, it would have served to unite and bind
in the firmest manner.

Ireland had the same reason to spurn at this power of external
legislation because it had been hitherto employed for the purpose only
of oppressing and distressing her. Had Ireland never been made
to feel this power as a curse, she never would have complained
of it, and the best and most effectual way to have kept it alive,

15

would have been, not to have made use of it ; Ireland would then have suffered this harmless power to exist in the statute book, she never would have called out for a renunciation of it. But, fatally for this country, this power of external legislation had been employed against Ireland as an instrument of oppression, to establish an impolitic monopoly in trade, to enrich one country at the expense of the other. . . . It was his intention not to pursue the footsteps of his predecessors ; and therefore he would agree to the demands of the Irish, relative to the 6 Geo. I, not because he was intimidated, and afraid to oppose them, but because he believed them to be founded in justice ; and he would have been as ready to grant them if Ireland made them now in the unarmed and modest manner in which she had preferred her complaints four years ago. . . . She [Ireland] therefore could have no reason to complain ; the terms acceded to by England, were proposed by herself, and all her wishes would now be gratified in the way which she herself liked best ; but as it was possible, that if nothing more was to be done than what he had stated to be his intention, Ireland might perhaps think of fresh grievances, and rise yearly in her demands, it was fit and proper that something should be now done towards establishing on a firm and solid basis, the future connexion of the two kingdoms. But that was not to be proposed by him here in parliament ; it would be the duty of the crown to look to that ; the business might be first begun by his majesty's servants in Ireland, and if afterwards it should be necessary to enter into a treaty, commissioners might be sent from the British parliament or from the crown, to enter upon it, and bring the negotiation to a happy issue by giving mutual satisfaction to both countries, and establishing a treaty which should be sanctified by the most solemn forms of the constitutions of both countries.

The parliamentary register (London), viii. 166–72.

19. DEBATE ON YELVERTON'S ACT, IRISH HOUSE OF COMMONS, 6 AND 7 JUNE 1782

Thursday, 6 June. In a committee on the bill for the modification of Poynings' law, Sir Richard Johnston in the chair

Mr. Yelverton remarked that as the bill then stood, the privy council were obliged to certify all bills which originated in parliament, and no other, without alteration.

The Right Hon. Henry Flood thought it not perfectly adequate to the idea held out and entertained by the nation, or what seemed necessary to do justice to the constitution. They ought either to declare against all usurpation, or by an effectual appeal to annihilate those pretensions in future. It was the opinion of the nine of Ireland [1] that this act [2] took away the power of originating bills and

---

[1] See the opinion of the Irish judges upon Poynings' law submitted to Lord Sidney in February 1692 (W. Harris, *The life and reign of William III* (Dublin 1749), appendix, pp. lxxxi–ii.   [2] Poynings' law.

gave it to the privy council. That should certainly be repealed, for he did not see, by any effect in the present bill, but the privy council might recall this power under a corrupt ministry, and it was not to be supposed that the breed of the Staffords in political principles, were yet extinct ; and an arbitrary government might at some future period take advantage of the negligence of the present hour. He understood, and the nation understood, that all they aimed at was a similar constitution with England, but the bill by implication cut them off from that benefit. He understood it to be the constitution of the land, that the whole business of legislation was to be done in public, but there was no provision made by this bill which could prevent the smothering of bills, or explain the reasons of a silent negative. . . .

Mr. Yelverton said that the right hon. gentleman certainly agreed in principle with him, and they differed only in mode. Their sentiments were certainly the same. He confessed the bill did not entirely restore what the constitution of England enjoyed, but circumstanced as Ireland was now, it was the best calculated that could be devised. The features of the two sister kingdoms were not exactly alike ; some little difference might be discovered in the traits, but they were actually and in fact the same. To restore the constitution of Ireland as it once stood, would in a great measure be restoring tumult and disorder, and going back to the necessity of laws, when a lord lieutenant had the same power as the king, made peace and war, and exercised all the privileges of sovereignty. . . . The Right Hon. Gentleman complained that the dissent to such bills as should come back were [sic] not to be publicly notified in parliament. He agreed with him that legislation should be as public as the courts of justice, but in the instance alluded to, he could not see any ill consequence which could possibly result from a silent negative. The question merely amounted to this, was the bill adequate to the constitution they demanded ? He thought it was. . . .

The Right Hon. the Prime Sergeant[1] observed, that the questions then before them, were, first whether the bill before them went sufficiently to the repeal of the obnoxious parts of Poynings' law, and secondly whether a private or a public dissent was the properest. The bill in his opinion was more eligible in its present form, than that of a specific repeal ; because it was virtually repealed by a general clause, there was not occasion for a specific one. The great difficulty of the friends of Ireland, was that England started at the idea of disunion, and they had looked at the law of Poynings as the greatest bond for the union of nations. He therefore thought, that an entire repeal would be cutting the bands which united the two countries asunder. They gained all they wanted, by that bill, without being glaringly offensive and went to conciliate and not to provoke the friends of this country in England. It was asked whether they preferred certainty to doubt ? He would answer if

[1] Walter Hussey Burgh.

the bill passed in its present form they ensured a certainty, if otherwise they rendered all they asked precarious. Lawyers, it was said, might create doubts hereafter. He did not look upon lawyers to be necromancers, who could conjure up doubts where a foundation for none was laid. Indeed he did not wish that an idea of such doubts should go abroad. The king being an absentee made a distinction between both nations necessary. In England the king was acquainted with the progress of each bill before it was ready for his assent, but as the same communication could not take place here, it was but reasonable to infer, that for the want of such communication, in some instances bills might be rejected.

Did gentlemen wish by a public rejection, parliament should be piqued into a declaration of its rights, and raise a commotion in the state ?—Many bills it may be for the good of the country to meet such a negative, and many had already received a dissent, which had they passed into laws, would have made that house mourn. He concluded by averring, that he was never more clear, than in the eligibility of the present bill.

Friday, 7 June. The engrossed bill for the repeal of Poynings' law being read. Mr. Walsh said, the more he considered the objections made yesterday, the more confident he was, that the present bill was defective. It was a bill which by no means met the idea that every Irishman formed of a constitution similar in every point to that of England, except the absence of the king. By the constitution of England, the king gives or refuses his assent publicly in person, or by his commissioners in the house of lords of England. The bill only transferred the power of altering from the Irish to the English privy council, and the English attorney-general. This was so far from amelioration of the present contest, that it was pregnant with implication and duplicity, and therefore nothing less than an express repeal would satisfy this nation. The king's public dissent was as necessary as his assent, to prevent their future acts from being smuggled under the cushion, before ever they received the eye of the sovereign.

Mr. Ogle said, he must approve of that bill which compelled a chief governor and privy council to transmit every bill that passed the two houses of parliament, without making the smallest alteration, nor could he see the force of what had been offered in regard to his majesty consulting with his English privy council, as it was totally out of the power of parliament to prevent him from consulting with whomsoever he pleased. . . .

The Parliamentary register (Dublin 1782), i. 383–92.

20. JOHN FITZGIBBON ON THE REGENCY QUESTION, IRISH HOUSE OF COMMONS, 11 FEBRUARY 1789

I shall in as few words as possible state my opinion. And first I maintain that the crown of Ireland and the crown of England are inseparably and indissolubly united. Secondly, I do maintain, that the Irish parliament is perfectly and totally independent of the British parliament.

The first position is your security ; the second is your freedom ; and when gentlemen talk any other language than this, they either talk to the separation of the crowns, or the subjugation of your parliament ; they invade either your security or your liberty ; further, the only security of your liberty is your connexion with Great Britain, and gentlemen who risk breaking the connexion must make up their mind to a union. God forbid I should ever see that day ; but if ever the day on which a separation shall be attempted, may come, I shall not hesitate to embrace a union rather than a separation.

Under the Duke of Portland's government the grievances of Ireland were stated to be, the alarming usurpation of the British parliament, a perpetual mutiny bill, and the powers assumed by the privy council.

These grievances were redressed, and in redressing them you passed a law repealing part of Poynings'. By your new law you enact, that all bills which pass the two houses here, which shall be certified into England, and which shall be returned under the great seal of England, without any addition, diminution, or alteration whatsoever, shall pass into law, and no other. By this you make the great seal of England essentially and indispensably necessary on the passing of laws in Ireland, you can pass no act without first certifying it into England, and having it returned under the great seal of that kingdom, insomuch that were the king of England and Ireland to come here in person and reside, he could not pass a bill without it first being certified to his regent in England, who must return it under the seal of that kingdom before his majesty could even in person assent to it. This bill was framed and introduced by a gentleman, certainly of as good intentions as any man in the kingdom. By this bill the great seal of England is the organ by which the king of England speaks, and the great seal of Ireland is the organ by which the king of Ireland speaks, and it is nonsense to say, that it is as king of Ireland he affixes the great seal of England to Irish acts, as well might you say that it is as king of Ireland he affixes the great seal of England to treaties of peace, alliance or commerce, which nevertheless include Ireland. I have stated, that his majesty could not, were he here in person, pass an act without having first the great seal of England affixed thereto. Let me now for a moment suppose, that we, in the dignity of our independence, appoint a regent for Ireland, being a different person from the regent of England, a case not utterly impossible, if the gentlemen insist on appointing the prince of Wales before it will be known whether he shall accept the regency of England ; and suppose we should go farther, and desire him to give the royal assent to bills, he would say ' My good people of Ireland, you here by your own law made the great seal of England absolutely and essentially necessary to be affixed to each bill before it passes in Ireland, that seal is in the hands of the chancellor of

England, who is a very sturdy fellow, that chancellor is an officer under the regent of England, I have no manner of authority over him, and so, my very good people, of Ireland, you had better apply to the regent of England, and request that he will order the chancellor of England to affix the great seal of England to your bills, otherwise, my very good people of Ireland, I cannot pass them ; . . .

Parliamentary Register (Dublin 1790), ix. 48–9.

21. THOMAS PELHAM AND HENRY GRATTAN ON THE POSITION OF IRISH MINISTERS, IRISH HOUSE OF COMMONS, 21 APRIL 1795

On a motion that the house go into committee on the state of the nation

Mr. Pelham—I believe all the sober part of the world, and all men conversant in public matters, will think I best discharge my duty, by not being betrayed into any indiscretion either by the attack of my adversaries, or by the zeal of my friends. A right hon. gentleman (Sir J. Blacquiere) has rightly stated, that the lord lieutenant and his secretary act under written instructions from the cabinet ; and that such instructions alone are the proper authority of their conduct. It is not, however, necessary at any time to discover those instructions—they are to be judged of by the goodness of the measures which are produced to this house and the public. . . .

Mr. Grattan said, that certain doctrines had been advanced on the subject of the British cabinet, to which he could not accede, that it had been argued that the British cabinet was to govern the executive power of Ireland, that the viceroy's function was only to obey orders, and to be the English agent in the kingdom of Ireland— that such a doctrine was fatal to monarchy in this country—that in its place it established the monarchy of clerks—a government to be carried on by post and under the dominion of spies, who were less than gentlemen, and more than ministers. It was such a base and dishonourable system that had excited the indignation of some of the whigs in England, the duke of Portland in particular. It was that system of national degradation and vice-regal extinction—that system where the clerks dominated and their betters obeyed, that had sunk a former administration, and had excited the scorn and indignation of the country. To the returning prevalence of such a system we must attribute in a great degree to [sic] the recall of the late chief governor.[1] The cabinet were misinformed, they heard appeals against him from the persons removed, and tried unsummoned on the testimony of partial witnesses, the representative of the king. . . . While I mention that the viceroy is the representative of the king and not of the minister, I do acknowledge that it is necessary for the viceroy to keep up with that minister a close communication, that the two executives may co-operate, and that when the English cabinet who advises the king, no longer co-operates with the viceroy it is prudent in him to withdraw. The king communicates with the viceroy through a cabinet officer. He consults

[1] Lord Fitzwilliam.

with that officer who probably consults with his colleagues touching the matter of the communication ; hence an interference of the British cabinet in the affairs of Ireland which will not be questioned until it is abused and becomes the domination instead of being communication.

The parliamentary register (Dublin 1795), xv. 189–90.

22. WILLIAM PITT ON THE UNION, BRITISH HOUSE OF COMMONS, 31 JANUARY 1799

. . . Thinking then, as we all must think, that a close connexion with Ireland is essential to the interests of both countries, and seeing how much this connexion is attacked, let it not be insinuated that it is unnecessary, much less improper, at this arduous and important crisis, to see whether some new arrangements, some fundamental regulations, are not necessary to guard against the threatened danger. . . .

When I last addressed the house on this subject, I stated that the settlement, which was made in 1782, so far from deserving the name of a final adjustment, was one that left the connexion between Great Britain and Ireland exposed to all the attacks of party, and all the effects of accident. That settlement consisted in the demolition of the system which before held the two countries together. Let me not be understood as expressing any regret at the termination of that system. I disapproved of it, because I thought it was one unworthy of the liberality of Great Britain, and injurious to the interests of Ireland. But to call that a system in itself—to call that a glorious fabric of human wisdom, which is no more than the mere demolition of another system, is a perversion of terms which, however prevalent of late, can only be the effect of gross misconception or of great hypocrisy. . . .

But when we consider the distinct powers possessed by the two legislatures on all the great questions of peace and war, of alliances and confederacies (for they each have in principle a right to discuss them and decide upon them, though one of them has hitherto been wisely restrained by discretion from the exercise of that right), have we not seen circumstances to induce us to think it possible, at least, that on some of these important questions the opinions and decisions of the two parliaments might have been at variance ? Are we talking of an indissoluble connexion, when we see it thus perpetually liable to be endangered ? Can we really think that the interests of the empire, or of its different branches, rest upon a safe and solid basis at present ? I am anxious to discuss this point closely with any man, either here or in Ireland. Will it be said, that the parliament of the latter country is bound by our decision on the question of peace or war ? And if not so bound, will any man, looking at human nature as it is, contend, that there is sufficient certainty that the decision on that important subject will always be the same in both countries ? . . .

This country is at this time engaged in the most important and momentous conflict that ever occurred in the history of the world ; a conflict in which Great Britain is distinguished for having made the only manly and successful stand against the common enemies of civilized society. We see the point in which that enemy thinks us the most assailable. Are we not then bound in policy and prudence to strengthen that vulnerable point, involved as we are in a contest of liberty against despotism—of property against plunder and rapine—of religion and order against impiety and anarchy ? . . .

Among the great and known defects of Ireland, one of the most prominent features is, its want of industry and a capital ; how are those wants to be supplied, but by blending more closely with Ireland the industry and the capital of this country ? But, above all, in the great leading distinction between the people of Ireland (I mean their religious distinctions), what is their situation ?—The protestant feels that the claims of the catholics threaten the existence of the protestant ascendancy ; while on the other hand, the great body of catholics feel the establishment of the national church, and their exclusion from the exercise of certain rights and privileges, a grievance. Between the two, it becomes a matter of difficulty in the minds of many persons, whether it would be better to listen only to the fears of the former, or to grant the claims of the latter.

I am well aware that the subject of religious distinction is a dangerous and delicate topic, especially when applied to a country such as Ireland, the situation of which is different in this respect from that of every other. Where the established religion of the state is the same as the general religion of the empire, and where the property of the country is in the hands of a comparatively small number of persons professing that established religion, while the religion of a great majority of the people is different, it is not easy to say, on general principles, what system of church establishment in such a country would be free from difficulty and inconvenience. By many I know it will be contended, that the religion professed by the majority of the people would, at least, be entitled to an equality of privileges. I have heard such an argument used in this house ; but those who apply it without qualification to the case of Ireland, forget surely the principles on which English interest and English connexion has been established in that country, and on which its present legislature is formed. No man can say, that, in the present state of things, and while Ireland remains a separate kingdom, full concessions could be made to the catholics, without endangering the state, and shaking the constitution of Ireland to its centre.

On the other hand, without anticipating the discussion or the propriety of agitating the question, or saying how soon or how late it may be fit to discuss it, two propositions are indisputable : first, when the conduct of the catholics shall be such as to make it safe for the government to admit them to the participation of the privileges granted to those of the established religion, and when the temper of the times shall be favourable to such a measure—when these events take place, it is obvious that such a question may be agitated in an united, imperial parliament, with much greater safety, than it could be in a separate legislature. In the second place, I think it certain that even for whatever period it may be thought necessary, after the union, to withhold from the catholics the enjoyment of those advantages, many of the objections which at present arise out of their situation would be removed, if the protestant legislature were no longer separate and local, but general and imperial ; and the catholics themselves would at once feel a mitigation of the most goading and irritating of their present causes of complaint.

How far, in addition to this great and leading consideration, it may also be wise and practicable to accompany the measure by some mode of relieving the lower orders from the pressure of tithes, which, in many instances, operate at present as a great practical evil, or to make, under proper regulations, and without breaking in on the security of the present protestant establishment, an effectual and adequate provision for the catholic clergy, it is not now necessary to discuss. It is sufficient to say, that these and all other subordinate points connected with the same subject, are more likely to be permanently and satisfactorily settled by a united legislature, than by any local arrangements. . . .

I have heard it asked, when I pressed the measure, What are the positive advantages that Ireland is to derive from it ? . . .

I might enumerate the general advantages which Ireland would derive from the effects of the arrangement to which I have already referred—the protection which she will secure to herself in the hour of danger, the most effectual means of increasing her commerce and improving her agriculture, the command of English capital, the infusion of English manners and English industry, necessarily tending to ameliorate her condition, to accelerate the progress of internal civilization, and to terminate those feuds and dissensions which now distract the country, and which she does not possess, within herself, the power either to control or to extinguish. She would see the avenue to honours, to distinctions, and exalted situations in the general seat of empire, opened to all those whose abilities and talents enable them to indulge an honourable and laudable ambition.

But, independent of all these advantages, I might also answer that the question is not what Ireland is to gain, but what she is to preserve, not merely how she may best improve her situation, but how she is to avert a pressing and immediate danger. In this view, what she gains is the preservation of all those blessings arising from the British constitution, and which are inseparable from her connexions with Great Britain ; . . .

I have thus, Sir, endeavoured to state to you the reasons, why I think this measure advisable ; why I wish it to be proposed to the parliament of Ireland, with temper and fairness ; and why it appears to me entitled, at least, to a calm and dispassionate discussion in that kingdom. I am aware, however, that objections have been urged against the measure, some of which are undoubtedly plausible, and have been but too successful in their influence on the Irish parliament. Of these objections I shall now proceed, as concisely as possible, to take some notice.

The first is, what I heard alluded to by the honourable gentleman opposite to me,[1] when his majesty's message was brought down ; namely, that the parliament of Ireland is incompetent to entertain and discuss the question, or rather, to act upon the measure proposed, without having previously obtained the consent of the people of Ireland. . . . For the present, I will assume that no man can deny the competency of the parliament of Ireland, representing as it does, in the language of our constitution, ' lawfully, fully, and freely, all the estates of the people of the realm,' to make laws to bind that people, unless he is disposed to distinguish that parliament from the parliament of Great Britain, and, while he maintains the independence of the Irish legislature, yet denies to it the lawful and essential powers of parliament. . . .

Sir, the next and not the least prevalent objection, is one which is contained in words which are an appeal to a natural and laudable, but what I must call an erroneous and mistaken, sense of national pride. It is an appeal to the generous and noble passions of a nation easily inflamed under any supposed attack upon its honour, I mean the attempt to represent the question of an union by compact between the parliaments of the two kingdoms as a question involving the independence of Ireland.—It has been said, that no compensation could be made to any country for the surrender of its national independence. Sir, on this, as well as on every part of the question, I am desirous gentlemen should come closely to the point, that they should sift it to the bottom, and ascertain upon what grounds and principles their opinion really rests. Do they mean to maintain that in any humiliating, in any degrading sense of the word which can be acted upon practically as a rule, and which can lead to any useful conclusion, that at any time when the government of any two separate countries unite in forming one more extensive empire, the individuals who composed either of the former narrow societies are afterwards less members of an independent country, or to any valuable and useful purpose less possessed of political freedom or civil happiness, than they were before ? It must be obvious to every gentleman who will look at the subject, in tracing the histories of all the countries, the most proud of their present existing independence, of all the nations in Europe, there is not one that could exist in the state in which it now stands, if that principle had been acted upon by our forefathers, and Europe must have remained to this hour in a state of ignorance and barbarism, from the perpetual warfare of independent and petty states. In the instance of our own country, it would be a superfluous waste of time to enumerate the steps by which all its parts were formed into one kingdom, but

[1] Richard Brinsley Sheridan.

will any man in general assert, that in all the different unions which have formed the principal states of Europe, their inhabitants have become less free, that they have had less of which to be proud, less scope for their own exertions, than they had in their former situation ? If this doctrine is to be generally maintained, what becomes of the situation at this hour of any one county of England, or of any one county of Ireland, now united under the independent parliament of that kingdom ? If it be pushed to its full extent, it is obviously incompatible with all civil society. . . .

But while I combat this general and abstract principle, which would operate as an objection to every union between separate states, on the ground of the sacrifice of independence, do I mean to contend that there is in no case just ground for such a sentiment ? Far from it ; it may become on many occasions the first duty of a free and generous people. If there exists a country which contains within itself the means of military protection, the naval force necessary for its defence, which furnishes objects of industry sufficient for the subsistence of its inhabitants, and pecuniary resources adequate to maintaining with dignity the rank which it has attained among the nations of the world, if, above all, it enjoys the blessings of internal content and tranquillity and possesses a distinct constitution of its own, the defects of which, if any, it is within itself capable of correcting, and if that constitution be equal, if not superior, to that of any other in the world, or (which is nearly the same thing) if those who live under it believe it to be so, and fondly cherish that opinion, I can indeed well understand that such a country must be jealous of any measure, which, even by its own consent, under the authority of its own lawful government, is to associate it as a part of a larger and more extensive empire.

But, Sir, if, on the other hand, it should happen that there be a country which, against the greatest of all dangers that threaten its peace and security, has not adequate means of protecting itself without the aid of another nation, if that other be a neighbouring and kindred nation, speaking the same language, whose laws, whose customs and habits are the same in principle, but carried to a greater degree of perfection, with a more extensive commerce and more abundant means of acquiring and diffusing national wealth, the stability of whose government—the excellence of whose constitution, is more than ever the admiration and envy of Europe, and of which the very country of which we are speaking, can only boast an inadequate and imperfect resemblance ;—under such circumstances, I would ask, what conduct would be prescribed by every rational principle of dignity, of honour, or of interest ? I would ask, whether this is not a faithful description of the circumstances which ought to dispose Ireland to an union ?—Whether Great Britain is not precisely the nation with which, on these principles, a country, situated as Ireland is, would desire to unite ? Does an union, under such circumstances, by free consent, and on just and equal terms, deserve to be branded as a proposal for subjecting Ireland to a foreign yoke ? Is it not rather the free and voluntary association of two great countries, which join for their common benefit, in one empire, where each will retain its proportional weight and importance, under the security of equal laws, reciprocal affection, and inseparable interests, and which want nothing but that indissoluble connexion to render both invincible ?

> Non ego nec Teucris Italos parere jubebo,
> Nec nova regna peto ; paribus se legibus ambae
> Invictae gentes aeterna in foedera mittant.

Sir, I have nearly stated all that is necessary for me to trouble the House with ; there are, however, one or two other objections which I wish not entirely to pass over.   One of them is, a general notion that an union with Great Britain must necessarily increase one of the great evils of Ireland, by producing depopulation in many parts of the country, and by increasing greatly the number of absentees.   I do not mean to deny that this effect would, to a limited extent, take place during a part of the year, but I think it will not be difficult for me to prove, that this circumstance will be more than counterbalanced by the operation of the system in other respects.

If it be true that this measure has an inevitable tendency to admit the introduction of that British capital which is most likely to give life to all the operations of commerce, and to all the improvements of agriculture, if it be that which, above all other considerations is most likely to give security, quiet, and internal repose to Ireland, if it is likely to remove the chief bar to the internal advancement of wealth and civilization, by a more intimate intercourse with England, if it is more likely to communicate from hence those habits which distinguish this country, and which, by a continued gradation, unite the highest and the lowest orders of the community without a chasm in any part of the system, if it is not only likely to invite (as I have already said) English capital to set commerce in motion, but to offer it the use of new markets, to open fresh resources of wealth and industry, can wealth, can industry, can civilization increase among the whole bulk of the people without much more than counterbalancing the partial effect of the removal of the few individuals who, for a small part of the year, would follow the seat of legislation ? . . .

There remains, Sir, another general line of argument, which I have already anticipated, and I hope answered, that the commercial privileges now enjoyed by Ireland, and to which it owes so much of its prosperity, would be less secure than at present.   I have given an answer to that already, by stating, that they are falsely imputed to the independence of the Irish parliament, for that they are, in fact, owing to the exercise of the voluntary discretion of the British parliament, unbound by compact, prompted only by its natural disposition to consider the interests of Ireland the same as its own, and if that has been done while Ireland is only united to us in the imperfect and precarious manner in which it is, while it has a separate parliament, notwithstanding the commercial jealousies of our own manufacturers ; if under these circumstances we have done so, if we have done so with no other connexion than that which now subsists, and while Ireland has no share in our representation, what fresh ground can there be for apprehension, when she will have her proportionate weight in the legislature, and will be united with us as closely as Lancashire or Yorkshire, or any other county in Great Britain ? . . .

Sir, the only other general topic of objection is that, upon which great pains have been taken to raise an alarm in Ireland—the idea that the main principle of the measure was to subject Ireland to a load of debt and an increase of taxes, and to expose her to the consequence of all our alleged difficulties and supposed necessities.

Sir, I hope the zeal, the spirit, and the liberal and enlarged policy of this country, has given ample proof that it is not from a pecuniary motive that we seek an union. If it is not desirable on the grounds I have stated, it cannot be recommended for the mere purpose of taxation. But to quiet any jealousy on this subject, here again let us look to Scotland : is there any instance where, with 45 members on her part and 513 on ours, that part of the united kingdom has paid more than its proportion to the general burdens ? Is it then, Sir, any ground for apprehension that we are likely to tax Ireland more heavily when she becomes associated with ourselves ? To tax in its due proportion the whole of the empire, to the utter exclusion of the idea of the predominance of one part of society over another, is the great characteristic of British finance, as equality of laws is of the British constitution.

Speeches of the Rt. Hon. William Pitt (1817), iii. 28–70.

THE VOLUNTEER MOVEMENT

23. THE ULSTER VOLUNTEER RESOLUTIONS, 1782

In December 1781 the officers and delegates of the first Ulster regiment summoned a meeting of delegates from the volunteers of Ulster. Representatives of 143 corps met at Dungannon in February 1782 and agreed to the resolutions given below.

Whereas it has been asserted, ' That volunteers, as such, cannot with propriety, debate or publish their opinions on political subjects, or on the conduct of parliament or public men.'

Resolved unanimously, That a citizen, by learning the use of arms, does not abandon any of his civil rights.

Resolved unanimously, That a claim of any body of men, other than the king, lords, and commons of Ireland to make laws to bind this kingdom, is unconstitutional, illegal, and a grievance.

Resolved (with one dissenting voice only), That the powers exercised by the privy council of both kingdoms, under, or under colour or pretence of the law of Poynings', are unconstitutional and a grievance.

Resolved unanimously, That the ports of this country are, by right, open to all foreign countries, not at war with the king, and that any burden thereupon, or obstruction thereto, save only by the parliament of Ireland, are unconstitutional, illegal, and a grievance

Resolved (with one dissenting voice only), That a mutiny bill, not limited in point of duration from session to session, is unconstitutional, and a grievance.

Resolved unanimously, That the independence of judges is equally essential to the impartial administration of justice in Ireland, as in England, and that the refusal or delay of this right to Ireland, makes a distinction where there should be no distinction, may excite jealousy where perfect union should prevail, and is, in itself, unconstitutional, and a grievance.

Resolved (with eleven dissenting voices only), That it is our decided and unalterable determination, to seek a redress of those grievances ; and we pledge ourselves to each other and to our country, as freeholders, fellow-citizens, and men of honour, that we will at every ensuing election, support those only, who have supported, and will support us therein, and we will use all constitutional means to make such pursuit of redress speedy and effectual.

Resolved (with one dissenting voice only), That the right honourable and honourable the minority in parliament, who have supported these our constitutional rights, are entitled to our most grateful thanks, and that the annexed address be signed by the chairman, and published with these resolutions.

Resolved unanimously, That four members from each county of the province of Ulster, eleven to be a quorum, be, and are hereby appointed a committee till next general meeting, to act for the volunteer corps here represented, and as occasions shall require, to call general meetings of the province. . . .

Resolved unanimously, That said committee do appoint nine of their members to be a committee in Dublin, in order to communicate with such other volunteer associations in the other provinces as may think proper to come to similar resolutions, and to deliberate with them on the most constitutional means of carrying them into effect.

Resolved unanimously, That the committee be, and are hereby instructed to call a general meeting of the province, within twelve months from this day, or in fourteen days after the dissolution of the present parliament, should such an event sooner take place.

Resolved unanimously, That the court of Portugal have acted towards this kingdom (being a part of the British empire) in such a manner as to call upon us to declare and pledge ourselves to each other that we will not consume any wine of the growth of Portugal, and that we will, to the extent of our influence, prevent the use of said wine, save and except the wine at present in this kingdom, until such time as our exports shall be received in the kingdom of Portugal, as the manufactures of part of the British empire.

Resolved (with two differing voices only, to this and the following resolution), That we hold the right of private judgment in matters of religion, to be equally sacred in others as in ourselves.

Resolved therefore, That as men and as Irishmen, as christians and as protestants, we rejoice in the relaxation of the penal laws against our Roman catholic fellow-subjects, and that we conceive the measure to be fraught with the happiest consequences to the union and prosperity of the inhabitants of Ireland.

> C. H. Wilson, *A complete collection of the resolutions of the volunteers, grand juries, etc. of Ireland* (Dublin, 1782), i. 1–4.

PLANS OF PARLIAMENTARY REFORM, 1794

24. THE WHIG BILL

Second reading moved by William Ponsonby, 4 March 1794. Rejected by 142 to 44.

A bill for amending and improving the state of the representation of the people in parliament

Whereas the state of the representation of the people in parliament is greatly defective, and it would tend much to protect the liberty of the subject, and to preserve our excellent constitution if the people of this realm were more fairly and equally represented in parliament, be it enacted . . . that from and after the expiration or dissolution of this present parliament assembled, the number of knights to be elected and returned to represent each county within this kingdom in any future parliament to be hereafter holden and kept within this realm, shall be three instead of two knights, as heretofore used and accustomed, and for that end and purpose the freeholders in each and every county within this kingdom (who have by law a right to vote for members to serve in parliament, and none other) are hereby authorized, empowered and required, at every general election to be hereafter holden for members to serve in parliament, to choose and elect three persons to serve as knights or representatives in parliament for said county, . . .

And be it enacted, . . . that from and after the expiration or dissolution of this present parliament, the number of citizens to be elected and returned to represent the city of Dublin in parliament shall be three ; and that the number of citizens to be elected and returned to represent the city of Cork in parliament shall be three. . . .

And whereas, enlarging the districts of the several cities and borough towns within this kingdom, would tend to render their elections of citizens and burgesses to serve in parliament much more free and independent, be it enacted that from and after the expiration or dissolution of this present parliament, the limits or precincts of every city, borough, town or manor having a right to send members to parliament, shall for the purposes of this act only, extend and be deemed and taken to extend to a space or distance of four miles from the said city, borough, town and manor, which space or distance is to be measured by a line to be drawn from some one place within the said city, borough, town or manor, as near the centre of the present site of the said city, borough, town or manor, as conveniently as may be done, and to extend in every direction to a distance of four miles from the said place, and no further, so as thereby to make the circuit of the district round the said city, borough, town or manor, equal to twenty-four miles in circumference or thereabouts, and which space contained within the said circuit shall be for the purposes of this act deemed and taken as the district of the said city, borough, town or manor. Provided always that where any city, borough, town or manor having a right to send members to serve in parliament shall be so situated, as that a line of four miles cannot conveniently be drawn or measured in the manner herein before directed, by reason of the vicinity of some other city, borough, town or manor, having also a right to send members to serve in parliament, or by reason of the proximity of the sea, then and in every such case a certain district shall be measured from the most central place within the said city, borough, town or manor, in such direction as can be best and most conveniently done, and which shall be equal or as nearly as may be to a space contained within a circumference of twenty-four miles, and which space shall be marked out and allotted as and for the district of the said city, borough, town or manor, situated as aforesaid, so as in all cases to give to every city, borough, town or manor, having a right to send members to parliament a district thereunto appertaining equal to twenty-four miles in circumference. . . .

Be it enacted, that when the district of the said city, town, borough or manor, shall be so allotted and marked out as aforesaid, every freeholder who shall be seized of a freehold of ten pounds value within the said district, shall have a right to vote for members to serve in parliament for the said city, borough, town or manor, any former law or usage to the contrary notwithstanding ; provided always, that the said person so claiming a right to vote at said election, shall have been seized of his freehold one whole year before the teste of the writ which issued for holding the said election, and shall have registered his freehold six months before the teste of the said writ, pursuant to the act made in the year of his present majesty for the due registering of freeholds. . . .

Be it further enacted, by the authority aforesaid, that from and after the   of   no person who shall be elected and admitted to the freedom of any corporation in any city or town corporate, shall by virtue of such election and admission have a right to vote for members to serve in parliament for the said city or town corporate, unless the said person shall have been seized of a freehold tenement of the value of five pounds by the year within the said city or town corporate, upon which he or his family shall have resided for one whole year before the time of such election and admission.

Provided always, that nothing herein contained shall extend to any person or persons who is or are admitted or who have a right to their freedom by reason of birth, marriage, or service to any

trade or calling, but that all such rights, shall remain in full force as
if this act had not been made.

Parliamentary Register (Dublin 1795), xiv. 62–8.

25. THE UNITED IRISHMEN'S PLAN OF PARLIAMENTARY REFORM

Published by the Dublin society of United Irishmen, March 1794

A plan of an equal representation of the people of Ireland in the
house of commons

Prepared for public consideration by the society of United Irishmen
of Dublin

I. That the nation, for the purposes of representation solely,
should be divided into 300 electorates, formed by combination of
parishes, and as nearly as possible equal in point of population.

II. That each electorate should return one representative to
parliament.

III. That each electorate should, for the convenience of carrying
on the elections at the same time, be subdivided into a sufficient
number of parts.

IV. That there should be a returning officer for each electorate,
and a deputy returning officer for each subdivision, to be respectively
elected.

V. That the electors of the electorate should vote, each in the subdivision in which he is registered, and has resided after specified.

VI. That the returning officers of the subdivisions should
severally return their respective polls to the returning officer of the
electorate, who should tot up the whole, and return the person
having a majority of votes, as the representative in parliament.

VII. That every man possessing the right of suffrage for a
representative in parliament, should exercise it in his own person
only.

VIII. That no person should have a right to vote in more than
one electorate at the same election.

IX. That every male of sound mind, who has attained the full
age of 21 years, and actually dwelt, or maintained a family establishment in any electorate for six months of the twelve immediately
previous to the commencement of the election (provided his residence
or maintaining a family establishment be duly registered) should be
entitled to vote for the representative of the electorate.

X. That there should be a registering officer, and a registry of
residence in every subdivision of each electorate ; and that in all
questions concerning residence, the registry should be considered
as conclusive evidence.

XI. That all elections in the nation should commence and close
on the same day.

XII. That the votes of all electors should be given by voice and
not by ballot.

XIII. That no oath of any kind should be taken by any elector.

16

XIV. That the full age of 25 years should be a necessary qualification to entitle any man to be a representative.

XV. That residence within the electorate should not, but that residence within the kingdom should be a necessary qualification for a representative.

XVI. That no property qualification should be necessary to entitle any man to be a representative.

XVII. That any person having a pension, or holding a place in the executive or judicial departments, should be thereby disqualified from being a representative.

XVIII. That representatives should receive a reasonable stipend for their services.

XIX. That every representative should, on taking his seat, swear that neither he, nor any person to promote his interest, with his privity, gave or was to give any bribe for the suffrage of any voter.

XX. That any representative convicted by a jury, of having acted contrary to the substance of the above oath, should for ever be disqualified from sitting or voting in parliament.

XXI. That parliaments should be annual.

XXII. That a representative should be at liberty to resign his delegation upon giving sufficient notice to his constituents.

XXIII. That absence from duty for   should vacate the seat of a representative.

Society of United Irishmen of Dublin (Dublin 1794), pp. 124–6.

THE UNITED IRISHMEN

The first societies of United Irishmen, founded in 1791, were radical clubs which aimed at educating and influencing public opinion. After 1795, however, Irish radicals strove to spread their propaganda and put pressure on the government through a network of secret societies organized in a military system.

26. THE ORGANIZATION OF THE UNITED IRISHMEN, 1797

The declaration, resolutions, and constitution
of the societies of United Irishmen

In the present era of reform, when unjust governments are falling in every quarter of Europe, when religious persecution is compelled to abjure her tyranny over conscience, when the rights of men are ascertained in theory, and that theory substantiated by practice, when antiquity can no longer defend absurd and oppressive forms, against the common sense and common interests of mankind, when all governments are acknowledged to originate from the people, and to be so far only obligatory, as they protect their rights, and promote their welfare, we think it our duty, as Irishmen, to come forward, and state what we feel to be our heavy grievance, and what we know to be its effectual remedy. We have no national government, we are ruled by Englishmen, and the servants of

Englishmen, whose object is the interest of another country, whose instrument is corruption, and whose strength is the weakness of Ireland ; and these men have the whole of the power and patronage of the country, as means to seduce and subdue the honesty of her representatives in the legislature. Such an extrinsic power, acting with uniform force, in a direction too frequently opposite to the true line of our obvious interest, can be resisted with effect solely by unanimity, decision, and spirit in the people, qualities which may be exerted most legally, constitutionally, and efficaciously, by that great measure, essential to the prosperity and freedom of Ireland, an equal representation of all the people in parliament.

Impressed with these sentiments, we have agreed to form an association, to be called the Society of United Irishmen, and we do pledge ourselves to our country, and mutually to each other, that we will steadily support, and endeavour by all due means to carry into effect the following resolutions :

1st. Resolved, That the weight of English influence in the government of this country is so great, as to require a cordial union among all the people of Ireland, to maintain that balance which is essential to the preservation of our liberties, and extension of our commerce.

2nd. That the sole constitutional mode by which this influence can be opposed is by a complete and radical reform of the representation of the people in parliament.

3rd. That no reform is practicable, efficacious, or just, which shall not include Irishmen of every religious persuasion.

Satisfied, as we are, that the intestine divisions among Irishmen have too often given encouragement and impunity to profligate, audacious, and corrupt administrations, in measures which, but for these divisions, they durst not have attempted, we submit our resolutions to the nation, as the basis of our political faith. We have gone to what we conceived to be the root of the evil. We have stated what we conceive to be remedy. With a parliament thus formed, everything is easy—without it, nothing can be done—and we do call on, and most earnestly exhort our countrymen in general to follow our example, and to form similar societies in every quarter of the kingdom, for the promotion of constitutional knowledge, the abolition of bigotry in religion and politics, and the equal distribution of the rights of man throughout all sects and denominations of Irishmen. The people, when thus collected, will feel their own weight, and secure that power which theory has already admitted as their portion, and to which, if they be not aroused by their present provocations to vindicate it, they deserve to forfeit their pretensions for ever.[1]

1st. This society is constituted for the purpose of forwarding a brotherhood of affection, a community of rights, and a union of power among Irishmen of every religious persuasion ; and thereby

---

[1] This declaration was drawn up and first issued by the Dublin Society of United Irishmen in November 1791.

to obtain a complete reform in the legislature, founded on the principles of civil, political, and religious liberty.

2nd. Every candidate for admission into this society shall be proposed by one member and seconded by another, both of whom shall vouch for his character and principles. The candidate to be balloted for on the society's subsequent meeting, and if one of the beans shall be black, he shall stand rejected.

3rd. Each society shall fix upon a weekly subscription suited to the circumstances and convenience of its numbers, which they shall regularly return to their baronial by the proper officer.

4th. The officers of this society shall be a secretary and treasurer, who shall be appointed by ballot every three months : on every first meeting in November, February, May and August.

5th. A society shall consist of no more than twelve members, and those as nearly as possible of the same street or neighbourhood, whereby they may be all thoroughly known to each other, and their conduct be subject to the censorial check of all.

6th. Every person elected a member of this society shall, previous to his admission, take the following test. But in order to diminish risk, it shall be taken in a separate apartment, in the presence of the persons who proposed and seconded him only, after which the new member shall be brought into the body of the society, and there vouched for by the same.

Test

In the awful presence of God, I, A.B., do voluntarily declare, that I will persevere in endeavouring to form a brotherhood of affection among Irishmen of every religious persuasion, and that I will also persevere in my endeavours to obtain an equal, full, and adequate representation of all the people of Ireland. I do further declare, that neither hopes, fears, rewards, or punishments, shall ever induce me, directly or indirectly, to inform on, or give evidence against, any member or members of this or similar societies for any act or expression of theirs, done or made collectively or individually in or out of this society, in pursuance of the spirit of this obligation.[1]

7th. No person, though he should have taken the test, will be considered as an United Irishman until he has contributed to the funds of the institution, or longer than he shall continue to pay such contribution.

8th. No communication relating to the business of the institution shall be made to any United Irishman on any pretence whatever,

---

[1] The oath taken by the societies founded in 1791 was as follows :—I A.B. in the presence of God do pledge myself to my country, that I will use all my abilities and influence in the attainment of an impartial and adequate representation of the Irish nation in parliament, and as a means of absolute and immediate necessity in the establishment of this chief good of Ireland, I will endeavour as much as lies in my ability to forward a brotherhood of affection, an identity of interests, a communion of rights, and a union of power among Irishmen of all religious persuasions, without which every reform in parliament must be partial, not national, inadequate to the wants, delusive to the wishes, and insufficient for the freedom and happiness of this country.

except in his own society or committee, or by some member of his own society or committee.

9th. When the society shall amount to the number of twelve members, it shall be equally divided by lot (societies in country places to divide as may best suit their local situation), that is, the names of all the members shall be put into a hat or box, the secretary or treasurer shall draw out six individually, which six shall be considered the senior society, and the remaining six the junior, who shall apply to the baronial committee, through the delegates of the senior society, for a number. This mode shall be pursued until the whole neighbourhood is organized.

Order of business at meetings

1st. New members read declaration and test, during which subscriptions to be collected.

2nd. Reports of committees received.

3rd. Communications called for.

4th. Candidates balloted for.

5th. Candidates proposed.

Constitution of committees

Baronial committees

1st. When any barony or other district shall contain from four to ten societies, the secretaries of these shall constitute a lower baronial committee, they should not exceed ten, and be numbered in the order of their formation.

2nd. An upper baronial, to consist of ten secretaries from ten lower baronials.

3rd. Baronial committees shall receive delegates from societies of a contiguous barony, provided said barony did not contain four societies.

County committees

1st. When any county shall contain four or more upper baronial committees, their secretaries shall assemble and choose deputies to form a county committee.

2nd. County committees shall receive delegates from baronial committees of adjacent counties, if said counties do not contain four baronial committees.

Provincial committees

1st. When two or more counties shall have county committees, two persons shall be elected by ballot from each to form a provincial committee (for three months).

2nd. Delegates from county committees in other provinces will be received, if such provinces do not contain two county committees.

National committees

That when two provincial committees are formed, they shall elect five persons each by ballot to form a national committee.

Societies first meetings in November, February, May and August to be on or before the 5th, baronial committees on or before the 8th, county committees on or before the 25th of the above months.

Baronial, county, and provincial committees, shall meet at least once in every month, and report to their constituents.

Names of committee men shall not be known by any person but by those who elect them.

Test for secretaries of societies or committees

In the awful presence of God I, A.B., do voluntarily declare that as long as I shall hold the office of secretary to this I will, to the utmost of my abilities faithfully discharge the duties thereof.

That all papers or documents received by me as secretary I will in safety keep ; I will not give any of them, or any copy or copies of them, to any person or persons, members or others, but by a vote of this   and that I will, at the expiration of my secretaryship deliver up to this   all such papers as may be in my possession. . . .

Commons journ., Ire, xvii., appendix, pp. 888–9.

SECTION V. THE NINETEENTH CENTURY AND AFTER

CATHOLIC EMANCIPATION

I. REPORT OF THE COMMITTEE APPOINTED BY THE CATHOLIC ASSOCIATION, 1824

The report was read to the association on the 18 February 1824 and after some discussion the resolutions incorporated in it were adopted.

The committee appointed to devise the best mode of raising a general subscription throughout Ireland beg leave respectfully to submit the following report.

The catholics of Ireland have long been engaged in a painful and anxious struggle to attain, by peaceful and constitutional means, those civil rights, to which every subject of these realms is, upon principle, and of justice entitled, and of which our forefathers were basely and perfidiously deprived, in defiance of the sacred claims of conscience, and in open and indecent violation of the faith of treaties.

Your committee are impressed with the melancholy conviction, that at no former period of this protracted struggle had the catholic people of Ireland so little reason to entertain hope of immediate success. A strange combination of events has occurred to cloud our prospects, and to render the expectation of redress remote and doubtful. . . .

The combination of all these untoward circumstances has almost extinguished hope ; and were it not forbidden to despair of the sacred cause of liberty and religion, your committee would feel it a duty to recommend a silent submission to events, over which we possess, alas, no control, and a tacit acquiescence in an evil system, which we want the power, or at least lawful and constitutional means, to crush, and to await, in the sullen silence of unconcealed discontent, for a more favourable opportunity, and better organized resources, to prove to Britain and the world—that we are men, and deserve to be free.

But your committee can never recommend such a course. They do not dare to despair. They know that their cause is just and holy. It is the cause of religion and liberty. It is the cause of their country and of their God. It never can be abandoned by the catholics of Ireland. . . .

But, in order effectually to exert the energies of the Irish people, pecuniary resources are absolutely necessary. Your committee have a just and entire confidence, that such resources can be procured with facility, and that it requires nothing more than a reasonable portion of exertion, on the part of a few individuals, to secure abundant pecuniary means to answer every legitimate object.

The purposes for which pecuniary resources are wanting should be clearly defined, and distinctly understood. They should be useful in their objects, and strictly legal and constitutional in all their details.

Your committee respectfully submit, that the following purposes are of obvious and paramount utility ; and that no doubt does or can exist of their being perfectly legal.

1st. To forward petitions to parliament, not only on the subject of catholic emancipation, but for the redress of all local or general grievances, affecting the Irish people.

Under this head should be included a salary for a permanent parliamentary agent in London.

Your committee conceive, that a sum of £5,000 per ann. would cover all the expenses under this first head.

2ndly. To procure legal redress for all such catholics, assailed or injured by Orange violence, as are unable to obtain it for themselves, to prevent, by due course of law, Orange processions and public insults, to bring before the high courts of criminal justice, all such magistrates as should participate in, or countenance the illegal proceedings, processions, etc., of the Orange faction, and to arrest, by the powerful arm of the law, that career of violence, by which principally in the north, but occasionally in the south, so many catholics have been murdered by Orangemen, many of whom are intrusted with arms by the government for far different purposes—and, in fine, to prosecute the Orange murderers, where we cannot prevent the murders.

There is also another head of legal relief of great importance. It is to procure for the catholics the actual enjoyment of all such rights in the several corporations in Ireland, to which they are by law entitled, and which have, for thirty years past, been perseveringly withheld from them by interested bigotry.

To this important object your committee would, in the first years, devote £15,000 per annum.

3rdly. To encourage and support a liberal and enlightened press, as well in Dublin as in London—a press which could readily refute the arguments of our enemies, and expose the falsehood of their calumnies upon us and our religion—a press which would publish and explain the real principles of the catholics, and, by the irresistible force of truth, either silence, or at least confound our calumniators.

For the last two centuries the British press, in all its exclusive ramifications, from the ponderous folio down to the most paltry ballad, has teemed with the most unfounded calumnies and the grossest falsehoods on the subject of the religion and principles of the catholics. The popular writers of the present day, even those who support our claims to emancipation, affect an air of candour by joining our worst enemies in traducing our most sacred religion.

It is time that this grievous mischief should be checked ; and your committee conceive that a less sum than £15,000 per annum ought not to be dedicated to this most useful purpose.

4thly. To procure for the various schools in the country cheap publications by means of which the catholic children may attain knowledge, without having their religion interfered with, or their social virtue checked by any thing unchristian or uncharitable. The money given by parliament for this purpose is shamefully misapplied ; and the necessity of a resource of this description is daily felt by the catholic prelates and pastors, who have the greatest anxiety to promote the education of their flocks, but are unable to afford sufficient sums of money for that purpose.

Your committee would, in the first instance, expend £5,000 per annum to remedy this evil ; they would recommend that all the savings on the foregoing heads of expenditure (which they trust will be considerable) should be applied then to advance education.

Your committee would respectfully submit the propriety of aiding the resources of the Irish and other catholics in North America, to procure for them a sufficient number of priests. The number of catholics in the United States is great and daily increasing. The want of catholic clergymen is felt as an extreme evil ; and it is thought that a sum of £5,000 a year could not be better applied than in remedying in some measure this deficiency.

Besides, the catholics in Great Britain are multiplying almost beyond hope. The French revolution supplied the English catholics with clergymen for many years. That resource is now gone ; and it would be suited to the charity and piety of the Irish people to supply their haughty and erratic neighbours with the means of instruction in that ancient faith which, since the first days of christianity, always was, and still is, and while the world lasts will be, the genuine source of every christian and social virtue.

Having detailed these five distinct objects, your committee beg leave to state, that as they conceive, that after exhausting those purposes, there ought to remain a sum of at least £5,000 per annum, at the disposal of the Association—they would recommend that such sum should be allowed to accumulate in the public funds, and that out of such accumulation, the Catholic Association should, from time to time, be at liberty to dedicate, in fair and reasonable proportions, in contributions, towards erecting schools, building catholic churches, and erecting and furnishing dwelling-houses for the clergy in the poorer parishes, and ameliorating, in other respects, the condition of the catholic clergy in Ireland.

Your committee confidently hope, that if the plan which they are about to suggest, be adopted, such accumulation will greatly exceed £5,000 per annum, and may be five times that sum, and thereby afford means of doing great and permanent good to the most estimable, laborious, learned, and pious clergy, with which it has ever pleased the eternal wisdom to bless a faithful and suffering people.

The basis of our plan is founded on the extent of the catholic population of Ireland. We may expect a good deal of assistance from the liberal portion of our protestant fellow countrymen, but our reliance for success must be placed upon the numbers and patriotism of the catholic people of Ireland. . . .

The detail of the plan of your committee is this. They propose—

1st. That a monthly subscription should be raised throughout Ireland, to be denominated, ' The monthly catholic rent.'

2nd. That the Association should forthwith appoint two of its members a secretary and assistant, in order to collect such subscriptions throughout Ireland.

3rd. That such secretary and assistant should immediately open an account with each parish in Ireland, and enter therein the particulars of all monies subscribed by such parish.

4th. That the Association should adopt the most speedy means of nominating in conjunction with the inhabitants of each parish, and if possible with the privity of the catholic clergyman, a number of persons not to exceed twelve, nor less than three, in order to collect the subscriptions.

5th. That monthly returns be procured from such persons, or from as many of them as possible, and that a monthly report, in writing, of the progress made in each parish be given in by the secretary for subscriptions to the secretary of the catholics of Ireland, to be by him laid before the Association.

6th. That care be taken to publish in, or at least as near each catholic chapel as may be permitted by the clergy, the particulars of the sums subscribed in such parish, with the names of each subscriber, unless where the individuals shall choose to insert the subscription under the head—anonymous.

7th. That accounts of subscriptions, debtor and creditor, be published annually, for the satisfaction of the subscribers and the public at large.

8th. That all subscriptions be paid, as soon as transmitted to Dublin, into the hands of the treasurer to the association.

9th. That an efficient committee of 21 members be appointed to superintend and manage the collection and expenditure of the subscription money, to be styled, and to act as, a committee of accounts.

10th. That no monies be expended without an express note of the Association, upon a notice regularly given.

11th. That the amount expected from each individual shall not exceed one penny per month, but that each individual shall be at liberty to give any greater monthly sum he pleases, not exceeding in the entire two shillings per month.

12th. That the guinea paid by each member of the Association on his admission, be deemed and taken as part of the entire of the contribution of the individual to the subscription thus proposed, and that each member be requested to allocate his guinea to some particular parish.

13th. That each subscriber be at liberty to allocate his subscription either to the fund generally or to any particular object heretofore specified, and that such allocation be in every respect, strictly, and without any deviation, attended to.

14th. That Daniel O'Connell Esq. be appointed secretary for subscriptions, and James Sugrue Esq. his assistant.

Your committee submit, that if only one million of the six millions of catholics, which this country contains, will contribute the small sum of one farthing a week each, the resources of the association will exceed the estimate of expenditures heretofore detailed. They cannot doubt the readiness with which the subscription will be raised if proper means are taken to apply for it universally.

Your committee cannot conclude without expressing their decided conviction, that if this plan shall be carried into complete operation, all the difficulties in the way of our emancipation will be speedily removed—and we shall have the glory, as well as the advantage, of carrying into effect the christian principle of liberty of conscience.

Daniel O'Connell, Chairman.
Dublin Evening Post, 19 February 1824.

2. THE CATHOLIC RELIEF BILL, 1829

An act for the relief of his majesty's Roman catholic subjects

Whereas by various acts of parliament certain restraints and disabilities are imposed on the Roman catholic subjects of his majesty, to which other subjects of his majesty are not liable, and whereas it is expedient that such restraints and disabilities shall be from henceforth discontinued, and whereas by various acts certain oaths and certain declarations, commonly called the declarations against transubstantiation and the invocation of saints and the sacrifice of the mass, as practised in the church of Rome, are or may be required to be taken, made, and subscribed, by the subjects of his majesty, as qualifications for sitting and voting in parliament, and for the enjoyment of certain offices, franchises, and civil rights, be it enacted . . . that from and after the commencement of this act all such parts of the said acts as require the said declarations, or either of them, to be made or subscribed by any of his majesty's subjects, as a qualification for sitting and voting in parliament, or for the exercise or enjoyment of any office, franchise, or civil right, be and the same are (save as hereinafter provided and excepted) hereby repealed.

II. And be it enacted, that . . . it shall be lawful for any person professing the Roman catholic religion, being a peer, or who shall after the commencement of this act be returned as a member of the house of commons, to sit and vote in either house of parliament respectively, being in all other respects duly qualified to sit and vote therein, upon taking and subscribing the following oath, instead of the oaths of allegiance, supremacy, and abjuration : I, A.B., do sincerely promise and swear, that I will be faithful and bear true allegiance to his majesty King George the fourth, and will defend him to the utmost of my power against all conspiracies and attempts whatever, which shall be made against his person, crown, or dignity. And I will do my utmost endeavour to disclose and make known to his majesty, his heirs and successors, all treasons and traitorous conspiracies which may be formed against him or them. And I do faithfully promise to maintain, support, and defend, to the utmost of my power, the succession of the crown, which succession, by an act, entitled *An act for the further limitation of the crown, and better securing the rights and liberties of the subject*, is and stands limited to the Princess Sophia, electress of Hanover, and the heirs of her body, being protestants ; hereby utterly renouncing and abjuring any obedience or allegiance unto any other person claiming or pretending a right to the crown of this realm. And I do further declare, that it is not an article of my faith, and that I do renounce, reject, and abjure the opinion, that princes excommunicated or deprived by the pope, or any other authority of the see of Rome, may be deposed or murdered by their subjects, or by any person whatsoever. And I do declare, that I do not believe that the pope of Rome, or any other foreign prince, prelate, person, state, or potentate, hath or ought to have any temporal or civil jurisdiction, power, superiority, or pre-eminence, directly or indirectly, within this realm. I do swear, that I will defend to the utmost of my power the settlement of property within this realm, as established by the laws, and I do hereby disclaim, disavow, and solemnly abjure, any intention to subvert the present church establishment as settled by law within this realm, and I do solemnly swear, that I never will exercise any privilege to which I am or may become entitled, to disturb or weaken the protestant religion or protestant government in the United Kingdom. And I do solemnly, in the presence of God, profess, testify, and declare, that I do make this declaration and every part thereof, in the plain and ordinary sense of the words of this oath, without any evasion, equivocation, or mental reservation whatsoever. So help me God.[1]

V. And be it further enacted, that it shall be lawful for persons professing the Roman catholic religion to vote at elections of members to serve in parliament for England and for Ireland, and also to vote at the elections of representative peers of Scotland and of Ireland, and to be elected such representative peers, being in all other respects duly qualified, upon taking and subscribing the oath hereinbefore appointed and set forth, . . .

X. And be it enacted, that it shall be lawful for any of his majesty's subjects professing the Roman catholic religion to hold, exercise and enjoy, all civil and military offices and places of trust or profit under his majesty, his heirs or successors ; and to exercise any other franchise or civil right, except as hereinafter excepted, upon taking and subscribing . . . the oath hereinbefore appointed. . . .

XII. Provided also, and be it further enacted, that nothing herein contained shall extend or be construed to extend to enable any person or persons professing the Roman catholic religion to hold or exercise the office of guardians and justices of the United

---

[1] The use of this oath in all circumstances was abolished by the Promissory oaths act, 1871.

Kingdom, or of regent of the United Kingdom, under whatever name, style, or title such office may be constituted, nor to enable any person, otherwise than as he is now by law enabled, to hold or enjoy the office of lord high chancellor, lord keeper or lord commissioner of the great seal of Great Britain or Ireland,[1] or the office of lord lieutenant, or lord deputy, or other chief governor or governors of Ireland,[2] or his majesty's high commissioner to the general assembly of the church of Scotland.

XIV. And be it enacted, that it shall be lawful for any of his majesty's subjects professing the Roman catholic religion to be a member of any lay body corporate, and to hold any civil office or place of trust or profit therein, and to do any corporate act or vote in any corporate election or other proceeding, upon taking and subscribing the oath hereby appointed and set forth, instead of the oaths of allegiance, supremacy, and abjuration, and upon taking also such other oath or oaths as may now by law be required to be taken by any persons becoming members of such lay body corporate. . . .

XVI. Provided also, and be it enacted, that nothing in this act contained shall be construed to enable any persons, otherwise than as they are now by law enabled, to hold, enjoy, or exercise any office, place, or dignity of, in, or belonging to the united church of England and Ireland, or the church of Scotland, or any place or office whatever of, in, or belonging to, any of the ecclesiastical courts of judicature of England and Ireland respectively, or any court of appeal from or review of the sentences of such courts, or of, in, or belonging to, the commissary court of Edinburgh, or of, in, or belonging to, any cathedral or collegiate or ecclesiastical establishment or foundation, or any office or place whatever of, in, or belonging to, any of the universities of this realm, or any office or place whatever, and by whatever name the same may be called, of, in, or belonging to, any of the colleges or halls of the said universities, . . . or any college or school within this realm ; or to repeal, abrogate, or in any manner to interfere with any local statute, ordinance, or rule, which is or shall be established by competent authority within any university, college, hall, or school, by which Roman catholics shall be prevented from being admitted thereto or from residing or taking degrees therein : . . .

XXIV. And whereas the protestant episcopal church of England and Ireland, and the doctrine, discipline, and government thereof, and likewise the protestant presbyterian church of Scotland, and the doctrine, discipline, and government thereof, are by the respective acts of Union of England and Scotland, and of Great Britain and Ireland, established permanently and inviolably, and whereas the right and title of archbishops to their respective provinces, of bishops to their sees, and of deans to their deaneries, as well in

---

[1] The disqualification regarding the office of lord chancellor of Ireland was removed by the Office and oath act, 1867.
[2] Under the provisions of the Government of Ireland Act, 1920, catholics were enabled to hold the office of lord lieutenant of Ireland.

England as in Ireland, have been settled and established by law, be it therefore enacted, that if any person, after the commencement of this act, other than the person thereunto authorized by law, shall assume or use the name, style, or title of archbishop of any province, bishop of any bishoprick, or dean of any deanery, in England or Ireland, he shall for every such offence forfeit and pay the sum of £100.

XXV. And be it further enacted, that if any person holding any judicial or civil office, or any mayor, provost, jurat, bailiff, or other corporate officer, shall after the commencement of this act, resort to or be present at any place or public meeting for religious worship in England, or in Ireland, other than that of the united church of England and Ireland, or in Scotland, other than that of the church of Scotland, as by law established, in the robe, gown, or other peculiar habit of his office, or attend with the ensign or insignia, or any part thereof, of or belonging to such his office, such person shall, being thereof convicted by due course of law, forfeit such office, and pay for every such offence the sum of £100.

XXVI. And be it further enacted, that if any Roman catholic ecclesiastic, or any member of any of the orders, communities, or societies herein-after mentioned, shall, after the commencement of this act, exercise any of the rites or ceremonies of the Roman catholic religion, or wear the habits of his order, save within the usual places of worship of the Roman catholic religion, or in private houses, such ecclesiastic or other person, shall being thereof convicted by due course of law, forfeit for every such offence the sum of £50.

XXXIV. And be it further enacted, that in case any person shall, after the commencement of this act, within any part of this United Kingdom, be admitted or become a jesuit, or brother, or member of any other such religious order, community, or society as aforesaid, such person shall be deemed and taken to be guilty of a misdemeanour, and being thereof lawfully convicted shall be sentenced and ordered to be banished from the United Kingdom, for the term of his natural life.[1]

XXXVII. Provided always, and be it enacted, that nothing herein contained shall extend or be construed to extend in any manner to affect any religious order, community, or establishment consisting of females bound by religious or monastic vows.

Public general statutes, 1829, pp. 105–15.

THE LAND QUESTION

3. RESOLUTIONS OF THE TENANT-RIGHT CONFERENCE OF 1850

Held in Dublin, the conference was attended by farmer-representatives from all over Ireland.

Section I

1. That a fair valuation of rent between landlord and tenant in Ireland is indispensible.

[1] By the Roman catholic relief act of 1926 section 26 and sections 28–36 of the act of 1829 were repealed.

2. That the tenant shall not be disturbed in his possession so long as he pays the rent fixed by the proposed law.

3. That the tenant shall have a right to sell his interest, with all its incidents, at the highest market value.

4. That where the rent has been fixed by valuation, no rent beyond the valued rent shall be recoverable by any process of law.

5. That cases of minors and other exceptional cases be considered hereafter in any measure to be introduced into parliament.

6. That it be an instruction to the league to take into consideration, at the earliest possible period, the condition of farm labourers, and suggest some measure for their permanent protection and improvement, in connection with the arrangement of the question between landlord and tenant.

Section II

1. That an equitable valuation of land for rent should divide between the landlord and the tenant the net profits of cultivation, in the same way as the profits would be divided between the partners in any other business where one of them is a dormant partner and the other the working capitalist who takes upon him the whole risk.

2. That nothing shall be included in the valuation or paid under the valuation to the landlord on account of improvements made by the tenant in possession, or those under whom he claims, unless these have been paid for by the landlord in reduced rent or in some other way.

3. That if the landlord shall at any time have made improvements either when the land is in his own occupation, or with the consent of the tenant in occupation, or if the landlord shall have bought the tenant's improvements, the landlord shall have the right, on letting the same to a new tenant, or on giving notice to the tenant in possession, to have such improvements valued for the purpose of adding to the rent.

4. That wherever in Ulster, or elsewhere, tenant-right custom has prevailed, the value of such right, according to the local custom, shall be considered in all respects as an improvement made by the tenant, and allowed for accordingly in valuing the rent.

5. That where land is held under lease, the lease shall not be disturbed unless at the request of the lessee or his assigns in possession ; and if on such requests the rent be altered by the valuators, the tenant shall hold in future at the altered rent.

6. That the valuation when once made, shall be permanent.

7. That every seven years there may and shall be a re-adjustment of the rent payable under the valuation, according to the rise or fall of the prices of agricultural produce, when the rise in prices be manifestly occasioned by the deficiency of the crops.

Section III

1. That the valuation shall be made by tribunals which shall unite as far as possible the advantages of *impartiality* between landlord and tenant, cheapness, accessibility, and *nomination* by the parties interested.

2. That these advantages may be secured to a reasonable degree —first by local tribunals, consisting of two valuators, one appointed by the landed proprietors and the other by the tenant farmers of the poor law union ; secondly by having valuators bound to value according to instructions embodied in the law ; and thirdly by having attached to each local tribunal a registrar or secretary, whose duty it shall be to register all the proceedings of the valuators, and keep them informed and reminded of the requirements of the instructions under which they act.

Rules of the League

1. That an association to be called The Irish Tenant League, be formed on the principles, and subject to the rules hereafter expressed ; and that such League be hereby established accordingly.

2. That the sole objects of the Tenant League are to protect the tenant, and to procure a good landlord-and-tenant law by the legal co-operation of persons of all classes and of all opinions on other subjects.

[Rules for the constitution and election of the council of the league.]

The Freeman's Journal, 7–9 August 1850.

4. RESOLUTION PASSED BY THE TENANT-RIGHT CONFERENCE OF 1852

At the general election of 1852 fifty members pledged to the support of tenant-right were returned.   But they failed to maintain cohesion as a party in parliament, and the movement collapsed.

That in the unanimous opinion of this conference it is essential to the proper management of this cause that the members of parliament who have been returned on tenant-right principles should hold themselves perfectly independent of, and in opposition to, all governments which do not make it a part of their policy and a cabinet question to give to the tenantry of Ireland a measure fully embodying the principles of Mr. Sharman Crawford's bill.

The Freeman's Journal, 9 September 1852.

5. LORD PALMERSTON ON THE IRISH LAND QUESTION, HOUSE OF COMMONS, 31 MARCH 1865

John Francis Maguire (Dungarvan) moved for a select committee on the law of landlord and tenant in Ireland.   After a debate he accepted a committee with more limited terms of reference.

Now, if there be one thing more than another which a nation in my opinion is bound to respect and regard, it is the rights of property, because upon those rights every man, however rich or however poor, must find it his interest to rest and to depend. And if laws are passed which infringe the rights of property, depend upon it that in the main those laws would be injurious to the nation in which they are passed, however tempting and apparent may be the advantage which for a time may be expected to arise from their operation. Now, Sir, I cannot bring my mind to the conviction that there can be any justice, and therefore that there can be any permanent advantage in doing that which the hon. member for Dungarvan pointed at in the latter part of his speech—namely, giving to one man the right of determining what should be done with respect to another man's property. The hon. member said—as I understood him—that in his opinion the veto of the landlord ought not to be sufficient to prevent the tenant from making unauthorized improvements upon the property of the landlord, but that some tribunal should be created—quarter sessions, or some other, I forget what was passing in his mind—which should determine as between landlord and tenant what changes—for I will not adopt the word improvements, for they may not be improvements—but what changes the tenant should make upon the landlord's property, and what should be the conditions of rent and of period of occupation which the tenant should be liable to and have a right to with regard to the landlord. Now it seems to me that an arrangement of that kind would violate the fundamental principles of justice.

Mr. Maguire said : I rise to order. (*Cries of ' Order ' and ' Chair.'*)

Mr. Speaker : The noble lord is in possession of the house, and if the hon. member has been misunderstood he will have the power of explanation after the noble lord.

Viscount Palmerston : No one would regret more than I should having misunderstood or unintentionally misrepresented what the hon. gentleman has said, and I accept with pleasure his disclaimer of the opinions which I conceived he had meant to express. But I have been quoted by him and other hon. members as having made the assertions which many have taken objection to, that the right of the tenant was the wrong of the landlord. Now, that is not what I said. What I stated upon the occasion to which I refer was this— that tenant-right, as I apprehend it to be understood in many parts of Ireland, was the landlord's wrong, and the tenant-right to which I then alluded was the right—I have just been discussing—proposed to be conferred upon him to deal with the property of the landlord without his consent and against his consent. That I consider to be the wrong of the landlord, especially when it is coupled with a reserved permission that, after a certain period, the tenant is to have the power to compel the landlord to pay for the changes which the landlord would not have made, and which he objected to being made at the time when they were made. Now, Sir, great complaints have been made, and in many respects justly, about the tide of emigration which has set from Ireland towards the shores of America. But how

17

any change in the relations of landlord and tenant is to check that emigration has not to my mind been satisfactorily explained by anybody who has taken part in this debate, and least of all by the hon. member who said that the great effect of the change contemplated would be to enable the small tenants to make improvements upon their holdings. Now, it has been well observed that no great agricultural improvements can be made except upon large holdings and with large capital. Everybody knows that the great majority of the tenants of Ireland have but small holdings of some five, ten, or fifteen acres, nor have they capital to improve any larger quantity of land which they might hold. But what does that condition of Ireland arise from ? It is not from the mis-government of England. England has nothing to do with the subdivision of holdings, by which an immense and—as many people have thought—a redundant population has been created in Ireland. It arose from the very cause which is now held out as the remedy of the evils complained of—it arose from comparative fixity of tenure.

But, upon the other hand, it is no doubt to the advantage, not only of Ireland, but of the United Kingdom, that encouragement should be held out to the tenant to make those real improvements which, according to the practice in Ireland, the landlord is not in the habit of making, as the landlord here is. No doubt for that purpose the tenant should have security that upon a change of occupation he should be reimbursed for improvements of a certain kind which he might have made upon the land which he holds. But then I say that the fundamental basis of that right ought to be mutual agreement and consent, and when hon. gentlemen say that these agreements are not made I really cannot imagine why. It seems to me to be the natural course of affairs between landlord and tenant, that if the latter should wish to make material improvements either in buildings, drains, or fences, or any other agricultural improvements, he should go to his landlord and say, ' The holding which I have wants these alterations, which you do not like or cannot afford to make. They will improve the estate. Well, then, I will make them, provided you, in the event of your turning me out within a certain period before I have been reimbursed by the length of my tenancy, will repay me a certain portion of my expenses before I quit your farm.' What reasonable landlord would object to that ? And what reasonable tenant would ask for more ? . . .

Parliamentary debates, series 3, clxxviii, cols. 618–22.

6. FOUNDATION OF THE NATIONAL LAND LEAGUE OF MAYO, 1879

Early in 1879 widespread agrarian agitation in Connaught led to a series of meetings. After some months it was decided to create ' a permanent organization for the control and direction of the new movement,' and the Mayo league was formed as a nucleus for a national body. In September a number of representative nationalists and land reformers summoned by Parnell, met in Dublin and founded the national land league (document 7).

A meeting in connexion with the land agitation in Mayo, . . .

took place at Castlebar to-day [1] in Daly's Hotel, and was attended by representative delegates from all parts of the county. . . . Mr. Michael Davitt read a document embodying the rules and objects of the proposed association.

This body shall be known as The National Land League of Mayo, and shall consist of farmers and others, who will agree to labour for the objects here set forth, and subscribe to the conditions of membership, principles, and rules specified below—

Objects : The objects for which this body is organized are—

1. To watch over the interests of the people it represents ; and protect the same, as far as may be in its power to do so, from an unjust or capricious exercise of power or privilege on the part of landlords or any other class in the community.

2. To resort to every means compatible with justice, morality, and right reason which shall not clash defiantly with the constitution upheld by the power of the British empire in this country, for the abolition of the present land laws of Ireland, and the substitution in their place of such a system as shall be in accord with the social rights and necessities of our people, the traditions and moral sentiments of our race, and which the contentment and prosperity of our country imperatively demand.

3. Pending a final and satisfactory settlement of the land question, the duty of this body will be to expose the injustice, wrong, or injury which may be inflicted upon any farmer in Mayo, either by rack-renting, eviction, or other arbitrary exercise of power which the existing laws enables the landlords to exercise over their tenantry, by giving all such arbitrary acts the widest possible publicity, and meeting their perpetration with all the opposition which the laws for the preservation of the peace will permit of. In furtherance of which the following plan will be adopted :—a. Returns to be obtained, printed, and circulated, of the number of landlords in this county ; the amount of acreage in possession of same, and the means by which such land was obtained ; farms let by each, with the conditions under which they are held by their tenants and excess of rent paid by same over the government valuation. b. To publish by placard, or otherwise, notice of contemplated evictions for non-payment of exorbitant rent, or other unjust cause, and the convening of a public meeting if deemed necessary or expedient, as near the scene of such evictions, as circumstances will allow, and on the day fixed upon for the same. c. The publication of a list of evictions carried out, together with cases of rack-renting, giving full particulars of same, names of landlords, agents, etc., concerned, and number of people evicted by such acts. d. The publication of the names of all persons who shall rent or occupy land or farms, from which others have been dispossessed for non-payment of exorbitant rents, or who shall offer a higher rent for land or farms than that paid by the previous occupier. e. The publication of reductions of rent, and acts of justice or kindness performed by landlords in the county.

[1] 16 August 1879.

4. This body to undertake the defence of such of its members, or those of local clubs affiliated with it, who may be required to resist by law the actions of landlords or their agents, who may purpose doing them injury, wrong, or injustice in connexion with their land or farms.

5. To render assistance when possible to such farmer-members as may be evicted or otherwise wronged by landlords or their agents.

6. To undertake the organizing of local clubs or defence associations in the baronies, towns, and parishes of this county, the holding of public meetings and demonstrations on the land question, and the printing of pamphlets on that and other subjects for the information of the farming classes.

7. And finally to act as a vigilance committee in Mayo, note the conduct of its grand jury, poor law guardians, town commissioners, and members of parliament and pronounce on the manner in which their respective functions are performed wherever the interests, social or political, of the people represented by this club renders it expedient to do so.

Conditions of membership : 1. To be a member of any local club or defence association in the county, and be selected by such club or association to represent the same on the central or county association. 2. A desire to co-operate in the carrying out of the foregoing objects and subscribing to the principles here enunciated with the view of propagating the same and labouring for their successful application in Ireland will qualify non-representative farmers or others for membership of this body, subject to the subscription and rules laid down for same. 3. To pay any sum not under five shillings a year towards the carrying out of the foregoing objects and the end for which this body is created—the obtaining of the soil of Ireland for the people of Ireland who cultivate it.

Declaration of principles. The land of Ireland belongs to the people of Ireland, to be held and cultivated for the sustenance of those whom God decreed to be the inhabitants thereof. Land being created to supply the necessities of existence, those who cultivate it to that end have a higher claim to its absolute possession than those who make it an article of barter to be used or disposed of for purposes of profit or pleasure. The end for which the land of a country is created requires an equitable distribution of the same among the people who are to live upon the fruits of their labour in its cultivation. Any restriction, therefore, upon such a distribution by a feudal land system embodying the laws of primogeniture and entail, the amassing of large estates, the claiming of proprietorship under penal obligations from occupiers, and preventing the same from developing the full resources of the land, must necessarily be opposed to the Divine purpose for which it was created, and to the social rights, security, and happiness of the people.

' Before the conquest the Irish people knew nothing of absolute property in land. The land virtually belonged to the entire sept, the chief was little more than the managing member of the association. The feudal idea, which views all rights as emanating from a head landlord, came in with the conquest, was associated with foreign dominion, and has never to this day been recognized by the moral sentiments of the people. Originally the offspring, not of industry, but of spoilation, the right has not been allowed to purify itself by protracted possession, but has passed from the original spoilators to others by a series of fresh spoilations, so as to be always connected with the latest and most odious oppression of foreign invaders. In the moral feelings of the Irish people, the right to hold the land goes, as it did in the beginning, with the right to till it.' These were the words of John Stuart Mill, the English political economist.

The landlord system which an alien government has imposed upon our country in the place of that which recognized no intermediate ownership between the cultivator of the soil and the state has reduced Ireland to a degree of poverty and social misery incompatible with the natural productiveness of its land and the progressive prosperity of other civilized nations.

The area of Ireland and the natural wealth of its soil is capable of supporting from twelve to twenty millions of inhabitants, if restrictive land laws did not operate against the full development of the country's resources and the unfettered cultivation of the land. Yet a population of 8,000,000 previous to the year 1847 was reduced by death, starvation and exile, consequent upon an artificial famine and continued impoverishment to little over 5,000,000 at the present day. Decreased population with its concomitant absorption of small-holdings into large estates has produced no beneficial changes in the condition of the existent farming classes who are compelled by the coercion of necessity in the absence of manufacturing industry to the acceptance of a non-alternative bargain in the shape of exorbitant rent in order to obtain the use of the soil. The dread of eviction or rack-renting must necessarily operate against that expenditure of labour and enterprise in the cultivation of the land and improvement of farm dwellings and premises which follow in every country where the fruits of the people's industry is protected by the state ; hence the soil of Ireland is worse and less cultivated, and the living and habitations of its agricultural classes more wretched than in any country in the civilized world. Over 6,000,000 acres of Irish land is owned by less than 300 individuals, twelve of whom are in possession of 1,297,888 acres between them, while 5,000,000 of the Irish people own not a solitary acre. For the protection of the proprietorial rights of the few thousand landlords in the country a standing army of semi-military police is maintained which the landless millions have to support, while the conduct of the landocracy in the exercise of its legal privileges occasions almost all the evils under which our people suffer.

Thus the rights of the soil cultivators, their security from arbitrary disturbance and incentives to social advancement, together with the general well-being, peace, and prosperity of the people at large are sacrificed for the benefit of a class insignificant in numbers, and of least account in all that goes towards the maintenance of a country, but which by the aid of existing land laws extracts some twenty million pounds annually from the soil of Ireland without conferring any single benefit in return on the same or the people by whose industry it is produced.

If the land in the possession of 744 landlords in this country were divided into 20-acre farms it would support in ease and comparative independence over two millions and a half of our people.

To substitute for such an unjust and anomalous system as the present land code—one that would show an equal protection and solicitude for the social rights and well-being of the labouring millions as that shown for those of the wealthy but non-operative few—is the principle upon which enlightened statesmanship aims at following in modern times to meet the growing necessities of that popular intelligence and awakening civilization which demands the sweeping away of those feudal laws opposed to the social progress and ideas of the age. Sacrificing the interests of the few to the welfare of the many by the abolition of feudal land codes, has laid the foundation of solid governments and secured the contentment of peoples in most European countries. The interests of the landlords of Ireland are pecuniary and can be compensated, but the interests of the people of Ireland, dependant upon the produce of the soil, is their very existence. In denouncing the existing land laws and demanding in their place such a system as will recognize and establish the cultivator of the said soil as its proprietor, we neither purpose nor demand the confiscation of the interest which the landlords now hold in the land, but ask that compensation be given them for loss of said rights when the state, for the peace, benefit and happiness of the people shall decree the abolition of the present system.

We appeal to the farmers of Ireland to be up and doing at once and organize themselves forthwith in order that their full strength may be put forth in behalf of themselves and their country in efforts to obtain what has brought security and comparative plenty to the farming classes of continental countries. Without an evidence of earnestness and practical determination being shown now by the farmers of Ireland and their friends in a demand for a small proprietary which alone can fully satisfy the Irish people or finally settle the great land question of the country, the tribunal of public opinion will neither credit the urgent necessity for such a change nor lend its influence in ameliorating the condition or redressing the social and political wrongs of which we complain. Let us remember, in the words of one of Ireland's greatest sons,[1] that ' the land is the fund whence we all ultimately draw ; and if the terms on which the land is cultivated be unfair—if the agricultural system of a country be unsound, then the entire structure is rotten and will inevitably come down. Let us never forget that mere appeals to the public to encourage native industry in other departments must be utterly

[1] John Mitchel. See Michael Davitt before the Parnell commission (*Special Commission act, 1888, reprint of the shorthand notes* . . . (London 1890), x. 573.

futile so long as the great and paramount native industry of the farmer is neglected. In vain shall we try to rouse national spirit if the very men who make the nation sink into paupers before our face. Paupers have no country, no rights, no duties ; and, in short, if we permit the small farmers to be reduced to pauperism—if we see them compelled to give up their land and throw themselves on public relief, there is an end of Ireland.'

The manifesto was unanimously adopted.

The Freeman's Journal, 18 August 1879. *The Connaught Telegraph*, 23 August 1879.

7. FOUNDATION OF THE IRISH NATIONAL LAND LEAGUE, 1879

In response to a circular from Mr. Parnell, M.P., a meeting was held in the Imperial Hotel, Dublin, yesterday, at two o'clock, for the purpose of forming a central body in connexion with the present land agitation. The chair was taken by Mr. A. J. Kettle, P.L.G. . . .

The Rev. Father Behan, C.C., proposed and Mr. William Dillon, B.L., seconded, the following resolution—' Resolved, That an association be hereby formed to be named the " Irish National Land League." ' Proposed by Mr. W. Kelly, seconded by Mr. Thos. Roe,—' That the objects of the league are, first, to bring out a reduction of rackrents ; second, to facilitate the obtaining of the ownership of the soil by the occupiers.' Proposed by Mr. Parnell, M.P., seconded by the Rev. Father Sheehy, C.C.—' That the objects of the league can be best attained by promoting organization among the tenant farmers, by defending those who may be threatened with eviction for refusing to pay unjust rents, by facilitating the working of the Bright clauses of the land act during the winter, and by obtaining such reform in the laws relating to land as will enable every tenant to become the owner of his holding by paying a fair rent for a limited number of years'.

Proposed by Mr. John Sweetman, seconded by Mr. T. D. Sullivan —' That Mr. Charles S. Parnell, M.P., be elected president of this league.' Proposed by Mr. George Delany, seconded by Mr. W. H. Cobbe, Portarlington—' That Mr. A. J. Kettle, Mr. Michael Davitt, and Mr. Thomas Brennan be appointed honorary secretaries of the league.' Proposed by Mr. Patrick Cummins, P.L.G., seconded by Mr. Laurence McCourt, P.L.G.,—' That Mr. J. G Biggar, M.P., Mr. W. H. O'Sullivan, M.P. and Mr. Patrick Egan be appointed treasurers.'

An appeal to the Irish race for the sustainment of the movement having been submitted, was approved and ordered to be circulated. On the motion of the Rev. Father Sheehy, seconded by Mr. Michael Davitt it was resolved that the president of this league, Mr. Parnell, be requested to proceed to America for the purpose of obtaining assistance from our exiled countrymen and other sympathisers, for the objects for which this appeal is issued.

Proposed by Mr. Thomas Ryan, seconded by Mr. J. F. Grehan—

'That none of the funds of this league shall be used for the purchase
of any landlord's interest in the land or for furthering the interests of
any parliamentary candidate.'

The Freeman's Journal, 22 October 1879.

8. CHARLES STEWART PARNELL ON THE LAND QUESTION, ENNIS,
19 SEPTEMBER 1880

. . . Depend upon it that the measure of the land bill of next
session will be the measure of your activity and energy this winter
(cheers)—it will be the measure of your determination not to pay
unjust rents—it will be the measure of your determination to keep
a firm grip of your homesteads (cheers). It will be the measure of
your determination not to bid for farms from which others have been
evicted, and to use the strong force of public opinion to deter any
unjust men amongst yourselves—and there are many such—from
bidding for such farms (hear, hear). If you refuse to pay unjust
rents, if you refuse to take farms from which others have been
evicted, the land question must be settled, and settled in a way that
will be satisfactory to you. It depends, therefore, upon yourselves,
and not upon any commission or any government. When you have
made this question ripe for settlement then and not till then will it
be settled (cheers). It is very nearly ripe already in many parts of
Ireland. It is ripe in Mayo, Galway, Roscommon, Sligo, and
portions of the county Cork (cheers). But I regret to say that the
tenant farmers of the county Clare have been backward in organization up to the present time. You must take and band yourselves
together in Land Leagues. Every town and village must have
its own branch. You must know the circumstances of the holdings
and of the tenures of the district over which the League has jurisdiction—you must see that the principles of the Land League are in-
culcated, and when you have done this in Clare, then Clare will take
her rank with the other active counties, and you will be included in
the next land bill brought forward by the government (cheers).
Now, what are you to do to a tenant who bids for a farm from which
another tenant has been evited?

Several voices. Shoot him.

Mr. Parnell. I think I heard somebody say shoot him (cheers).
I wish to point out to you a very much better way—a more christian
and charitable way, which will give the lost man an opportunity of
repenting (laughter, and hear). When a man takes a farm from
which another has been evicted you must shun him on the roadside
when you meet him—you must shun him in the streets of the town
—you must shun him in the shop—you must shun him in the fair-
green and in the market place, and even in the place of worship, by
leaving him alone, by putting him into a moral Coventry, by isolating
him from the rest of his country as if he were the leper of old—you
must show him your detestation of the crime has he committed.
If you do this, you may depend on it there will be no man so full of
avarice—so lost to shame—as to dare the public opinion of all the

right-thinking men in the county and transgress your unwritten code of laws. People are very much engaged at present in discussing the way in which the land question is to be settled, just the same as when a few years ago Irishmen were at each other's throats as to the sort of parliament we would have if we got one. I am always thinking it is better first to catch your hare before you decide how you are going to cook him (laughter). I would strongly recommend public men not to waste their breath too much in discussing how the land question is to be settled, but rather to help and encourage the people in making it, as I said just now, ripe for settlement (applause). When it is ripe for settlement you will probably have your choice as to how it shall be settled and I said a year ago that the land question would never be settled until the Irish landlords were just as anxious to have it settled as the Irish tenants (cheers).

A voice. They soon will be.

Mr. Parnell. There are, indeed, so many ways in which it may be settled that it is almost superfluous to discuss them ; but I stand here to-day to express my opinion that no settlement can be satisfactory or permanent which does not ensure the uprooting of that system of landlordism which has brought the country three times in a century to famine. The feudal system of land tenure has been tried in almost every European country and it has been found wanting everywhere ; but nowhere has it brought more exile, produced more suffering, crime and destitution than in Ireland (cheers). It was abolished in Prussia by transferring the land from the landlords to the occupying tenants. The landlords were given government paper as compensation. Let the English government give the landlords their paper to-morrow as compensation (laughter). We want no money—not a single penny of money would be necessary. Why, if they gave the Irish landlords—the bad section of them—the four or five millions a year that they spend on the police and military (groans) in helping them to collect their rents, that would be a solution of it (cheers), and a very cheap solution of it. But, perhaps, as with other reforms, they will try a little patchwork and tinkering for a while until they learn better (hear, hear). Well, let them patch and tinker if they wish. In my opinion the longer the landlords wait, the worse the settlement they will get (cheers). Now is the time for them to settle before the people learn the power of combination. We have been accused of preaching communistic doctrines when we told the people not to pay an unjust rent, and the following out of that advice in a few of the Irish counties had shown the English government the necessity for a radical alteration in the land laws. But how would they like it if we told the people some day or other not to pay any rent until this question is settled (cheers). We have not told them that yet, and I suppose it may never be necessary for us to speak in that way (hear). I suppose the question will be settled peaceably, fairly, and justly to all parties (hear, hear). If it should not be settled, we cannot continue to allow this milestone to hang round the neck of our country, throttling its industry, and preventing its progress (cheers).

It will be for the consideration of wiser heads than mine whether, if the landlords continue obdurate, and refuse all just concessions, we shall not be obliged to tell the people of Ireland to strike against rent until this question has been settled (cheers). And if the five hundred thousand tenant farmers of Ireland struck against the ten thousand landlords, I would like to see where they would get police and soldiers enough to make them pay (loud cheers).

The Freeman's Journal, 20 September 1880.

9. THE LAND ACT OF 1881

By the act of 1870 Gladstone had given the tenant the right to compensation for improvements and disturbance. The act of 1881, by giving the tenant security of tenure, established a system of dual ownership. Clauses 24–28 following the precedent set by the Irish church act, 1869, and the ' Bright clauses ' of the 1870 act, foreshadowed the ultimate solution of the question, state-aided purchase by the tenant.

An act to further amend the law relating to the occupation and ownership of land in Ireland, and for other purposes relating thereto

Be it enacted . . . as follows :

1. The tenant for the time being of every holding, not hereinafter specially excepted from the provisions of this act, may sell his tenancy for the best price that can be got for the same, subject to the following regulations and subject also to the provisions in this act contained with respect to the sale of a tenancy subject to statutory conditions :

(1) Except with the consent of the landlord, the sale shall be made to one person only :

(2) The tenant shall give the prescribed notice to the landlord of his intention to sell his tenancy :

(3) On receiving such notice the landlord may purchase the tenancy for such sum as may be agreed upon, or in the event of disagreement may be ascertained by the court to be the true value thereof :

(4) Where the tenant shall agree to sell his tenancy to some other person than the landlord, he shall, upon informing the landlord of the name of the purchaser, state in writing therewith the consideration agreed to be given for the tenancy :

(5) If the tenant fails to give the landlord the notice or information required by the foregoing sub-sections, the court may, if it think fit and that the just interests of the landlord so require, declare the sale to be void :

(6) Where the tenancy is sold to some other person than the landlord, the landlord may within the prescribed period refuse on reasonable grounds to accept the purchaser as tenant. In case of dispute the reasonableness of the landlord's refusal shall be decided by the court : . . .

(7) Where the tenancy is subject to any such conditions as are in this act declared to be statutory conditions, and the sale is made in consequence of proceedings by the landlord for the purpose of

recovering possession of the holding by reason of the breach of any of such conditions, the court shall grant to the landlord out of the purchase moneys payment of any debt, including arrears of rent, due to him by the tenant. . . .

(8) Where permanent improvements on a holding have been made by the landlord or his predecessors in title . . . and the landlord . . . consents that his property in such improvements shall be sold along with the tenancy . . . the purchase money shall be apportioned by the court as between the landlord's property in such improvements, and the tenancy, . . .

(9) When a tenant sells his tenancy to any person other than the landlord, the landlord may at any time within the prescribed period give notice both to the outgoing tenant and to the purchaser of any sums which he may claim from the outgoing tenant for arrears of rent or other breaches of the contract or conditions of tenancy. And

(a) If the outgoing tenant does not within the prescribed period give notice to the purchaser that he disputes such claims or any of them, the purchaser shall out of the purchase moneys pay the full amount thereof to the landlord ; and

(b) If the outgoing tenant disputes such claims or any of them, the purchaser shall out of the purchase moneys pay to the landlord so much (if any) of such claims as the outgoing tenant admits, and pay the residue of the amount claimed by the landlord into court in the prescribed manner.

Until the purchaser has satisfied the requirements of this subsection, it shall not be obligatory on the landlord to accept the purchaser as his tenant.

(11) A tenant who has sold his tenancy on any occasion of quitting his holding shall not be entitled on the same occasion to receive compensation for either disturbance or improvements ; and a tenant who has received compensation for either disturbance or improvements on any occasion of quitting his holding shall not be entitled on the same occasion to sell his tenancy.

(12) The tenant of a holding subject to the Ulster tenant-right custom or to a usage corresponding to the Ulster tenant-right custom may sell his tenancy either in pursuance of that custom or usage, or in pursuance of this section, . . .

4. Where the landlord demands an increase of rent from the tenant of a present tenancy . . . or demands an increase of rent from the tenant of a future tenancy beyond the amount fixed at the beginning of such tenancy, then,

(1) Where the tenant accepts such increase, until the expiration of a term of fifteen years from the time when such increase was made (in this act referred to as a statutory term) such tenancy shall (if it so long continues to subsist) be deemed to be a tenancy subject to statutory conditions, with such incidents during the continuance of the said term as are in this act in that behalf mentioned.

(2) Where the tenant of any future tenancy does not accept such increase and sells his tenancy, the same shall be sold subject

to the increased rent, and in addition to the price paid for the tenancy, he shall be entitled to receive from his landlord the amount (if any) by which the court may, on the application of the landlord or tenant, decide the selling value of his tenancy to have been depreciated below the amount which would have been such selling value if the rent had been a fair rent, . . .

(3) Where the tenant does not accept such increase and is compelled to quit the tenancy by or in pursuance of a notice to quit, but does not sell the tenancy, he shall be entitled to claim compensation as in the case of disturbance by the landlord.

(4) The tenant of a present tenancy may in place of accepting or declining such increase apply to the court in manner hereafter in this act mentioned to have the rent fixed.

5. A tenant shall not, during the continuance of a statutory term in his tenancy, be compelled to pay a higher rent than the rent payable at the commencement of such term, and shall not be compelled to quit the holding of which he is tenant except in consequence of the breach of some one or more of the conditions following (in this act referred to as statutory conditions), that is to say,

(1) The tenant shall pay his rent at the appointed time.

(2) The tenant shall not, to the prejudice of the interest of the landlord in the holding, commit persistent waste . . .

(3) The tenant shall not, without the consent of his landlord in writing, subdivide his holding or sub-let the same. . . . Agistment or the letting of land for the purpose of temporary depasturage, or the letting in conacre of land for the purpose of its being solely used . . . for the growing of potatoes or other green crops, the land being properly manured, shall not be deemed a sub-letting for the purposes of this act.

(5) The landlord, or any person or persons authorized by him in that behalf (he or they making reasonable amends and satisfaction for any damage to be done or occasioned thereby), shall have the right to enter upon the holding for any of the purposes following (that is to say), mining or taking minerals, or digging or searching for minerals ; . . . cutting or taking timber or turf, . . . opening or making roads, fences, drains, and watercourses ; passing and re-passing to and from the sea shore with or without horses and carriages for exercising any right of property or royal franchise belonging to the landlord, viewing or examining at reasonable times the state of the holding and all buildings or improvements thereon ; hunting, shooting, fishing . . .

(6) The tenant shall not on his holding, without the consent of his landlord, open any house for the sale of intoxicating liquors.

Nothing contained in this section shall prejudice or affect any ejectment for nonpayment of rent instituted by a landlord whether before or after the commencement of a statutory term, in respect of rent accrued due for a holding before the commencement of such term.

During the continuance of a statutory term in a tenancy, save as hereinafter provided, the court may, on the application of the landlord, and upon being satisfied that he is desirous of resuming the holding or part thereof for some reasonable and sufficient purpose authorize the resumption thereof by the landlord upon such conditions as the court may think fit, . . .

Provided that the rent of any holding subject to statutory conditions may be increased in respect of capital laid out by the landlord under agreement with the tenant to such an amount as may be agreed upon between landlord and tenant.

6. . . . . The compensation payable . . . in the case of a tenant disturbed in his holding by the act of a landlord after the passing of this act shall be as follows, in the case of holdings where the rent is thirty pounds or under, a sum not exceeding seven years rent ; where the rent is above thirty pounds and not exceeding fifty pounds, a sum not exceeding five years rent ; where the rent is above fifty pounds and not exceeding one hundred pounds, a sum not exceeding four years rent ; where the rent is above one hundred pounds and not exceeding three hundred pounds, a sum not exceeding three years rent ; where the rent is above three hundred pounds and not exceeding five hundred pounds, a sum not exceeding two years rent ; where the rent is above five hundred pounds, a sum not exceeding one year's rent.

8. (1) The tenant of any present tenancy to which this act applies, or such tenant and the landlord jointly, or the landlord, . . . may from time to time during the continuance of such tenancy apply to the court to fix the fair rent to be paid by such tenant to the landlord for the holding, . . .

(3) Where the judicial rent [the rent fixed by the court] of any present tenancy has been fixed . . . then, until the expiration of a term of fifteen years from the rent day next succeeding the day on which the determination of the court has been given (in this act referred to as a statutory term), such present tenancy shall (if it so long continue to subsist) be deemed to be a tenancy subject to statutory conditions . . .

(6) Subject to rules made under this act, the landlord and tenant of any present tenancy to which this act applies, may . . . by writing under their hands, agree and declare what is then the fair rent of the holding ; and such agreement and declaration on being filed in court in the prescribed manner, shall have the same effect and consequences in all respects as if the rent so agreed on were a judicial rent . . .

10. The landlord and tenant of any ordinary tenancy and the landlord and proposed tenant of any holding to which this act applies which is not subject to a subsisting tenancy, may agree, the one to grant and the other to accept a lease for a term of thirty-one years or upwards (in this act referred to as a judicial lease), on such conditions and containing such provisions as the parties to such lease may mutually agree upon, and such lease . . . shall be substituted for the former tenancy, if any, in the holding . . .

13. (1) Where proceedings are or have been taken by the landlord to compel a tenant to quit his holding, the tenant may sell his tenancy

at any time before but not after the expiration of six months from the
execution of a writ or decree for possession in an ejectment for non-
payment of rent, and at any time before but not after the execution
of such writ or decree in any ejectment other than for nonpayment
of rent; and any such tenancy so sold shall be and be deemed to
be a subsisting tenancy notwithstanding such proceedings, without
prejudice to the landlord's rights, in the event of the said tenancy
not being redeemed within said period of six months ; and, if any
judgment or decree in ejectment has been obtained before the passing
of this act, such tenant may within the same periods respectively
apply to the court to fix the judicial rent of the holding, but subject
to the provisions herein contained such application shall not invalidate
or prejudice any such judgment or decree, which shall remain in
full force and effect.

(3) Where any proceedings for compelling the tenant of a present
tenancy to quit his holding shall have been taken before or after an
application to fix a judicial rent and shall be pending before such
application is disposed of, the court before which such proceedings
are pending shall have power . . . to postpone or suspend such
proceedings until the termination of the proceedings on the application for such judicial rent ; . . .

(6) A tenant compelled to quit his holding during the continuance
of a statutory term in his tenancy, in consequence of the breach by
the tenant of any statutory condition, shall not be entitled to compensation for disturbance.

22. A tenant whose holding or the aggregate of whose holdings
is valued under the act relating to the valuation of rateable property
in Ireland at an annual value of not less than one hundred and fifty
pounds, shall be entitled by writing under his hand to contract
himself out of any of the provisions of this act or of the *Landlord
and Tenant (Ireland) Act*, 1870.

24. (1) The land commission, out of moneys in their hands, may,
if satisfied with the security, advance sums to tenants for the purpose
of enabling them to purchase their holdings, that is to say,—

(*a*) Where a sale of a holding is about to be made by a landlord
to a tenant in consideration of the payment of a principal sum, the
land commission may advance to the tenant for the purposes of such
purchase, any sum not exceeding three fourths of the said principal
sum.

(*b*) Where a sale of a holding is about to be made by a landlord
to a tenant in consideration of the tenant paying a fine and engaging
to pay to the landlord a fee farm rent, the land commission may
advance to the tenant for the purposes of such purchase, any sum
not exceeding one half of the fine payable to the landlord.

26. (1) Any estate may be purchased by the land commission
for the purpose of reselling to the tenants of the lands comprised in
such estate their respective holdings, if the land commission are
satisfied . . . that a competent number of the tenants are able and
willing to purchase their holdings from the land commission.

(2) The sale by the land commission of a holding to the tenant thereof may be made either in consideration of a principal sum being paid as the whole price . . . or in consideration of a fine and of a fee farm rent, with this qualification, that the amount of the fee farm rent shall not exceed seventy-five per cent of the rent which in the opinion of the land commission would be a fair rent for the holding.

(3) For the purposes of this section a competent number of tenants means a body of tenants who are not less in number than three fourths of the whole number of tenants on the estate, and who pay rent not less than two thirds of the whole rent of the estate, . . .

28. (1) Any advance made by the land commission for the purpose of supplying money for the purchase of a holding from a landlord or of a holding or parcel from the land commission, shall be repaid by an annuity in favour of the land commission for thirty-five years of five pounds for every hundred pounds of such advance, and so in proportion for any less sum.

37. (1) The expression 'the court' as used in this act shall mean the civil bill court of the county where the matter requiring the cognizance of the court arises.

(3) Any proceedings which might be instituted before the civil bill court may, at the election of the person taking such proceedings, be instituted before the land commission, . . .

40. Any matter capable of being determined by the court under this act, may, if the parties so agree, be decided by arbitration, . . . and where the amount of rent is decided by arbitration, such rent shall for the purposes of this act be deemed to be the judicial rent.

41. A land commission shall be constituted under this act consisting of a judicial commissioner and two other commissioners.

43. The lord lieutenant may from time to time, with the consent of the treasury as to number, appoint and by order in council remove assistant commissioners, . . .

44. Any power or act by this act vested in or authorized to be done by the land commission, except the power of hearing appeals, may be exercised or done by any one member of the land commission or by any sub-commission, . . .

Public general acts, 1881, pp. 139–64.

10. WYNDHAM'S ACT, 1903

Under Ashbourne's act of 1885 the tenant for the first time was permitted to borrow the whole of the purchase money for his holding from the state. Further acts extending the facilities for land purchase were passed in 1888, 1891, and 1896. Wyndham's act of 1903 based on the recommendations of a conference of landlord and tenant representatives, offered a bonus on the purchase money as an inducement to landlords to sell.

An act to amend the law relating to the occupation and ownership of land in Ireland and for other purposes relating thereto and to amend the labourers (Ireland) acts

Be it enacted . . . as follows :

1. (1) In the case of the sale of an estate, whether to the land

commission or otherwise, when application is made for an advance under the land purchase acts of the whole purchase money of a holding and the land commission are satisfied that the tenant is in occupation of the holding, then . . . the land commission shall sanction the advance in the following cases, namely ;

(*a*) In the case of the purchase of a holding subject to a judicial rent fixed or agreed to since the passing of the act of 1896, if the purchase annuity, created under this act payable in respect of the advance, will be not less than ten nor more than thirty per cent below the existing rent ; and

(*b*) In the case of the purchase of a holding subject to a judicial rent fixed or agreed to before that date, if the said purchase annuity will be not less than twenty nor more than forty per cent below that rent.

6. (1) Where the owner of an estate makes an application in the prescribed form to the land commission, requesting them to enquire into the circumstances of the estate with a view to the sale thereof under this part of this act, the land commission may, after due enquiry, propose to purchase the estate, and in estimating the price shall have regard to the foregoing provisions of this act in respect of advances, and to the prices which the tenants and other persons are willing to give for the holdings and other parcels of land comprised in the estate.

(2) If within the prescribed time the owner of the estate agrees to sell the estate at the estimated price, and tenants of holdings on the estate, to the extent of not less than three-fourths in number and rateable value, undertake to purchase from the land commission their holdings, or other designated parcels of land in lieu thereof, for the respective amounts on the basis of which the price of the tenanted portion of the estate was estimated by the commission, the commission may agree to purchase the estate for the estimated price.

19. Where an estate is purchased by the land commission and tenants on the estate to the extent of three-fourths in number and rateable value have agreed to purchase their holdings, the estates commissioners may . . . order that the remaining tenants, or any of them, shall be deemed to have accepted the offers made to them, and the land purchase acts shall apply accordingly, where the tenant could have obtained an advance of the entire purchase money, and the land commission have offered in the prescribed manner to make the advance.

23. (1) The jurisdiction, powers and duties of the land commission, under the foregoing provisions of this act, shall be exercised and performed exclusively by three members of the commission (in this act referred to as 'the estates commissioners') . . .

(5) The estates commissioners shall hold office during pleasure, but any estates commissioner shall only be removed from his office by an order in council, and any such order shall be laid before each house of parliament forthwith, and, if an address is presented to his majesty by either house of parliament, within the next subsequent

forty days on which that house has sat next after any such order is laid before it, praying that the order may be annulled, his majesty in council may annul the order, and it shall therefore be void.

27. Advances for the purposes of the land purchase acts shall, in the case of agreements entered into after the passing of this act, be made by means of money and not by means of guaranteed land stock ; and any sums required for those purposes shall be issued out of a special fund, to be under the control of the national debt commissioners and to be called the ' Irish land purchase fund.'

28. (1) For the purpose of raising the money required for the Irish land purchase fund, the treasury may, by warrant addressed to the bank of England or bank of Ireland, direct the creation of a new capital stock (to be called ' guaranteed two and three-quarters per cent. stock,' and in this act referred to as ' the stock ') consisting of perpetual annuities, yielding dividends at the rate of two and three-quarters per cent. per annum on the nominal amount of the capital.

29. (1) The dividends on the stock shall be paid out of the income of the Irish land purchase fund and, if that income is insufficient, shall be charged on and paid out of the consolidated fund of the United Kingdom or the growing produce thereof.

(2) Any sums so paid out of the consolidated fund shall be treated as a temporary advance to the Irish land purchase funds and shall be made good out of the guarantee fund.[1]

45. As regards advances under the land purchase acts, in pursuance of agreements entered into after the passing of this act, every advance shall be repaid, in the manner and at the times prescribed by the treasury, by means of a purchase annuity calculated at the rate of three pounds five shillings for every hundred pounds of the advance and so, in proportion, for any less sum : . . .

48. (1) For the purpose of aiding the sale of estates under this act, the land commission may . . . pay to the vendor of each estate sold a sum calculated at the rate of twelve per cent. on the amount of the purchase money advanced under the land purchase acts.

Public general acts, 1903, pp. 187–225.

ANGLO-IRISH CONSTITUTIONAL RELATIONS

11. DANIEL O'CONNELL ON REPEAL, MULLINGAR, 14 MAY 1843

One of a series of speeches made when the repeal agitation was at its height.

My first object is to get Ireland for the Irish (loud cheers). I am content that the English should have England, but they have had the domination of this country too long, and it is time that the Irish should at length get their own country—that they should get

---

[1] The guarantee fund, set up by the land act of 1891, consisted of sums paid from the imperial exchequer for purely Irish purposes.

18

the management of their own country—the regulation of their own country—the enjoyment of their own country—that the Irish should have Ireland (great cheers). Nobody can know how to govern us as well as we would know how to do it ourselves—nobody could know how to relieve our wants as well as we would ourselves— nobody could have so deep an interest in our prosperity, or could be so well fitted for remedying our evils, and procuring happiness for us as we would ourselves (hear, hear). Old Ireland and liberty ! (loud cheers). That is what I am struggling for (hear, hear). If I was to tell the Scotch that they should not have Scotland—if I was to tell the English that they should not have England—if I was to tell the Spaniards that they should not have Spain—or the French that they should not have France, they would have a right to laugh at, to hate, to attack, or to assail me in whatever manner they chose. But I do not say any such thing. What I say is, that as all these people have their own countries, the Irish ought to have Ireland (hear, and cheers). What numberless advantages would not the Irish enjoy if they possessed their own country ? A domestic parliament would encourage Irish manufactures. The linen trade, and the woollen would be spreading amongst you. An Irish parliament would foster Irish commerce, and protect Irish agriculture. The labourer, the artizan, and the shopkeeper would be all benefited by the repeal of the union ; but if I were to describe all the blessings that it would confer I would detain you here crowding on each other's backs until morning before I would be done (laughter). In the first place, I ask did you ever hear of the tithe rent charge (groans). Are you satisfied to be paying parsons who do not pray for you (no, no). It is time, therefore, that they should be put an end to (hear, hear). The people of England do not pay for the church of the minority.

A voice. No, nor the people of Scotland either.

You are quite right, though I think I heard the remark before (laughter). But carry home my words with you, and tell them to your neighbours. I tell you the people of Ireland will not be much longer paying them (hear, hear, and cheers). I next want to get rid of the poor rates (cheers). England does charity in the way a person will throw a bone to a dog, by slashing it in between his teeth (hear, hear). That is the poor law charity, the charity of the commissioners and assistant-commissioners, and all concerned under them except the poor themselves, and when they do give relief they take up the poor as if they were criminals, or as if poverty were a crime to be punished by perpetual imprisonment (hear and cheers). . . . I know it will be said that I want to leave the poor destitute. I do not want to do any such thing. Would I not have the tithe rent-charge and the ecclesiastical revenues to apply for their relief ? And would I not with their aid be able to maintain hospitals for the sick, the lame, the impotent, the aged, and all those who are real objects of charity, and for whom the doors would be open at every hour of the day and during a part of the night, so that anybody who did not like to remain might go out when they liked (hear, hear, and cheers) ? I would thus do you two pieces of service by the repeal of the Union. I would relieve the poor without the imposition of poor rates, and I would prevent you from paying any clergy but your own (loud cheers). I should not have used the word prevent, because if any of you wished to pay both you might do it if you pleased (laughter). I often asked protestants how would they like to pay for the support of the catholic clergy by force, and they always said they would not like it at all ; and why should the catholics like it one bit the better (hear) ? Cobbett had a phrase for it. He used to say ' what's sauce for the goose is sauce for the gander,' (laughter). The next thing that the repeal would abolish is the grand jury cess (cheers). I believe it grinds some of you (cries of ' It does so '). There is not a more iniquitous tax in the world, for it comes on the occupier instead of on the country at large. Give me the repeal, and the national treasury will pay for the making and repairing of all the roads, bridges, and public buildings ; and instead of the poor farmers and occupiers paying the money themselves, it will come from the treasury, and would go in giving employment to those who now have to pay it (hear, hear). I will tell you another thing I want to do. I want that every head of a family, every married man and every householder should have a right to vote for members of parliament. They say that I would have an interest in that, because I would then have more votes ; but my answer is, if I would it is because the people know I am acting honestly by them, and everybody else who does the same will be equally supported. The landlords now persecute those who vote differently from their wishes, but I would institute the ballot-box. Every married man should have a vote, and any blackguard who could not get a wife anywhere I would not pity him to be without the vote (cheers and laughter). The good landlord would then be sure to be supported by his tenants ; but if he were a scoundrel, whether he was a catholic, a protestant, or a presbyterian, he would deserve to be turned out (hear, hear). If he was serving notices to quit, or holding up his head in the street, and not looking his tenants in the face and speaking to them, or if he was a man who would not salute their wives and children as he passed them, or if, when he sat upon the bench, he was always fining, fining, fining (loud laughter), the tenant would always have the advantage of using the ballot-box against that fellow (hear, hear, and cheers). The next advantage is one that does not much concern the majority of you. It is the giving the management of their own affairs to the inhabitants of towns, instead of their having the miserable municipal reform that they now possess ; but I will not trouble you farther with that. You know that the landlords have duties as well as rights, and I would establish the fixity of tenure (loud cheers) to remind them of these duties. I will tell you what my plan is, and you can consider it among yourselves. My plan is that no landlord could recover rent unless he made a lease for twenty-one years to the tenant—no lease or no rent say I (loud cheers). Unless he made a lease, he would have no more business looking for his rent than a dog would have barking at the moon (cheers and laughter). It may be said that the landlords would, in that case, put too high a rent on their lands, but I have a remedy for that too in my plan (laughter, and cries of ' more power '). At present, if a man goes to register his vote, he must prove on oath what a solvent tenant could pay to his landlord for his holding, and in the same manner I would give the tenant an opportunity of proving what a solvent tenant ought to give for his land, in order to fix the amount of rent he would have to pay (cheers). I would give the poor man the benefit of a trial by jury in such case, so that it would be impossible for a landlord to get more than the fair value of his land. It may be said that the poor man would be turned out of his holding at the expiration of his lease, and his land given to another, but I have a cure for that also (cheers). I would allow the tenant by law every year to register, as he can now register trees that he plants, all the improvements that he makes on his holding, and if the landlord did not pay him the full value of these improvements, he could not turn him out, but would be obliged to give him a new holding. Every tenant would be then building a better house for his pigs than he now inhabits himself, as he would be sure to get every farthing he laid out on his holding before he could be deprived of possession at the end of his lease (hear, hear, and cheers). Is it not, I ask you, worth while to look for a repeal of the union for that alone (cheers)? Would it not do more to produce happiness and prosperity in the country, and put an end to the horrible wholesale murders of the landlords who now send their tenants to die by twenties in the ditches, and the fearful retaliations, by assassination, that so frequently take place on the other side (hear). But that is not all. Every year since the Union nine millions of money has been sent out of Ireland, after being raised from the produce of the soil (cries of ' Oh, murder, murder '). It is no wonder you should cry ' murder ' for there is no country in the world where such a system would exist that must not be poor. The only countries except Ireland where anything like it occurs are Sicily and Sardinia, and both of these, from having absentee landlords, are miserably poor. There is not, however, a country in the world so impoverished as Ireland, where it has been found that there are 2,300,000 persons in a state of destitution every year. Lord Eliot the other day gave a proof of that, for he had to admit that out of 83,000 poor rate payers, 44,000 were rated under £5. For the last ten years no less than ninety millions have been drawn out of Ireland, but if we get the Union [1] there will be ninety millions spent in Ireland that would otherwise be taken from her (hear, hear, and cheers). This will leave an average of £750,000 a month, or £125,000 a week of six days, to be spent in wages and in giving employment to the people (cheers). I have all this within my grasp if the people join me. Now, what is there in all this that Wellington should stammer at in his old age, and that Peel should bluster, and get very angry about it (groans). Do not take the trouble of groaning

[1] Presumably misprint for ' Repeal.'

him (renewed groans). I suppose you groan not so much to dispute with what I ask you as because you do not find it a trouble but a pleasure to groan him. They say we want separation from England, but what I want is to prevent separation taking place, and there is not a man in existence more loyally attached than I am to the Queen —God bless her. The present state of Ireland is nearly unendurable, and if the people of Ireland had not some person like me to lead them in the paths of peace and constitutional exertion, I am afraid of the result (hear). While I live I will stand by the throne (hear, hear). But what motive could we have to separate if we obtain all those blessings and advantages I have been enumerating ? They would all serve as solid golden links of connexion with England. But I would be glad to know what good did the Union do (hear, hear) ? What I want you to do is, for every one of you to join me in looking for Repeal. As many of you as are willing to do so let them hold up their hands (here every person in the immense assemblage raised his hands aloft amidst loud and continued cheers). I see you have ready hands, and I know you have stout hearts too. But what do I want you to do ? Is it to turn out into battle or war (cries of no, no) ? Is it to commit riot or crime (cries of no, no) ? Remember ' whoever commits a crime gives strength to the enemy ' (hear, hear, and cheers). . . . I want you to do nothing that is not open and legal, but if the people unite with me and follow my advice it is impossible not to get the Repeal (loud cheers and cries of ' we will '). And our country deserves that we should exert ourselves for her. Other countries changed their religious opinions at the fantasy of their governors, but Ireland is the only country that for centuries set her governors at defiance, and she is also the only country that was converted to christianity in the short space of four years (hear, hear, hear). . . .

But nothing could be more true, that there was no pursuit of Roman catholic interests as opposed to protestant, and that the object in view was to benefit the whole nation ; and because it was a national movement it should never be abandoned until justice was done to the nation (loud cheers). Even their enemies should admit the progress they had made ; and let him have but three millions of Repealers, and then he would make his arrangements for obtaining Repeal. He would have the Repealers send up three hundred gentlemen, chosen from various parts of the country, each entrusted with £100, that would be £30,000. They should meet in Dublin to consult upon the best means of obtaining legislative independence. They would not leave Dublin till they would agree to an act of parliament to establish a domestic legislature, household suffrage, vote by ballot, fixity of tenure, and a law against absentees having estates in the country. Many estates would then be sold, in lots and purchased by those who would become small proprietors ; and it was a fact well ascertained that in proportion as the owners in fee were numerous in any country, so in proportion were the people prosperous (hear, hear). It was truly said by Mr. Martin, their chairman, that if they had their own parliament, taxation would be diminished to almost nothing—for in five or six years they would be able to pay off their portion of the national debt—the duty upon every exciseable article would be reduced—they would have a pound of tea for little more than was now paid for a couple of ounces, and a pound of sugar at the price of a quarter of a pound, the duty on tobacco would be reduced, so that there was not an old woman in the country who might not have her pipe lighted from morning to night if she pleased (laughter). . . .

The Nation, 20 May 1843.

12. WILLIAM SHARMAN CRAWFORD ON FEDERALISM, 1844

Crawford, a northern liberal, wrote a series of letters advocating federalism as an alternative to repeal.

Local legislature for Ireland. No. 3

Sir, I have in the preceding sections shown, first, the evils produced to Ireland through the want of local legislation by a local body. I have shown, secondly, that it is the principle of British policy to grant local legislative bodies to portions of the empire so circumstanced, and I have taken the constitution of Canada as an example of their construction. I now proceed to inquire on what basis a legislature could be constructed for Ireland, which would secure to her these two things ; 1st, protection for her rights, and 2dly, the management of her own resources—and would, at the same time, avoid any danger to the integrity of the empire by leaving in the hands of an imperial parliament those matters of legislation which imperial interests require.[1]

As it is always prudent to adopt a precedent in existence when not inconsistent with the purposes sought to be obtained, I shall take as my basis the act for the constitution of Canada, already referred to in my second section. I shall suppose, then, that a legislature is constituted for Ireland, consisting of two houses—a house of lords, which may be considered analogous to the legislative council of Canada, and a house of commons, analogous to their house of assembly. I shall not now enter into the particular details of construction ; I shall at once refer to the power with which such a parliament may be invested.

1. That this parliament shall be competent (with the royal assent) to make all laws necessary for Ireland, and to impose and apply all necessary taxes, subject to the limitations and regulations hereinafter stated.

2. That all bills which may be passed by the local parliament, which make any provisions with regard to religion or religious worship, or pecuniary grants or payments for the purposes of religion, or any bills which relate to   ,[2] shall be subject to the regulations

---

[1] In his second letter Crawford had explained that since the imperial parliament would retain a measure of control over Irish affairs Ireland should continue to be represented in it.   [2] Blank in original.

contained in the 42d section of the Canada act—viz. that before the royal assent be given to any such bills, they shall lie for thirty days on the tables of the houses of the imperial parliament, and in case the said houses shall address the sovereign to withhold the royal assent, such assent shall not be given. (Note.—Upon the subject of this exception with regard to religion, I may remark, that before any new political constitution can be established, I conceive that some equitable settlement with regard to the Irish church and its revenues must be effected ; such being made, it is only a reasonable concession to the apprehension of many persons well affected to local legislation, to provide that such settlement shall not be disturbed by any act of the local legislature without the approval of the imperial parliament ; and I would further add, by any act of the imperial parliament without the approval of the local parliament. It would be a matter for consideration whether any bills, regarding any other laws than those relating to religion, should be made subject to the same rules.

3. That all acts of the imperial legislature which regard the succession to the throne, or the appointment of a regent (if such should be necessary), shall be binding on Ireland without being referred to the local legislature.

4. That the local parliament shall have power to impose and apply, with the assent of the crown, all taxation necessary for the purposes of Ireland, subject to the regulations and limitations hereinafter stated.

5. That the imperial parliament shall retain a power similar to that provided by the 43rd section of the Canada act—to impose all duties necessary for the purposes of commerce over the united kingdom.

6. That the net produce of all duties so imposed shall—in conformity with the proviso contained in the 43rd section of the Canada act—be paid into the Irish exchequer, and placed at the disposal of the local parliament, in same manner as all taxes imposed by the local authority.

7. That if any bill be passed by the local parliament, proposing to alter or repeal, with regard to Ireland, any duty which had been so imposed by the imperial parliament, or to impose any new duty on any article of foreign or colonial produce imported into Ireland, such bill shall be subjected, previous to the royal assent being declared, to the same regulations as provided under the second head with regard to certain laws to be submitted to the consideration of the imperial parliament.

8. That it be a fundamental law that no duties shall be imposed by either parliaments which would impede the perfect freedom of trade between Great Britain and Ireland.

9. That Ireland shall pay a certain quota to the military and naval establishments, and other expenses of the empire, that this quota shall be a sum fixed for a certain number of years, not to be increased under any circumstances during the time specified,

except by a free grant of the parliament of Ireland, that at the termination of the period specified a new arrangement of the quota may be made, if both parliaments consent.

10. That Ireland shall pay the expenses of all her civil establishments and institutions out of her own revenue.

11. That no law made, nor tax imposed by the local parliament of Ireland shall have operation beyond the limits of Ireland ; and that all foreign and colonial legislation, of every description, shall remain under the control and authority of the imperial parliament.

12. That no law, or act of the imperial parliament, made after the passing of this act, and operating locally in Ireland, shall be binding on Ireland, unless assented to by her local parliament— with the exception of those matters reserved in proposition no. 3, and the power of imposing duties reserved in no. 5.

13. That all laws and statutes now in force shall be binding on Ireland till altered or repealed according to the power given by this act.

If the above propositions be examined, I think they shall be found to define with sufficient accuracy the general powers which I would propose to vest in a local and imperial parliament. They are not powers or distinctions which are the mere creations of my imagination—they are taken from the laws of England, as developed in her legislation towards her colonial possessions, . . .

I am aware that these propositions will not meet the views of those who claim for Ireland a separate national existence—they will allege that my propositions would place her rather in the position of a colony of a nation. I cannot help this ; I repeat what I have often before stated—that I cannot conceive no means of separate national existence, except by a separation of the crown as well as of the parliament. By this I mean a perfectly independent condition, and I think this condition cannot be obtained, and if temporarily obtained, could not be preserved. I care not what name may be given to the position in which Ireland may be placed, if it gives the best practical security for her rights and her interests. Ireland is now in the position of a conquered country, held only by the military power of England ; I wish to redeem her from that state by founding the connexion on a just and useful basis.

The Freeman's Journal, 15 November 1844.

13. RESOLUTIONS OF THE HOME RULE CONFERENCE OF 1873

In the autumn of 1873 a requisition was circulated calling on the friends of Irish home rule to hold a conference. The requisition which was strongly supported by the Home Government Association, received about 25,000 signatures. In November the conference met. Nine hundred tickets were issued to requisitionists, and among those who attended were 28 M.P.s.

1. That as the basis of the proceedings of this conference, we declare our conviction that it is essentially necessary to the peace

and prosperity of Ireland that the right of domestic legislation on all Irish affairs should be restored to our country.

2. That, solemnly reasserting the inalienable right of the Irish people to self-government, we declare that the time in our opinion has come when a combined and energetic effort should be made to obtain the restoration of that right.

3. That, in accordance with the ancient and constitutional rights of the Irish nation, we claim the privilege of managing our own affairs by a parliament assembled in Ireland, and composed of the sovereign, the lords, and the commons of Ireland.

4. That, in claiming these rights and privileges for our country, we adopt the principle of a federal arrangement, which would secure to the Irish parliament the right of legislating for and regulating all matters relating to the internal affairs of Ireland, while leaving to the imperial parliament the power of dealing with all questions affecting the imperial crown and government, legislation regarding the colonies and other dependencies of the crown, the relations of the empire with foreign states, and all matters appertaining to the defence and stability of the empire at large, as well as the power of granting the supplies necessary for imperial purposes.

5. That, such an arrangement does not involve any change in the existing constitution of the imperial parliament, or any interference with the prerogatives of the crown or disturbance of the principles of the constitution.

6. That to secure to the Irish people the advantages of constitutional government, it is essential that there should be in Ireland an administration for Irish affairs, controlled, according to constitutional principles, by the Irish parliament, and conducted by ministers constitutionally responsible to that parliament.

7. That in the opinion of this conference, a federal arrangement, based upon these principles, would consolidate the strength and maintain the integrity of the empire, and add to the dignity and power of the imperial crown.

8. That while we believe that in an Irish parliament the rights and liberties of all classes of our countrymen would find their best and surest protection, we are willing that there should be incorporated in the federal constitution articles supplying the amplest guarantees that no change shall be made by that parliament in the present settlement of property in Ireland, and that no legislation shall be adopted to establish any religious ascendancy in Ireland, or to subject any person to disabilities on account of his religious opinions.

9. That this conference cannot separate without calling on the Irish constituencies at the next general election, to return men earnestly and truly devoted to the great cause which this conference has been called to promote, and who in any emergency that may arise may be ready to take counsel with a great national conference, to be called in such a manner as to represent the opinions and feelings of the Irish nation ; and that, with a view of rendering members of parliament and their constituents more in accord on

all questions affecting the welfare of the country, it is recommended by this conference that at the close of each session of parliament the representatives should render to their constituents an account of their stewardships.

10. That in order to carry these objects into practical effect, an association be now formed to be called ' The Irish Home Rule league ' of which the essential and fundamental principles shall be those declared in the resolutions adopted at this conference, and of which the object, and the only object, shall be to obtain for Ireland by peaceable and constitutional means, the self-government claimed in those resolutions.

Proceedings of the home rule conference held in the Rotunda, Dublin, the 18, 19, 20, and 21 November 1873 (Dublin 1874), pp. 201–2.

14. ISAAC BUTT ON HOME RULE, HOUSE OF COMMONS, 30 JUNE 1874

Butt moved that the house go into committee to consider relations between Great Britain and Ireland. The motion was rejected by 458 to 51.

The resolutions [1] he now submitted to the house were very clear, and if they were debated, it would be seen that they were quite sufficient to guide the house to a conclusion. In the next place, he would direct their attention to this fact—that they involved no change in the constitution, and he was anxious that the house should clearly understand this. He proposed no change in the imperial parliament, and if his scheme were adopted, the house would meet next year just as it had done this ; there would not be a single change in members or constituencies ; there would be the members for Leeds, Glasgow, Dublin, and Limerick, the only change would be to take from that assembly some of the duties which it now discharged in reference to Irish business, and to relegate them to another. That being so, he was tempted to ask, whether the removal of the Irish business from that house would be regarded by the hon. members as an intolerable grievance ? Some might be of opinion that it would be no great grievance if the Irish members were sent away ; but the great majority, he believed, would be of opinion that if the Irish business were transacted elsewhere, more time would be left for the transaction of the legitimate business of the house. Now, he might be asked what he called Irish business ; and further, if, should Irish members go into a parliament of their own to transact their own business, they would still claim the power and privilege of voting on English questions in this house ? He would answer the second question by saying emphatically ' No ' ; . . .

[1] ' That this house resolve itself into a committee of the whole house, to consider the present parliamentary relations between Great Britain and Ireland.'
' That it is expedient and just to restore to the Irish nation the right and power of managing all exclusively Irish affairs in an Irish parliament ; and that provision should be made at the same time for maintaining the integrity of the empire and the connexion between the countries by reserving to this imperial parliament full and exclusive control over all imperial affairs.'

The English parliament, including the Scotch members—he would perhaps have a word to say on the last point presently—would meet to discuss purely English affairs, and when there was any question affecting the empire at large, Irish members might be summoned to attend. He saw no difficulty in the matter. The English parliament could manage English affairs as before the Union; but now the English parliament undertook a duty it was unable to perform—namely, to manage the internal affairs of Ireland to the satisfaction of the Irish people. He did not seek to interfere with the right of taxing Ireland for imperial purposes, providing always that Ireland had a voice in imperial matters. He was asking only for a constitutional government, and the benefit of those free institutions which made England great. If he succeeded in showing that Ireland had not a constitutional government, then he thought he could rely on the justice and generosity of the English parliament and of the commons at large to give it to her. What was constitutional government? It consisted of adequate representation in parliament—a control of the administration of affairs by a representative assembly of the people, so as to bring the government of the country into harmony with the feeling, the wants, and the wishes of the people. Did the representation by 103 Irish members in the English house of commons amount to that? Could it be said that that house discharged the great function of constitutional government to Ireland? If it did not, then it followed that Ireland was deprived of that constitutional government which was its inherent right. He knew it might be said that this involved the question whether Ireland and England were not so blended into one nation, that the same house might discharge the duties of a representative assembly for both. That, again, was a matter of fact. The house might wish that they were all West Britons, but wishes would not alter facts. . . . The two countries were not blended together, because in every department in Ireland the distinction was marked. They had a separate government, a separate lord lieutenant, separate courts of law, and exceptional laws were passed for Ireland which would never be tolerated for England. How, then, could one representative assembly act for both? Was not the consequence that the weaker country had no constitutional government? In this country there was constitutional government. The house of commons administered the affairs of the nation in harmony with the sentiments of the English people. Statesmen in that house breathed an atmosphere of English feeling; they discussed English questions in an English assembly; they were driven of necessity to mould the administration of the government in accordance with the wants and wishes of the people. They asked the same for Ireland, and they asked for no more. . . .

As a matter of fact, the whole government of Ireland was based upon distrust of all classes in the community. Stipendary magistrates were substituted for the resident gentry of the country, and a sub-inspector of constabulary was a more influential person than the lord-lieutenant of a county. The whole record of the legislation for Ireland since the Union was made up of successive Arms Acts, suspensions of the Habeas Corpus Act, to Party Processions Prevention Acts, and Coercion Acts, each one being more severe than its predecessor. And this record was the more gloomy because it was a record of the doings of well-intentioned parliaments. Notwithstanding all that had been done, the curfew bell of the Norman conquerors was rung in many parts of the country, and in others blood money was exacted after the example of the Saxons. Even if it were true—which he denied—that such a course of legislation had been necessary, that very fact would be its most grievous condemnation. He was therefore justified in saying that up to now the government of the country had failed, and in asking that the Irish people might have an opportunity of managing their own affairs. He was told that parliament having passed the land act and the church act, the Irish people were ungrateful in coming forward and demanding home rule also. It was even said that such a course was an act of ingratitude towards the individual minister who had been mainly instrumental in passing those acts. All he could say was that such assertions showed the faultiness of the system under which they could be possible. Who ever spoke of the English people being grateful for the passing of a good act ? . . . Was there an Englishman in the house who would not be glad to get rid of the opprobriums attaching to the government of Ireland ? If the wish was really entertained, the way to get rid of it was by allowing the Irish people an opportunity of trying to govern themselves. If they succeeded, great and glorious would be the reward of those who gave the opportunity ; if they failed, theirs alone would be the blame. And where was there to be found any valid objection to granting what they asked ? The imperial parliament would hold the army, the navy, and all that was connected with affairs purely imperial, and no difficulty would be found in separating from imperial questions those with which an Irish parliament might properly deal. The United States of America afforded an illustration of a successful federal government with independent state legislatures, and in some of our own colonies they found instances of people owning the imperial sway of England, but at the same time managing their own internal affairs. Even supposing that there might be some disaffected members of an Irish parliament—and this he did not admit—they would be in a miserable minority, and the fact of their disaffection being open to the light would give the strongest assurance of its speedy extinction. In two English colonies were to be found men who, driven out of Ireland because they could no longer endure the system of government existing there, had become ministers under the British crown, and were doing honour alike to the colonies in which they served and to the sovereign who had appointed them. Sir George Grey, the governor of the Cape of Good Hope, wrote strongly in favour of giving a federal parliament to Ireland, and he believed in his soul that it would be the means of effecting a complete union with England. Wrong had driven a large proportion of the Irish people into the madness of insurrection or sympathy with insurrection. It was, indeed, the consciousness of this fact which made him set himself earnestly to work to devise a means of stopping this miserable series of abortive insurrections and revolts by which Ireland had been torn and some of the best and bravest of her sons driven into exile. He believed he had devised a plan which would satisfy the just demands of the people without producing a disintegration of the empire ; therefore, he had asked the people to give up the madness of revolt and join with him in constitutionally and peacefully making an appeal to England. Many of the people who supported this moderate proposal would waste their lives in useless struggles against England, if they saw no other redress for the sufferings of their country. . . . He believed the Irish people were essentially conservative. It was only misgovernment that had driven them into revolt. Give them fair play, and there was no people on earth who would be more attached to true conservative principles than the Irish nation. The geographical position of Ireland made it her interest to be united with England. They were allied to England by ties of kindred and ties of self-interest which bound them to maintain inviolate the connexion with this country, and the way to maintain that connexion was to give them justice in the management of their own internal affairs. . . . Give us—continued the hon. and learned gentleman—a full participation in your freedom, and make us sharers in those free institutions which have made England so great and glorious. Give us our share which we have not now in that greatest and best of all free institutions—a free parliament, representing indifferently the whole people. Then, indeed, we might speak the words which were spoken before in this house.

' Non ego nec Teucris Italos parere jubebo,
Nec nova regna peto : paribus se legibus ambae
Invictae gentes aeterna in foedera mittant.'—

Parliamentary debates, series 3, ccxx cols. 700–17.

15. THE IRISH PARTY PLEDGE, 1884

In 1884 T. M. Healy drew up a pledge, which was taken by the candidate for Co. Waterford. Improved by Healy in 1885 it became ' the standard test for nationalists at all elections.' [1]

General election

Parliamentary pledge

I pledge myself, that in the event of my election to parliament, I will sit, act, and vote with the Irish parliamentary party ; and if at a meeting of the party, convened upon due notice, specially to consider the question, it be determined by resolution, supported by

[1] T. M. Healy, *Letters and leaders of my day* (London 1928), pp. 205, 493–4.

a majority of the Irish party, that I have not fulfilled the above pledges, I hereby undertake to resign my seat.

Signature   Thomas Sexton
Date   June 30th, 1892
Witness   Michael Davitt
Chairman of Convention

Davitt MSS.

16. CHARLES STEWART PARNELL ON HOME RULE, CORK, 21 JANUARY 1885

During the general election campaign of 1885 Parnell emphasized the intention of his party to secure home rule and gave some indications of the sort of scheme he would accept. In May 1886 he supported Gladstone's Home Rule bill.

. . . At the election in 1880 I laid certain principles before you, and you accepted them (applause, and cries of ' we do '). I said and I pledged myself, that I should form one of an independent Irish party to act in opposition to every English government which refused to concede the just rights of Ireland (applause). And the longer time which is gone by since then, the more I am convinced that that is the true policy to pursue so far as parliamentary policy is concerned, and that it will be impossible for either or both of the English parties to contend for any long time against a determined band of Irishmen acting honestly upon these principles, and backed by the Irish people (cheers). But we have not alone had that object in view—we have always been very careful not to fetter or control the people at home in any way, not to prevent them from doing any thing by their own strength which it is possible for them to do. Sometimes, perhaps, in our anxiety in this direction we have asked them to do what is beyond their strength, but I hold that it is better even to encourage you to do what is beyond your strength even should you fail sometimes in the attempt than to teach you to be subservient and unreliant (applause). You have been encouraged to organize yourselves, to depend upon the rectitude of your cause for your justification, and to depend upon the determination which has helped Irishmen through many centuries to retain the name of Ireland and to retain her nationhood. Nobody could point to any single action of ours in the house of commons or out of it which was not based upon the knowledge that behind us existed a strong and brave people, that without the help of the people our exertions would be as nothing, and that with their help and with their confidence we should be, as I believe we shall prove to be in the near future, invincible and unconquerable (great applause). . . . We shall struggle, as we have been struggling, for the great and important interests of the Irish tenant farmer. We shall ask that his industry shall not be fettered by rent. We shall ask also from the farmer in return that he shall do what in him lies to encourage the struggling manufactures of Ireland, and that he shall not think it too great a sacrifice to be called upon when he wants anything, when he has to purchase anything, to consider how he may get it of Irish material and manufacture (hear, hear), even supposing he has to pay a little more for it (cheers). I am sorry if the agricultural population has shown itself somewhat deficient in its sense of duty in this respect up to the present time, but I feel convinced that the matter has only to be put before them to secure the opening up of most important markets in this country for those manufactures which have always existed, and for those which have been reopened anew, as a consequence of the recent exhibitions, the great exhibition in Dublin, and the other equally great one in Cork, which have been recently held (cheers). We shall also endeavour to secure for the labourer some recognition and some right in the land of his country (applause). We don't care whether it be the prejudices of the farmer or of the landlord that stands in his way (hear, hear). We consider that whatever class tries to obstruct the labourer in the possession of those fair and just rights to which he is entitled, that class should be put down, and coerced if you will, into doing justice to the labourer. . . . Well, but gentlemen, I go back from the consideration of these questions to the land question, in which the labourers' question is also involved and the manufacturers' question. I come back, and every Irish politician must be forcibly driven back, to the consideration of the great question of national self-government for Ireland (cheers). I do not know how this great question will be eventually settled. I do not know whether England will be wise in time and concede to constitutional arguments and methods the restitution of that which was stolen from us towards the close of the last century (cheers). It is given to none of us to forecast the future, and just as it is impossible for us to say in what way or by what means the national question may be settled, in what way full justice may be done to Ireland, so it is impossible for us to say to what extent that justice should be done. We cannot ask for less than restitution of Grattan's parliament (loud cheers), with its important privileges and wide and far-reaching constitution. We cannot under the British constitution ask for more than the restitution of Grattan's parliament (renewed cheers), but no man has the right to fix the boundary to the march of a nation (great cheers). No man has a right to say to his country, ' Thus far shalt thou go and no further,' and we have never attempted to fix the *ne plus ultra* to the progress of Ireland's nationhood, and we never shall (cheers). But, gentlemen, while we leave those things to time, circumstances and the future, we must each one of us resolve in our own hearts that we shall at all times do everything that within us lies to obtain for Ireland the fullest measure of her rights (applause). In this way we shall avoid difficulties and contentions amongst each other. In this way we shall not give up anything which the future may put in favour of our country ; and while we struggle to-day for that which may seem possible for us with our combination, we must struggle for it with the proud consciousness that we shall not do anything to hinder or

prevent better men who may come after us from gaining better
things than those for which we now contend (prolonged applause).

The Freeman's Journal, 22 January 1885.

17. CHARLES STEWART PARNELL ON HOME RULE, WICKLOW, 5 OCTOBER 1885

When I last spoke in public in Ireland I expressed my conviction
that in the new parliament we should be able to form our platform
of a single plank, and that plank the plank of legislative independence
(cheers), and that we should carry that plank to a successful issue
in the same way as during the last parliament we have carried other
subordinate planks, such as the extension of the franchise and so
forth (cheers). My declaration has been received by the English
press and by some, although not by all, the English leaders with a
storm of disapproval, and they have told us that the yielding of an
independent parliament to Ireland is a matter of impossibility.
But nothing that has been said in this interval has in the slightest
degree diminished my confidence in the near success of our efforts
(loud cheers). On the contrary, very much that has been said by
our enemies in reference to this claim of ours has very much increased
my confidence (cheers). They practically admit that things cannot
be allowed to go on as they are ; that it is impossible to keep an
unwilling people and unwilling representatives in forced legislative
connexion with the other two kingdoms (hear, hear). They admit
that there must be some change ; but the two conditions that they
put forward in regard to this change, and as a condition of this change,
are—firstly, that the separation of Ireland from England shall not
be a consequence of the grant of legislative independence to Ireland ;
and, in the second place, they claim that we shall not be allowed to
protect our manufactures at the cost of those of England. . . . To
take the last point first, and to deal with the question of the protection of Irish manufactures, I have claimed for Ireland a parliament
that shall have power to protect these Irish manufactures (cheers), if
it be the will of the parliament and of the Irish people that they
should be protected (cheers). But it is not for me to say beforehand
what the action of such a freely elected Irish assembly would be. I
may have my own opinion as to the best course for that assembly
to take, but I have claimed that no parliamentary assembly will work
satisfactorily which has not free power over Irish affairs (applause) ;
which has not free power to raise a revenue for the purpose of
government in Ireland as shall seem fit and best to that assembly
(applause). I am of the opinion—an opinion that I had expressed
before now—that it would be wise to protect certain Irish industries
at all events for a time (hear, hear) ; that it is impossible for us to
make up for the loss of the start in the manufacturing race which
we have experienced owing to adverse legislation in times past against
Irish industries by England, unless we do protect these industries,
not many in number, which are capable of thriving in Ireland

(applause). I am not of the opinion that it would be necessary for us to protect these industries very long, possibly protection continued for two or three years would give us that start which we have lost, owing to the nefarious legislative action of England in times past (hear, hear). I think also that Ireland could never be a manufacturing nation of such importance as to compete to any great extent with England. I believe there are several industries which would thrive, and could be made to thrive, in Ireland. But I think that, as regards many other branches of manufacture, of which we have now to seek our supply from the English markets, we should still have to go to their markets for supply on account of natural reasons which I have not time to enter into at the present moment. But I claim this for Ireland, that if the Irish parliament of the future considers that there are certain industries in Ireland which could be benefited by protection, which could be nursed by protection, and which could be placed in such a position as to enable them to compete with similar industries in other countries by a course of protection extending over a few years, the parliament ought to have power to carry out that policy (cheers). It is not for me to predict the extent to which that power should be used ; but I tell English radicals and English liberals that it is useless for them to talk of their desire to do justice to Ireland when, from motives of selfishness, they refused to repair that most manifest injustice of all—namely, the destruction of our manufactures by England in times past, when they refused to repair that injustice by giving us the power which we think would be sufficient to enable us to build up these comparatively few industries which Ireland is adapted by her circumstances to excel in (applause). I will proceed a little further, and I will deal with the claim that has been put forward, that some guarantee should be given that the granting of legislative powers to Ireland should not lead to the separation of Ireland from England. This claim is one which at first sight may seem a fair one. It may appear preposterous, and it undoubtedly would be preposterous, to ask England to concede to us an engine which we announced our intention of using to bring about either separation of the two countries, or which we accepted silently with the intention of so using it ; but there is a great difference between having such an intention, or announcing such an intention, and giving counter guarantees against such an intention. It is not possible for human intelligence to forecast the future in these matters ; but we can point to this—we can point to the fact that under 85 years of parliamentary connexion with England, Ireland has become intensely disloyal and intensely disaffected (applause) ; that notwithstanding the whig policy of so-called conciliation, alternative conciliation and coercion, and ameliorative measures, that disaffection has broadened, deepened and intensified from day to day (cheers). Am I not, then, entitled to assume that one of the roots of this disaffection and feeling of disloyalty is the assumption by England of the management of our affairs (cheers). It is admitted that the present system can't go on,

19

and what are you going to put in its place ? (Cries of ' Home Rule.')
My advice to English statesmen considering this question would be
this—trust the Irish people altogether or trust them not at all
(cheers). Give with a full and open hand—give our people the
power to legislate upon all their domestic concerns, and you may
depend upon one thing, that the desire for separation, the means of
winning separation at least, will not be increased or intensified
(cheers). Whatever chance the English rulers may have of drawing
to themselves the affection of the Irish people lies in destroying the
abominable system of legislative union between the two countries
by conceding fully and freely to Ireland the right to manage her own
affairs. It is impossible for us to give guarantees, but we can point
to the past ; we can show that the record of English rule is a constant
series of steps from bad to worse (cheers), that the condition of English
power is more insecure and more unstable at the present moment
than it has ever been (applause). We can point to the example
of other countries ; of Austria and of Hungary—to the fact that
Hungary having been conceded self-government became one of the
strongest factors in the Austrian empire. We can show the powers
that have been freely conceded to the colonies—to the greater
colonies—including this very power to protect their own industries
against and at the expense of those of England. We can show that
disaffection has disappeared in all the greater English colonies,
that while the Irishman who goes to the United States of America
carries with him a burning hatred of English rule (cheers) ; that
while that burning hatred constantly lives in his heart, never leaves
him, and is bequeathed to his children, the Irishman coming from
the same village, and from the same parish, and from the same
townland, equally maltreated, cast out on the road by the relentless
landlord, who goes to one of the colonies of Canada or one of the
colonies of Australia, and finds there another and a different system
of English rule to that which he has been accustomed to at home,
becomes to a great extent a loyal citizen and a strength and a prop
to the community amongst whom his lot has been cast ; that he
forgets the little memories of his experience of England at home,
and that he no longer continues to look upon the name of England
as a symbol of oppression, and the badge of the misfortunes of his
country (cheers). I say that it is possible, and that it is the duty of
English statesmen at the present day to inquire and examine into
these facts for themselves with their eyes open ; and to cease the
impossible task, which they admit to be impossible, of going forward
in the continued misgovernment of Ireland and persisting in the
government of our people by a people outside herself who know not
her real wants (cheers) ; and if these lessons be learned, I am convinced that the English statesman who is great enough, and who is
powerful enough to carry out these teachings, to enforce them on
the acceptance of his countrymen, to give to Ireland full legislative
liberty, full power to manage her own domestic concerns, will be
regarded in the future by his countrymen as one who has removed

the greatest peril to the English empire (hear, hear)—a peril, I firmly believe, which if not removed will find some day, perhaps not in our time—some year, perhaps not for many years to come, but will certainly find sooner or later, and it may be sooner than later, an opportunity of revenging itself—(loud cheers)—to the destruction of the British empire for the misfortunes, the oppressions, and the misgovernment of our country (loud cheers).

The Freeman's Journal, 6 October 1885.

18. WILLIAM EWART GLADSTONE ON HOME RULE, HOUSE OF COMMONS, 8 APRIL 1886

Gladstone introduced his Government of Ireland bill on 8 April 1886. It was defeated on the second reading by 341 to 311.

I could have wished, Mr. Speaker, on several grounds, that it had been possible for me on this single occasion to open to the house the whole of the policy and intentions of the government with respect to Ireland. The two questions of land and of Irish government are, in our view, closely and inseparably connected, for they are the two channels through which we hope to find access, and effectual access, to that question which is the most vital of all—namely the question of social order in Ireland. As I have said, those two questions are in our view—whatever they may be in that of anyone else—they are in our view, for reasons which I cannot now explain, inseparable the one from the other. But it is impossible for me to attempt such a task. . . .

Since the last half-century dawned we have been steadily engaged in extending, as well as in consolidating, free institutions. I divide the period since the act of union with Ireland into two—the first from 1800 to 1832, the epoch of what is still justly called the great reform act ; and secondly, from 1833 to 1885. I do not know whether it has been as widely observed as I think it deserves to be that, in the first of those periods—32 years—there were no less than 11 years—it may seem not much to say, but wait for what is coming —there were no less than 11 of those 32 years in which our statute book was free throughout the whole year from repressive legislation of an exceptional kind against Ireland. But in the 53 years since we advanced far in the career of liberal principles and actions—in those 53 years, from 1833 to 1885—there were but two years which were entirely free from the action of this special legislation for Ireland. Is not that of itself almost enough to prove we have arrived at the point where it is necessary that we should take a careful and searching survey of our position ? . . .

Well, Sir, what are the results that have been produced ? This result above all—and now I come to what I consider to be the basis of the whole mischief—that rightly or wrongly, yet in point of fact, law is discredited in Ireland, and discredited in Ireland upon this ground especially—that it comes to the people of that country with a foreign aspect, and in a foreign garb. These coercion bills of ours, of course—for it has become a matter of course—I am speaking of the facts and not of the merits—these coercion bills are stiffly resisted by the members who represent Ireland in parliament. The English mind, by cases of this kind and by the tone of the press towards them, is estranged from the Irish people and the Irish mind is estranged from the people of England and Scotland. I will not speak of other circumstances attending the present state of Ireland, but I do think that I am not assuming too much when I say that I have shown enough in this comparatively brief review —and I wish it could have been briefer still—to prove that, if coercion is to be the basis for legislation, we must no longer be seeking, as we are always laudably seeking, to whittle it down almost to nothing at the very first moment we begin, but we must, like men, adopt it, hold by it, sternly enforce it, till its end has been completely attained—with what results to peace, good will and freedom I do not now stop to inquire. Our ineffectual and spurious coercion is morally worn out. . . .

Now, I enter upon another proposition to which I hardly expect broad exception can be taken. I will not assume, I will not beg, the question, whether the people of England and Scotland will ever administer that sort of effectual coercion which I have placed in contrast with our timid and hesitating repressive measures ; but this I will say, that the people of England and Scotland will never resort to that alternative until they have tried every other. Have they tried every other ? Well, some we have tried, to which I will refer. I have been concerned with some of them myself. But we have not yet tried every alternative, because there is one—not unknown to human experience—on the contrary, widely known to various countries in the world, where this dark and difficult problem has been solved by the comparatively natural and simple, though not always easy, expedient of stripping law of its foreign garb, and investing it with a domestic character. I am not saying that this will succeed ; I by no means beg the question at this moment ; but this I will say, that Ireland, as far as I know, and speaking of the great majority of the people of Ireland, believes it will succeed and that experience elsewhere supports that conclusion. The case of Ireland, though she is represented here not less fully than England or Scotland, is not the same as that of England or Scotland. England, by her own strength, and by her vast majority in this house, makes her own laws just as independently as if she were not combined with two other countries. Scotland—a small country, smaller than Ireland, but a country endowed with a spirit so masculine that never in the long course of history, excepting for two brief periods, each of a few years, was the superior strength of England such as to enable her to put down the national freedom beyond the border—Scotland, wisely recognized by England, has been allowed and encouraged in this house to make her own laws as freely and as effectually as if she had a representation six times as strong. The consequence is that the mainspring of law in England is felt by the people to be English ; the mainspring of law in Scotland is felt by the people to be Scotch ; but the mainspring of law in Ireland is not felt by the people to be Irish, and I am bound to say—truth extorts from me the avowal—that it cannot be felt to be Irish in the same sense as it is English and Scotch. The net results of this statement which I have laid before the house, because it was necessary as the groundwork of my argument, are these—in the first place, I admit it to be little less than a mockery to hold that the state of law and of facts conjointly, which I have endeavoured to describe, conduces to the real unity of this great, noble, and world-wide empire. In the second place, something must be done, something is imperatively demanded from us to restore to Ireland the first conditions of civil life—the free course of law, the liberty of every individual in the exercise of every legal right, the confidence of the people in the law, apart from which no country can be called, in the full sense of the word, a civilized country, nor can there be given to that country the blessings which it is the object of civilized society to attain. Well, this is my introduction to the task I have to perform, and now I ask attention to the problem we have before us.

It is a problem not unknown in the history of the world ; it is really this—there can be no secret about it as far as we are concerned —how to reconcile imperial unity with diversity of legislation. Mr. Grattan not only held these purposes to be reconcilable, but he did not scruple to go the length of saying this—' I demand the continued severance of the parliaments with a view to the continued and everlasting unity of the empire.' Was that a flight of rhetoric, an audacious paradox ? No ; it was the statement of a problem which other countries have solved, and under circumstances much more difficult than ours. We ourselves may be said to have solved it, for I do not think that anyone will question the fact that, out of the six last centuries, for five centuries at least Ireland has had a parliament separate from ours. That is a fact undeniable. Did that separation of parliament destroy the unity of the British empire ? Did it destroy it in the 18th century ? Do not suppose that I mean that harmony always prevailed between Ireland and England. We know very well there were causes quite sufficient to account for a recurrence of discord. But I take the 18th century alone. Can I be told that there was no unity of empire in the 18th century ? Why, Sir, it was the century which saw our navy come to its supremacy. It was the century which witnessed the foundation of that great, gigantic manufacturing industry which now over-shadows the whole world. It was, in a pre-eminent sense, the century of empire, and it was in a sense, but too conspicuous, the century of wars. Those wars were carried on, that empire was maintained and enormously enlarged, that trade was established, that navy was brought to supremacy when England and Ireland had separate parliaments. Am I to be told that there was no unity of empire in that state of things ? Well, Sir, what has happened elsewhere ? Have any other countries had to look this problem in the face ? The last half-century—the last 60 or 70 years since the great war—has been particularly rich in its experience of this subject and in the lessons which it has afforded to us. There are many cases to which I might refer to show how practicable it is, or how practicable it has been found by others whom we are not accustomed to look upon as our political superiors—how practicable it has been found by others to bring into existence what is termed local autonomy, and yet not to sacrifice, but to confirm imperial unity. . . .

What is the essence of the union ? That is the question. It is impossible to determine what is and what is not the repeal of the union, until you settle what is the essence of the union. Well, I define the essence of the union to be this—that before the act of union there were two independent, separate, co-ordinate parliaments ; after the act of union there was but one. A supreme statutory authority of the imperial parliament over Great Britain, Scotland, and Ireland as one United Kingdom was established by the act of union. That supreme statutory authority it is not asked, so far as I am aware, and certainly it is not intended, in the slightest degree to impair. . . .

I will deviate from my path for a moment to say a word upon the state of opinion in that wealthy, intelligent, and energetic portion of the Irish community which, as I have said, predominates in a certain portion of Ulster. Our duty is to adhere to sound general principles, and to give the utmost consideration we can to the opinions of that energetic minority. The first thing of all, I should say, is that if, upon any occasion, by any individual or section, violent measures have been threatened in certain emergencies, I think the best compliment I can pay to those who have threatened us is to take no notice whatever of the threats, but to treat them as momentary ebullitions, which will pass away with the fears from which they spring, and at the same time to adopt on our part every reasonable measure for disarming those fears. I cannot conceal the conviction that the voice of Ireland, as a whole, is at this moment clearly and constitutionally spoken. I cannot say it is otherwise when five-sixths of its lawfully-chosen representatives are of one mind in this matter. There is a counter voice ; and I wish to know what is the claim of those by whom that counter voice is spoken, and how much is the scope and allowance we can give them. Certainly, sir, I cannot allow it to be said that a protestant minority in Ulster, or elsewhere, is to rule the question at large for Ireland. I am aware of no constitutional doctrine tolerable on which such a conclusion could be adopted or justified. But I think that the protestant minority should have its wishes considered to the utmost practicable extent in any form which they may assume.

Various schemes, short of refusing the demand of Ireland at large, have been proposed on behalf of Ulster. One scheme is, that Ulster itself, or, perhaps with more appearance of reason, a portion of Ulster, should be excluded from the operation of the bill we are about to introduce. Another scheme is, that certain rights with regard to certain subjects—such, for example, as education and some other subejcts—should be reserved and should be placed, to a certain extent, under the control of provincial councils. These, I think, are the suggestions which reached me in different shapes ; there may be others. But what I wish to say of them is this—there is no one of them which has appeared to us to be so completely justified, either upon its merits or by the weight of opinion supporting and recommending it, as to warrant our including it in the bill and proposing it to parliament upon our responsibility. What we think is that such suggestions deserve careful and unprejudiced consideration. It may be that free discussion, which I have no doubt will largely take place after a bill such as we propose shall have been laid on the table of the house, may give to one of these proposals, or to some other proposals, a practical form, and that some such plan may be found to be recommended by a general or pedominating approval. If it should be so, it will, at our hands, have the most favourable consideration, with every disposition to do what equity may appear to recommend. . . .

In 1782 there were difficulties that we have not now before us. At any time it might have been very fairly said that no one could tell how a separate legislature would work unless it had under its control what is termed a responsible government. We have no such difficulty and no such excuse now. The problem of responsible government has been solved for us in our colonies. It works very well there ; and in, perhaps, a dozen cases in different quarters of the globe it works to our perfect satisfaction. It may be interesting to the house if I recount the fact that that responsible government in the colonies was, I think, first established by one of our most distinguished statesmen, Earl Russell, when he held the office of colonial secretary in the government of Lord Melbourne. But it was a complete departure from established tradition ; and, if I remember right, not more than two or three years before that generous and wise experiment was tried, Lord Russell had himself written a most able despatch to show that it could not be done ; that with responsible government in the colonies you would have two centres of gravity and two sources of motion in the empire ; while a united empire absolutely required that there should be but one, and that consequently the proposition could not be entertained. . . .

There is only one subject more on which I feel it still necessary to detain the house. It is commonly said in England and Scotland— and in the main it is, I think, truly said—that we have for a great number of years been struggling to pass good laws for Ireland. We have sacrificed our time, we have neglected our own business, we have advanced our money—which I do not think at all a great favour conferred on her—and all this in the endeavour to give Ireland good laws. That is quite true in regard to the general course of legislation since 1829. But many of those laws have been passed under influences which can hardly be described otherwise than as influences of fear. Some of our laws have been passed in a spirit of grudging and of jealousy. . . .

But, sir, I do not deny the general good intentions of parliament on a variety of great and conspicuous occasions, and its desire to pass good laws for Ireland. But let me say that, in order to work out the purposes of government, there is something more in this world occasionally required than even the passing of good laws. It is sometimes requisite not only that good laws should be passed, but also that they should be passed by the proper persons. The passing of many good laws is not enough in cases where the strong permanent instincts of the people, their distinctive marks of character, the situation and history of the country require not only that these laws should be good, but that they should proceed from a congenial and native source, and besides being good laws should be their own laws.

Parliamentary debates, series 3, ccciv. cols. 1036–85.

19. GOVERNMENT OF IRELAND ACT, 1914

In twenty-five years the liberals introduced three home rule bills. The first (1886) was rejected by the commons, the second (1893) by the lords. The third (1912) having been passed by the commons in three successive sessions received the royal assent in September 1914. But by the Suspensory act its coming into operation was postponed until the end of the war.

An act to amend the provision for the government of Ireland. Be it enacted by the king's most excellent majesty, by and with the advice and consent of the commons, in this present parliament assembled, in accordance with the provisions of *The parliament act*, 1911, and by authority of the same, as follows :

1. (1) On and after the appointed day there shall be in Ireland an Irish parliament consisting of his majesty the king and two houses, namely, the Irish senate and the Irish house of commons.

(2) Notwithstanding the establishment of the Irish parliament or anything contained in this act, the supreme power and authority of the parliament of the United Kingdom shall remain unaffected and undiminished over all persons, matters, and things in Ireland and every part thereof.

2. Subject to the provisions of this act, the Irish parliament shall have power to make laws for the peace, order, and good government of Ireland with the following limitations, namely, that they shall not have power to make laws except in matters exclusively relating to Ireland or some part thereof, and (without prejudice to that general limitation) that they shall not have power to make laws in respect of the following matters in particular, or any of them, namely—

(1) The crown, or the succession to the crown, or a regency, . .

(2) The making of peace or war or matters arising from a state of war ; . . .

(3) The navy, the army, the territorial force, or any other naval or military force, or the defence of the realm, . . .

(4) Treaties, or any relations, with foreign states, or relations with other parts of his majesty's dominions, . . .

(5) Dignities, or titles of honour ; . . .

(6) Treason, treason felony, alienage, naturalization, . . .

(7) Trade with any place out of Ireland (except so far as trade may be affected by the exercise of the powers of taxation given to the Irish parliament, or by the regulation of importation for the sole purpose of preventing contagious disease, or by steps taken, by means of inquiries or agencies out of Ireland, for the improvement of Irish trade or for the protection of Irish traders from fraud) ; the granting of bounties on the export of goods ; quarantine ; or navigation, including merchant shipping (except as respects inland waters, the regulation of harbours, and local health regulations) ; . . .

(8) Any postal services . . .

(9) Lighthouses, buoys, or beacons, . . .

(10) Coinage, . . .

(11) Trade marks, . . .

3. In the exercise of their power to make laws under this act the Irish parliament shall not make a law so as either directly or indirectly to establish or endow any religion, or prohibit or restrict the free exercise thereof, or give a preference, privilege, or advantage, or impose any disability or disadvantage, on account of religious belief or religious or ecclesiastical status. . . .

4. (2) . . . the lord lieutenant or other chief executive officer or officers for the time being appointed in his place, on behalf of his majesty, shall exercise any prerogative or other executive power of his majesty the exercise of which may be delegated to him by his majesty.

(3) The powers so delegated shall be exercised through such Irish departments as may be established by Irish act or, subject to any alteration by Irish act, by the lord lieutenant, and the lord lieutenant may appoint officers to administer those departments, and those officers shall hold office during the pleasure of the lord lieutenant.

5. (1) The public services in connexion with the administration of the acts relating to the Royal Irish Constabulary and the management and control of that force, shall by virtue of this act be transferred from the government of the United Kingdom to the Irish government on the expiration of a period of six years from the appointed day [1] . . .

7. The lord lieutenant shall give or withhold the assent of his majesty to bills passed by the two houses of the Irish parliament, subject to the following limitations ; namely—

(1) He shall comply with any instructions given by his majesty in respect of any such bill ; and

---

[1] A date not later than fifteen months after the passing of the act, to be fixed by order in council.

(2) He shall, if so directed by his majesty, postpone giving the assent of his majesty to any such bill . . .

8. (1) The Irish senate shall consist of forty senators nominated as respects the first senators by the lord lieutenant subject to any instructions given by his majesty in respect of the nomination, and afterwards elected by the four provinces of Ireland as separate constituencies . . .

(2) The election of senators shall be according to the principle of proportional representation, the electors being the same electors as the electors of members returned by constituencies in Ireland to serve in the parliament of the United Kingdom, . . .

9. (1) The Irish house of commons shall consist of one hundred and sixty-four members, returned by the constituencies in Ireland named in the first part of the first schedule . . .

11. (1) If the Irish house of commons pass any public bill which is sent up to the Irish senate at least before the end of the session and the Irish senate reject or fail to pass it, or pass it with amendments to which the Irish house of commons will not agree, and if the Irish house of commons in the next session again pass the bill with or without any amendments which have been made or agreed to by the Irish senate, and the Irish senate reject or fail to pass it, or pass it with amendments to which the Irish house of commons will not agree, the lord lieutenant may during that session convene a joint sitting of the members of the two houses.

(2) The members present at any such joint sitting may deliberate and shall vote together upon the bill as last proposed by the Irish house of commons, and upon the amendments (if any) which have been made therein by the one house and not agreed to by the other ; and any such amendments which are affirmed by a majority of the total number of members of the two houses present at the sitting, shall be taken to have been carried.

13. Unless and until the parliament of the United Kingdom otherwise determine, the following provisions shall have effect :—

(1) After the day of the first meeting of the Irish parliament the number of members to be returned by constituencies in Ireland to serve in the parliament of the United Kingdom shall be forty-two, . . .

14. (1) There shall be an Irish exchequer and an Irish consolidated fund separate from those of the United Kingdom.

(2) The proceeds of all taxes levied in Ireland, whether under the authority of the parliament of the United Kingdom or of the Irish parliament, shall be paid into the exchequer of the United Kingdom, but . . . there shall be charged on and paid out of the consolidated fund of the United Kingdom or the growing produce thereof in each year to the Irish exchequer a sum (in this act referred to as ' the transferred sum ') consisting of—

(a) Such sum as may be determined by the joint exchequer board established under this act . . . to represent the net cost to the exchequer of the United Kingdom at the time of the passing of this act of Irish services ; and (*b*) a sum of five hundred thousand pounds, diminishing in each year after the third year of payment by the sum of fifty thousand pounds until it is reduced to the sum of two hundred thousand pounds ; and

(*c*) a sum equal to the proceeds as determined by the joint exchequer board of any Irish taxes imposed in Ireland by the Irish parliament under the powers given to them by this act.

15. (1) The Irish parliament shall have power to vary (either by way of addition, reduction, or discontinuance) any imperial tax so far as respects the levy of that tax in Ireland, and to impose in Ireland any independent tax not being in the opinion of the joint exchequer board substantially the same in character as an imperial tax, subject to the following limitations :—

(*a*) The Irish parliament shall not have power to impose or charge a customs duty, whether an import or an export duty, on any article unless that article is for the time being liable to a customs duty of a like character levied as an imperial tax, and shall not have power to vary, except by way of addition, any customs duty levied as an imperial tax or any excise duty so levied where there is a corresponding customs duty ; and

(*c*) The power of the Irish parliament to vary an imperial tax, so far as income tax (not including super-tax) is concerned, shall only be exercised so as to alter the conditions under which any exemption, abatement, or relief from the tax may be granted to persons resident in Ireland without varying the rate of the tax, and, so far as any customs duty or any death duty is concerned, shall only be exercised so as to vary the rate of the duty without otherwise altering the provisions with respect to the duty, or discriminating in that variation between persons, articles, or property, and where the duty is one of two or more correlated duties, or is a duty levied at a varying rate, shall not be exercised without varying proportionately all the correlated duties or all the rates of duty ; and

(*f*) The Irish parliament shall not, in the exercise of their powers of taxation under this provision, make any variation of customs or excise duties the effect of which will be, in the opinion of the joint exchequer board, to cause the customs duty on an article of a class produced, prepared, or manufactured in Ireland, to exceed the excise duty by more than an amount reasonably sufficient to cover any expenses due to revenue restrictions, or any variation of customs or excise drawbacks or allowances which would cause the amount of drawback or allowance payable in respect of any article to be more than reasonably sufficient, in the opinion of the joint exchequer board, to cover the duty paid thereon and any expenses due to revenue restrictions ;

17. (2) In the event of the reduction or discontinuance of any imperial tax by the Irish parliament, the transferred sum shall be reduced in each year by such sum as may be determined by the joint exchequer board to represent the amount by which the proceeds

of the tax are diminished in that year in consequence of the reduction or discontinuance.

22. (1) For the purposes of the financial provisions of this act there shall be established a board to be called the joint exchequer board, consisting of two members appointed by the treasury and two members appointed by the Irish treasury and a chairman appointed by his majesty.

28. (1) The appeal from courts in Ireland to the house of lords shall cease ; and where any person would, but for this act, have a right to appeal from any court in Ireland to the house of lords, that person shall have the right to appeal to his majesty the king in council ; . . .

(4) Any person who is aggrieved by any decision of the court of appeal in any proceedings taken by way of certiorari, mandamus, quo warranto, or prohibition, shall have a right to appeal to his majesty the king in council in the same manner as if he had such a right to appeal to the house of lords before the passing of this act.

29. (1) If it appears to the lord lieutenant or a secretary of state expedient in the public interest that steps shall be taken for the speedy determination of the question whether any Irish act or any provisions thereof, or any Irish bill or any provision thereof, is beyond the powers of the Irish parliament, or whether any service is an Irish service within the meaning of this act or not, or if the joint exchequer board, or any two members of the board, in the execution of their duties under this act, are desirous of obtaining the decision of any question of the interpretation of this act, or other question of law, which arises in connexion with those duties, the lord lieutenant, secretary of state, or board, or members thereof, as the case may be, may represent the same to his majesty in council, and thereupon, if his majesty so directs, the said question shall be forthwith referred to and heard and determined by the judicial committee of the privy council, constituted as if hearing an appeal from a court in Ireland.

(3) Nothing in this act shall prejudice any other power of his majesty in council to refer any question to the judicial committee or the right of any person to petition his majesty for such reference.

30. (1) Where any decision of the court of appeal in Ireland involves the decision of any question as to the validity of any law made by the Irish parliament . . . an appeal shall lie to his majesty the king in council by virtue of this section, but only by leave of the court of appeal or his majesty.

(2) Where any decision of a court in Ireland involves the decision of any question as to the validity of any law made by the Irish parliament, and the decision is not subject to any appeal to the court of appeal in Ireland, an appeal shall lie to the court of appeal in Ireland by virtue of this section.

(3) If any person is dissatisfied with the decision of the joint exchequer board on the question whether a tax is an independent tax not substantially the same in character as an imperial tax, that

person may petition his majesty in council to refer the question to the judicial committee of the privy council ; and if his majesty so direct, the question shall be referred to and heard and determined by that committee as if hearing an appeal from a court in Ireland ; and the determination of the judicial committee on the question shall have effect with respect to the question decided as if it were the decision of the joint exchequer board. If any decision of the joint exchequer board under this act involves a decision with respect to any question of law, any person may petition his majesty in council to refer the question of law to the judicial committee. . . .

41. (1) The Irish parliament shall not have power to repeal or alter any provision of this act (except as is specially provided by this act), or of any act passed by the parliament of the United Kingdom after the passing of this act and extending to Ireland, although that provision deals with a matter with respect to which the Irish parliament have power to make laws.

Public general acts, 1914, pp. 406–51.

20. GOVERNMENT OF IRELAND ACT, 1920

Introduced into the house of commons, 25 February, received the royal assent 23 December 1920.

An act to provide for the better government of Ireland

Be it enacted . . .

1. (1) On and after the appointed day [1] there shall be established for Southern Ireland a parliament to be called the parliament of Southern Ireland consisting of his majesty, the senate of Southern Ireland, and the house of commons of Southern Ireland, and there shall be established for Northern Ireland a parliament to be called the parliament of Northern Ireland consisting of his majesty, the senate of Northern Ireland, and the house of commons of Northern Ireland.

(2) For the purposes of this act, Northern Ireland shall consist of the parliamentary counties of Antrim, Armagh, Down, Fermanagh, Londonderry and Tyrone, and the parliamentary boroughs of Belfast and Londonderry, and Southern Ireland shall consist of so much of Ireland as is not comprised within the said parliamentary counties and boroughs.

2. (1) With a view to the eventual establishment of a parliament for the whole of Ireland, and to bringing about harmonious action between the parliaments and governments of Southern Ireland and Northern Ireland, and to the promotion of mutual intercourse and uniformity in relation to matters affecting the whole of Ireland, and to providing for the administration of services which the two parliaments mutually agree should be administered uniformly throughout the whole of Ireland, or which by virtue of this act are

---

[1] A date not later than fifteen months after the passing of the act, to be fixed by order in council.

to be so administered, there shall be constituted, as soon as may be after the appointed day, a council to be called the council of Ireland.

(2) Subject as hereinafter provided, the council of Ireland shall consist of a person nominated by the lord lieutenant acting in accordance with instructions from his majesty who shall be president, and forty other persons, of whom seven shall be members of the senate of Southern Ireland, thirteen shall be members of the house of commons of Southern Ireland, seven shall be members of the senate of Northern Ireland, and thirteen shall be members of the house of commons of Northern Ireland.

The members of the council of Ireland shall be elected in each case by the members of that house of the parliament of Southern Ireland or Northern Ireland of which they are members. . . .

(3) The constitution of the council of Ireland may from time to time be varied by identical acts passed by the parliament of Southern Ireland and the parliament of Northern Ireland, and the acts may provide for all or any of the members of the council of Ireland being elected by parliamentary electors, . . .

3. (1) The parliaments of Southern Ireland and Northern Ireland may, by identical acts agreed to by an absolute majority of members of the house of commons of each parliament at the third reading (hereinafter referred to as constituent acts), establish, in lieu of the council of Ireland, a parliament for the whole of Ireland consisting of his majesty and two houses. . . . .

(2) On the date of Irish union the council of Ireland shall cease to exist and there shall be transferred to the parliament and government of Ireland all powers then exercisable by the council of Ireland, . . .

(3) There shall also be transferred to the parliament and government of Ireland, except so far as the constituent acts otherwise provide, all the powers and duties of the parliaments and governments of Southern Ireland and Northern Ireland. . . .

4. (1) Subject to the provisions of this act, the parliament of Southern Ireland and the parliament of Northern Ireland shall respectively have power to make laws for the peace, order, and good government of Southern Ireland and Northern Ireland with the following limitations, namely, that they shall not have power to make laws except in respect of matters exclusively relating to the portion of Ireland within their jurisdiction, or some part thereof, and (without prejudice to that general limitation) that they shall not have power to make laws in respect of the following matters in particular, namely : [practically a repetition of clause 2 of the Government of Ireland act, 1914].

6. (1) Neither the parliament of Southern Ireland nor the parliament of Northern Ireland shall have power to repeal or alter any provision of this act (except as is specially provided by this act), or of any act passed by the parliament of the United Kingdom after the appointed day and extending to the part of Ireland within their jurisdiction, . . .

7. (1) The council of Ireland shall have power to make orders with respect to matters affecting interests both in Southern Ireland and Northern Ireland, in any case where the matter—

(a) Is of such a nature that if it had affected interests in one of those areas only it would have been within the powers of the parliament for that area ; and

(b) Is a matter to affect which, it would apart from this provision, have been necessary to apply to the parliament of the United Kingdom by petition for leave to bring in a private bill.

8. (2) As respects Irish services, the lord lieutenant . . . shall exercise any prerogative or other executive power of his majesty, the exercise of which may be delegated to him by his majesty : . . .

(3) Subject to the provisions of this act relating to the council of Ireland, powers so delegated shall be exercised—

(a) In Southern Ireland, through such departments as may be established by act of the parliament of Southern Ireland, or, subject to any alteration by act of that parliament, by the lord lieutenant ; and

(b) in Northern Ireland, through such departments as may be established by act of the parliament of Northern Ireland, or, subject to any alteration by act of that parliament, by the lord lieutenant ; and the lord lieutenant may appoint officers to administer those departments, and those officers shall hold office during the pleasure of the lord lieutenant.

9. (1) The Royal Irish Constabulary and the Dublin Metropolitan Police . . . shall be reserved matters until such date, not being later than the expiration of three years after the appointed day as his majesty in council may determine, . . .

(2) The following matters, namely :

(a) the postal service ; (b) the Post Office Savings Bank and Trustee Savings Bank ; (c) designs for stamps, whether for postal or revenue purposes ; (d) the registration of deeds and the Public Record Office of Ireland ; shall be reserved matters until the date of Irish union, . . . and on that date if there should be no provision to the contrary in the constituent acts . . . the public services in connexion with the administration of those matters, except in so far as they are matters with respect to which the parliament of Ireland have not power to make laws, shall, by virtue of this act, be transferred from the government of the United Kingdom to the government of Ireland, . . .

10.(1) The parliaments of Southern Ireland and Northern Ireland may, by identical acts, delegate to the council of Ireland any of the powers of the parliaments and governments of Southern Ireland and Northern Ireland, and such acts may determine the manner in which the powers so delegated are to be exercisable by the council.

(2) With a view to the uniform administration throughout Ireland . . . any powers (not being powers relating to reserved matters) exercisable by any department of the government of the

United Kingdom at the appointed day with respect to railways and fisheries and the contagious diseases of animals in Ireland and the power of making laws with respect to railways and fisheries and the contagious diseases of animals shall, as from the appointed day, become powers of the council of Ireland, . . .

(3) The council may consider any questions which may appear in any way to bear on the welfare of both Southern Ireland and Northern Ireland, and may, by resolution, make suggestions in relation thereto as they may think proper, but suggestions so made shall have no legislative effect, . . .

12. The lord lieutenant shall give and withhold the assent of his majesty to bills passed by the senate and house of commons of Southern Ireland or the senate and house of commons of Northern Ireland, and to orders of the council of Ireland, subject to the following limitations :

(1) He shall comply with any instructions given by his majesty in respect of any such bill or order ; and

(2) He shall, if so directed by his majesty, reserve any such bill or order for the signification of his majesty's pleasure, . . .

19. Unless and until the parliament of the United Kingdom otherwise determine, . . . the number of members to be returned by constituencies in Ireland to serve in the parliament of the United Kingdom shall be forty-six, . . .

20. (1) There shall be an exchequer and consolidated fund of Southern Ireland and an exchequer and consolidated fund of Northern Ireland separate from one another and from those of the United Kingdom.

21. (1) The power of the parliaments of Southern Ireland and Northern Ireland to make laws shall include power to make laws with respect to the imposing, charging, levying, and collection of taxes within their respective jurisdictions, other than customs duties, excise duties on articles manufactured and produced, and excess profits duty, corporation profits tax, and any other tax on profits, and (except to the extent hereinafter mentioned) income tax (including super-tax), or any tax substantially the same in character as any of those duties or taxes, . . .

22. (1) The imposing, charging, levying, and collection of customs duties and of excise duties on articles manufactured and produced and the granting of customs and excise drawbacks and allowances, and, except to the extent hereinafter mentioned, the imposing, charging, levying, and collection of income tax (including super-tax) and excess profits duty, corporation profits tax, and any other tax on profits shall be reserved matters, and the proceeds of those duties and taxes shall be paid into the consolidated fund of the United Kingdom.

(2) The joint exchequer board shall in each year determine what part of the proceeds of the said duties and taxes . . . are properly attributed to Ireland . . . and the sum so determined to be the Irish share of the proceeds of the said duties and taxes is hereinafter referred to as the Irish share of reserved taxes.

23. (1) Ireland shall in each year make a contribution towards the imperial liabilities and expenditure . . .

(3) The proportion of imperial liabilities and expenditure to be so contributed shall be such as the joint exchequer board may . . . determine to be just ; . . .

(4) The said contribution shall be apportioned as between Southern Ireland and Northern Ireland in the following manner, that is to say :

(a) So long as the contribution remains at the rate of eighteen million pounds a year, fifty-six per centum thereof shall be apportioned to Southern Ireland and forty-four per centum thereof to Northern Ireland :

(b) Thereafter such part shall be apportioned to Southern Ireland and Northern Ireland respectively as the joint exchequer board may determine to correspond to their relative taxable capacities. . . .

24. (1) There shall in respect of each year be charged on and paid out of the consolidated fund of the United Kingdom to the exchequers of Southern Ireland and Northern Ireland a sum equal to the Irish share of reserved taxes in that year after deducting—

(a) The amount of the Irish contribution towards imperial liabilities and expenditure ; and

(b) whilst any services remain reserved services, the net cost to the exchequer of the United Kingdom during the year of the services . . .

(3) In determining the apportionment as between the exchequers of Southern and Northern Ireland of the Irish residuary share of reserved taxes, the joint exchequer board shall act on the following principles :

(a) So far as the amount of the said share depends on the proceeds of any tax, they shall determine what parts of the proceeds are properly attributable to Southern and Northern Ireland respectively, and shall allot the amount so determined accordingly :

(b) So far as the amount of the said share depends on the amount of the Irish contribution towards imperial liabilities and expenditure, they shall allot to Southern Ireland and Northern Ireland their respective shares in that contribution determined in manner hereinbefore provided.

(c) So far as the amount of the said share depends on the cost of any service, they shall, where the cost of the service in Southern and Northern Ireland respectively can be ascertained, allot to Southern and Northern Ireland the cost of the service in Southern and Northern Ireland respectively ; and where the cost of the service in Southern and Northern Ireland cannot in their opinion be ascertained with sufficient accuracy, they shall divide the cost between them in proportion to population.

26. (1) Purchase annuities payable in respect of land situate in Southern Ireland and Northern Ireland respectively, including any arrears thereof due or accruing due on the appointed day, shall be

20

collected by the governments of Southern Ireland and Northern Ireland, and the amounts so collected shall be paid into their respective exchequers, but nothing in this act shall confer on either such government any powers with respect to the redemption of purchase annuities.

32. (1) For the purposes of the financial provisions of this act, there shall be established a board to be called the joint exchequer board, consisting of two members appointed by the treasury, one member appointed by the treasury of Southern Ireland, one member appointed by the treasury of Northern Ireland, and a chairman appointed by his majesty.

38. The supreme court of judicature in Ireland shall cease to exist, and there shall be established in Ireland the following courts, that is to say, a court having jurisdiction in Southern Ireland, to be called the supreme court of judicature of Southern Ireland, a court having jurisdiction in Northern Ireland, to be called the supreme court of judicature in Northern Ireland, and a court having appellate jurisdiction throughout the whole of Ireland, to be called the high court of appeal for Ireland.

43. (1) An appeal shall lie to the high court of appeal for Ireland from any decision of the court of appeal in Southern Ireland or the court of appeal in Northern Ireland, and all questions which under the *Crown cases act*, 1848, would be reserved for the decision of the judges of the high court shall be reserved for the decision of the high court of appeal for Ireland, whose decision shall, except as hereinafter provided, be final, . . .

49. An appeal shall lie from the high court of appeal for Ireland to the house of lords—

(*a*) in any case where under existing enactments such an appeal would lie from the existing court of appeal in Ireland to the house of lords ;

(*b*) in any case where a person is aggrieved by any decision of the high court of appeal for Ireland in any proceedings taken by way of certiorari, mandamus, quo warranto or prohibition ;

(*c*) in any case where a decision of the high court of appeal for Ireland involves a decision of any question as to the validity of any law made by or having the effect of an act of the parliament of Southern Ireland or Northern Ireland . . .

51. If it appears to the lord lieutenant or a secretary of state expedient in the public interest that steps shall be taken for the speedy determination of the question whether any act, or order having the effect of an act of the parliament of Southern Ireland or Northern Ireland, or any provision thereof, or any bill introduced in either of those parliaments, or any provision thereof or any legislative proposal before the council of Ireland, is beyond the powers of such parliament or council, whether any service is an Irish service within the meaning of this act or not, or if the joint exchequer board, or any two members of the board, in the execution of their duties under this act, are desirous of obtaining the decision of any question of the interpretation

of this act, or other question of law, which arises in connexion with those duties, the lord lieutenant, secretary of state, or board, or members thereof, as the case may be, may represent the same to his majesty in council, and thereupon, if his majesty so directs, the said question shall be forthwith referred to and heard and determined by the judicial committee of the privy council.

Public general acts, 1920, pp. 394–461.

THE OPPOSITION TO HOME RULE

21. PROTEST ADOPTED BY A MEETING OF SOUTHERN UNIONISTS IN DUBLIN, 10 OCTOBER 1911

We, Irishmen belonging to the three southern provinces, being of all creeds and classes, representing many separate interests, and sharing a common desire for the honour and welfare of our country, hereby declare our unalterable determination to uphold the legislative union between Great Britain and Ireland.

We protest against the creation of a separate parliament for Ireland whether independent or subordinate.

We protest against the creation of an executive dependent for its existence upon the pleasure of such a parliament.

We do so upon the following grounds : because any measure for the creation of a separate Irish parliament, and a separate Irish executive, would produce most dangerous social confusion, involving a disastrous conflict of interests and classes, and a serious risk of civil war. Because such a measure would endanger the commercial relations between Ireland and Great Britain, and would cause in Ireland widespread financial distrust, followed by a complete paralysis of enterprise.

Because such a measure would imperil personal liberty, freedom of opinion, and the spirit of tolerance in Ireland.

Because such a measure, instead of effecting a settlement, would inevitably pave the way for further efforts towards the complete separation of Ireland from Great Britain.

Because no statutory limitations restricting the authority of an Irish legislative assembly, or the power of an Irish executive, could protect the freedom and the rights of minorities in this country. Because such a measure would hand over Ireland to the government of a party which, notwithstanding professions, the political purpose of which is obvious, has proved itself during its long course of action unworthy of the exercise of power by its repeated defiance of the law and disregard of the elementary principles of honesty and justice.

Because the great measures enacted in recent years by the imperial parliament have resulted in such industrial, agricultural, social and educational progress that our country has been steadily advancing in prosperity, and we view with the gravest alarm an experiment which must in large measure destroy the good work already done and hinder the progress now in operation.

Finally regarding the question from a wider point of view than that which concerns alone the internal government of Ireland, highly prizing as we do the advantages we derive from our present imperial position, and being justly proud of the place we Irishmen have long held amongst those to whom the empire owes its prosperity and fame, having been always faithful in our allegiance to our sovereigns and upholders of the constitution, we protest against any change that will deprive us of our birthright, by which we stand on equal ground with our fellow-countrymen of Great Britain as subjects of our king and citizens of the British empire.

The Times, 11 October 1911.

22. ULSTER'S SOLEMN LEAGUE AND COVENANT, 1912

Signed 28 September 1912 by 471,000 persons[1]

Being convinced in our consciences that Home Rule would be disastrous to the material well-being of Ulster as well as of the whole of Ireland, subversive of our civil and religious freedom, destructive of our citizenship, and perilous to the unity of the empire, we, whose names are underwritten, men of Ulster, loyal subjects of His Gracious Majesty King George V, humbly relying on the God whom our fathers in days of stress and trial confidently trusted, do hereby pledge ourselves in solemn covenant throughout this our time of threatened calamity to stand by one another in defending for ourselves and our children our cherished position of equal citizenship in the United Kingdom, and in using all means which may be found necessary to defeat the present conspiracy to set up a Home Rule parliament in Ireland. And in the event of such a parliament being forced upon us we further solemnly and mutually pledge ourselves to refuse to recognize its authority. In sure confidence that God will defend the right we hereto subscribe our names. And further, we individually declare that we have not already signed this covenant. God save the king.

23. SIR EDWARD CARSON, ON THE POSITION OF ULSTER, HOUSE OF COMMONS, 11 FEBRUARY 1914

In the debate on the address. Earlier in the debate Asquith announced that the government intended to bring forward proposals for dealing with the Ulster problem.

. . . The speech from the throne talks of the fears of these men. Yes, they have, I think, genuine fears for their civil and religious liberty under the bill, but do not imagine that that is all that these men are fighting for. They are fighting for a great principle, and a great ideal. They are fighting to stay under the government which they were invited to come under, under which they have flourished, and under which they are content, and to refuse to come under a

[1] For the text of this document and an account of its drafting see R. McNeill, *Ulster's stand for union* (London 1922), pp. 103–5.

government which they loath and detest. Men do not make sacrifices or take up the attitude these men in Ulster have taken up on a question of detail or paper safeguards. I am not going to argue whether they are right or wrong in resisting. It would be useless to argue it, because they have thoroughly made up their minds, but I say this : If these men are not morally justified when they are attempted to be driven out of one government with which they are satisfied and put under another which they loath, I do not see how resistance ever can be justified in history at all. There was one point made by the prime minister yesterday, and repeated by Lord Morley in another place which I should like to deal with for one moment, although it has been already referred to by my right hon. friend last night. The prime minister said, it is ' as the price of peace that any suggestion we make will be put forward ' (Official Report, 10 February 1914, col. 82) and he elaborated that by saying that he did not mean the mere abandonment of resistance, but that he meant that the bill, if these changes were made, as I understand him, should as the price of the changes be accepted generally by opponents in Ireland, and in the unionist party, so as to give, as he hoped, a good chance and send-off to the bill. If he means that as the condition of the changes in the bill we are to support the bill or take any responsibility whatever for it, I tell him we never can do it. Ulster looms very largely in this controversy, simply because Ulster has a strong right arm, but there are unionists in the south and west who loath the bill just as much as we Ulster people loath it, whose difficulties are far greater, and who would willingly fight, as Ulster would fight, if they had the numbers. Nobody knows the difficulties of these men better than I do. Why, it was only the other day some of them ventured to put forward as a business proposition that this bill would be financial ruin to their businesses, saying no more, and immediately they were boycotted, and resolutions were passed, and they were told that they ought to understand as protestants that they ought to be thankful and grateful for being allowed to live in peace among the people who are there. Yes, we can never support the bill which hands these people over to the tender mercies of those who have always been their bitterest enemies. We must go on whatever happens, opposing the bill to the end. That we are entitled to do ; that we are bound to do. But I want to speak explicitly about the exclusion of Ulster. . . . If the exclusion of Ulster is not shut out, and if at the same time the prime minister says he cannot admit anything contrary to the fundamental principles of the bill, I think it follows that the exclusion of Ulster is not contrary to the fundamental principles of the bill. If that is so, are you really going on to these grave difficulties in the future that the gracious speech from the throne deals with, and not going to make your offer now, at once, with a view, not to our adopting the bill, but to putting an end to resistance in Ulster. Why do you hesitate ? Surely something that is not fundamental to the principles of the bill is a thing that you may readily concede, rather than face these grave difficulties which you yourselves admit to exist. I can only say this to the prime minister : If the exclusion for that purpose is proposed, it will be my duty to go to Ulster at once and take counsel with the people there ; for I certainly do not mean that Ulster should be any pawn in any political game. I say once more, that no responsible leader, unless he were a lunatic, as the secretary of state says I am—

The Secretary of State for War (Colonel Seely) : Mr. Speaker, if I have ever said an unkind thing about the right hon. gentleman, I unreservedly withdraw it ; perhaps he will unreservedly withdraw the unkind things which he may have said about me. (An Hon. member : ' They are always eating their words.')

Sir E. Carson : No responsible man, whether he was a leader or follower, could possibly go to the people, under any condition, and say, ' We are offered something,' but say to them that, for political purposes, ' You ought to prepare to fight for it rather than accept it' ; and I am not going to do anything of the kind.

On the other hand I say this, that if your suggestions—no matter what paper safeguards you put, or no matter what other methods you may attempt to surround these safeguards with for the purpose of raising what I call ' your reasonable atmosphere '—if your suggestions try to compel these people to come into a Dublin parliament, I tell you I shall, regardless of personal consequences, go on with these people to the end with their policy of resistance. Believe me, whatever way you settle the Irish question, there are only two ways to deal with Ulster. It is for statesmen to say which is the best and right one. She is not a part of the community which can be bought. She will not allow herself to be sold. You must therefore either coerce her if you go on, or you must, in the long run, by showing that good government can come under the Home Rule bill, try and win her over to the case of the rest of Ireland. You probably can coerce her—though I doubt it. If you do, what will be the disastrous consequences not only to Ulster, but to this country and the empire ? Will my fellow-countryman, the leader of the Nationalist party, have gained anything ? I will agree with him—I do not believe he wants to triumph any more than I do. But will he have gained anything if he takes over these people and then applies for what he used to call—at all events his party used to call—the enemies of the people to come in and coerce them into obedience ? No, sir, one false step taken in relation to Ulster will, in my opinion, render for ever impossible a solution of the Irish question. I say this to my nationalist fellow-countrymen, and, indeed also to the government : you have never tried to win over Ulster. You have never tried to understand her position. You have never alleged, and can never allege, that this bill gives her one atom of advantage. Nay, you cannot deny that it takes away many advantages that she has as a constituent part of the United Kingdom. You cannot deny that in the past she had produced the most loyal and law-abiding part of the citizens of Ireland. After all that, for these two years, every time we came before you your only answer to us—the majority of you, at all events—was to insult us, and to make little of us. I say to the leader of the Nationalist party, if you want Ulster, go and take her, or go on and win her. You have never wanted her affections ; you have wanted her taxes.

Parliamentary debates, series 5, lviii. cols. 171–7.

YOUNG IRELAND

From 1844 there was a growing divergency in outlook between O'Connell and the group of younger nationalists whose organ was the *Nation*. In the middle of July 1846 O'Connell's supporters on the committee of the Repeal Association passed a report containing a series of statements condemning the use of physical force in politics under any circumstances. These ' peace resolutions ' were discussed by the association on 27 and 28 July. As a result of this two days' debate the Young Irelanders withdrew from the association.

24. THOMAS FRANCIS MEAGHER ON THE USE OF PHYSICAL FORCE, DUBLIN, 28 JULY 1846

I will commence as my friend Mr Mitchel concluded, by an allusion to the whigs (hear, hear). I fully concur with my friend that the ' most comprehensive measures ' which the whig minister may propose, and the English parliament may adopt will fail to lift this country up to that position which she has the right to occupy, and the power to maintain (cheers). A whig minister, I admit, may improve the province, he will not restore the nation. Franchises, ' equal laws,' tenant compensation bills, ' liberal appointments,' in a word ' full justice ' as they say, may ameliorate, they will not exalt (cheers). They may meet the necessities, they will not call forth the abilities of the country. The errors of the past may be repaired. The hopes of the future will not be fulfilled. . . . From the stateliest mansion down to the poorest cottage in the land, the inactivity, the meanness, the debasement, which provincialism engenders will be perceptible. These are not the crude sentiments of youth, though the mere commercial politician who has deduced his ideas of self-government from the table of imports and exports may satirize them as such. . . .

Voter's books and reports, these are the only weapons we can employ (hear). Therefore, my lord, I do advocate the peaceful policy of this association (cheers). It is the only policy we can and should adopt (cheers). If that policy be pursued with truth, with courage, with stern determination of purpose, I do firmly believe that it will succeed (loud and enthusiastic cheers). But, my lord, I dissented from the resolutions in question for other reasons (hear, hear). . . . I dissented from these resolutions, for I felt that by assenting to them I should have pledged myself to the unqualified repudiation of physical force in all countries, at all times, and in every circumstance. This I could not do, for my lord, I do not abhor the use of arms in the vindication of national rights (cheers).

There are times when arms will alone suffice, and when political ameliorations call for a drop of blood—(cheers)—and many thousand drops of blood (enthusiastic cheering and cries of 'Oh, Oh'). Opinion I admit will operate against opinion. But, as the hon. member for Kilkenny observed, force must be used against force (cheers and some confusion). The soldier is proof against an argument but he is not proof against a bullet. The man that will listen to reason, let him be reasoned with, but it is the weaponed arm of the patriot that can alone avail against battalioned despotism (loud cheers). Then, my lord, I do not disclaim the use of force as immoral, nor do I believe that it is the truth to say that the God of Heaven withholds His sanction from the use of arms. From the day on which in the valley of Bethulia He nerved the arm of the Jewish girl to smite the drunken tyrant in his tent, down to the hour in which He blessed the insurgent chivalry of the Belgium priests, His Almighty hand has ever been stretched forth from His throne of light, to consecrate the flag of freedom, to bless the patriot's sword (loud and enthusiastic cheering). Be it for the defence or be it for the assertion of a nation's liberty, I look upon the sword as a sacred weapon ('No, No' from the Rev. Mr Hopkins). And if my lord it has sometimes reddened the shroud of the oppressor, like the annointed rod of the high priest, it has at other times blossomed into flowers to deck the freeman's brow (vehement applause). Abhor the sword and stigmatize the sword? No, my lord, for in the cragged passes of the Tyrol it cut in pieces the banner of the Bavarian, and won an immortality for the peasant of Innsbruck (hear). Abhor the sword and stigmatize the sword? No, my lord, for at its blow a giant nation sprung up from the waters of the far Atlantic, and by its redeeming magic the fettered colony became a daring free republic. Abhor the sword and stigmatize the sword? No, my lord, for it scourged the Dutch marauders out of the fine old towns of Belgium, back into their own phlegmatic swamps— (cheers)—and knocked their flag, and laws, and sceptre, and bayonets, into the sluggish waters of the Scheldt (enthusiastic cheers).

The Nation, 1 August 1846.

THE FENIAN MOVEMENT

In 1858 the Irish Revolutionary Brotherhood, frequently referred to as the Fenian Brotherhood, was founded in New York. It received considerable support from the Irish in America, and in 1863 a convention representing the branch societies met in Chicago. In 1867 the movement was responsible for a number of revolutionary outbreaks in Ireland.

25. THE FENIAN OATHS, 1858–9

The oath, first drawn up in 1858 (a) was redrafted in 1859 after the trial of some members of a Fenian society in Skibbereen. The revision (b) made it possible for Fenians to contend that they did not form a secret society.

(a) I, A.B., do solemnly swear, in the presence of Almighty God that I will do my utmost, at every risk, while life lasts, to make Ireland an independent, democratic republic, that I will yield implicit obedience, in all things not contrary to the law of God, to the commands of my superior officers, and that I shall preserve inviolable secrecy regarding all the transactions of this secret society that may be confided to me. So help me God! Amen.

(*b*) I, A.B., in the presence of Almighty God, do solemnly swear allegiance to the Irish republic, now virtually established, and that I will do my utmost, at every risk, while life lasts, to defend its independence and integrity, and finally, that I will yield implicit obedience in all things, not contrary to the laws of God, to the commands of my superior officers. So help me God! Amen.

J. O'Leary, *Recollections of Fenians and Fenianism*
(London 1896), i. 81–2, 119–21.

26. RESOLUTION PASSED BY THE CHICAGO CONGRESS, NOVEMBER 1863

Whereas, it has been proved to the Fenian Brotherhood, not alone through the authorized reports of the Head Centre, but also through the forced acknowledgements conveyed in certain recent denunciations emanating from the enemies of the Irish race, that there exists among the men of Ireland a numerous and widely extended national organization, which was heretofore named The Irish Revolutionary Brotherhood, but which having grown in numbers and power, in subordination to its constituent authorities, and in discipline under the wise and able directions of its central executive, is now known as the Irish Republic, be it resolved— That we, the centres and delegates of the Fenian Brotherhood, assembled in this convention, do hereby proclaim the Republic of Ireland to be virtually established, and moreover that we pledge ourselves to use all our influence, and every legitimate privilege within our reach, to promote the full acknowledgement of its independence by every free government in the world.

John O'Mahony, President and Head Centre
H. O'C. McCarthy.
Jas. A. Stewart.
Richard Doherty, Ind. ⎫
Daniel Grady, D.C.   ⎬ Vice presidents.
Daniel Carmody, Wis. ⎭

Report of the proceedings . . . of the special commission . . . for the trial of Thomas Clarke Luby (Dublin 1866), pp. 219–20.

THE GAELIC REVIVAL

In 1893 the Gaelic League, whose object was 'to keep the Irish language spoken in Ireland,' was founded with Douglas Hyde as president.

27. DOUGLAS HYDE ON THE NECESSITY FOR DE-ANGLICIZING IRELAND, DUBLIN, 25 NOVEMBER 1892

An address delivered before the Irish National Literary Society

If we take a bird's-eye view of our island to-day, and compare it with what it used to be, we must be struck by the extraordinary fact that the nation which was once, as every one admits, one of the most classically learned and cultured nations in Europe, is now one of the least so ; how one of the most reading and literary peoples has become one of the *least* studious and most *un*-literary, and how the present art products of one of the quickest, most sensitive, and most artistic races on earth are now only distinguished for their hideousness.

I shall endeavour to show that this failure of the Irish people in recent times has been largely brought about by the race diverging during this century from the right path, and ceasing to be Irish without becoming English. I shall attempt to show that with the bulk of the people this change took place quite recently, much more recently than most people imagine, and is, in fact, still going on. I should also like to call attention to the illogical position of men who drop their own language to speak English, of men who translate their euphonious Irish names into English monosyllables, of men who read English books, and know nothing about Gaelic literature, nevertheless protesting as a matter of sentiment that they hate the country which at every hand's turn they rush to imitate.

I wish to show you that in anglicizing ourselves wholesale we have thrown away with a light heart the best claim which we have upon the world's recognition of us as a separate nationality. What did Mazzini say ? What is Goldwin Smith never tired of declaiming ? What do the *Spectator* and *Saturday Review* harp on ? That we ought to be content as an integral part of the United Kingdom because we have lost the notes of nationality, our language and customs.

It has always been very curious to me how Irish sentiment sticks in this half-way house—how it continues to apparently hate the English, and at the same time continues to imitate them ; how it continues to clamour for recognition as a distinct nationality, and at the same time throws away with both hands what would make it so. If Irishmen only went a little further they would become good Englishmen in sentiment also. But—illogical as it appears—there seems not the slightest sign or probability of their taking that step.

It is the curious certainty that come what may Irishmen will continue to resist English rule, even though it should be for their good, which prevents many of our nation from becoming unionists upon the spot. It is a fact, and we must face it as a fact, that although they adopt English habits and copy England in every way, the great bulk of Irishmen and Irishwomen over the whole world are known to be filled with a dull, ever-abiding animosity against her, and—right or wrong—to grieve when she prospers, and joy when she is hurt. Such movements as Young Irelandism, Fenianism, Land Leagueism, and parliamentary obstruction seem always to gain their sympathy and support. It is just because there appears no earthly chance of their becoming good members of the empire that I urge that they should not remain in the anomalous position they are in, but since they absolutely refuse to become the one thing, that they become the other ; cultivate what they have rejected, and build up an Irish nation on Irish lines.

But you ask, why should we wish to make Ireland more Celtic than it is—why should we de-anglicize at it all ? I answer because the Irish race is at present in a most anomalous position, imitating England and yet apparently hating it. How can it produce anything good in literature, art, or institutions as long as it is actuated by motives so contradictory ? Besides, I believe it is our Gaelic past which, though the Irish race does not recognize it just at present, is really at the bottom of the Irish heart, and prevents us becoming citizens of the empire, as, I think, can be easily proved. . . .

Let us suppose for a moment—which is impossible—that there were to arise a series of Cromwells in England for the space of one hundred years, able administrators of the empire, careful rulers of Ireland, developing to the utmost our national resources, whilst they unremittingly stamped out every spark of national feeling, making Ireland a land of wealth and factories, whilst they extinguished every thought and every idea that was Irish, and left us, at last, after a hundred years of good government, fat, wealthy, and populous, but with all our characteristics gone, with every external that at present differentiates us from the English lost or dropped ; all our Irish names of places and people turned into English names ; the Irish language completely extinct ; the O's and the Macs dropped ; our Irish intonation changed, as far as possible by English schoolmasters into something English ; our history no longer remembered or taught ; the names of our rebels and martyrs blotted out ; our battlefields and traditions forgotten ; the fact that we are not of Saxon origin dropped out of sight and memory, and let me now put the question—How many Irishmen are there who would purchase material prosperity at such a price ? It is exactly such a question as this and the answer to it that shows the difference between the English and Irish race. Nine Englishmen out of ten would jump to make the exchange, and I as firmly believe that nine Irishmen out of ten would indignantly refuse it.

And yet this awful idea of complete anglicization, which I have put here before you in all its crudity is, and has been, making silent inroads upon us for nearly a century. Its inroads have been silent, because, had the Gaelic race perceived what was being done, or had they been once warned of what was taking place in their own midst, they would, I think, never have allowed it. When the picture of complete anglicization is drawn for them in all its nakedness Irish sentimentality becomes suddenly a power and refuses to surrender its birthright.

What lies at the back of the sentiments of nationality with which the Irish millions seem so strongly leavened, what can prompt them to applaud such sentiments as :

' They say the British empire owes much to Irish hands,
That Irish valour fixed her flag o'er many conquered lands ;
And ask if Erin takes no pride in these her gallant sons,
Her Wolseleys and her Lawrences, her Wolfes and Wellingtons.
Ah ! these were of the empire—we yield them to her fame,
And ne'er in Erin's orisons are heard their alien name ;
But those for whom her heart beats high and benedictions swell,
They died upon the scaffold and they pined within the cell.'

Of course it is a very composite feeling which prompts them ; but I believe that what is largely behind it is the half unconscious feeling that the race which at one time held possession of more than half Europe, which established itself in Greece, and burned infant Rome, is now—almost extirpated and absorbed elsewhere—making its last stand for independence in this island of Ireland ; and do what they may the race of to-day cannot wholly divest itself from the mantle of its own past. Through early Irish literature, for instance, we can best form some conception of what that race really was, which, after overthrowing and trampling on the primitive peoples of half Europe, was itself forced in turn to yield its speech, manners, and independence to the victorious eagles of Rome. We alone of the nations of Western Europe escaped the claws of those birds of prey ; we alone developed ourselves naturally upon our own lines outside of and free from all Roman influence ; we alone were thus able to produce an early art and literature, *our* antiquities can best throw light upon the pre-Romanized inhabitants of half Europe, and—we are our father's sons. . . .

What we must endeavour to never forget is this, that the Ireland of to-day is the descendant of the Ireland of the seventh century ; then the school of Europe and the torch of learning. It is true that Northmen made some minor settlements in it in the ninth and tenth centuries, it is true that the Normans made extensive settlements during the succeeding centuries, but none of these broke the continuity of the social life of the island. Dane and Norman drawn to the kindly Irish breast issued forth in a generation or two fully Irishized, and more Hibernian than the Hibernians themselves, and even after the Cromwellian plantation the children of numbers of the English soldiers who settled in the south and midlands, were after forty years' residence, and after marrying Irish wives, turned into good Irishmen, and unable to speak a word of English, while several Gaelic poets of the last century have, like Father English, the most unmistakably English names. In two points only was the continuity of the Irishism of Ireland damaged. First, in the north-east of Ulster, where the Gaelic race was expelled and the land planted with aliens, whom our dear mother Erin, assimilative as she is, has hitherto found it difficult to absorb, and in the ownership of the land, eight-ninths of which belongs to people many of whom have always lived, or live, abroad, and not half of whom Ireland can be said to have assimilated.

During all this time the continuation of Erin's national life centred, according to our way of looking at it, not so much in the Cromwellian or Williamite landholders who sat in College Green, and governed the country, as in the mass of the people whom Dean Swift considered might be entirely neglected, and looked upon as mere hewers of wood and drawers of water ; the men who, nevertheless, constituted the real working population, and who were living on in the hopes of better days ; the men who have since made America, and have within the last ten years proved what an important factor they may be in wrecking or in building the British empire. These are the men of whom our merchants, artisans, and farmers mostly consist, and in whose hands is to-day the making or marring of an Irish nation. But, alas, *quantum mutatus ab illo !* What the battleaxe of the Dane, the sword of the Norman, the wile of the Saxon were unable to perform, we have accomplished ourselves. We have at last broken the continuity of Irish life, and just at the moment when the Celtic race is presumably about to largely recover possession of its own country, it finds itself deprived and stripped of its Celtic characteristics, cut off from the past, yet scarcely in touch with the present. It has lost since the beginning of this century almost all that connected it with the era of Cuchullain and of Ossian, that connected it with the christianizers of Europe, that connected it with Brian Boru and the heroes of Clontarf, with the O'Neills and O'Donnells, with Rory O'More, with the wild geese, and even to some extent with the men of '98. It has lost all that they had— language, traditions, music, genius and ideas. Just when we should be starting to build up anew the Irish race and the Gaelic nation— as within our own recollection Greece has been built up anew—we find ourselves despoiled of the bricks of nationality. The old bricks that lasted eighteen hundred years are destroyed ; we must now set to, to bake new ones, if we can, on other ground and of other clay. Imagine for a moment the restoration of a German-speaking Greece. . . .

The revival of Irish literature and other addresses (London 1894), pp. 118–29.

SINN FÉIN

28. RESOLUTIONS PASSED ON THE 28 NOVEMBER 1905, AT THE PUBLIC
    MEETING WHICH FOLLOWED THE FIRST ANNUAL CONVENTION OF
    THE NATIONAL COUNCIL OF SINN FÉIN, 1905

From 1899 Griffith as editor of *The United Irishman* was advocating absention from parliament, passive resistance to British rule in Ireland, and national economic development. During the early years of the twentieth century a number of Sinn Féin clubs were founded in Ireland. Some of the supporters of the movement, however, were willing to use force to attain their ends if they saw any prospect of success.[1]

1. That the people of Ireland are a free people, and that no law made without their authority or consent is or can ever be binding on their conscience. That the general council of county councils presents the nucleus of a national authority, and we urge upon it to extend the scope of its deliberation and action ; to take within its purview every question of national interest and to formulate lines of procedure for the nation.

2. That national self-development through the recognition of the duties and rights of citizenship on the part of the individual, and by the aid and support of all movements originating from within Ireland, instinct with national tradition, and not looking outside Ireland for the accomplishment of their aims, is vital to Ireland.

The United Irishman, 9 December 1905.

29. ARTHUR GRIFFITH'S SPEECH AT THE FIRST ANNUAL NATIONAL
    COUNCIL CONVENTION OF SINN FÉIN, 28 NOVEMBER 1905

. . . I am in economics largely a follower of the man who thwarted England's dream of the commercial conquest of the world, and who made the mighty confederation before which England has fallen commercially and is falling politically—Germany. His name is a famous one in the outside world, his works are the text books of economic science in other countries—in Ireland his name is unknown and his works unheard of—I refer to Frederick List, the real founder of the German Zollverein— . . .

Brushing aside the fallacies of Adam Smith and his tribe, List points out that between the individual and humanity stands, and must continue to stand, a great fact—the nation. The nation, with its special language and literature, with its peculiar origin and history, with its special manners and customs, laws and institutions, with the claims of all these for existence, independence, perfection, and continuance for the future, with its separate territory, a society which, united by a thousand ties of minds and interests, combines itself into one independent whole, which recognizes the law of right for and within itself, and in its united character is still opposed to other societies of a similar kind in their national liberty, and

[1] For an account of nationalist opinion in the first two decades of this century see R. M. Henry, *The evolution of Sinn Fein* (Dublin 1920).

consequently can, only under the existing conditions of the world, maintain self-existence and independence by its own power and resources. As the individual chiefly obtains by means of the nation and in the nation, mental culture, power of production, security and prosperity, so is the civilization of the human race only conceivable and possible by means of the civilization and development of individual nations. But as there are amongst men infinite differences in condition and circumstances, so there are in nations—some are strong, some are weak, some are highly civilized, some are half civilized, but in all exists as in the unit the impulse of self-preservation and the desire for improvement. It is the task of national politics to ensure existence and continuance to the nation to make the weak strong, the half civilized more civilized. It is the task of national economics to accomplish the economical development of the nation and fit it for admission into the universal society of the future. . . .

We in Ireland have been taught by our British lords lieutenant, our British educational boards, and our Barrington lecturers, that our destiny is to be the fruitful mother of flocks and herds—that it is not necessary for us to pay attention to our manufacturing arm, since our agricultural arm is all sufficient. The fallacy is apparent to the man who thinks—but it is a fallacy which has passed for truth in Ireland. With List I reply : a nation cannot promote and further its civilization, its prosperity, and its social progress equally as well by exchanging agricultural products for manufactured goods as by establishing a manufacturing power of its own. A merely agricultural nation can never develop to any extent a home or foreign commerce, with inland means of transport, and its foreign navigation, increase its population in due proportion to their well-being or make notable progress in its moral, intellectual, social and political development ; it will never acquire important political power or be placed in a position to influence less advanced nations and to form colonies of its own. A mere agricultural state is infinitely less powerful than an agricultural-manufacturing state. The former is always economically and politically dependent on those foreign nations who take from it agriculture in exchange for manufactured goods. . . . An agricultural nation is a man with one arm who makes use of an arm belonging to another person, but cannot, of course, be sure of having it always available. An agricultural-manufacturing nation is a man who has both arms of his own at his own disposal. . . . We must offer our producers protection where protection is necessary ; and let it be clearly understood what protection is. Protection does not mean the exclusion of foreign competition ; it means the enabling of the native manufacturer to meet foreign competition on an equal footing. It does not mean that we shall pay a higher profit to any Irish manufacturer, but that we shall not stand by and see him crushed by mere weight of foreign capital. If an Irish manufacturer cannot produce an article as cheaply as an English or other foreigner, solely because his foreign competitor has had larger resources at his disposal, then it is the first duty of the Irish nation to accord protection to the Irish manufacturer. If, on the other hand, an Irish manufacturer can produce as cheaply, but charges an enhanced price, such a man deserves no support—he is in plain words a swindler. It is the duty of our public bodies in whose hands the expenditure of £4,000,000 annually is placed to pay where necessary an enhanced price for Irish manufactured articles, when the manufacturers show them they cannot produce them at the lesser price—this is protection. . . . With the development of her manufacturing arm will proceed the rise of a national middle class in Ireland and a trained national democracy and—I here again quote List against the charlatans who profess to see in a nation's language and tradition things of no economic value—' in every nation will the authority of national language and national literature, the civilizing arts and the perfection of municipal institutions keep pace with the development of the manufacturing arm.' How are we to accord protection to and procure the development of our manufacturing arm ? First, by ourselves individually—secondly, through our county, urban, and district councils, and poor law guardians, thirdly, by taking over control of those inefficient bodies known as harbour commissioners ; fourthly, by stimulating our manufacturers and our people to industrial enterprise ; and fifthly, by inviting to aid in our development, on commercial lines, Irish-American capital. In the first case, every individual knows his duty, whether he practises it or not—it is, unless where fraud is attempted, to pay if necessary an enhanced price for Irish goods, and to use whenever possible none but Irish goods. As to our public elective bodies which annually control the expenditure of our local taxation, their duty is the same. The duty of our harbour bodies is to arrange the incidence of port dues so that they shall fall most heavily on manufactured goods coming into the country, and to keep and publish a table of all goods imported and to whom consigned. . . .

We propose the formation of a Council of Three Hundred, composed of members of the general council of county councils and representatives of the urban councils, rural councils, poor law boards, and harbour boards of the country to sit in Dublin and form a *de facto* Irish parliament. Associated and sitting and voting with this body, which might assemble in Dublin in the spring and in the autumn, could be the persons elected for Irish constituencies, who decline to confer on the affairs of Ireland with foreigners in a foreign city. On its assembly in Dublin this national assembly should appoint committees to especially consider and report to the general assembly on all subjects appertaining to the country. On the reports of these committees the council should deliberate and formulate workable schemes, which, once formulated, it would be the duty of all county councils, rural councils, urban councils, poor law boards, and other bodies to give legal effect to so far as their powers permit, and where their legal powers fall short, to give it the moral force of law by inducing and instructing those whom they represent to honour and obey the recommendations of the Council of Three Hundred individually and collectively.

The United Irishman, 9 December 1905.

THE REBELLION OF 1916

30. THE PROCLAMATION OF THE REPUBLIC

Issued 24 April 1916, the day the rebellion in Dublin began.[1]

Poblacht na h-Eireann

The Provisional Government of the Irish republic to the people of Ireland

Irishmen and Irishwomen : In the name of God and of the dead generations from which she receives her old tradition of nationhood, Ireland, through us, summons her children to her flag and strikes for her freedom.

Having organized and trained her manhood through her secret revolutionary organization, the Irish Republican Brotherhood, and through her open military organizations, the Irish Volunteers, and the Irish Citizen Army, having patiently perfected her discipline, having resolutely waited for the right moment to reveal itself, she now seizes that moment, and, supported by her exiled children in America and by gallant allies in Europe, but relying in the first on her own strength, she strikes in full confidence of victory.

We declare the right of the people of Ireland to the ownership of Ireland, and to the unfettered control of Irish destinies, to be sovereign and indefeasible. The long usurpation of that right by a foreign people and government has not extinguished the right, nor can it ever be extinguished except by the destruction of the Irish people. In every generation the Irish people have asserted their right to national freedom and sovereignty ; six times during the past three hundred years they have asserted it in arms. Standing on that fundamental right and again asserting it in arms in the face of the world, we hereby proclaim the Irish republic as a sovereign independent state, and we pledge our lives and the lives of our comrades-in-arms to the cause of its freedom, of its welfare, and of its exaltation among the nations.

The Irish republic is entitled to, and hereby claims, the allegiance of every Irishman and Irishwoman. The republic guarantees religious and civil liberty, equal rights and equal opportunities to all its citizens, and declares its resolve to pursue the happiness and prosperity of the whole nation and of all its parts, cherishing all the children of the nation equally, and oblivious of

---

[1] For a facsimile of the proclamation and an account of its publication see *Publications of the Biblographical Society, Ire.*, v. 43–54.

the differences carefully fostered by an alien government, which have divided a minority from the majority in the past.

Until our arms have brought the opportune moment for the establishment of a permanent national government, representative of the whole people of Ireland, and elected by the suffrages of all her men and women, the Provisional Government, hereby constituted, will administer the civil and military affairs of the republic in trust for the people. We place the cause of the Irish republic under the protection of the Most High God, whose blessing we invoke upon our arms, and we pray that no one who serves that cause will dishonour it by cowardice, inhumanity, or rapine. In this supreme hour the Irish nation must, by its valour and discipline, and by the readiness of its children to sacrifice themselves for the common good, prove itself worthy of the august destiny to which it is called.

Signed on behalf of the provisional government,

Thomas J. Clarke, Sean MacDiarmada, Thomas MacDonagh, P. H. Pearse, Eamonn Ceannt, James Connolly, Joseph Plunkett.

DÁIL ÉIREANN, 1919

On 21 January 1919 the Sinn Féin members returned at the general election of 1918 met in Dublin, declared themselves the parliament of Ireland, and adopted the declaration of independence and the democratic programme (documents 28, 29). The first Dáil functioned until May 1921 when it was replaced by the Second Dáil comprised of persons elected to the house of commons of the parliaments of Northern and Southern Ireland.

31. THE IRISH DECLARATION OF INDEPENDENCE, 21 JANUARY 1919

Whereas the Irish people is by right a free people :

And whereas for seven hundred years the Irish people has never ceased to repudiate and has repeatedly protested in arms against foreign usurpation :

And whereas English rule in this country is, and always has been, based upon force and fraud and maintained by military occupation against the declared will of the people :

And whereas the Irish Republic was proclaimed in Dublin on Easter Monday 1916, by the Irish Republican Army, acting on behalf of the Irish people :

And whereas the Irish people is resolved to secure and maintain its complete independence in order to promote the common weal, to re-establish justice, to provide for future defence, to insure peace at home and good will with all nations and to constitute a national polity based upon the people's will with equal right and equal opportunity for every citizen :

And whereas at the threshold of a new era in history the Irish electorate has in the general election of December of 1918, seized the first occasion to declare by an overwhelming majority its firm allegiance to the Irish Republic :

Now therefore, we, the elected representatives of the ancient Irish people in national parliament assembled, do in the name of the Irish nation, ratify the establishment of the Irish Republic and pledge ourselves and our people to make this declaration effective by every means at our command :

We ordain that the elected representatives of the Irish people alone have power to make laws binding on the people of Ireland, and that the Irish parliament is the only parliament to which that people will give its allegiance :

We solemnly declare foreign government in Ireland to be an invasion of our national right which we will never tolerate, and we demand the evacuation of our country by the English garrison :

We claim for our national independence the recognition and support of every free nation in the world, and we proclaim that independence to be a condition precedent to international peace hereafter :

In the name of the Irish people we humbly commit our destiny to Almighty God Who gave our fathers the courage and determination to persevere through long centuries of a ruthless tyranny, and strong in the justice of the cause which they have handed down to us, we ask His Divine blessing on this the last stage of the struggle we have pledged ourselves to carry through to freedom.

Minutes of the proceedings of the first parliament of the republic of Ireland, pp. 15–16.

32. THE DEMOCRATIC PROGRAMME, 21 JANUARY 1919

We declare in the words of the Irish republican proclamation the right of the people of Ireland, to the ownership of Ireland and to the unfettered control of Irish destinies to be indefeasible, and in the language of our first president, Pádraig MacPhiarais, we declare that the nation's sovereignty extends not only to all men and women of the nation, but to all its material possessions, the nation's soil and all its resources, all the wealth and all the wealth-producing processes within the nation, and with him we reaffirm that all right to private property must be subordinated to the public right and welfare.

We declare that we desire our country to be ruled in accordance with the principles of liberty, equality, and justice for all, which alone can secure permanence of government in the willing adhesion of the people.

We affirm the duty of every man and woman to give allegiance and service to the commonwealth, and declare it is the duty of the nation to assure that every citizen shall have opportunity to spend his or her strength and faculties in the service of the people. In return for willing service, we, in the name of the republic, declare the right of every citizen to an adequate share of the produce of the nation's labour.

It shall be the first duty of the government of the republic to make provision for the physical, mental and spiritual well-being of the children, to secure that no child shall suffer hunger or cold from lack of food, or clothing, or shelter, but that all shall be provided with the means and facilities requisite for their proper education and training as citizens of a free and Gaelic Ireland.

The Irish republic fully realizes the necessity of abolishing the present odious, degrading, and foreign poor law system, substituting therefor a sympathetic native scheme for the care of the nation's aged and infirm, who shall not be regarded as a burden, but rather entitled to the nation's gratitude and consideration. Likewise it shall be the duty of the republic to take such measures that will safeguard the health of the people and ensure the physical as well as the moral well-being of the nation.

It shall be our duty to promote the development of the nation's resources, to increase the productivity of its soil, to exploit its mineral deposits, peat bogs and fisheries, its waterways and harbours, in the interests and for the benefit of the Irish people.

It shall be the duty of the republic to adopt all measures necessary for the recreation and invigoration of our industries, and to ensure their being developed on the most beneficial and progressive co-operative industrial lines. With the adoption of an extensive Irish consular service, trade with foreign nations shall be revived on terms of mutual advantage and goodwill, and while undertaking the organization of the nation's trade, import and export, it shall be the duty of the republic to prevent the shipment from Ireland of food and other necessaries until the wants of the Irish people are fully satisfied and the future provided for.

It shall also devolve upon the national government to seek [the] co-operation of the governments of other countries in determining a standard of social and industrial legislation with a view to a general and lasting improvement in the conditions under which the working classes live and labour.

Minutes of the proceedings of the first parliament of the republic of Ireland, pp. 22–3.

33. THE PRESIDENT'S STATEMENT TO THE DÁIL, 10 APRIL 1919

. . . There is in Ireland at this moment only one lawful authority, and that authority is the elected government of the Irish republic. . . .

Our attitude towards the powers that maintain themselves here against the expressed will of the people shall then, in a word, be this : We shall conduct ourselves towards them in such a way as will make it clear to the world that we acknowledge no right of theirs. Such use of their laws as we shall make will be dictated solely by necessity, and only in so far as we deem them for the public good.

In order to secure for our own *de jure* government, and for the

Irish republic which the Irish people have willed to set up, the necessary international recognition, we shall send at once our accredited representatives to Paris to the peace conference and to the League of Nations. . . .

We shall send also to other countries a number of duly accredited ambassadors and consuls to see that the position of Ireland is understood as it truly is, and not as English propaganda would represent it, and in general to see that the interests of Ireland in these countries are in no way neglected. We shall thus resume that intercourse with other peoples which befits us as a separate nation, that intercourse which it has been the chief aim of English statescraft to cut off and which indeed English power has succeeded in cutting off for over a century.

At the present time of general world-reconstruction it is most important that the internal interests of this country at home be also looked after, and by Irishmen. It will be the duty of our ministry to secure co-operation and to co-ordinate the activities of the various bodies which have taken voluntarily to themselves the safeguarding and advancement of these interests. Towards English legislation interfering with these interests we shall act in accordance with the general principles I have already indicated, that is, we shall act as we think best for the general good.

To measures such as the English Ways and Communications bill, designed, as regards Ireland, to prevent Irishmen from using the natural resources of their own country to benefit their own nation, handing over on set purpose to an English bureau complete control of the communications of this country, so that they may be used solely in the interests of England—to such measures we shall offer all the resistance we can command as being both injurious and unjust. It shall be the especial duty of our director of trade to examine, in co-operation with public bodies, how best to make our resistance effective.

The ministers and directors at the heads of the other departments —labour, industries, agriculture, local government—will similarly be charged with seeking co-operation with all interested in their departments. The minister of national defence is, of course, in close association with the voluntary military forces which are the foundation of the national army.

It is obvious that the work of our government cannot be carried on without funds.

The minister of finance is accordingly preparing a prospectus, which will shortly be published, for the issue of a loan of one million sterling—£500,000 to be offered to the public for immediate subscription, £250,000 at home and £250,000 abroad, in bonds of such amounts as to meet the needs of the small subscriber.

Minutes of the proceedings of the first parliament of the republic of Ireland,
pp. 45-7.

THE TREATY

After negotiations lasting for some months the treaty [1] between Great
Britain and Ireland was signed on 6 December 1921.

34. ARTICLES OF AGREEMENT FOR A TREATY BETWEEN GREAT BRITAIN AND IRELAND, DATED THE SIXTH DAY OF DECEMBER 1921

1. Ireland shall have the same constitutional status in the
community of nations known as the British Empire as the Dominion
of Canada, the Commonwealth of Australia, the Dominion of New
Zealand, and the Union of South Africa, with a parliament having
powers to make laws for the peace and good government of Ireland
and an executive responsible to that parliament, and shall be styled
and known as the Irish Free State.

2. Subject to the provisions hereinafter set out the position of
the Irish Free State in relation to the imperial parliament and
government and otherwise shall be that of the Dominion of Canada,
and the law, practice and constitutional usage governing the relationship of the crown or the representative of the crown and of the
imperial parliament to the Dominion of Canada shall govern their
relationship to the Irish Free State.

3. The representative of the crown in Ireland shall be appointed
in like manner as the governor-general of Canada, and in accordance
with the practice observed in the making of such appointments.

4. The oath to be taken by members of the parliament of the
Irish Free State shall be in the following form : I   do solemnly
swear true faith and allegiance to the constitution of the Irish Free
State as by law established and that I will be faithful to H.M. King
George V, his heirs and successors by law in virtue of the common
citizenship of Ireland with Great Britain and her adherence to and
membership of the group of nations forming the British Commonwealth of nations.[2]

5. The Irish Free State shall assume liability for the service of
the public debt of the United Kingdom as existing at the date
hereof and towards the payment of war pensions as existing at that
date in such proportion as may be fair and equitable, having regard
to any just claims on the part of Ireland by way of set off or counter-
claim, the amount of such sums being determined in default of
agreement by the arbitration of one or more independent persons
being citizens of the British empire.

6. Until an arrangement has been made between the British
and Irish governments whereby the Irish Free State undertakes her
own coastal defence, the defence by sea of Great Britain and Ireland
shall be undertaken by his majesty's imperial forces, but this shall
not prevent the construction or maintenance by the government of

---

[1] The document was officially referred to in Ireland as the treaty, in England
as the articles of agreement.
[2] The oath of allegiance was deleted from the Free State constitution by a bill
which became law in May 1933.

the Irish Free State of such vessels as are necessary for the protection of the revenue or the fisheries.

The foregoing provisions of this article shall be reviewed at a conference of representatives of the British and Irish governments to be held at the expiration of five years from the date hereof with a view to the undertaking by Ireland of a share in her own coastal defence.

7. The government of the Irish Free State shall afford to his majesty's imperial forces :

(a) In time of peace such harbour and other facilities as are indicated in the annex hereto, or such other facilities as may from time to time be agreed between the British government and the government of the Irish Free State ; and

(b) In time of war or of strained relations with a foreign power such harbour and other facilities as the British government may require for the purposes of such defence as aforesaid.[1]

8. With a view to securing the observance of the principle of international limitation of armaments, if the government of the Irish Free State establishes and maintains a military defence force, the establishments thereof shall not exceed in size such proportion of the military establishments maintained in Great Britain as that which the population of Ireland bears to the population of Great Britain.

9. The ports of Great Britain and the Irish Free State shall be freely open to the ships of the other country on payment of the customary port and other dues.

10. The government of the Irish Free State agrees to pay fair compensation on terms not less favourable than those accorded by the act of 1920 to judges, officials, members of police forces, and other public servants who are discharged by it or who retire in consequence of the change of government effected in pursuance hereof.

Provided that this agreement shall not apply to members of the Auxiliary Police Force or to persons recruited in Great Britain for the Royal Irish Constabulary during the two years next preceding the date hereof. The British government will assume responsibility for such compensation or pensions as may be payable to any of these excepted persons.

11. Until the expiration of one month from the passing of the act of parliament for the ratification of this instrument, the powers of the parliament and the government of the Irish Free State shall not be exercisable as respects Northern Ireland, and the provisions of the *Government of Ireland Act*, 1920, shall, so far as they relate to Northern Ireland, remain of full force and effect, and no election shall be held for the return of members to serve in the parliament of the Irish Free State for constituencies in Northern Ireland, unless

[1] By the terms of the agreement made between the governments of Great Britain and Eire in May 1938, the provisions of articles 6 and 7 of the treaty ceased to have effect.

a resolution is passed by both houses of the parliament of Northern Ireland in favour of the holding of such elections before the end of the said month.

12. If before the expiration of the said month, an address is presented to his majesty by both houses of the parliament of Northern Ireland to that effect,[1] the powers of the parliament and government of the Irish Free State shall no longer extend to Northern Ireland, and the provisions of the *Government of Ireland Act*, 1920 (including those relating to the council of Ireland), shall so far as they relate to Northern Ireland, continue to be of full force and effect, and this instrument shall have effect subject to the necessary modifications.

Provided that if such an address is so presented a commission consisting of three persons, one to be appointed by the government of the Irish Free State, one to be appointed by the government of Northern Ireland, and one who shall be chairman to be appointed by the British government shall determine in accordance with the wishes of the inhabitants, so far as may compatible with economic and geographic conditions the boundaries between Northern Ireland and the rest of Ireland, and for the purposes of the *Government of Ireland Act*, 1920, and of this instrument, the boundary of Northern Ireland shall be such as may be determined by such commission.[2]

13. For the purpose of the last foregoing article, the powers of the parliament of Southern Ireland under the *Government of Ireland Act*, 1920, to elect members of the council of Ireland shall after the parliament of the Irish Free State is constituted be exercised by that parliament.

14. After the expiration of the said month, if no such address as is mentioned in article 12 hereof is presented, the parliament and government of Northern Ireland shall continue to exercise as respects Northern Ireland the powers conferred on them by the *Government of Ireland Act*, 1920, but the parliament and government of the Irish Free State shall in Northern Ireland have in relation to matters in respect of which the parliament of Northern Ireland has not the power to make laws under that act (including matters which under the said act are within the jurisdiction of the council of Ireland) the same powers as in the rest of Ireland, subject to such other provisions as may be agreed in manner hereinafter appearing.

15. At any time after the date hereof the government of Northern Ireland and the provisional government of Southern Ireland hereinafter constituted may meet for the purpose of discussing the pro-

---

[1] Such an address was presented on the 7 December 1922.
[2] By the terms of a tripartite pact concluded in December 1925 between the governments of Great Britain, the Irish Free State and Northern Ireland the boundaries of Northern Ireland as defined by the Government of Ireland Act, 1920, remained unchanged, the Free State was relieved of its obligations under article V of the treaty, and the powers of the council of Ireland in relation to Northern Ireland were transferred to the parliament and government of Northern Ireland.

visions subject to which the last foregoing article is to operate in the event, of no such address as is therein mentioned being presented, and those provisions may include :

(*a*) Safeguards with regard to patronage in Northern Ireland.

(*b*) Safeguards with regard to the collection of revenue in Northern Ireland.

(*c*) Safeguards with regard to import and export duties affecting the trade or industry of Northern Ireland.

(*d*) Safeguards for minorities in Northern Ireland.

(*e*) The settlement of the financial relations between Northern Ireland and the Irish Free State.

(*f*) The establishment and powers of a local militia in Northern Ireland and the relation of the defence forces of the Irish Free State and of Northern Ireland respectively,

and if at any such meeting provisions are agreed to, the same shall have effect as if they were included amongst the provisions subject to which the powers of the parliament and government of the Irish Free State are to be exercisable in Northern Ireland under Article 14 hereof.

16. Neither the parliament of the Irish Free State nor the parliament of Northern Ireland shall make any law so as to either directly or indirectly to endow any religion or prohibit or restrict the free exercise thereof or give any preference or impose any disability on account of religious belief or religious status or affect prejudicially the right of any child to attend a school receiving public money without attending the religious instruction at the school or make any discrimination as respects state aid between schools under the management of different religious denominations or divert from any religious denomination or any educational institution any of its property except for public utility purposes and on payment of compensation.

17. By way of provisional arrangement for the administration of Southern Ireland during the interval which must elapse between the date hereof and the constitution of a parliament and government in accordance therewith, steps shall be taken forthwith for summoning a meeting of members of parliament elected for constituencies in Southern Ireland since the passing of the *Government of Ireland Act*, 1920, and for constituting a provisional government, and the British government shall take the steps necessary to transfer to such provisional government the powers and machinery requisite for the discharge of its duties, provided that every member of such provisional government shall have signified in writing his or her acceptance of this instrument. But this arrangement shall not continue in force beyond the expiration of twelve months from the date hereof.

18. This instrument shall be submitted forthwith by his majesty's government for the approval of parliament and by the Irish signatories to a meeting summoned for the purpose of the members

elected to sit in the house of commons of Southern Ireland, and if approved shall be ratified by the necessary legislation.

(Signed)

On behalf of the British Delegation,	On behalf of the Irish Delegation,
D. Lloyd George.	Art O Gríobhtha (Arthur
Austen Chamberlain.	Griffith).
Birkenhead.	Mícheál O Coileáin.
Winston S. Churchill.	Riobárd Bartún.
L. Worthington-Evans.	Eudhmenn S. O. Dugáin.
Hamar Greenwood.	Seórsa Ghabháin Uí Dhubh-
Gordon Hewart.	thaigh.

6th December 1921.

Saorstat Éireann, public general acts, 1922, pp. 44–8.

35. DAVID LLOYD GEORGE ON THE TREATY, HOUSE OF COMMONS, 14 DECEMBER 1921

On the British side we have allegiance to the crown, partnership in the empire, security of our shores, non-coercion of Ulster. These are the provisions we have over and over again laid down, and they are here, signed in this document.

On the Irish side there is one supreme condition—that the Irish people as a nation should be free in their own land to work out their own national destinies in their own way. These two nations, I believe, will be reconciled. Ireland, within her own boundaries, will be free to marshal her own resources, direct her own forces— material, moral and spiritual—and guide her own destinies. She has accepted allegiance to the crown, partnership in the same empire, and subordinated her external relations to the judgment of the same general council of the empire as we have. She has agreed to freedom of choice for Ulster. The freedom of Ireland increases the strength of the empire by ending the conflict which has been carried on for centuries with varying success, but with unvarying discredit, for centuries. Incidents of that struggle have done more to impair the honour of this country than any aspect of its world dominion throughout the ages. It was not possible to interchange views with the truest friends of Britain without feeling that there was something in reference to Ireland to pass over. This brings new credit to the empire, and it brings new strength. It brings to our side a valiant comrade.

During the trying years of the war we set up for the first time in the history of this empire a great imperial war cabinet. There were present representatives of Canada, Australia, South Africa, New Zealand, and India, but there was one vacant chair, and we all were conscious of it. It was the chair that ought to have been filled by Ireland. In so far as it was occupied, it was occupied by the shadow of a fretful, resentful, angry people—angry not merely for ancient wrongs, but angry because, while every nation in the empire had its nationhood honoured, the people who were a nation when the oldest Dominion had not even been discovered had its nationhood ignored. The youngest Dominion marched into the war under its own flag. As for the flag of Ireland, it was torn from the hands of men who had volunteered to die for the cause which the British empire was championing. The result was a rebellion, and, at the worst moment of the war, we had to divert our minds to methods of dealing with the crisis in Ireland. Henceforth that chair will be filled by a willing Ireland, radiant because her long quarrel with Great Britain will have been settled by the concession of liberty to her own people, and she can now take part in the partnership of empire, not merely without loss of self-respect, but with an accession of honour to herself and of glory to her own nationhood.

By this agreement we win to our side a nation of deep abiding and even passionate loyalties. What nation ever showed such loyalty to its faith under such conditions? Generations of persecution, proscription, beggary and disdain—she faced them all. She showed loyalty to kings whom Britain had thrown over. Ireland stood by them, and shed her blood to maintain their inheritance— that precious loyalty which she now avows to the throne, and to the partnership and common citizenship of empire. It would be taking too hopeful a view of the future to imagine that the last peril of the British empire has passed. There are still dangers lurking in the mists. Whence will they come? From what quarter? Who knows? But when they do come, I feel glad to know that Ireland will be there by our side, and the old motto that ' England's danger is Ireland's opportunity ' will have a new meaning. As in the case of the Dominions in 1914, our peril will be her danger, our fears will be her anxieties, our victories will be her joy.

The parliamentary debates, series 5, cxlix. cols. 25–49.

36. ÉAMON DE VALERA ON THE TREATY, DÁIL ÉIREANN, 19 DECEMBER 1921

We were elected by the Irish people, and did the Irish people think we were liars when we said that we meant to uphold the republic, which was ratified by the vote of the people three years ago, and was further ratified—expressly ratified—by the vote of the people at the elections last May? When the proposal for negotiation came from the British government asking that we should try by negotiation to reconcile Irish national aspirations with the association of nations forming the British empire, there was no one here as strong as I was to make sure that every human attempt should be made to find whether such reconciliation was possible. I am against this treaty because it does not reconcile Irish national aspirations with association with the British government. I am against this treaty, not because I am a man of war, but a man of peace. I am against this treaty because it will not end the centuries of conflict between the two nations of Great Britain and Ireland.

We went out to effect such a reconciliation and we have brought back a thing which will not even reconcile our own people much less reconcile Britain and Ireland.

If there was to be reconciliation, it is obvious that the party in Ireland which typifies national aspirations for centuries should be satisfied, and the test of every agreement would be the test of whether the people were satisfied or not. A war-weary people will take things which are not in accordance with their aspirations. You may have a snatch election now and you may get a vote of the people, but I will tell you that treaty will renew the contest that is going to begin the same history that the union began, and Lloyd George is going to have the same fruit for his labours as Pitt had. When in Downing Street the proposals to which we could unanimously assent in the cabinet were practically turned down at the point of the pistol and immediate war was threatened upon our people. It was only then that this document has been signed, and that document has been signed by plenipotentiaries, not perhaps individually under duress, but it has been signed, and would only affect this nation as a document signed under duress, and this nation would not respect it.

I wanted, and the cabinet wanted, to get a document we could stand by, a document that could enable Irishmen to meet Englishmen and shake hands with them as fellow-citizens of the world. That document makes British authority our masters in Ireland. It was said that they had only an oath to the British king in virtue of common citizenship, but you have an oath to the Irish constitution, and that constitution will be a constitution which will have the king of Great Britain as head of Ireland. You will swear allegiance to that constitution and to that king ; and if the representatives of the republic should ask the people of Ireland to do that which is inconsistent with the republic, I say they are subverting the republic. It would be a surrender which was never heard of in Ireland since the days of Henry II ; . . .

I am as anxious as anyone for the material prosperity of Ireland and the Irish people, but I cannot do anything that would make the Irish people hang their heads. I would rather see the same thing over again than that Irishmen should have to hang their heads in shame for having signed and put their hands to a document handing over their authority to a foreign country. The Irish people would not want me to save them materially at the expense of their national honour. I say it is quite within the competence of the Irish people if they wished to enter into an association with other peoples, to enter into the British empire ; it is within their competence if they want to choose the British monarch as their king, but does this assembly think the Irish people have changed so much within the past year or two that they now want to get into the British empire after seven centuries of fighting ? Have they changed that they now want to choose the person of the British monarch, whose forces they have been fighting against, and who have been associated with all the barbarities of the past couple of years ; have they changed so much that they want to choose the king as their monarch ? It is not King George as a monarch they choose ; it is Lloyd George, because it is not the personal monarch they are choosing, it is British power and authority as sovereign authority in this country. The sad part of it, as I was saying, is that a grand peace could at this moment be made, and to see the difference . . . I am against the treaty, because it does not do the fundamental thing and bring us peace. The treaty leaves us a country going through a period of internal strife just as the act of union did.

Iris Dháil Éireann official report : debate on the treaty, pp. 24–6.

37. ARTHUR GRIFFITH ON THE TREATY, DAIL EIREANN, 7 JANUARY 1922

. . . We were sent to make some compromise, bargain or arrangement ; we made an arrangement ; the arrangement we made is not satisfactory to many people. Let them criticise on that point, but do not let them say that we were sent to get one thing and that we got something else. We got a different type of arrangement from that which many wished ; but when they charge us or insinuate that we went there with a mandate to demand a republic, and nothing but a republic, then they are maligning us ; if we got that mandate we would have finished up in five minutes in Downing Street. . . . We went there to London, not as republican doctrinaires, but looking for the substance of freedom and independence. If you think what we brought back is not the substance of independence that is a legitimate ground for attack upon us, but to attack us on the ground that we went there to get a republic is to attack us on false and lying grounds ; and some of those who criticise on that ground know perfectly the conditions under which we went. . . .

You say we are dishonourable men ; this does not affect the fact of the treaty which has been discussed on the basis of the failure, at least, of the plenipotentiaries, and not discussed on what was in it. It has been discussed in the way that Carlyle once described—and I have thought of this many times while listening to the criticism of the treaty—he describes the fly that crawled along the front of the Cologne cathedral and communicated to all the other flies what a horribly rough surface it was, because the fly was unable to see the edifice. Now, as to that treaty, an effort has been made to put us in the position of saying that this treaty is an ideal thing ; an effort has been made to put us into a false position. That treaty is not an ideal thing ; it has faults. I could draw up a treaty—any of us could draw up a treaty which would be more satisfactory to the Irish people ; we could ' call spirits from the vasty deep,' but will they come when you call them ? We have a treaty signed by the heads of the British government ; we have nothing signed against it. I could draw up a much better treaty myself, one that would suit myself ; but it is not going to be passed. We are, therefore, face to face with a practical situation. Does this treaty give away the interests and the honour of Ireland ? I say it does not. I say it serves the interests of Ireland ; it is not dishonourable to Ireland. It is not an ideal thing ; it could be better. It has no more finality than that we are the final generation on the face of the earth (applause). No man is going, as was quoted here—I have used it all my life—' No man can set bounds to the march of a nation.' But we here can accept the treaty, and deal with it in good faith with the English people, and through the files of events reach, if we desire it, any further status that we desire or require after. Who is going to say what the world is to be like in ten years hence ? We can make peace on the basis of that treaty ; it does not for ever bind us not to ask for any more. England is going beyond where she is at present ; all nations are going beyond where they are at present ; and in the meantime we can move on in comfort and peace to the ultimate goal. This treaty gives the Irish people what they have not had for centuries ; it gives them a foothold in their own country ; it gives them solid ground on which to stand ; and Ireland has been a quaking bog for three hundred years, where there was no foothold for the Irish people. Well, reject this treaty ; throw Ireland back into what she was before this treaty came—I am not a prophet, though I have listened to many prophets here, and I can't argue with prophets ; but I know where Ireland was twenty or thirty years ago, I know where Ireland was when there was only a few dozen of us up in Dublin trying to keep the national idea alive, not trying to keep it alive, because the Irish people never deserted it, but a few of us who had faith in our people and faith in our country, stood by her—you are going to throw Ireland back to that ; to dishearten the men who made the fight, and to let back into Irish politics the time-servers and men who let down Ireland before and who will, through their weakness, if not through dishonesty, let down Ireland again. You can take this treaty and make it the basis of an Irish Ireland. You can reject this treaty and you can throw Ireland back into where she was years ago, into where she was before—well, I do not like to speak about the dead—before the sacrifice that the dead men have made raised her up : . . .

I have heard in this assembly statements about the people of Ireland. The people of Ireland sent us here—we have no right and no authority except what we derive from the people of Ireland —we are here because the people of Ireland elected us, and our only right to speak is to seek what they want. I am told that the people of Ireland elected us to get a republic. They elected us in 1918 to get rid of the parliamentary party ; they elected us in 1921 as a gesture, a proper gesture of defiance to the Black-and-Tans ; they elected us, not as doctrinaire republicans, but as men looking for freedom and independence. When we agreed to enter into negotiations with England with the object of producing a treaty we were bound, I hold, to respect whatever the Irish people—the people of Ireland—thought of that treaty. I have heard one deputy saying here that it does not matter what his constituents say. I tell him it does. If representative government is going to remain on the earth, then a representative must voice the opinion of his constituents ; if his conscience will not let him do that he has only one way out and that is to resign and refuse to misrepresent them ; but that men who know their constituents want this treaty should come here and tell us that, by virtue of the vote they derive from these constituents, they are going to vote against the treaty—that is the negation of all democratic right ; it is the negation of all freedom. . . .

Ibid., pp. 336–40.